Moderate Modernity

Social History, Popular Culture, and Politics in Germany
Kathleen Canning, Series Editor

Recent Titles
Moderate Modernity: The Newspaper Tempo *and the Transformation of Weimar Democracy*
   Jochen Hung
African Students in East Germany, 1949-1975
   Sara Pugach
The Arts of Democratization: Styling Political Sensibilities in Postwar West Germany
   Jennifer M. Kapczynski and Caroline A. Kita, Editors
Decolonizing German and European History at the Museum
   Katrin Sieg
Spaces of Honor: Making German Civil Society, 1700–1914
   Heikki Lempa
Bankruptcy and Debt Collection in Liberal Capitalism: Switzerland, 1800–1900
   Mischa Suter
Marking Modern Movement: Dance and Gender in the Visual Imagery of the Weimar Republic
   Susan Funkenstein
Anti-Heimat Cinema: The Jewish Invention of the German Landscape
   Ofer Ashkenazi
Dispossession: Plundering German Jewry, 1933–1953
   Christoph Kreutzmüller and Jonathan R. Zatlin, Editors
Sex between Body and Mind: Psychoanalysis and Sexology in the German-speaking World, 1890s–1930s
   Katie Sutton
Imperial Fictions: German Literature Before and Beyond the Nation-State
   Todd Kontje
White Rebels in Black: German Appropriation of Black Popular Culture
   Priscilla Layne
Not Straight from Germany: Sexual Publics and Sexual Citizenship since Magnus Hirschfeld
   Michael Thomas Taylor, Annette F. Timm, and Rainer Herrn, Editors
Passing Illusions: Jewish Visibility in Weimar Germany
   Kerry Wallach
Cosmopolitanisms and the Jews
   Cathy S. Gelbin and Sander L. Gilman
Bodies and Ruins: Imagining the Bombing of Germany, 1945 to the Present
   David Crew
The Jazz Republic: Music, Race, and American Culture in Weimar Germany
   Jonathan Wipplinger
The War in Their Minds: German Soldiers and Their Violent Pasts in West Germany
   Svenja Goltermann

For a complete list of titles, please see www.press.umich.edu

Moderate Modernity

The Newspaper Tempo *and the Transformation of Weimar Democracy*

JOCHEN HUNG

UNIVERSITY OF MICHIGAN PRESS
Ann Arbor

Copyright © 2023 by Jochen Hung
All rights reserved

For questions or permissions, please contact um.press.perms@umich.edu

Published in the United States of America by the
University of Michigan Press
Manufactured in the United States of America
Printed on acid-free paper
First published February 2023

A CIP catalog record for this book is available from the British Library.

Library of Congress Cataloging-in-Publication data has been applied for.

ISBN 978-0-472-13332-1 (hardcover : alk. paper)
ISBN 978-0-472-22090-8 (e-book)

Contents

List of Illustrations   vii

Introduction.
   "Germany's Most Modern Newspaper"   1
   Tempo, Ullstein, and the Late Weimar Republic   25

Chapter 1.
   1928–1929: Banging the Drum for Democracy   44
   "Every Day a Race against Time!" Technology, Speed,
      and *Sachlichkeit* in *Tempo*   61
   Forging Rational Citizens: *Tempo*'s Definition of Democracy   71
   Young Germans as Consumer-Citizens: Representations
      of Modern Masculinity and Femininity   82

Chapter 2.
   1930–1931: Adapting to the Crisis   123
   Consuming against the Crisis: *Tempo*'s Vision of a
      German Consumer Society after 1930   146
   Technology vs. the Soul: *Tempo*'s Discourse of Technology
      and Speed after 1930   158
   Citizen-Consumers during a Time of Crisis: *Tempo*'s
      Construction of Modern Masculinity and Femininity
      after 1930   160

Chapter 3.
   1932–1933: "Nobody but Ourselves Can Save Us"   182
   "We Vow to Be Happy!" Consumption as Duty in 1932   195

The Political Appeal of Slowness: Technology and Speed during the Crisis	201
The Oldest Guard Leads the Way: Constructions of Modern Masculinity and Femininity in 1932	202
30 January 1933: Ullstein under Hitler	208
"Everybody Will Have Their Own Car!" Dreams of a *Volkswagen* in *Tempo*	212
Youthful Pessimism: Young Men and Women under Chancellor Hitler	215
The End of *Tempo*	220
Conclusion: Creative Adaptations of Modernity in the Interwar Period	222
Bibliography	241
Index	261

Digital materials related to this title can be found on the Fulcrum platform via the following citable URL: https://doi.org/10.3998/mpub.9294519

List of Illustrations

Figure 1. Front page, *Tempo*, 11 September 1928, evening edition.   3
Figure 2. Inside page, *Tempo*, 11 September 1928, 9.   4
Figure 3. Film still, *M—Eine Stadt sucht einen Mörder*, directed by Fritz Lang (Nero, 1931).   6
Figure 4. Film still, *Emil und die Detektive*, directed by Gerhard Lamprecht (Ufa, 1931).   7
Figure 5. Detail from "Ein Exemplar des *Roten Tempo*," *Tempo*, 10 May 1929, 12.   8
Figure 6. John Heartfield, "Wer Bürgerblätter liest wird blind und taub," *Arbeiter Illustrierte Zeitung*, 9 February 1930.   31
Figure 7. "Preisausschreiben 'Ferienfreude'," *Tempo*, 23 September 1929, 12.   58
Figure 8. Advertisement, *Ullstein-Berichte*, October 1928, 2.   67
Figure 9. Emery Kelen, "Die Partei-Tenöre," *Tempo*, 16 November 1928, 2.   80
Figure 10. Advertisement, *Ullstein-Berichte*, January 1930, 7.   93
Figure 11. "Kameradschaftsehe," *Tempo*, 20 October 1928, 8.   97
Figure 12. "Die vollkommene Sportsfrau als vollkommene Hausfrau," *Tempo*, 2 October 1928, 3.   104
Figure 13. "Möchten Sie mit mir boxen?," *Tempo*, 21 September 1928, 11.   107
Figure 14. Hans Boht, "Brigittchen," *Tempo*, 16 October 1928, 8.   108
Figure 15. "Revue-Girl," *Tempo*, 19 November 1928, 8.   110
Figure 16. "Die Premiere des 'Revuegirls' bei den Revuegirls," *Tempo*, 24 November 1928, 3.   111
Figure 17. "Welcher die 1000 M.?," *Tempo*, 16 March 1929, 5.   116

viii List of Illustrations

Figure 18. Erna Koch, *Tempo*, 21 February 1929, 4. 119
Figure 19. "*Tempo*-Girls und die Schönheits-Siegerin Erna Koch,"
Tempo, 6 April 1929, 8. 120
Figure 20. Detail from "Wie und womit die Parteien agitieren,"
Tempo, 10 September 1930, 3. 130
Figure 21. "Sonne, See, Sand und Schweben," *Tempo*,
6 September 1930, 4. 154
Figure 22. "Kamera-Glück in den Ferien," *Tempo*, 15 August 1931, 6. 155
Figure 23. "Kleinstadtidyll auf dem Potsdamer Platz," *Tempo*,
18 August 1931, 3. 160
Figure 24. "Anita Page näht . . . ," *Tempo*, 9 January 1931, 5. 169
Figure 25. "Frau Christine," *Tempo*, 6 September 1930, 10. 173
Figure 26. "Mutter Deutschland und ihre Sorgenkinder," *Tempo*,
31 December 1932, 1. 196
Figure 27. "Herbst-Ausverkauf beginnt," *Tempo*, 1 August 1932, 3. 199
Figure 28. Ottmar Starke, "Kleiner *Tempo*-Bilderbogen:
Des Mädchens Wandlung," *Tempo*, 8 August 1932, 7. 207
Figure 29. Detail from S. W.-N., "Die Ersten und Einzigen," *Tempo*,
25 March 1933, 6. 219

Introduction

"Germany's Most Modern Newspaper"

On 11 September 1928, at four o'clock in the afternoon, a new name could be heard on the streets of Berlin, a word that seemed to encapsulate the busyness and frantic pace of Germany's metropolis: *Tempo*. For weeks, the name had greeted Berliners from posters and advertising columns on Alexanderplatz, Kurfürstendamm, and Potsdamer Platz, announcing the imminent arrival of a totally new type of publication: "*Tempo*—the newspaper of our time!" Now the cries of the paperboys also carried it through the streets: "*Tempo! Tempo!*" The bearer of this breathless name, the new publication they thrust at passers-by on Berlin's boulevards, claimed to be nothing less than "Germany's most modern newspaper"—an up-to-date display of the most sensational news from the most important centers of the nation and the globe.

A sophisticated marketing campaign had counted down the launch of the newspaper, with billboards announcing "You're lacking *Tempo*!," "You'll soon have *Tempo*!," and "Tomorrow you'll have *Tempo*!"[1] On the day *Tempo* finally appeared, the curious Berliners who took a copy off the paperboys' hands were presented with a modern world full of danger, adventure, and scintillating glamour. Printed on pink paper, *Tempo*'s very first front page carried the head-

---

1. Carl Jödicke, "Als die Werbung noch Propaganda hieß," in *Hundert Jahre Ullstein, 1877–1977*, ed. W. Joachim Freyburg and Hans Wallenberg, vol. 3 (Berlin: Ullstein, 1977), 140–42. According to Bernhard Fulda, *Tempo*'s teaser campaign was copied from the Nazi newspaper *Der Angriff*, which was introduced a year earlier, see Bernhard Fulda, "Industries of Sensationalism: German Tabloids in Weimar Germany," in *Mass Media, Culture and Society in Twentieth-Century Germany*, ed. Karl Christian Führer and Corey Ross (Basingstoke: Palgrave Macmillan, 2006), 202. This practice, however, was nothing new: it was famously introduced in 1913 by R. J. Reynolds Tobacco for their *Camel* brand of cigarettes, see P. David Marshall and Joanne Morreale, *Advertising and Promotional Culture: Case Histories* (Macmillan International Higher Education, 2017), 50.

line about a "dreadful" murder on a high-speed train from Hamburg to Bremen (Fig. 1). Most of the page was filled with large photographs of recent events from around the nation and the world: images of the wreckage of a capsized steamship in Hamburg, the mangled remains of a fatal car accident north of Berlin, the funeral of the crew of a recently recovered British submarine that had been sunk during the war, and the return of "Iron Gustav," a Berlin hackney coach driver who had found fame by taking his carriage to Paris and back. On the following pages, readers were informed about the ongoing League of Nations conference in Geneva as well as the murder of infamous local con woman and courtesan Pussy Uhl. The business pages brought the latest financial news from Berlin, Frankfurt, Hamburg, London, Paris, and New York. In the section "The World of Ideas and Adventures," Kurt Tucholsky commented on the new popularity of detective novels, and in the culture section, called "Under Berlin's City Lights," the production of Tolstoy's play *The Living Corpse* at Berlin's Volksbühne theater was reviewed. The most prominent part of this section was a large photograph of a naked Josephine Baker, announcing her arrival in Berlin—an image that was guaranteed to raise eyebrows among the newspaper's first readers (Fig. 2). While many German illustrated magazines regularly printed photos of naked men and women, most readers of daily newspapers still had moral qualms about photos of scantily clad women.[2] On the back page, a column titled "At the Last Minute" relayed the news that had come in just before going to print: the arrest of an "internationally operating pickpocket" at Hamburg's main station, the announcement of new rules for professional car races to protect spectators from crashes, and the preparations for the new Zeppelin airship's maiden voyage. *Tempo*, that much was clear from its first issue, was nothing less than the nation's "most radical proponent of American-style tabloid journalism, . . . outdoing everything Berlin had read so far."[3]

Tempo's arrival caused immediate controversy among the German public. With an explicit reference to the revealing photo of Josephine Baker, the veterans organization Young German Order (Jungdeutscher Orden) denounced the newspaper as a "flower of the asphalt" that every patriotic reader should boycott: "Every German worth his salt should do without such 'Tempo,' which has only been created to make money from whipping up and titillating the hoi polloi."[4] The high-brow conservative journal *Die Tat*

---

2. Bernhard Fulda, *Press and Politics in the Weimar Republic* (Oxford: Oxford University Press, 2009), 32.
3. Fulda, *Press and Politics in the Weimar Republic*, 35.
4. "Ein feines Tempo," *Der Jungdeutsche*, 13 September 1928. Unless otherwise indicated, all translations are by the author.

Figure 1. Front page, *Tempo*, 11 September 1928, evening edition. © Axel Springer AG. Used with permission.

Figure 2. Inside page, *Tempo*, 11 September 1928, 9. © Axel Springer AG. Used with permission.

mocked *Tempo* as a newspaper that applied "the principle of Ford's conveyor belt" to journalism.⁵ The communist *Rote Fahne* accused the new publication of flooding Berlin and Germany with "junk, gossip, snobbery" to sedate the working class.⁶ Others, however, were positively exuberant: in the first few days after its launch, the paper published several letters sent in by enthusiastic readers eulogizing the new publication as "honest, *a tempo* and unabashed" and a "kindred spirit" of the modern woman.⁷

Over the following years, *Tempo* left its mark on the national consciousness. For many contemporary observers, the publication became the ultimate symbol of the "Americanized" mass culture that seemed to have taken over Berlin and other urban centers in Germany. In 1931, *Tempo* appeared as the embodiment of Weimar's urban press in *M—Eine Stadt sucht einen Mörder*, Fritz Lang's film about a city in the grip of fear of an unknown killer. In one of the central scenes, *Tempo* fans the flames of public outrage by publishing a letter by the fugitive criminal.⁸ The paper eventually lands on the desk of the interior minister, who calls the publication a "scandal" (Fig. 3). In the same year, *Tempo* formed a significant part of the backdrop in Gerhard Lamprecht's adaption of Erich Kästner's popular children's book *Emil und die Detektive*.⁹ In one of the central parts of the film, when Emil arrives in Berlin from his rural hometown, shots of busy traffic and large advertisements around Kaiser Wilhelm Memorial Church and Friedrichstraße station create a disorienting feeling of the big city. *Tempo* is among the most visible brands in these scenes (Fig. 4).¹⁰ In Irmgard Keun's novel *The Artificial Silk Girl*, published in 1932,

---

5. "Tempo," *Die Tat*, October 1928, 559.

6. Joe Lengle, "Glosse vom Tage," *Die Rote Fahne*, 11 September 1928, 10.

7. "Tribüne für Alle: Das neue Schlagwort," *Tempo*, 13 September 1928, 2; "Tribüne für Alle: Ich halte mit!" *Tempo*, 18 September 1928, 2. Unless otherwise indicated, all citations from *Tempo* are from its first daily edition.

8. *M—Eine Stadt sucht einen Mörder*, dir. Fritz Lang (Nero, 1931). The mock front page is shown in a close-up (13:42) and several times on the desks of the superintendent (14:13) and the interior minister (14:02). The paper might have even provided some inspiration for the film's script: at the beginning of the year, *Tempo* had offered a reward of one thousand marks for any leads in a recent murder case and printed daily news about the hunt for the fugitive killer on its front page, see "1000 Mark *Tempo*-Belohnung für Aufklärung des Kino-Mords," *Tempo*, 21 January 1931, 1. On the day of the premiere of the film, *Tempo* published an article by Lang, warning of the seemingly normal criminals "among us," see Fritz Lang, "Das Gesicht des Mörders," *Tempo*, 11 May 1931, 5.

9. *Emil und die Detektive*, dir. Gerhard Lamprecht (Ufa, 1931). The film's script was written by *Tempo* contributor Billy Wilder.

10. *Tempo*'s logo appears on an advertisement in front of a café (21:59) and on a newspaper kiosk Emil is hiding behind (22:25). In one of the following scenes, a poster with the

6   Moderate Modernity

Figure 3. Film still, *M—Eine Stadt sucht einen Mörder*, directed by Fritz Lang (Nero, 1931).

Tempo also forms part of the colorful panorama of the city that the protagonist Doris experiences vicariously for her blind neighbor:

> I saw a man with a placard round his neck—"I will do any work".... And the placard was white with black on it. And lots of newspapers, very gay, the *Tempo* lilac-pink, and late editions with a red stroke across and a yellow one from corner to corner—and I saw Kempinsky's [*sic*] with fine timbering and taxis in front of it with a pattern of white diamonds on them, and chauffeurs with sunk heads, because they are always waiting.[11]

Like Lamprecht, Keun treats *Tempo*, with its pinkish paper, as a colorful feature of the city, as important as its buildings, such as the famous Kempinski restaurant on Friedrichstraße.

---

slogan "Be up to date by reading *Tempo!*" is centrally placed in the shot (25:11). I am indebted to Erhard Schütz for directing my attention to *Tempo*'s appearances in *Emil und die Detektive* and *M*.

11. Irmgard Keun, *The Artificial Silk Girl*, trans. Basil Creighton (London: Chatto & Windus, 1933), 128; the paragraph has been cut in Katharina von Ankum's more recent translation, see Irmgard Keun, *The Artificial Silk Girl*, trans. Katharina von Ankum (New York: Other Press, 2002), 87. In the German original, the text also references the newspaper *Nachtausgabe*, translated here as "Late Editions," and the magazine *Querschnitt* with its famous yellow jacket, see Irmgard Keun, *Das Kunstseidene Mädchen* (Berlin: List, 2004), 101–2.

Figure 4. Film still, *Emil und die Detektive*, directed by Gerhard Lamprecht (Ufa, 1931).

Tempo's editors were well aware of the cultural impact of their newspaper and reported with relish when its striking design was appropriated, which happened with astonishing regularity. For example, over only a few days in May 1929, both a new Berlin ice cream parlor and a Communist newsletter—called *The Red Tempo*—copied the paper's distinctive logotype (Fig. 5).[12] According to the newspaper's own reporters, the Communist copy was sold on the streets of Berlin with the catchphrase "*Tempo* now in red—as red as the Red Flag," referring to the original's pink hue and the name of the flagship newspaper of the Communist Party of Germany (Kommunistische Partei Deutschlands, KPD). *Tempo*'s notoriety even spread beyond Germany's borders, a fact the newspaper noticed with pride. It referred to a Danish tabloid using its logo and quoted from an article in a Norwegian newspaper that described the calls of *Tempo*'s paperboys on the streets of Berlin as "the city's very own war cry."[13] When a new Swedish supermarket copied the paper's logo, it proudly pointed out its role in the worldwide spread of a culture of speed:

> Tempo!—That is the word. A word that describes the meaning of a whole time, a word that rules not only economy and technology—this era's two great powers—, but also the lives of individuals. . . . Well, we do not want

---

12. "Namensvetter," *Tempo*, 6 May 1929, 3; "Ein Exemplar des *Roten Tempo*," *Tempo*, 10 May 1929, 12.

13. "Ein kleines Plagiat in Danemärk," *Tempo*, 20 December 1930, 1; "Tempo, Tempo— Berliner Eindrücke einer Norwegerin," *Tempo*, 14 May 1930, 7.

Figure 5. Detail from "Ein Exemplar des *Roten Tempo*," *Tempo*, 10 May 1929, 12. © Axel Springer AG. Used with permission.

> to sell ourselves short: we, the newspaper *Tempo*, played a not entirely insignificant role in this sudden spread of this word that is so symbolic for our time.[14]

While this was an obvious exaggeration, the many instances in which *Tempo* was appropriated, embraced, or rejected by contemporaries show that the newspaper was perceived as an integral part of—and a potent symbol for—the urban experience and the popular culture of the new democratic Germany.

Only nine months after this proud declaration and five years after its launch, on 5 August 1933, *Tempo* ceased publication. In a farewell note to its readers on the last page of its final issue, the paper gave a remarkable reason for this decision. The culture of speed it supposedly had contributed to so much, *Tempo* argued, had run its course:

> Founded in the autumn of 1928, in the years of the utmost public agitation, it was *Tempo*'s mission to express certain aspects of the last "postwar years." ... The steady progress of the new Germany that has replaced this epoch of excited restlessness and fierce struggling for meaning has

---

14. "Tempo, Tempo überall!," *Tempo*, 28 October 1932, 3.

changed the preconditions for our service to the reader. *Tempo* considers its mission to be accomplished; consequently, it will cease publication with today's issue.[15]

The short notice implied that the advent of yet another "new" Germany—the Nazis' "Third Reich"—had put an end to the cosmopolitan modernity of the Weimar Republic and, with it, to *Tempo* and its self-defined mission of giving a voice to this culture.

These dates—*Tempo*'s sensational appearance in 1928 and its muted end in 1933—mark one of the most significant periods in German history, when Weimar's phase of relative stabilization deteriorated into an acute political, social, and economic crisis, leading to the establishing of the Nazi dictatorship—events that would determine the course of global history.[16] This book investigates the culture and mentalities of this pivotal time in German history through the in-depth, intensive analysis of this newspaper. To call this "microhistory" might overstretch the definition of that approach, but this study does share some of its methodological and theoretical positions, most of all "the belief that microscopic observation will reveal factors previously unobserved."[17] Microhistory describes the particular and puts it in its historically specific context, not primarily to explain its meaning, but to reveal "the fragmentation, contradictions and plurality of viewpoints" of that context.[18] Most importantly, despite studying small objects, microhistory focuses on the "great historical questions," while preserving the agency of individual actors.[19] The historical question the present study addresses is the paradox of the failure of Weimar's liberal press, despite its formidable reach and influence, to prevent the rise of the Nazis and the demise of the democratic Republic. This question has puzzled historians for a long time and their answers have generally fallen into two camps: in the 1970s, a range of studies blamed structural factors, such as the economic model of the commercial press, while more recent studies have identified the radicalization of Weimar's political climate—and the role of the media in this process—as the main reason for the failure of the liberal press to stop the rise of the Nazis. In his pioneering study of the Weimar press, pub-

---

15. "*Tempo* heute zum letzten Mal," *Tempo*, 5 August 1931, 10.
16. Eberhard Kolb, *The Weimar Republic* (Abingdon: Routledge, 2005), 101.
17. Giovanni Levi, "On Microhistory," in *New Perspectives on Historical Writing*, ed. Peter Burke (Cambridge: Polity, 1991), 97.
18. Levi, "On Microhistory," 107.
19. Sigurður Gylfi Magnússon and István M. Szíjártó, *What Is Microhistory? Theory and Practice* (London: Routledge, 2013), 5.

lished in 1972, Kurt Koszyk argued that the lack of "internal press freedom"—that is, the financial dependency on advertisement revenue—forced Weimar's mass-market press to embrace populist politics and kept it from effective opposition.[20] In 1975, Modris Eksteins offered a similar explanation, but differentiated between idealistic editors and pragmatic publishers, who "were by and large more conservative in their liberal orientation than the leading editors of their newspapers" and often put commercial interests first.[21] The tension between the two, Eksteins argued, was exacerbated by the depression that hit Germany in the early 1930s and ultimately hobbled Weimar's great democratic publishing houses in their fight for the Republic's survival. In 1976, Bernd Sösemann argued that during Weimar's final crisis between 1930 and 1933 liberal editors like Theodor Wolff and Julius Elbau did their best to shore up support for Weimar democracy and offer constructive advice on how to steer it into safer waters. However, they lacked any direct political influence and the ability to "correct any oversights by politicians or convert moral authority into political action."[22] In the same year, Michael Bosch claimed that the liberal publishing houses failed to adapt to the radicalized and emotionalized political culture of the late Weimar Republic and thus did not reach their audiences anymore, even if they continued to read their newspapers.[23] Overall, these studies painted an image of the liberal press as an upright yet ultimately powerless defender of Weimar democracy. Nearly forty years later, the question of the role of the liberal press in Weimar's demise was taken up again by a number of historians operating with concepts informed by communication studies and cultural studies, such as political culture and opinion climate. Karl Christian Führer has blamed the extreme partisanship of German journalists for a "poisoning" of the political climate that contributed to the demise of the Weimar Republic.[24] Corey Ross has argued that "the increasingly consumerist orienta-

---

20. Kurt Koszyk, *Deutsche Presse 1914–1945* (Berlin: Colloquium, 1972), 444–53.

21. Modris Eksteins, *The Limits of Reason: The German Democratic Press and the Collapse of Weimar Democracy* (Oxford: Oxford University Press, 1975), 309. See also Modris Eksteins, "The Frankfurter Zeitung: Mirror of Weimar Democracy," *Journal of Contemporary History* 6, no. 4 (1971): 3–28.

22. Bernd Sösemann, *Das Ende der Weimarer Republik in der Kritik demokratischer Publizisten. Theodor Wolff, Ernst Feder, Julius Elbau, Leopold Schwarzschild* (Berlin: Colloquium, 1976), 181.

23. Michael Bosch, *Liberale Presse in der Krise. Die Innenpolitik der Jahre 1930 bis 1933 im Spiegel des Berliner Tageblatts, der Frankfurter Zeitung und der Vossischen Zeitung* (Frankfurt/Main: Peter Lang, 1976), 298–305.

24. Karl Christian Führer, "Politische Kultur und Journalismus. Tageszeitungen als politische Akteure in der Krise der Weimarer Republik 1929–1933," *Jahrbuch für Kommunikationsgeschichte* 10 (2008): 27.

tion" of much of the liberal newspapers meant that most their readers bought them for their entertainment value and not for their political messages—which they ignored at the ballot box.[25] In the most extensive study on this question to date, Bernhard Fulda argued that newspapers of all political colors undermined Weimar democracy by collectively perpetuating the feeling of permanent crisis and entrenching political differences.[26]

This study takes a different approach: rather than addressing the question of the failure of Weimar's liberal press with a comparative macro-level approach like the works mentioned above, it uses the history of one newspaper to interrogate the validity of this question itself. The present work suggests that drawing well-defined battle lines between staunch defenders and rabid enemies of democracy ignores the plurality and fluidity of Weimar's public discourse. Only in hindsight are these lines easy to draw—as will be shown below, the contemporary public debate was characterized by shifting meanings of the period's central concepts and keywords, which included the meaning of democracy itself. Particularly during Weimar's later years, the central issue was not being for or against the democratic order, but what "kind" of democracy was needed. A microhistorical approach is a very helpful instrument to reveal this fluidity, as it pays close attention to the individuals—the editors, the publishers, the writers, and the readers—and their opinions, viewpoints, and beliefs that are frequently ascribed to publications themselves, as if they were living beings holding "conservative," "right-wing," or "liberal" worldviews. While most newspapers have an explicit or implicit editorial line that its journalists are meant to follow, this line is interpreted and negotiated daily and often swings between different political positions depending on the issue and the historical context. An in-depth study of a single newspaper can retrace this negotiation process and the gradual change over time of the central ideological beliefs, opinions, and keywords articulated in it.

Why, then, choose *Tempo* as the subject of such a micro-level study? The proper object of study in microhistory has often been defined as the "exceptional normal," historical actors that are marginal, obscure, or undistinguished, yet—through their deviant lifestyle or the extraordinary fate that befell them—exceptional in some way.[27] However, this approach is not limited to humans—

---

25. Corey Ross, *Media and the Making of Modern Germany: Mass Communications, Society, and Politics from the Empire to the Third Reich* (Oxford: Oxford University Press, 2008), 178.

26. Fulda, *Press and Politics*, 211.

27. Edoardo Grendi, "Micro-Analisi e Storia Sociale," *Quaderni storici* 12, no. 35 (1977):

recently, it has also been applied to places and objects.[28] The present study applies this approach to the media. In many ways, *Tempo* was an "exceptionally normal" publication: as a mass-market tabloid newspaper, it firmly belongs to the realm of the everyday, the popular, and pedestrian, yet its unusual design and style as well as its fate mark it out as an exception among the press of the time.

Because of its popular nature and its relatively short life span, *Tempo* has hardly attracted any scholarly attention until now. Koszyk, in his magisterial four-volume history of the German press, mentions the newspaper only once in passing.[29] Eksteins describes it only fleetingly as "sensational to the hilt" and "crammed full of pictures."[30] Despite arguing that *"Tempo* was . . . an important aspect of Berlin's media landscape and, from a sociological perspective, much more representative of the city's character and spirit in the 1920s than its readers realized at the time," Peter de Mendelssohn dedicated less than a page of his history of the Berlin press to the newspaper he considered to be so typical of it.[31] In his formative book *Weimar Culture*, Peter Gay briefly mentions *Tempo* as a "racy tabloid."[32] In more recent studies, *Tempo* has been acknowledged as a serious historical source, but without delving further into its whole history.[33] Perhaps not surprisingly, Tempo has found more attention in current popular culture than in historical scholarship: in the third season of the hugely popular German television series Babylon Berlin, a newspaper of the same name – and obviously modelled on its real-life namesake – plays a central role as the representative of the sensationalist press of Weimar-era Berlin.[34]

506–20; Levi, "On Microhistory," 33; Matti Peltonen, "Clues, Margins, and Monads: The Micro-Macro Link in Historical Research," *History and Theory* 40, no. 3 (2001): 347–51.

28. See, for example, Alison K. Smith, "A Microhistory of the Global Empire of Cotton: Ivanovo, the 'Russian Manchester,'" *Past & Present* 244, no. 1 (2019): 163–93; Robin Wolfe Scheffler, "Interests and Instrument: A Micro-History of Object Wh.3469 (X-Ray Powder Diffraction Camera, ca. 1940)," *Studies in History and Philosophy of Science* 40, no. 4 (2009): 396–404.

29. Koszyk, *Deutsche Presse*, 255.

30. Eksteins, *Limits*, 122.

31. Peter de Mendelssohn, *Zeitungsstadt Berlin. Menschen und Mächte in der Geschichte der deutschen Presse* (Berlin: Ullstein, 1982), 361.

32. Peter Gay, *Weimar Culture: The Outsider as Insider* (London: Penguin, 1968), 134.

33. Jonathan O. Wipplinger, *The Jazz Republic: Music, Race, and American Culture in Weimar Germany* (Ann Arbor: University of Michigan Press, 2017); Moritz Föllmer, *Individuality and Modernity in Berlin: Self and Society from Weimar to the Wall* (Cambridge: Cambridge University Press, 2013), 53–55; Fulda, "Industries"; Moritz Föllmer, "Auf der Suche nach dem eigenen Leben. Junge Frauen und Individualität in der Weimarer Republik," in *Die "Krise" der Weimarer Republik. Zur Kritik eines Deutungsmusters*, ed. Moritz Föllmer and Rüdiger Graf (Frankfurt/Main: Campus, 2005), 287–317.

34. Jochen Hung, "Modernity in Babylon: The Media as Proponents of Modern Life in

This book argues that *Tempo* was representative for a certain liberal and progressive current in the contemporary debate about the very character of the Weimar Republic that has often been neglected in the study of its demise. As will be shown throughout this book, its publisher Ullstein—a giant in the German newspaper industry at the time and an important actor in Weimar politics—used *Tempo* more unscrupulously than the rest of its wide range of publications as a vehicle to express these views. Most importantly, the Ullstein company posited *Tempo* at the forefront of the discursive struggle over what it meant to be "modern" in Weimar Germany. Since Detlev Peukert's seminal interpretation of Weimar as "the crisis of classical modernity," a period when the conflicting potentials of modernization came to a head, the concept of modernity is central to the historiography of Weimar Germany.[35] The experience of modernization and the debate about its consequences, meaning, and future was pivotal to the political and cultural life in Weimar Germany. As Eric Weitz put it, "[a]ll of Weimar's protagonists, whatever their political and cultural proclivities, grappled with this tension-bound world of modernity."[36] One of Peukert's important innovations, rooted in his Weberian understanding of modernity, was the interpretation of the demise of Weimar's liberal democracy and the rise of the Nazi regime not as a failure, but as "a legitimate, if extreme, outcome" of Weimar-era experimentations.[37] In this perspective, the establishing of the "Third Reich" was not a consequence of Germany's incomplete modernization, as the followers of the *Sonderweg* thesis had argued, but of an excessive application of "bureaucratization, rationalization, and a deep investment in science and medicine, as tools for the engineering of a 'therapeutic' modernity."[38] According to Peukert, the "crisis years" of 1928–33—*Tempo*'s years of publication—were the pivotal period in the transformation of Weimar's reformist, optimistic modernity governed by science-based progressivism into the exclusionary "alternative vision" that would ultimately lead to the "Final Solution."[39]

Babylon Berlin," in *Babylon Berlin*, ed. Hester Baer and Jill S. Smith (London: Bloomsbury, forthcoming).

35. Detlev Peukert, *The Weimar Republic: The Crisis of Classical Modernity*, trans. Richard Deveson (New York: Hill and Wang, 1992).

36. Eric D. Weitz, *Weimar Germany: Promise and Tragedy* (Princeton: Princeton University Press, 2007), 4.

37. Peter Fritzsche, "Did Weimar Fail?," *Journal of Modern History* 68, no. 3 (1996): 631.

38. Geoff Eley, Jennifer L. Jenkins, and Tracie Matysik, "Introduction: German Modernities and Contest of Futures," in *German Modernities from Wilhelm to Weimar: A Contest of Futures*, ed. Geoff Eley, Jennifer L. Jenkins, and Tracie Matysik (London: Bloomsbury, 2016), 2.

39. Detlev J. K. Peukert, "The Genesis of the 'Final Solution' from the Spirit of Science,"

Since the publication of Peukert's pathbreaking interpretation of Weimar's history, the "decentering" and "provincializing" of Western modernity has given rise to the concept of "multiple" or "alternative" modernities—the idea, as Dilip P. Gaonkar put it, that "modernity always unfolds within a specific cultural or civilizational context and that different starting points . . . lead to different outcomes."[40] This has enhanced and complicated the thinking about modernity after Peukert: the Kaiserreich and Weimar, for example, have recently been analyzed as specific "German modernities."[41] The concept of "multiple modernities" has three salient points for this book. First, we need to look at the history of early twentieth-century Germany not as a deviation, but as one of many historically specific instances of the unfolding of modernity. Second, the path this process took in Germany was not preordained. There was a "plurality of visions and efforts aiming to make claims on the future" that competed with each other over the shaping of the unfolding of German modernity.[42] As Peter Fritzsche and others have shown, the mass media played a crucial role in constructing and disseminating visions of this future, presenting their audience with "seemingly self-evident facts of 'das neue Leben,' 'das Leben von morgen,' and 'die neue Zeit'."[43] This brings us to the third, and most important, point: in the febrile atmosphere of Weimar Germany, when the shape of the future was struggled over furiously, it was not only the Communists and the Nazis who developed an "alternative modernity."[44] German liberals offered their own vision of a specifically German modernity, particularly after the Great Depression dethroned the United States as the model of Western

---

in *Nazism and German Society, 1933–1945*, ed. David F. Crew (London: Routledge, 1994), 438–43.

40. Dilip Parameshwar Gaonkar, "On Alternative Modernities," ed. Dilip Parameshwar Gaonkar (Durham, N.C.: Duke University Press, 1999), 17; Dipesh Chakrabarty, *Provincializing Europe: Postcolonial Thought and Historical Difference* (Princeton: Princeton University Press, 2000).

41. Eley, Jenkins, and Matysik, *German Modernities*; Roger Griffin, *Modernism and Fascism: The Sense of a Beginning under Mussolini and Hitler* (London: Palgrave Macmillan, 2007). For a discussion of this strand of interpretation, see Mark Roseman, "National Socialism and the End of Modernity," *American Historical Review* 116, no. 3 (2011): 688–701.

42. Eley, Jenkins, and Matysik, "Introduction," 5. See also Rüdiger Graf, *Die Zukunft der Weimarer Republik. Krisen und Zukunftsaneignungen in Deutschland, 1918–1933* (Munich: Oldenbourg, 2008).

43. Peter Fritzsche, "Historical Time and Future Experience in Postwar Germany," in *Ordnungen in der Krise. Zur politischen Kulturgeschichte Deutschlands 1900–1933*, ed. Wolfgang Hardtwig (Munich: Oldenbourg, 2007), 148. See also Graf, *Zukunft*, 225–50.

44. Shmuel N. Eisenstadt, "Multiple Modernities," *Daedalus* 129, no. 1 (2000): 11.

modernity. Ullstein, with *Tempo* as its most eye-catching representative, was a significant protagonist in this struggle over the *Deutungshoheit* over German modernity.

Geoff Eley has argued that, in light of these new approaches, historical phenomena like the Wandervogel youth movement or the aspects of the *Lebensreform* lifestyle have to be interpreted not as a rejection of modernity, but as a specifically German way to negotiate and grapple with it.[45] We should add that these were specifically middle-class ways of negotiating modernity. The idea of a "different" modernity that reconciled German tradition with progress had long been discussed among the German bourgeoisie, and after the First World War the feeling that the future of the modern world could—and should—actively be shaped only intensified.[46] This study introduces the concept of "moderate modernity" to describe this middle-class blend of progressive and conservative elements. This term has sometimes been used as an aesthetic category, most prominently by Theodor W. Adorno, who applied it to music that "swims with the tide of the new, but still takes great care to keep to the ingrained listening habits and expectations of the audience."[47] Adelheid von Saldern has used the term in her historical analysis of German cultural conservatism, which promoted a middle course between tradition and supposedly "excessive" modernism. This position was popular among the urban middle classes, which "wanted to be up-to-date, even 'modern'—but just not 'too modern.'"[48] Such alternative modernities on the liberal spectrum have often been ignored in the "contest of futures" of the Weimar period.[49] Rather than radical visions of a thoroughly transformed society like the ones formulated by Communists and Nazis, the moderate modernity of Weimar's liberals aimed for a reconciliation of old and new, achieved in measured, evolutionary steps rather than through violent revolution. Modern technology played a central

---

45. Geoff Eley, "What Was German Modernity and When?," in Eley, Jenkins, and Matysik, *German Modernities*, 46.

46. Thomas Rohkrämer, *Eine andere Moderne? Zivilisationskritik, Natur und Technik in Deutschland 1880–1933* (Paderborn: Schöningh, 1999), 245–70.

47. Theodor W. Adorno, "Neue Musik heute," in *Musikalische Schriften V*, vol. 18, Gesammelte Schriften (Frankfurt/Main: Suhrkamp, 2003), 14485. He used the term "moderate modernity" for the first time in 1929, see Theodor W. Adorno, "Mai 1929," in *Musikalische Schriften VI*, vol. 19, Gesammelte Schriften (Frankfurt/Main: Suhrkamp, 2003), 16013.

48. Adelheid von Saldern, "'Art for the People': From Cultural Conservatism to Nazi Cultural Policies," in *The Challenge of Modernity: German Social and Cultural Studies, 1890–1960*, trans. Bruce Little (Ann Arbor: University of Michigan Press, 2002), 311.

49. Eley, Jenkins, and Matysik, "Introduction," 1–6. One notable exception is Graf, *Zukunft*.

role in this vision as the force that would help make it a reality. While concerns about the dangers of technology for spiritual life and nature had been widespread among the German bourgeoisie before the war, in the Weimar Republic many liberals sought to overcome these negative aspects of modern life with *more* technology.[50] Particularly in everyday life, modern technologies such as the motor car, the radio, and the flush toilet, which slowly became available to broader parts of the population, promised to address problems of a society increasingly perceived as a controllable technical system that could easily be tweaked and perfected.

Tempo was a vocal proponent of the idea of a "moderate modernity." The newspaper fashioned itself as a representative, even a leader, of an extremely modern, up-to-date approach to life—an approach, however, that still operated in the framework of bourgeois society and that was aimed at strengthening the status quo of Weimar democracy. It constructed an alternative modernity on the liberal spectrum that was characterized by the ideas of a participatory political order, egalitarian social and gender relations, modernist mass culture, and an advanced consumer society, which competed with conservative, Social Democratic, Communist, and National Socialist modernities. *Tempo*'s vision was partially realized in the Weimar Republic, which the paper supported more or less enthusiastically. But in some respects, the vision touted in *Tempo* was quite radically different from the—often dispiriting—realities of Weimar Germany. The brashness with which the paper championed its vision of a modern Germany has usually not been located on the center-left of Weimar's political spectrum. *Tempo* was relentlessly positive about the future of modern Germany, and, in an astonishing feat of circular reasoning, it often claimed that this optimism would overcome the obstacles that still stood in the way of making its rosy vision a reality. The guiding ideal, at least during the first years of its publication, was the United States of America, which occupied a singularly important place in the German imagination of the early twentieth century.[51] In 1920s Germany, "'Americanism' became a catchword for untrammeled modernity."[52] In *Tempo*, "America" was portrayed as a country of prosperity, with a peaceful society and a rational political culture. Nearly every day, *Tempo*'s audience read news and anecdotes about the United States, particularly

---

50. Rohkrämer, *Moderne*, 245.
51. Graf, *Zukunft*, 261–68; Egbert Klautke, *Unbegrenzte Möglichkeiten. "Amerikanisierung" in Deutschland und Frankreich, 1900–1933* (Stuttgart: Steiner, 2003); Alf Lüdtke, Inge Marszolek, and Adelheid von Saldern, eds., *Amerikanisierung. Traum und Alptraum im Deutschland des 20. Jahrhunderts* (Stuttgart: Steiner, 1996).
52. Peukert, *Weimar*, 178.

about spectacular American achievements: the construction of the world's biggest airships, the opening of the world's longest bridge, a new transcontinental air speed record.[53] But there were also many accounts of America's mundane everyday life, such as the use of nonreturnable milk bottles in Chicago.[54] When it came to popular culture, America stood for everything that was modern: in contrast to many German intellectuals, *Tempo*'s writers celebrated Hollywood films, jazz music, and chorus girls.[55] To be sure, their image of the United States was not entirely positive. *Tempo*'s writers frequently criticized American dominance in world affairs and still saw their own country as more culturally mature.[56] Americans were often portrayed as a materially blessed "people of eighteen-year olds"—slightly naïve, shallow, and materialistic.[57] With this image of the *homo americanus* as a youthful loudmouth, *Tempo* fit into the mainstream of the European reaction to the American challenge.[58] And yet the sheer number of articles and images in the newspaper seemed to bring American everyday life closer to its audience. Germany's European neighbors, such as France, Austria, or Britain, often appeared only in the political and economic news, and German society and culture seemed to share more with "America" than with these countries. However, despite its Americanism and modernist stylings, the vision *Tempo* advocated was a middle course between tradition and change—a "moderate modernity" that contained the promise of modest material and social progress without the need for drastic political measures. The central question was how to adapt the American model to suit German postwar society, in other words, how to follow the American ideal without losing Germany's "soul," its cultural heritage and traditions, which even *Tempo*'s authors, most of them members of the educated bourgeoisie, still held in high regard. They did not want Germans to become Americans: rather, *Tempo* promoted a German take on American modernity, without the supposed excesses of the latter. The path to this moderate modernity, according to *Tempo*,

---

53. "Neuer Rekord New York–Los Angeles," *Tempo*, 27 October 1928, 12; "Die längste Brücke der Welt," *Tempo*, 30 November 1928, 12; "Amerika baut die größten Zeppeline," *Tempo*, 4 December 1928, 4.

54. "In Amerika werden Milchflaschen grundsätzlich weggeworfen," *Tempo*, 1 November 1928, 12.

55. For the reaction by German intellectuals to American mass culture, see Klautke, *Unbegrenzte Möglichkeiten*, 239–68.

56. See, for example, Roda Roda, "Fragen des Tages: Onkel Sam und sein europäischer Neffe," *Tempo*, 2 October 1928, 2; Roda Roda, "Fragen des Tages: Der strenge Pauker," *Tempo*, 8 December 1928, 2.

57. Heaven, "Fragen des Tages: Ei, ei, Amerika!," *Tempo*, 11 January 1929, 2.

58. Klautke, *Unbegrenzte Möglichkeiten*, 275.

was "common sense" and "objectivity" (*Sachlichkeit*)—its vision of Germany's future was not to be realized by revolution, but by a policy of small steps. In this sense, *Tempo* offered what Ulrich Herbert has described as the widespread need, beyond social and political boundaries, for guidance and meaning in a confusing, fast-changing world of modernity.[59] The example of *Tempo* shows that it was not only the *völkisch* right that tried to offer such reassurance, but the political center, too—not by invoking old customs and tradition in opposition to the "new life" but by constructing an unthreatening, moderated version of it.

The main currents of *Tempo*'s vision of a moderate modernity were democracy, citizenship, and consumerism. As one of Ullstein's major new publications after 1918, *Tempo* embodied the company's democratic ideology like no other newspaper, and it was founded at a decisive moment in Weimar's history. At the end of the 1920s, in contrast to the beginning of the decade, there was a widespread belief among pro-democratic forces that the biggest threat for the Republic was not a direct, violent coup d'état anymore, but the undermining of its popular legitimacy. After the new state and its Constitution had prevailed for ten years, the legal scholar Hugo Sinzheimer noted in August 1929, the battle had now shifted to the hearts and minds of the population:

> The enemies of the Republic do no longer plan any immediate violent putsches. They think differently. They are now bent on the political and psychological demoralization of the people's democratic will. Accordingly, the Republican defense against this must not rely primarily on the police force, but rather on the convincing power of political leadership; not on mechanical pressure, but on the democratic spirit and will.[60]

This was echoed a few months later by the Prussian interior minister Albert Grezinski, who stressed the need "to educate the people in democratic thought and action" to strengthen the Republic.[61] By this time, the democratic foundation of the German state had—often grudgingly—been accepted by most polit-

---

59. Ulrich Herbert, "Europe in High Modernity. Reflections on a Theory of the 20th Century," *Journal of Modern European History* 5, no. 1 (2007): 12.

60. Hugo Sinzheimer and Ernst Fraenkel, *Die Justiz in der Weimarer Republik. Eine Chronik* (Neuwied: Luchterhand, 1968), 188; see also Michael Dreyer, "Weimar as a 'Militant Democracy,'" in *Beyond Glitter and Doom: The Contingency of the Weimar Republic*, ed. Jochen Hung, Godela Weiss-Sussex, and Geoff Wilkes (Munich: iudicium, 2012), 81.

61. Ross, *Media and the Making of Modern Germany*, 246.

ical camps.[62] Not the formal existence of the Republic was fought over anymore, but its governance: "democracy" remained a malleable and contested term in Weimar Germany, even ten years after the abdication of the Kaiser.[63] It was one of the essential keywords of the time and, as such, highly politicized: all serious political movements of Weimar Germany associated their ideology with some form of popular government (*Volksherrschaft*).[64] There was a multitude of competing notions of democratic rule, from representative to direct, social to national, soviet (*Rätedemokratie*) and people's democracy (*Volksdemokratie*).[65] Even pronounced enemies of the Weimar state like the

---

62. Tim B. Müller, *Nach dem ersten Weltkrieg. Lebensversuche moderner Demokratien* (Hamburg: Hamburger Edition, 2014), 69; Anthony McElligott, "Political Culture," in *Weimar Germany*, ed. Anthony McElligott (Oxford: Oxford University Press, 2009), 26–49; Kolb, *Weimar Republic*, 3–22; Boris Barth, *Dolchstoßlegenden und politische Desintegration. Das Trauma der deutschen Niederlage im Ersten Weltkrieg 1914–1933* (Düsseldorf: Droste, 2003), 302–21; Thomas Mergel, *Parlamentarische Kultur im Reichstag der Weimarer Republik. Politische Kommunikation, symbolische Politik und Öffentlichkeit im Reichstag* (Düsseldorf: Droste, 2002), 323–31; Klaus Reimus, "'Aber das Reich muss uns doch bleiben!' Die nationale Rechte," in *Politische Identität und nationale Gedenktage. Zur politischen Kultur in der Weimarer Republik*, ed. Detlef Lehnert and Klaus Megerle (Opladen: Westdeutscher Verlag, 1989), 232.

63. Riccardo Bavaj, "Pluralizing Democracy in Weimar Germany: Historiographical Perspectives and Transatlantic Vista," in *Transatlantic Democracy in the Twentieth Century: Transfer and Transformation*, ed. Paul Nolte (Munich: Oldenbourg, 2016), 54–61; Heidrun Kämper, "Demokratisches Wissen in der frühen Weimarer Republik," in *Demokratiegeschichte als Zäsurgeschichte. Diskurse der frühen Weimarer Republik*, ed. Heidrun Kämper, Peter Haslinger, and Thomas Raithel (Berlin: de Gruyter, 2014), 19–96; Marcus Llanque, "Massendemokratie zwischen Kaiserreich und westlicher Demokratie," in *Demokratisches Denken in der Weimarer Republik*, ed. Christoph Gusy (Baden-Baden: Nomos, 2000), 38–39; Thomas Childers, "Languages of Liberalism: Liberal Political Discourse in the Weimar Republic," in *In Search of a Liberal Germany: Studies in the History of German Liberalism from 1789 to the Present*, ed. Konrad J. Jarausch and Larry E. Jones (New York: Berg, 1990), 323–59. See also Jochen Hung, "'Bad' Politics and 'Good' Culture: New Approaches to the History of the Weimar Republic," *Central European History* 49, nos. 3–4 (2016): 448.

64. Christian Schottmann, *Politische Schlagwörter in Deutschland zwischen 1929 und 1934* (Stuttgart: Hans-Dieter Heinz, 1997), 111–26; Werner Conze, "Demokratie," in *Geschichtliche Grundbegriffe. Historisches Lexikon zur politisch-sozialen Sprache in Deutschland*, ed. Otto Brunner, Werner Conze, and Reinhart Koselleck, vol. 1 (Stuttgart: Klett, 1972), 896–97.

65. Bavaj, "Pluralizing Democracy," 61–70; Kämper, "Demokratisches Wissen"; Marcus Llanque, *Politische Ideengeschichte. Ein Gewebe politischer Diskurse* (Munich: Oldenbourg, 2008), 406–41; Christoph Gusy, "Demokratisches Denken in der Weimarer Republik—Entstehungsbedingungen und Vorfragen," in Gusy, *Demokratisches Denken*, 12–13.

National Socialists espoused concepts like "Germanic" or "organic" democracy or offered the "people's community" (*Volksgemeinschaft*) as an alternative.[66] These competing definitions centered around two forms of democracy, either as a parliamentary "party state" (*Parteienstaat*) in Western fashion or a more directly plebiscitary state, with the latter allowing for a more authoritarian form of government as long as it had the support of the population.[67] This debate about the "right" form of democracy was by no means confined to Germany, but was an international trend after the war, even in the US.[68] The diversity of notions of democracy was reflected in the Weimar Constitution itself, which incorporated different democratic models, with parliamentarianism existing alongside strong aspects of plebiscitary democracy in the direct election of the president and the referendum system (*Volksbegehren* and *Volksentscheid*).[69] Most significantly, the first article of the Constitution effectively declared "the people" not only the source but also the bearer of popular sovereignty. This could be interpreted—and was, even by most legal experts of the time—in essentialist, organic terms as "the people" standing above the Constitution, a precept that does not explicitly call for a parliamentary order.[70]

Closely related to the discursive battle over the meaning of democracy was the question of citizenship, "one of the crucially unresolved dilemmas of Germany's modernity."[71] Because the unfolding of modernity in Germany involved dramatic changes of national boundaries, war, revolution, and disso-

---

66. Anja Lobenstein-Reichmann, "Der völkische Demokratiebegriff," in Kämper, Haslinger, and Raithel, *Demokratiegeschichte*, 285–306; Llanque, *Politische Ideengeschichte*, 424; Schottmann, *Politische Schlagwörter*, 119.

67. McElligott, "Political Culture," 26; Oliver Lepsius, "Staatstheorie und Demokratiebegriff in der Weimarer Republik," in Gusy, *Demokratisches Denken*, 366–414.

68. Boris Barth, *Europa nach dem großen Krieg. Die Krise der Demokratie in der Zwischenkriegszeit 1918–1938* (Frankfurt/Main: Campus, 2016), 148–80; Tim B. Müller and Adam Tooze, "Demokratie nach dem Ersten Weltkrieg," in *Normalität und Fragilität. Demokratie nach dem Ersten Weltkrieg*, ed. Tim B. Müller and Adam Tooze (Hamburg: Hamburger Edition, 2015), 9–33; Anthony McElligott, "Rethinking the Weimar Paradigm: Carl Schmitt and Politics without Authority," in Hung, Weiss-Sussex, and Wilkes, *Beyond Glitter and Doom*, 100; Llanque, *Politische Ideengeschichte*, 424–34; Benjamin L. Alpers, *Dictators, Democracy, and American Public Culture: Envisioning the Totalitarian Enemy, 1920s–1950s* (Chapel Hill: University of North Carolina Press, 2003), 15–76.

69. McElligott, "Weimar Paradigm," 91–92; Llanque, *Politische Ideengeschichte*, 415.

70. Jörn Retterath, "Der Volksbegriff in der Zäsur des Jahres 1918/19," in Kämper, Haslinger, and Raithel, *Demokratiegeschichte*, 97–122.

71. Kathleen Canning, "War, Citizenship, and Rhetorics of Sexual Crisis: Reflections on States of Exception in Germany, 1914–20," in Eley, Jenkins, and Matysik, *German Modernities*, 236.

lutions and new formations of the state, citizenship—understood as a political status, a set of social practices, a discursive framework, and as experience and subjectivity—was a crucial field of contest in which Germans negotiated their public relationship to the modern world they inhabited.[72] Naturally, the changes in political citizenship that the Weimar Republic had brought to Germany, manifested most prominently in the extending of suffrage to women and young people, were welcomed by the paper. However, *Tempo* took these changes as a given and did not discuss them in detail, but constructed a complementing consumer citizenship, which people could practice in everyday life. This put the newspaper at the forefront of a transformative intellectual trend that developed globally during the interwar period. While the 1950s and 1960s are traditionally seen as the era of the breakthrough of the mature consumer society in the West, more recently the interwar years have been identified as the pivotal transition period during which "the vision of a society of producers faded into one of consumers."[73] The 1920s were also the first decade that "promoted a powerful link between everyday consumption and modernization," positing "consumerism as the shining path to modernity."[74] Competing interwar regimes, from US democracy to republican China and Nazi Germany, constructed visions of a consumer modernity to "embed citizens in national collectives . . . and institutionalize consumerism as the basis of citizenship and national identity."[75] The study of the cultural and political history of consumption has long been a focus of historians of the United States. Charles McGovern has argued that the idea of consumer citizenship had a long tradition in America, but it was only during the prolonged period of prosperity after the

---

72. Kathleen Canning, "Claiming Citizenship: Suffrage and Subjectivity in Germany after the First World War," in *Weimar Publics/Weimar Subjects: Rethinking the Political Culture of Germany in the 1920s*, ed. Kerstin Barndt, Kathleen Canning, and Kristin McGuire (New York: Berghahn, 2010), 116–37; Geoff Eley and Jan Palmowski, "Citizenship and National Identity in Twentieth-Century Germany," in *Citizenship and National Identity in Twentieth-Century Germany*, ed. Geoff Eley and Jan Palmowski (Stanford: Stanford University Press, 2008), 3–23; Kathleen Canning and Sonya O. Rose, "Gender, Citizenships and Subjectivities: Some Historical and Theoretical Considerations," in *Gender, Citizenships and Subjectivities*, ed. Kathleen Canning and Sonya O. Rose (Oxford: Blackwell, 2002), 1–17.

73. Joe Perry, "Consumer Citizenship in the Interwar Era: Gender, Race, and the State in Global-Historical Perspective," *Journal of Women's History* 18, no. 4 (2006): 159. See also Ruth Oldenziel, Adri Albert de la Bruhèze, and Onno de Wit, "Europe's Mediation Junction: Technology and Consumer Society in the 20th Century," *History and Technology* 21, no. 1 (March 1, 2005): 116.

74. Don Slater, *Consumer Culture and Modernity* (Cambridge: Polity, 1997), 12.

75. Perry, "Consumer Citizenship," 159.

First World War that consuming began to be equated with being American.[76] At the same time, the consumer's choice became the dominant metaphor for American democracy, pushed mainly by advertisers who created the ideal of a "democracy of goods" eclipsing class differences and uniting the nation in shared consumer lifestyles.[77] The Great Depression did not fundamentally undermine the success of this narrative—in fact, it was through the political struggle to address the crisis that "American people fitfully but firmly came to equate the consumer with the citizen, a consumer standard of living with democracy."[78] Lizabeth Cohen has shown how during the Depression this view of the "purchaser consumer," who mainly exercised their democratic role as citizen through their purchasing power, won out over the ideal of the citizen-consumer as an activist directly involved in political decision-making.[79]

In most of interwar Europe, despite the beginning shift toward a consumerist worldview, producerist ideas still dominated the ideological landscape.[80] In Weimar Germany, growing consumer desires and a shifting "horizon of expectations" regarding the standard of living were met with the realities of a struggling postwar economy.[81] Most Germans looked to the new state to address the gap between expectations and reality, leading to an immense amount of initiatives, interventions, and visions directed at controlling and steering consumption.[82] While Julia Sneeringer has shown how from the mid-1920s Americanized metaphors of the citizen-consumer found their way into German political culture, they did not reach widespread acceptance similar to

---

76. Charles F. McGovern, *Sold American: Consumption and Citizenship, 1890–1945* (Chapel Hill: University of North Carolina Press, 2009), 96–131.

77. Roland Marchand, *Advertising the American Dream: Making Way for Modernity, 1920–1940* (Berkeley: University of California Press, 1985), 217–28.

78. Charles McGovern, "Consumption and Citizenship in the United States, 1900–1940," in *Getting and Spending: European and American Consumer Societies in the Twentieth Century*, ed. Susan Strasser, Charles McGovern, and Matthias Judt (Cambridge: Cambridge University Press, 1998), 37.

79. Lizabeth Cohen, *A Consumers' Republic: The Politics of Mass Consumption in Postwar America* (New York: Vintage, 2003), 18–61.

80. Victoria de Grazia, *Irresistible Empire: America's Advance through Twentieth-Century Europe* (Cambridge: Harvard University Press, 2006), 1–14; Hannes Siegrist, "Konsum, Kultur und Gesellschaft im modernen Europa," in *Europäische Konsumgeschichte. Zur Gesellschafts-und Kulturgeschichte des Konsums (18. bis 20. Jahrhundert)*, ed. Hartmut Kaelble, Jürgen Kocka, and Hannes Siegrist (Frankfurt/Main: Campus, 1997), 13–48.

81. Claudius Torp, *Konsum und Politik in der Weimarer Republik* (Göttingen: Vandenhoek & Ruprecht, 2011), 65–97.

82. Torp, *Konsum und Politik*, 335.

the United States.[83] Claudius Torp concluded that a dominant sociopolitical vision centered around the figure of the consumer did not exist in Weimar Germany.[84] In this context, *Tempo*'s construction of a German consumer modernity was extraordinary. While the newspaper was clearly influenced by the American discourse, *Tempo* offered its readers the vision of a particularly German consumer-citizen, which combined the pleasures of conspicuous consumption with the democratic system. At least for the first few years of its existence, *Tempo* created an emphatic, optimistic, and quite radical vision of a German consumerist democratic society, collapsing the traditional boundaries between the frivolous world of consumption and the serious world of politics. The paper's readers were constantly reminded of their role as citizen-consumers: private consumption was framed as a necessary and explicitly political act, one that would help make *Tempo*'s vision of a prosperous modern Germany a reality. Modern technology was an essential aspect of this vision, but not as an awesome force shaping people's lives, but in the form of consumer products used to achieve a modern, convenient lifestyle. Young people of both genders were treated as the foremost agents of this form of citizenship, and their ways of using technology, dressing, socializing, and consuming were presented as the representative ways to practice it. But *Tempo* also gave its readers room for what Aihwa Ong called the process of "self-making" in citizenship—space to debate, negotiate, and apply the newspaper's vision of German modernity to their own lives, through content that involved the audience, such as contests, advice columns, film reviews written by readers, and by printing letters sent in to the editors.[85] This positive approach toward consuming and its role in selfhood and citizenship set *Tempo* apart from the generally negative attitude toward mass consumption that dominated Europe in the interwar years.[86]

While these three elements of *Tempo*'s vision of modernity—democracy, citizenship, consumerism—remained in place over the course of its lifetime, they changed their meaning or importance during these momentous five years. Particularly after the Great Depression had dethroned its American role model,

---

83. Julia Sneeringer, "The Shopper as Voter: Women, Advertising, and Politics in Post-Inflation Germany," *German Studies Review* 27, no. 3 (2004): 476–501.

84. Torp, *Konsum und Politik*, 325.

85. Aihwa Ong, "Cultural Citizenship as Subject-Making: Immigrants Negotiate Racial and Cultural Boundaries in the United States," *Current Anthropology* 37, no. 5 (1996): 738.

86. Andreas Wirsching, "From Work to Consumption: Transatlantic Visions of Individuality in Modern Mass Society," *Contemporary European History* 20, no. 1 (February 2011): 14.

Tempo's definition of modernity changed from a byword for American-style consumer democracy to a combination of plebiscitary government, social conservatism, and an advanced consumer society. While Ullstein, like the rest of Weimar's liberal press, was an outspoken enemy of the Nazis, the worldview the company espoused through *Tempo* in the early 1930s did not differ as sharply from the National Socialist vision as many historians of the Weimar press have argued. As von Saldern has shown, the concept of a "moderate modernity" brings these cultural continuities between Weimar and Nazi Germany into sharper focus.[87] However, the purpose of this argument is not to apportion blame for the "enabling" of Hitler, but to show that National Socialism was part and parcel of Weimar modernity.

In this book, the development of *Tempo*'s vision of a German modernity is traced in three chapters, which generally follow the chronological development of the history of the Weimar Republic. The first chapter covers the years from 1928 to 1929, which are usually regarded as the turning point from Weimar's relatively stable "golden years" to its final phase of disintegration. The new state finally seemed to have found safer waters politically and Germans enjoyed prewar levels of income for the first time since 1914, but the economy already showed the first signs of crisis. During this short time, *Tempo* operated in the economic, political, and cultural context Ullstein had developed it for, and this chapter sets up the main facets of the newspaper's vision, constructed through its coverage of the everyday life of Weimar Germany, in which consumer products, modern technology, and leisure culture featured prominently. At the same time, *Tempo* offered direct and full-throated support to the new democratic system, most visibly during significant political dates, such as the tenth anniversary of the founding of the Republic in 1928. An important part of this vision were its supposed representatives—the young men and women of Weimar—who *Tempo* set up as the agents of its moderate modernity. The second chapter covers the development of these facets during the years from 1930 to 1931, with a particular focus on the momentous year of 1930, when the Republic was rocked by multiple crises: the Great Depression arrived in Germany, while Chancellor Brüning's first "presidential cabinet" in March and the surprising success of the Nazis in the general election in September seriously undermined Weimar democracy. *Tempo* had to adjust to these fundamental challenges to its vision of a modern Germany. This chapter also puts a focus on internal politics at the

---

87. Saldern, "Art for the People," 299–347; Adelheid von Saldern, "Volk and Heimat: Culture in Radio Broadcasting during the Period of Transition from Weimar to Nazi Germany," *Journal of Modern History* 76, no. 2 (2004): 312–46.

Ullstein house: the company entered a deep crisis of its own during this time, triggered by a family dispute among the owners, which impacted the way *Tempo* was able to operate in the volatile political climate of the early 1930s. Weimar's final years from 1932 to 1933 are covered in the third chapter, which is divided by the appointment of Hitler as chancellor at the beginning of 1933. Before this date, at the height of the political and economic crisis, without hope for quick improvement, *Tempo*'s quintessential nature as a political project—rather than just a newspaper—showed most clearly. While it adjusted its vision of a modern Germany, rather than reporting on the crisis the paper put an extraordinary optimistic spin on everyday life under these pressures. After 30 January 1933, *Tempo*'s moderate modernity was confronted with powerful Nazi visions of a German future, and this second part of the chapter chronicles the newspaper's attempts to find a compromise between the two.

Tempo, Ullstein, and the Late Weimar Republic

While this study focuses on a single newspaper, it is in many respects also the history of its publisher, the Ullstein company, and of the late Weimar Republic itself.[88] This context is essential to understand *Tempo*'s historical significance. In many ways, 1928 was the Weimar Republic's best year: the German economy reached its highest rate of production of the whole Weimar era and real wages had climbed back to prewar levels for the first time.[89] In the general election of 20 May, the Social Democrats had broadened their share of the vote considerably, and while the liberal parties had incurred losses, the liberal press interpreted the results as a clear demonstration of the electorate's support for the new state and democracy as a whole.[90] There certainly were signs, such as the Ruhr lockout in November, that showed the continuing volatility and instability of Weimar society. But many observers in Germany and abroad still believed that ten years after its foundation, the Republic had finally reached safer waters.[91]

---

88. Parts of this subchapter have been published in Jochen Hung, "The 'Ullstein Spirit': The Ullstein Publishing House, the End of the Weimar Republic and the Making of Cold War German Identity, 1925–77," *Journal of Contemporary History* 53, no. 1 (2018): 158–84.

89. Torp, *Konsum und Politik*, 37; Werner Abelshauser and Dieter Petzina, *Deutsche Wirtschaftsgeschichte im Industriezeitalter. Konjunktur, Krise, Wachstum* (Königstein: Athenäum, 1981), 56.

90. Sösemann, *Ende*, 60–62; Bosch, *Liberale Presse*, 77–81; Eksteins, *Limits*, 141.

91. Graf, *Zukunft*, 65–82; Eksteins, *Limits*, 68.

The newspaper industry, always a very sensitive gauge for the overall economic climate, reflected Weimar's relative stability. In 1928, 900 million marks were spent on newspaper advertising in Germany.[92] *Deutsche Presse*, the official organ of the Reich Association of the German Press, reported on the "almost miraculous growth" of the number of newspapers worldwide and the "gigantic boom" of the growing advertising market.[93] No other media organization represented this boom better than the Ullstein publishing house. Founded in Berlin in 1877 by Leopold Ullstein, son of a Jewish paper merchant from Fürth, by the 1920s it had grown into "the giant of German publishing."[94] The architects of the company's success were Leopold's five sons, who had taken over the company after his death in 1899. The effective cooperation of Hans, Louis, Franz, Hermann, and Rudolf Ullstein was legendary and seen as one of the company's most important assets.[95] When Franz Ullstein was asked in 1927 to record a message for the Berlin University's sound archive, he began the recording with a reference to the company's shared ownership:

> Ullstein is a multeity of five brothers and thus we should really record a choir. . . . Because we decide unanimously in the Ullstein house. This is necessary for the forceful implementation of our decisions and the reason why our multiplicity does not hinder our progress but fuels it.[96]

Just like for the Weimar Republic as a whole, 1928 marked Ullstein's peak. That year, the firm's newspapers reported their highest ever circulation and, in its annual report, the company recorded a substantial increase in revenue.[97] By then, the company not only owned the country's biggest daily, the

---

92. Eksteins, *Limits*, 222.
93. "Gewaltige Entwicklung des Zeitungswesens in aller Welt," *Deutsche Presse* 18 (1928), 478–79.
94. Fulda, *Press and Politics*, 2. For a general overview of Ullstein's history, see also Eksteins, *Limits*, 111–22; Kurt Koszyk, *Deutsche Presse im 19. Jahrhundert* (Berlin: Colloquium, 1966), 283–90; Koszyk, *Deutsche Presse 1914–1945*, 251–58. The official company history should be used with care: Erik Lindner, ed., *125 Jahre Ullstein. Presse-und Verlagsgeschichte im Zeichen der Eule* (Berlin: Axel Springer, 2002); Freyburg and Wallenberg, *Hundert Jahre Ullstein*; Max Osborn, ed., *Fünfzig Jahre Ullstein 1877–1927* (Berlin: Ullstein, 1927).
95. Eksteins, *Limits*, 104–14.
96. Franz Ullstein, *Das Ullsteinhaus*, 20 January 1927, in Wissenschaftliche Sammlungen der Humboldt-Universität zu Berlin (WSHU), Lautarchiv, LA 833.
97. "Geschäftsbericht Ullstein 1928," *Zeitungs-Verlag*, 28 July 1928. See also Oron J. Hale, *The Captive Press in the Third Reich* (Princeton: Princeton University Press, 1964), 135.

Berliner Morgenpost, Europe's biggest weekly, the *Berliner Illustrirte Zeitung*, and the *Vossische Zeitung*, one of Germany's most respected broadsheet newspapers, but also held a considerable share of the book market. Its latest project, the illustrated magazine *Die Grüne Post*, had turned out to be an enormous success: in April 1928, a year after its founding, it already had over 450,000 subscribers, a number that rose to over 810,000 by the end of the year.[98] According to the company's own numbers from 1929, Ullstein employed close to 10,000 people and its presses printed 350 million newspaper copies and 115 million magazine copies a year.[99] With its network of uniformly designed Ullstein shops—eighty in Berlin alone and seventy in the rest of the country, where people could buy not only Ullstein newspapers and magazines and its distinctive line of cheap, red-jacketed Ullstein-Romane but also purchase sewing patterns and book holiday cruises—the company made sure most Germans had access to its products.[100] Ullstein's success was registered even beyond the country's borders. In 1920, the *New York Times* depicted the company as a formidable force in the society of the new German state and reported with awe on its economic and cultural clout:

> This enormous chain publishing industry is unmatched by any similar organization in the United States. Naturally it wields tremendous power in Germany. The combined circulations of its newspapers and periodicals number millions and its influence extends into nearly every field, for there is scarcely a home throughout the length and breadth of the land that is not reached by at least one Ullstein publication.[101]

In his book on the "new Germany," published in 1928, the French journalist Jacques Mortane devoted a whole chapter to Ullstein, describing its headquarters as a bustling, well-organized, cosmopolitan hub of activity, whose size

---

98. *Ullstein-Chronik*, 1928, unpaginated, in Berlin, Unternehmensarchiv Axel Springer (UAS), Ullstein files. The *Ullstein-Chronik* is a handwritten, unpaginated company diary presented to the owners by the staff to mark the firm's fiftieth anniversary. It was continuously updated every year until 1941. For the *Grüne Post*, see also Richard Katz, "Die Grüne Post," in Freyburg and Wallenberg, *Hundert Jahre Ullstein*, 2:167–76.

99. "Der größte deutsche Verlag in Zahl und Bild," in *Der Verlag Ullstein zum Weltreklamekongress Berlin 1929* (Berlin: Ullstein, 1929), 81–85.

100. "Zahlen aus den Ullstein Betrieben," *Ullstein-Berichte*, April 1929, 6. For a description of the Ullstein branches, see Max Krell, *Das alles gab es einmal* (Frankfurt/Main: Scheffler, 1961), 121.

101. "Ullstein Verlag, Power in the Reich," *New York Times*, October 5, 1920.

and dynamism surpassed all similar ventures in his own country.[102] A year later, the British trade journal *Newspaper World* praised the company as an international leader of the publishing industry: "In every phase of publishing, printing, and advertising service, the Ullstein organization is thoroughly up-to-date."[103]

In Germany, however, Ullstein's success and influence were seen more critically. In 1928, the pacifist and playwright Herbert Eulenberg complained about Ullstein threatening the diversity of German culture:

There is no other publishing company that finds advertising as easy as Ullstein, as it can promote its books as cheaply as possible in its own countless newspapers and magazines. In the future, this will be ever more profitable for the company, and consequently there might come a day when all publishers in Germany have become one single Ullstein house.[104]

Two years later, the conservative literary critic Conrad Wandrey used the term "Ullstein-German" as a catchphrase for anyone uncritically embracing Weimar's modern mass culture.[105] This kind of criticism reflected the general anxiety of many Weimar intellectuals about a supposed homogenization, commercialization, and commodification of German culture that was condensed in the catchphrase of "Americanization."[106] Ullstein, with its many popular newspapers and magazines, range of cheap paperbacks and nationwide presence, became a symbol for this perceived development.

The criticism of Ullstein's commercialism sometimes veered into outright anti-Semitism.[107] In the polemic *The German Book Trade and the Jewry*, issued

---

102. Jacques Mortane, *Sous les Tilleuls. La Nouvelle Allemagne* (Paris: Baudiniere, 1928), 277–82.

103. "The German Press: The 'Big Three' of German Publishers," *Newspaper World*, August 17, 1929, 20.

104. Herbert Eulenberg, "Wie die großen deutschen Verlage gegründet wurden. Das Haus Ullstein," *Die literarische Welt*, 17 August 1928, 3.

105. Conrad Wandrey, "Thomas Mann und die Forderung des Tages," in *Thomas Mann im Urteil seiner Zeit. Dokumente 1891–1955*, ed. Klaus Schröter (Frankfurt/Main: Vittorio Klostermann, 2000), 187.

106. Klautke, *Unbegrenzte Möglichkeiten*, 269–314; Rohkrämer, *Moderne*, 270–300.

107. Leopold Ullstein's five sons were baptized Christians and while the company employed a great number of Jewish editors, writers, and journalists, its publications never defined themselves as "Jewish" newspapers. See Hans Wallenberg, "Zum jüdischen Beitrag. Biographische Miniaturen," in Freyburg and Wallenberg, *Hundert Jahre Ullstein*, 1:407–53; Eksteins, *Limits*, 133–34.

in 1925 by the anti-Semitic publishing house Hammer-Verlag, Ullstein was described as "the department store of German intellectual life" that appealed to the basest instincts of its audience.[108] Ullstein was also "a target for concentrated Nazi hate" as the epitome of the image of the "Jewish press" poisoning the minds of the German people.[109] One particularly vivid example is the Nazi publication *The Press as Jewish Instrument of Power*, published in 1930, which devoted a whole chapter to Ullstein, calling the company's high output undeniable proof of "the poisoning of our public sphere by the Jewry."[110] The Nazi satirical magazine *Die Brennessel* also regularly attacked the company in articles and illustrations.[111]

The Communists, on the other hand, attacked Ullstein as an agent of the capitalist system, peddling escapist entertainment that kept the working class away from political engagement. In a series of reports on "Hindenburg's country" published in 1925, the Soviet journalist Larissa Reissner depicted Ullstein as one of the "national sanctuaries" from which the nation was "invisibly ruled."[112] She likened the company to a "clever brothel keeper," with its many different publications as her prostitutes, catering to every taste. The illusion they sold was a consumerist fantasy of material prosperity—"a luxurious villa and a car in the garage"—that their audience saw in American movies: "Millions of European workers live with a dream about Russia. . . . But Ullstein's reader, the petty-bourgeois, goes to the pictures to see his promised land."[113] For Communist critics of the company, *Tempo* was the embodiment of Ullstein escapism: in February 1930, John Heartfield used the newspaper in one of his most famous collages for the *Arbeiter Illustrierte Zeitung (AIZ)*.[114] Captioned "Whoever reads bourgeois newspapers goes blind and deaf!," the

---

108. Lynkeus, *Der deutsche Buchhandel und das Judentum. Ein Menetekel* (Leipzig: Hammer, 1925), 17–19.

109. Hale, *Captive Press*, 131.

110. Anton Meister, *Die Presse als Machtmittel Judas* (Munich: Eher, 1930), 58.

111. Lancelot, "Erwachendes Ullstein-Christentum," *Die Brennessel*, 20 April 1931, 182; "Ullsteinredakteure unterwegs," *Die Brennessel*, 22 June 1932, front page; "Georg Bernhard gegen Deutschland," *Die Brennessel*, 31 Mai 1933, 262.

112. Larissa Reissner, *Hamburg at the Barricades and Other Writings on Weimar Germany*, trans. Richard Chappell (London: Pluto Press, 1977), 113–63.

113. Reissner, *Hamburg at the Barricades*, 163.

114. John Heartfield, *Wer Bürgerblätter liest wird blind und taub. Weg mit den Verdummungsbandagen!*, published in *Arbeiter Illustrierte Zeitung* 9 (1930), 103. The *Tempo* edition used by Heartfield is from 9 January 1930, the full headline reads "Apotheker-Skandal in Schöneberg. Wie man einen Menschen in den Tod treibt." I am indebted to Judith Brodie for this information.

collage shows a laborer whose head is wrapped in newspapers (Fig. 6). The two publications visible in the collage are the Social Democratic Party (Sozialdemokratische Partei Deutschlands, SPD) paper *Vorwärts* and *Tempo*; the only word visible of *Tempo*'s front page is "scandal." The message of the image is clear: the liberal media are dumbing down the working class and keeping workers from organized political action. The fact that Heartfield chose *Tempo* as a metaphor for the supposed sensationalism and superficiality of the bourgeois press suggests that the paper had become an easily recognizable brand among the audience of the *AIZ*. These political attacks on Ullstein by Nazis and Communists were not surprising. The company's leaders were a powerful political force and did not shy away from using their influence. Their editorial conferences consisted of daily briefings on foreign and domestic politics, where strategic alliances were forged with party envoys, newspapers were positioned against or in favor of individual policies, and visions for Germany's future were drawn up and dismissed.[115]

Ullstein publications traditionally took a liberal stance. Before the First World War, they regularly opposed the German government and called for a free press and civil rights. This earned the company not only multiple lawsuits for libel and lèse-majesté but also—after the Social Democratic press had been banned in 1878—a growing readership among the working class.[116] Ullstein supported Germany's aggressive politics during the war, but after 1918 it quickly backed the new democratic regime and "came to be regarded as a pillar of the Weimar state."[117] Although the company generally avoided open political partisanship, Ullstein was perceived by many as one of the mouthpieces of the German Democratic Party (Deutsche Demokratische Partei, DDP).[118] Georg Bernhard, the influential editor-in-chief of the *Vossische Zeitung* and the company's political figurehead, was an early member of the DDP, and Hermann Ullstein took a close interest in the party's fortunes.[119] The DDP, founded

---

115. Hermann Ullstein, "We Blundered Hitler into Power," *Saturday Evening Post*, July 13, 1940, 36. See also Hans Schäffer's records of editorial conferences during his time as Ullstein's general director: Schäffer diary, New York, Leo Baeck Institute (LBI), AR 7177/MF 512, 9–10.

116. Georg Bernhard, "Die Geschichte des Hauses," in *Fünfzig Jahre Ullstein 1877–1927*, ed. Max Osborn (Berlin: Ullstein, 1927), 22–28.

117. Eksteins, *Limits*, 192.

118. Fulda, *Press and Politics*, 41; Joachim Stang, *Die Deutsche Demokratische Partei in Preußen 1918–1933* (Düsseldorf: Droste, 1994), 41–42; Bruce B. Frye, *Liberal Democrats in the Weimar Republic: The History of the German Democratic Party and the German State Party* (Carbondale: Southern Illinois University Press, 1985), 217; Eksteins, *Limits*, 111–37.

119. Eksteins, *Limits*, 54–58, 205–10.

Figure 6. John Heartfield, "Wer Bürgerblätter liest wird blind und taub," *Arbeiter Illustrierte Zeitung*, 9 February 1930. © The Heartfield Community of Heirs, c/o Pictoright Amsterdam 2021

in 1918 by the left-wing forces of German liberalism, had a decisive influence, through the party's cofounder Hugo Preuß, on the drafting of the Constitution and remained its staunchest defender throughout the Weimar era.[120] Its main aim was to act as a bridge between liberalism and social democracy; its core program stressed traditional liberal values, such as individual responsibility and personal freedom, but also incorporated demands such as an extension of the welfare state, strong trade unions, and the eight-hour day.[121] The DDP was the only liberal party that unequivocally supported the new democratic system, and it was instrumental in tying the liberal press to the fate of the Republic.[122] In many respects, the definition of democracy that ruled the Ullstein house overlapped with the DDP's. For both, democracy was not merely a form of government, but a way of life, a *Weltanschauung*.[123] The DDP espoused a "democratic nationalism," an attempt to fuse the idea of Western democracy with the ideal of the German nation, a vision that Georg Bernhard supported enthusiastically.[124] At the heart of DDP liberalism was a pedagogical impulse to educate the German people in a new "sense of citizenship" (*staatsbürgerliche Gesinnung*).[125] In 1928, celebrating the tenth anniversary of the founding of the Republic, the historian and DDP member Wilhelm Mommsen emphasized the party's central mission of enforcing the values of democracy and citizenship:

> Democracy and the republic not only grant the individual new rights, they also come with even more duties. Because every German has the right to have their say in the affairs of the state and the nation, they also have the duty to exercise this right of co-determination with a responsibility towards all others. Furthermore, this thinking in terms of state and nation

---

120. Dieter Langewiesche, *Liberalismus in Deutschland* (Frankfurt/Main: Suhrkamp, 1988), 255–56.

121. Langewiesche, *Liberalismus*, 251–72; Frye, *Liberal Democrats*, 59–60.

122. Childers, "Languages," 327–28; Eksteins, *Limits*, 158.

123. Childers, "Languages," 329–30; Sösemann, *Ende*, 176–77; Bosch, *Liberale Presse*, 30–36.

124. Michael Klein, *Georg Bernhard. Die politische Haltung des Chefredakteurs der Vossischen Zeitung, 1918–1930* (Frankfurt/Main: Lang, 1999), 54–56; Jürgen C. Heß, *"Das ganze Deutschland soll es sein." Demokratischer Nationalismus in der Weimarer Republik am Beispiel der Deutschen Demokratischen Partei* (Stuttgart: Klett-Cotta, 1978), 317–69.

125. "Programm der Deutschen Demokratischen Partei," *Mitteilungen für die Mitglieder der Deutschen Demokratischen Partei*, February 1920, 41–47, reprinted in part in *Deutsche Parteiprogramme vom Vormärz bis zur Gegenwart*, ed. by Wilhelm Mommsen (Munich: Isar, 1952), 121–22.

must be complemented with a truly social idea that overcomes the thinking along class lines and, beyond all political and social differences, sees in every citizen first and foremost a German compatriot (*Volksgenosse*). If we succeed in waking and strengthening this attitude in all classes of German society, then the form and idea of the democratic republic will be indestructible.[126]

As the appeal shows, Mommsen was well aware that the idea of the individual, responsible, classless, democratic citizen, wielding his or her right to vote with common sense and consideration, still had to take root among the wider population. In fact, his essay was not just a regurgitating of DDP ideology, but a call to arms in defense of democracy and parliamentarianism, as these liberal notions of representative democracy were already on the back foot in Germany by 1928. After a surge of popularity in the early days of the Republic, the DDP and the idea of liberal democracy it represented lost the majority of its support already in the first parliamentary elections of the following year.[127] Still, the DDP was represented in nearly all governments of the Weimar Republic and thus had significant influence on the political discourse.[128] Perhaps even more important in this respect was the continued support of the liberal press for the DDP and its notions of democratic citizenship.[129] Newspapers such as the *Berliner Tageblatt*, the *Vossische Zeitung*, and the *Frankfurter Zeitung* defined themselves—and were perceived by the wider public, in particular by antidemocratic forces—as the foremost proponents of democracy and as "guardians of the Constitution."[130] Together, the DDP and the liberal press tried to instill a new, republican culture that rescued the notion of "the nation" from conservatives and the far right and connected it with the new democratic order.[131]

However, while Mosse and Sonnemann—the respective publishers of the venerable liberal newspapers *Berliner Tageblatt* and *Frankfurter Zeitung*—

---

126. Wilhelm Mommsen, "Wie die deutsche Republik wurde," in *Zehn Jahre deutsche Republik. Ein Handbuch für republikanische Politik*, ed. by Anton Erkelenz (Berlin: Sieben Stäbe, 1928), 15.

127. Llanque, *Politische Ideengeschichte*, 415. For the general crisis of liberal democracy in Weimar Germany, see Jörn Leonhard, "Semantische Deplazierung und Entwertung. Deutsche Deutungen von *liberal* und *Liberalismus* nach 1850 im europäischen Vergleich," *Geschichte und Gesellschaft* 29, no. 1 (2003): 31–34; Langewiesche, *Liberalismus*, 233–86.

128. Childers, "Languages," 327–31; Langewiesche, *Liberalismus*, 272.

129. Bosch, *Liberale Presse*, 65–69; Eksteins, *Limits*, 104–37.

130. Bosch, *Liberale Presse*, 30–31.

131. Childers, "Languages," 323; Harold James, *A German Identity: 1770 to the Present Day* (London: Phoenix Press, 2000), 112, 22–25; Langewiesche, *Liberalismus*, 265–67.

were directly involved in the founding of the party, Ullstein had maintained a critical distance. This had as much to do with Georg Bernhard's personality as with political differences.[132] In the company's corporate philosophy, Germany's democratic transformation featured less as a revolutionary act than as a decidedly apolitical, commonsense reaction by the German people to a historical cataclysm. In the lavishly produced, 400-page strong celebratory volume commemorating the company's fiftieth anniversary in 1927, Bernhard depicted Ullstein as an exemplary realization of this vision—the core of, and model for, the new state.[133] In the same book, Ullstein's personnel director, Georg Sydow, described the traditional in-house labor agreements as arrangements between equal partners that benefitted both sides and thus the company as a whole:

> During the fifty years of its existence, the company has always upheld the democratic principle of acknowledging the workers as equal partners in all labor agreements. . . . It has always been the fundamental tendency of all labor policy at the Ullstein house to work with the workers, not against them.[134]

This harmonious relationship in the Ullstein company, Sydow argued, contrasted with the prewar "lord-of-the-manor attitude" (*Herr-im-Hause-Standpunkt*) of German industrialists that had been swept away in 1918.[135] Thus, he suggested, Ullstein had already practiced the social pact between unions and employers that would later form the sociopolitical foundation of the Weimar Republic. However, Sydow added, the peaceful cooperation at Ullstein also had to be defended against excessive government intervention—for example, the comprehensive labor agreements enshrined in law after the war.[136] These enforced contracts were, in Sydow's view, unnecessary or even harmful to the free and voluntary cooperation between the owners and their employees.

Ullstein's image of the German Republic as an expression of the political will of the whole people beyond boundaries of class and party affiliations, which contrasted sharply with the reality of Weimar's highly partisan political

---

132. Eksteins, *Limits*, 54–58.
133. Bernhard, "Geschichte," 1–146.
134. Georg Sydow, "Die Sozialpolitik des Hauses Ullstein," in Osborn, *Fünfzig Jahre Ullstein*, 364.
135. For the "lord of the manor" debate and Weimar social policy, see Andreas Wirsching, *Die Weimarer Republik. Politik und Gesellschaft* (Munich: Oldenbourg, 2000), 24–27.
136. Sydow, "Sozialpolitik," 366.

culture, was also reflected in the company's publication for the 1929 World Advertising Congress in Berlin. The trilingual, glossy, and opulent book introduced international visitors to the company's view of the new state and "the position held by the Ullstein Publishing Company in German economic and cultural life."[137] In a chapter on the "Germany of Today," Albrecht Graf Montgelas, one of the *Vossische Zeitung*'s political editors, painted the picture of a sound economy and of strong democratic institutions enthusiastically supported by the public.[138] The Republic had weathered political and economic storms, he argued, but had outlived its internal enemies "due to the discipline, the sense of order, the education and, most of all, the national ideals of the biggest part of the German workers."[139] In the same publication, Richard Lewinsohn, financial editor of the *Vossische Zeitung*, described German consumers as "the least conservative audience in the whole of Europe," eager to try out new products and with a great demand for branded goods.[140] According to Max Osborn, the company's foremost art critic, *Tempo* was the publication that reflected the "new Germany" like no other Ullstein publication: "*Tempo* is born from a new idea. It is not just 'one more newspaper,' added to the existing ones, but a publication that . . . in its whole attitude reflects the particular mood and demands of our changed times."[141]

Both Ullstein books concluded with the same essay by Paul Schlesinger, the company's popular legal correspondent, about the "spirit of the house."[142] Similarly to Bernhard and Sydow, Schlesinger described Ullstein as a company embodying the new democratic Germany, where everybody, from the lowly worker to the directors, worked together under meritocratic principles, with no place for the old authoritarian culture:

---

137. "Preface," in *Der Verlag Ullstein zum Weltreklamekongress*, 3. All texts in this volume were published in German, French, and English, and it was well received by the foreign press, see "The German Press," 20.

138. Albrecht Graf Montgelas, "Deutschland von Heute," in *Der Verlag Ullstein zum Weltreklamekongress*, 1–8.

139. Montgelas, "Deutschland von Heute," 4.

140. Richard Lewinsohn, "Deutschland, das Land der Arbeit und der Organisation," in *Der Verlag Ullstein zum Weltreklamekongress*, 13.

141. Max Osborn, "Wie Ullstein entstand," in *Der Verlag Ullstein zum Weltreklamekongress*, 105.

142. Sling (i.e., Paul Schlesinger), "Und der Geist des Hauses. Betrachtungen eines Unverantwortlichen," in *Fünfzig Jahre Ullstein 1877–1927*, ed. Max Osborn (Berlin: Ullstein, 1927), 385–93; "Und der Geist des Hauses," in *Der Verlag Ullstein zum Weltreklamekongress*, 249–63.

36   Moderate Modernity

> We are all workers for the same purpose. Our work progresses continuously, but not because some Napoleon thinks he must command and shout orders. There are no servants in uniform, opening the doors. Nobody bows before anyone. Our politeness does not need any formalities. In our house, there is more respect from above for the ones below than the other way around. Our democracy is perfect.[143]

While there is no doubt that Ullstein was a strong supporter of the Republic, it is remarkable that the most important institutions of a representative democracy—parliament, political parties—played virtually no role in the company's vision of a democratic Germany. Instead, the company promoted the idea of democracy as an egalitarian national community—and of itself as its exemplary institution, aloof from the murkiness of the party system. This optimistic image deliberately glossed over the deep social and political divides in German society as well as Ullstein's own commercial interests. A vivid sign of the precariousness of the Republic and of Ullstein's position had been the occupation of the company headquarters in Berlin's Kochstraße by Spartacist troops during the January uprising of 1919 that had caused a major disruption of production.[144] Thus, Ullstein's ideal of a peaceful and prosperous Republic with content and spend-happy citizens, based on the equal and free relationship between employers and workers, was not only a political vision but also in the best commercial interest of the company.

If we see Ullstein in this light, as both a political actor and a commercial venture, we can pinpoint three strategic goals the company pursued with the introduction of *Tempo*, which influenced the editorial orientation of the paper over the course of its existence. First, the newspaper addressed a gap in the company's portfolio: by 1928, it had become clear that Ullstein had missed the development of a new type of publication—evening tabloids published around 5 p.m., which had emerged as the most lucrative and popular form of these mass-market newspapers.[145] In Berlin, this market segment was dominated by the liberal *8-Uhr-Abendblatt*, the right-wing *Nachtausgabe*, and the Communist newspaper *Welt am Abend*. Earlier in the year, even the SPD had jumped on the bandwagon and launched *Der Abend*, an evening tabloid version of the party organ *Vorwärts*.[146] The acquisition, in 1927, of the *8-Uhr-Abendblatt* by

---

143. Sling, "Geist des Hauses," 386.
144. Mendelssohn, *Zeitungsstadt*, 284–87.
145. Fulda, *Press and Politics*, 32.
146. Fulda, *Press and Politics*, 35; Volker Schulze, "Vorwärts (1876–1933)," in *Deutsche Zeitungen des 17. bis 20. Jahrhunderts*, ed. Heinz Dietrich Fischer (Pullach: Dokumentation, 1972), 342.

the Mosse company, one of Ullstein's biggest rivals in Berlin, had increased the pressure on the company to act if it wanted to keep its edge on the competition.[147] For the trade press, it was clear that the introduction of *Tempo* was an attempt by Ullstein to claim its share of this growing market.[148] However, according to Ullstein, *Tempo* did not just offer more of the same, but a uniquely modern and cosmopolitan perspective that was missing among the existing evening tabloids:

> Until now, an evening paper for Berlin has been lacking among our publications. Since 11 September 1928, this gap has been filled by a new publication with the fitting name *Tempo*. This paper maintains a definitive individual touch compared to Berlin's evening papers. One may even say that this publication translates Anglo-Saxon methods into German with undeniable skill—an interpretation, not an imitation.[149]

Ullstein described *Tempo* as standing in an Anglo-American newspaper tradition, modeled after successful tabloids such as the London *Daily Mirror* and the New York *Daily News*, papers for quick consumption by urban commuters, with an emphasis on visual content and entertainment.[150]

With this German take on modern American journalism, Ullstein hoped to fulfil its second goal: to reach young, male and female white-collar consumers. According to the *Ullstein-Berichte*, a magazine for the company's advertising clients, *Tempo* had "a distinctive focus on the particular interests and needs of the younger businessman, the engineer and the female employee."[151] Commercially, this made perfect sense: the prewar years had seen one of the highest birth rates in German history.[152] According to the 1925 census, the age group born between 1900 to 1910 made up over 18 percent of the population—over

---

147. Fulda, *Press and Politics*, 35; Walter Matuschke, "Führend in Deutschland, anerkannt in der Welt. Technik im Hause Ullstein/Axel Springer," in Freyburg and Wallenberg, *Hundert Jahre Ullstein*, 3:32; Hermann Ullstein, *The Rise and Fall of the House of Ullstein* (New York: Simon and Schuster, 1943), 206.

148. "Eine neue Berliner Abendzeitung," *Deutsche Presse*, 22 September 1928, 496.

149. "Der Verlag Ullstein," *Zeitungs-Verlag. Festausgabe des Zeitungs-Verlags zur Hauptversammlung des Vereins Deutscher Zeitungs-Verleger 5. Oktober 1928*, 6 October 1928, 8.

150. "Der Verlag Ullstein," 8; "Tempo—Die Zeitung der Zeit," *Ullstein-Berichte*, October 1928, 4.

151. "Tempo—Die Zeitung der Zeit," 4.

152. Peukert, *Weimar*, 86–89. See also Josef Ehmer, *Bevölkerungsgeschichte und historische Demographie 1800–2000* (Munich: Oldenbourg, 2004), 7.

735,000 inhabitants—in Berlin alone, *Tempo*'s core market.[153] Thus, simply by their sheer number, Weimar's twentysomethings—the age group who had spent their formative years at the home front and under the new democratic order—were a very potent group of new consumers. At the same time, the proportion of white-collar workers in the German labor force had been growing rapidly since the beginning of the twentieth century: from 5.2 percent in 1907 to 13.6 percent in 1925; during this time their number nearly tripled, from around 1.3 million to over 3.8 million.[154] This rise was especially pronounced in urban areas: in Berlin alone, over 665,000 people were working in white-collar jobs by the mid-1920s.[155] According to Ullstein, *Tempo* was the first newspaper that catered to the lifestyle and interests of this new group of young white-collar workers: "Until now, there really was no newspaper tailored to the particular needs of the younger generation. All existing newspapers still reflected the taste and the opinions of the prewar generation."[156] Instead, *Tempo* offered quickly digestible information in text and images—"following the English and American model"—and addressed the topics younger Germans were interested in: "the problems of marriage, children and sexuality, sport and body culture, and their will to educate themselves socially and intellectually."[157] The explicit focus on sports, reflected in the newspaper's dedicated sports section, was significant: competitive physical culture was perceived as an integral aspect of modernity in Weimar Germany.[158] In its entertainment section, Ullstein claimed, *Tempo* "naturally catered only to modern tastes" and, on its business pages, it specifically addressed the demands of the "younger businessman." An important way to address this young audience was through images. Ullstein allocated considerable financial resources to the visual content of its new publication: *Tempo* spent more money on illustrations and similar images

---

153. Statistisches Amt der Stadt Berlin, *Statistisches Jahrbuch der Stadt Berlin* (Berlin: Grunert, 1928), 6.

154. Günther Schulz, *Die Angestellten seit dem 19. Jahrhundert* (Munich: Oldenbourg, 2000), 6. Heinz-Jürgen Priamus gives slightly different figures, but also talks of a "growth with explosive character," see Heinz-Jürgen Priamus, *Angestellte und Demokratie. Die nationalliberale Angestelltenbewegung in der Weimarer Republik* (Stuttgart: Klett-Cotta, 1979), 12.

155. Preußisches Statistisches Landesamt, *Statistisches Jahrbuch für den Freistaat Preußen 1926* (Berlin: Verlag des Preußischen Statistischen Landesamts, 1926), 46.

156. "*Tempo*—Die Zeitung der Zeit," 3.

157. "*Tempo*—Die Zeitung der Zeit," 4.

158. Erik Norman Jensen, *Body by Weimar: Athletes, Gender, and German Modernity* (Oxford: Oxford University Press, 2013), 3–14.

than any of the company's other newspapers.[159] Its heavy reliance on images, the paper claimed, was an expression of a new kind of journalism:

> We use more images than German dailies normally do, and we are the first newspaper to use the image not as mere "illustration," but as news in itself. We report in two languages: in the language of words and the vivid language of images.[160]

Tempo's focus on a new "language of images" was reflected in the new post of "editor-in-chief of visual content" (*Chefredakteur des Bilderteils*).[161] *Tempo* aimed to be not only the newspaper with the most images but also with the most sensational and most current ones. For example, only four days after the passenger steamship *Vestris* had sunk off the coast of Virginia on 12 November 1928, the paper published a photograph from the deck of the sinking ship.[162] In the accompanying text, the fact that the image had been transmitted so quickly after the event, using the new technology of image telegraphy, was described as a bigger sensation than the disaster itself.

This focus on a younger audience was directly linked to the third goal Ullstein hoped to address with *Tempo*. Without a newspaper catering to their needs and interests, the company warned its advertising clients, young people had fallen prey to the ideological agitation of a "propaganda press promoting extreme radicalism or class warfare."[163] By the end of the 1920s, as the generation of the prewar baby boom reached the eligible age to vote, the youth vote had become a central political battleground of the Weimar Republic. However, the middle-class parties of the Weimar Republic struggled to recruit young voters.[164] The general election in May 1928 was something of a watershed

---

159. "Gesamtkosten Tageszeitungen 1931," unpaginated, in UAS, Ullstein files. The numbers are for 1931; that year, *Tempo*'s expenses for illustrations amounted to RM 102,599, while the *B.Z. am Mittag* spent only RM 70,728.

160. "Eine neue Zeitung," 2.

161. See the imprint in *Tempo*, 11 September 1928, 12. See also *Jahrbuch der Tagespresse*, 1929, 82.

162. "Funkphoto von der Vestris," *Tempo*, 16 November 1928, 1.

163. "*Tempo*—Die Zeitung der Zeit," 4.

164. Barbara Stambolis, *Mythos Jugend—Leitbild und Krisensymptom. Ein Aspekt der politischen Kultur im 20. Jahrhundert* (Schwalbach: Wochenschau, 2003), 165–80; Larry E. Jones, *German Liberalism and the Dissolution of the Weimar Party System, 1918–1933* (Chapel Hill: University of North Carolina Press, 1988), 323–37; Hans Mommsen, "Generationskonflikt und Jugendrevolte in der Weimarer Republik," in *"Mit uns zieht die neue Zeit": Der Mythos Jugend*, ed. Thomas Koebner, Rolf-Peter Janz, and Frank Trommler (Frankfurt/

moment for the political role of the youth, showing the need for middle-class parties to address and activate younger voters, as most of them, from the national-conservative German National People's Party (Deutschnationale Volkspartei, DNVP) to the liberal parties such as the DDP, lost votes.[165] For the journalist Rüdiger Robert Beer, the neglect of young voters by the liberal press was to blame for the poor result:

> Without a doubt, the loss of votes for all middle-class (*bürgerliche*) parties in the last election can be partly explained by the ignorance of their press regarding young people and their problems, because, as is well known, around four million young voters exercised their noble right to vote in the election in May.[166]

The Social Democrats, the biggest winners of the 1928 election, had a similar view.[167] It seems reasonable to assume that the same conclusions were drawn by the Ullstein management and that a mouthpiece for liberal politics catering especially to young voters was considered essential if liberal parties such as the DDP—and liberal politics as a whole—could stand a chance in the next election. Thus, *Tempo*'s "great political mission," Ullstein claimed, was to convince its young audience of the superiority of the new democratic order: "*Tempo* hopes to lead great parts of this generation towards a productive mind-set of citizenship by showing them all the possibilities for success that real life holds."[168]

Tempo employed some of the best-known journalists and writers of its time to achieve these three goals. Kurt Tucholsky, Stefan Großmann, and Billy Wilder wrote regularly for the paper.[169] The socialist reporter Maria Leitner often conducted interviews with members of the general public.[170] Erika Mann,

---

Main: Suhrkamp, 1985), 58–59. For a detailed account of liberal youth politics, see Wolfgang Krabbe, *Die gescheiterte Zukunft der Ersten Republik. Jugendorganisationen bürgerlicher Parteien im Weimarer Staat* (Opladen: Westdeutscher Verlag, 1995).

165. Jones, *German Liberalism*, 326.
166. Rüdiger Robert Beer, "Jugendfragen," *Die Tat*, December 1928, 794.
167. Kurt Koszyk, *Zwischen Kaiserreich und Diktatur. Die sozialdemokratische Presse von 1914 bis 1933* (Heidelberg: Quelle & Meyer, 1958), 181.
168. Koszyk, *Zwischen Kaiserreich und Diktatur*, 181.
169. For Wilder's articles in *Tempo*, see Billy Wilder, *Der Prinz von Wales geht auf Urlaub. Berliner Reportagen, Feuilletons und Kritiken der zwanziger Jahre*, ed. Klaus Siebenhaar (Berlin: Fannei & Walz, 1996).
170. For Leitner's articles, see Maria Leitner, *Mädchen mit drei Namen. Reportagen aus Deutschland und ein Berliner Roman 1928–1933*, ed. by Helga Schwarz and Wilfried Schwarz (Berlin: Aviva, 2013).

daughter of Nobel laureate Thomas Mann, published her first journalistic articles in *Tempo*.[171] Sporadic contributors included such esteemed writers like Erich Kästner, Gina Kaus, Franz Hessel, Ödon von Horwarth, Eugenie Schwarzwald, and a whole range of celebrities such as Valeska Gert, Gustav Gründgens, Elisabeth Bergner, and Max Schmeling. One of *Tempo*'s most prolific authors was the popular satirist Alexander Roda Roda. Born in 1872 in Slavonia, he had been one of the most widely read German-language authors before the First World War.[172] In *Tempo*, he published one or two opinion pieces daily, commenting on world news and current events, either in the politics section or his own column called "Roda Roda's Tales" (*Roda Roda erzählt*). Many of *Tempo*'s articles, however, were written under pseudonyms, such as "Sky," "C. Enseo," "Heaven," and "Billie." The many English pseudonyms show that even in the choice of pen names, *Tempo* tried to appear as "American" as possible. These authors gave *Tempo* a unique character: in comparison to Ullstein's flagship tabloid *B.Z. am Mittag*, *Tempo* had many more opinion-focused features and formats, taking its cue more from the magazine, a format that had been introduced to Germany only recently, than from *Generalanzeiger*, a commercial mass-market newspaper.

Gustav Kauder, one of Ullstein's most experienced newspapermen, was appointed as *Tempo*'s editor-in-chief. Kauder, who had worked for Ullstein as correspondent in London and Paris and then as political editor of the *B.Z. am Mittag*, was one of Berlin's celebrated journalists, not quite of the international reputation of Georg Bernhard or the *Berliner Tageblatt*'s Theodor Wolff, but a renowned newspaperman nonetheless.[173] In its first years, *Tempo*'s news desk was staffed with political editor Felix von Eckardt and Carl Adolf Bratter, a well-known expert on foreign policy, while Ferdinand Friedrich Zimmermann edited the economics section.[174] Manfred Georg, Heinrich Mühsam, theatre and fashion editor Lucy von Jacobi, and film critic Hanns G. Lustig oversaw

---

171. Erika Mann, *Blitze überm Ozean. Aufsätze, Reden, Reportagen*, ed. Irmela von der Lühe (Reinbek: Rowohlt, 2000), 470.

172. For the following, see Max Kaiser, "Roda Roda, Alexander," in *Neue Deutsche Biographie*, ed. Hans Günther Hockerts (Berlin: Duncker & Humblot, 1953–2008), 21:687–89; "Roda Roda, Alexander," in *Reichshandbuch der deutschen Gesellschaft. Das Handbuch der Persönlichkeiten in Wort und Bild*, ed. Robert Volz (Berlin: Deutscher Wirtschaftsverlag, 1931), 2:1541–42; "Alexander Roda Roda," in *Wer ist's?*, ed. Herrmann Degener (Berlin: Degener, 1928), 1278–79.

173. "Kauder, Gustav," in *Reichshandbuch*, 1:891.

174. Deutsches Institut für Zeitungskunde, *Jahrbuch der Tagespresse* (Berlin: Duncker, 1929), 82.

the culture section.[175] Jacobi, a former theatre actress and Germany's first female dramaturge, was one of the very few women employed as full-time editors in the Weimar press.[176] Manfred Georg was undoubtedly an important presence at *Tempo*: he acted as the paper's managing editor and remained a fixture while *Tempo*'s staff changed over the years.[177] In 1928, he was already a well-established journalist, public lecturer, and political activist, who had worked as an editor for the *8-Uhr-Abendblatt*, had published several novels and plays, spoke regularly on the radio, and was a long-standing contributor to left-liberal magazines such as *Die Weltbühne* and *Die Literarische Welt*.[178] Himself a Jew, Georg wrote an acclaimed biography of Theodor Herzl, the founder of modern political Zionism.[179] In 1924, he became chairman of the Republican Party of Germany (Republikanische Partei Deutschlands), a pro-democratic splinter party formed by a group of intellectuals including Carl von Ossietzky, Karl Vetter, Stefan Großmann, and Fritz von Unruh.[180] His candor earned him the admiration of his colleagues: Axel Eggebrecht praised him as "a man of conviction" and Ludwig Marcuse remarked that "Georg belongs to the small number of excellent journalists who are newspapermen to the bone—and still have a very specific purpose in life."[181]

The three goals Ullstein pursued with *Tempo*, and for which the company

---

175. *Jahrbuch der Tagespresse*, 1929, 82. For Jacobi, see *Lucy von Jacobi. Journalistin*, ed. Rolf Aurich et al. (Munich: Text + Kritik, 2009); for Lustig, see Jan Lustig (i.e., Hanns G. Lustig), *Ein Rosenkranz von Glücksfällen. Protokoll einer Flucht* (Bonn: Weidle, 2001); Wallenberg, "Zum jüdischen Beitrag," 440–42.

176. Irene Below, "Wege der Professionalisierung," in Aurich et al., *Lucy von Jacobi*, 15.

177. Georg is listed as "*verantwortlicher Redakteur*" in the paper's imprint, see *Tempo*, 11 September 1928, 2.

178. Jennifer Borrmann, ed., *Manfred George. Journalist und Filmkritiker* (Munich: Edition Text+Kritik, 2014); Frank C. Steiner, "Manfred George: His Life and Works" (PhD diss., State University of New York, 1977), 10–19; Walther G. Oschilewski, *Zeitungen in Berlin. Im Spiegel der Jahrhunderte* (Berlin: Haude und Spenersche Verlagsbuchhandlung, 1975), 146. See also "Georg, Manfred," in *Reichshandbuch*, 1:534; "Georg, Manfred," in Degener, *Wer ist's?*, 475.

179. Manfred Georg, *Theodor Herzl. Sein Leben und sein Vermächtnis* (Berlin: Höger, 1932). For its reception, see Steiner, "Manfred George," 96–102.

180. "Vorstandswahl beim Republikanischen Parteitag," *Vossische Zeitung*, 29 September 1924, 3. See also Steiner, "Manfred George," 15. For the German Republican Party, see Werner Fritsch, "Republikanische Partei Deutschlands (RPD)," in *Lexikon zur Parteiengeschichte. Die bürgerlichen und kleinbürgerlichen Parteien und Verbände in Deutschland 1789–1945*, ed. Dieter Fricke (Cologne: Pahl-Rugenstein, 1986), 4:94–96.

181. Axel Eggebrecht, "Buch-Chronik," *Die Literarische Welt*, 20 May 1927, 6; Ludwig Marcuse, "Aufstand im Warenhaus," *Die Weltbühne*, 11 September 1928, 422.

had assembled such an impressive team of journalists, were all rooted in the fundamental objective of shoring up the political and economic foundations of the Weimar Republic. *Tempo* was supposed to provide a positive vision of Germany's future—a German modernity—in order to bind its audience to the new state, and through this popular support give it the legitimacy and stability to put this vision into practice.

Finally, this book is also a study of how to report on the rise of extremist antidemocratic movements in a modern democracy. The challenges faced by a mainstream, commercial publisher like Ullstein in finding an effective way to cover the activities of the Nazis foreshadowed the questions today's journalists in Europe and the US are asking themselves during a time of populist attacks on democratic norms and institutions: How can we fulfill our mission of objectively informing the public without supplying these movements with the oxygen of unwarranted publicity and inflating their real influence? Ullstein and *Tempo* did not find a straightforward answer to this question and this study does not pretend to provide one either. However, the history of *Tempo* shows how complex and difficult the terrain is that journalists and publishers have to navigate today and that there are probably no easy solutions to this problem.

CHAPTER I

1928–1929

Banging the Drum for Democracy

The sensationalist front page of *Tempo*'s inaugural issue of 11 September 1928 got people's attention, but its actual vision of a German modernity was developed on the inside pages, in the many reports and images recording and commenting on modern everyday life. The curious buyers of the first issue who flicked past the first page encountered, for example, the column "Technology Everybody Needs," which praised the American invention of a new type of plug for electric consumer products. This "Columbus's egg of electrical fittings" was made of soft rubber and supposedly solved the problem of shattering ceramic plugs that German consumers still had to contend with.[1] This short column reflected many of the central themes of the new publication: a focus on issues of urban everyday life, an infatuation with technological progress and consumer products, and an intense interest in all things American. In "Technology Everybody Needs," one of its longest-running series, the newspaper promoted new entertainment and household appliances on a daily basis, from a portable radio praised as "working just like in a fairy tale" to an immersion heater lauded for giving the busy urbanite mobile access to hot water, and an electrical egg cooker, which was introduced as a necessary companion to other new appliances such as the coffee machine and the toaster.[2] Soon, the author claimed in a column about a new electric drill for home use, every German household would be equipped with such modern, affordable, and easy-to-use electrical appliances.[3] These columns did not offer information for potential shoppers to find the best purchase among

---

1. "Technik, die jeder braucht," *Tempo*, 11 September 1928, 6.
2. "Technik, die jeder braucht," *Tempo*, 15 September 1928, 4; 26 November 1929, 4; 4 September 1929, 4.
3. "Technik, die jeder braucht," *Tempo*, 18 October 1929, 4.

a range of electrical goods. Rather, *Tempo* promoted the ownership of modern consumer goods itself: all products were presented as perfect, revolutionary, and convenient—and thus necessary purchases.

In October 1928, a few weeks before the tenth anniversary of the founding of the Weimar Republic, an article in the paper painted a picture of the lifestyle these products supposedly made possible. The text, running over half a page and titled "Ten Years in a Day, or: Don't You Think We Are Making Progress?," recounted the—fictitious—daily routine of a common Berlin citizen in 1928, getting up in the morning in his new, modern apartment, showering and shaving with instant hot water, and speeding to work on the underground.[4] In his office he converses via telephone with a colleague in Stuttgart, then meets a friend to see an American sound film, and finally returns to his flat at the end of the day, where he unwinds listening to a live transmission on the radio of a jazz concert at London's Savoy Hotel. Two hundred years earlier, in 1728, the author argues, this citizen of Berlin would have had to spend ten years to achieve everything he now manages to do in one busy day. The modern technology of 1928 and the speed it brought to the common man's life were celebrated as a means to achieve an existence full of comfort, excitement, and national and international understanding.

To be sure, the lifestyle of this imaginary Berliner differed very much from the daily experience of most Germans, even in the country's urban centers. The life of the majority of the population in the Weimar Republic was still characterized by scarcity, and many of the products they encountered in the media were out of reach.[5] *Tempo*'s writers were very much aware of this: in the third installment of "Technology Everybody Needs," a new type of electric fridge was introduced that, the author conceded, was too expensive for most German households.[6] In other cases, such as the new type of plug lauded in the column's first installment, the products had only just been introduced in the United States and were not available to German customers, even the ones who could afford them.[7] The American consumer society was the aspirational context of these consumer products, and *Tempo* presented them as embodiments of that promise. But the newspaper repeatedly assured its readers that it was only a matter of time until all Germans could enjoy them, too. In the case of the new fridge, the capitalist order and competition on the free market, the author

---

4. Dr. F. K., "Zehn Jahre in einem Tag. Oder: Meinen Sie nicht, dass es vorwärts geht?," *Tempo*, 3 October 1928, 8.
5. Torp, *Konsum und Politik*, 27–97.
6. "Technik, die jeder braucht," *Tempo*, 13 September 1928, 4.
7. "Technik, die jeder braucht," *Tempo*, 11 September 1928, 4.

claimed, would "soon deliver cheaper and even more reliable models" that were attainable for the common German consumer.[8]

The diffusion of electrical household appliances, which began in the 1920s, was closely linked to the modernity discourse in interwar Germany. Fridges, washing machines, and toasters were seen as "insignia of a modern age . . . and the carriers of progress," which brought the masculine world of technology, industrialization, and rationalization into the feminine sphere of the home.[9] With the column "Technology Everybody Needs," *Tempo* expanded its vision of modernity to the domestic sphere and painted an image of a modern home that rivaled American standards. In a broader sense, the column also tapped into the idea of a German consumer society that gained popularity during Weimar's short phase of relative stabilization.[10] This vision was "imagined," in the literal sense of the word, by Weimar's mass media—commercial cinema, billboards, illustrated magazines, and shop window displays—that introduced broad sections of the population to new mass-produced consumer goods such as radios, electric home appliances, and cars.[11] Newspapers played a central role in this process, not merely as a carrier for advertising, but by establishing consumption as a value in itself.[12] *Tempo* was an ardent proponent of unfettered consumption, actively encouraging the purchase of consumer goods. It did not really matter that only a minority of its readers could afford them—*Tempo* offered its readers a "virtual" participation in the consumer society.[13] This offer of "virtual consumption" was thoroughly political: in Weimar

8. "Technik, die jeder braucht," *Tempo*, 13 September 1928, 4.
9. Martina Hessler, "*Mrs. Modern Woman.*" Zur Sozial-und Kulturgeschichte der Haushaltstechnisierung (Frankfurt/Main: Campus, 2001), 13–14.
10. Martina Hessler, "Visionen des Überflusses. Entwürfe künftiger Massenkonsumgesellschaften im 20. Jahrhundert," in *Wirtschaftsgeschichte als Kulturgeschichte. Dimensionen eines Perspektivenwechsels*, ed. Hartmut Berghoff and Jakob Vogel (Frankfurt: Campus, 2004), 460–63.
11. Torp, *Konsum und Politik*, 81–90; Kaspar Maase, "Massenmedien und Konsumgesellschaft," in *Die Konsumgesellschaft in Deutschland 1890–1990*, ed. Heinz-Gerhard Haupt and Claudius Torp (Frankfurt: Campus, 2009), 62–78; Janet Ward, *Weimar Surfaces: Urban Visual Culture in 1920s Germany* (Berkeley: University of California Press, 2001), 194–233.
12. Gideon Reuveni, "Lesen und Konsum. Der Aufstieg der Konsumkultur in Presse und Werbung Deutschlands bis 1933," *Archiv für Sozialgeschichte* 41 (2001): 113–16. See also Gideon Reuveni, "Reading, Advertising and Consumer Culture in the Weimar Period," in Führer and Ross, *Mass Media, Culture and Society*, 204–16; Gideon Reuveni, "Wohlstand durch Konsum. Straßenhandel und Versicherungszeitschriften in den zwanziger Jahren," in Föllmer and Graf, *Die "Krise" der Weimarer Republik*, 267–86.
13. For the concept of "virtual consumption," see Hartmut Berghoff, "Träume und Alpträume. Konsumpolitik im Nazionalsozialistischen Deutschland," in Haupt and Torp, *Die*

Germany, the enshrining of the welfare state in the Constitution, together with policies aimed at improving the general standard of living after the experiences of hardship during the war, raised hopes and desires for an unbounded prosperity.[14] Thus, fridges, cars, radios, and other new consumer products played an important role as signifiers of a better future.

The most powerful model for this imagined future was the United States, where mass consumption had generated sustained economic growth and a rise in the standard of living after the war, promising an integrative, classless society based on democratic, liberal values.[15] According to its proponents, the motor of the American "democracy of goods" was a virtually unlimited demand for nonessential goods such as household appliances and cars, spurred by a highly developed marketing and mass media industry.[16] The American success story of a consumer-driven economy created great interest in Weimar Germany, and books by esteemed businessmen, such as investment banker Paul Myer Mazur's *American Prosperity*, published in 1928 and translated into German by the prestigious Fischer publishing house in the same year, enjoyed great popularity.[17] In his book, Mazur described the "unparalleled torrent of modern consumer demand" for luxury and convenience goods, stimulated by

---

Konsumgesellschaft in Deutschland, 268–88; Hartmut Berghoff, "Enticement and Deprivation: The Regulation of Consumption in Pre-War Nazi Germany," in *The Politics of Consumption: Material Culture and Citizenship in Europe and America*, ed. Martin Daunton and Matthew Hilton (New York: Berg, 2001), 165–84.

14. Hartmut Berghoff, "Consumption Politics and Politicized Consumption: Monarchy, Republic, and Dictatorship in Germany, 1900–1939," in *Decoding Modern Consumer Societies*, ed. Hartmut Berghoff and Uwe Spiekermann (New York: Palgrave Macmillan, 2012), 132–34; Claudius Torp, "Das Janusgesicht der Weimarer Konsumpolitik," in Haupt and Torp, *Die Konsumgesellschaft in Deutschland*, 261; Young-Sun Hong, *Welfare, Modernity, and the Weimar State, 1919–1933* (Princeton: Princeton University Press, 1998), 44–75.

15. Adelheid von Saldern, "Transatlantische Konsumleitbilder und Übersetzungspraktiken 1900–1945," in Haupt and Torp, *Die Konsumgesellschaft in Deutschland*, 389–402; Wolfgang König, *Geschichte der Konsumgesellschaft* (Stuttgart: Steiner, 2000), 108–22; McGovern, "Consumption and Citizenship," 37–58; Victoria de Grazia, "Amerikanisierung und wechselnde Leitbilder der Konsum-Moderne (consumer-modernity) in Europa," in *Europäische Konsumgeschichte. Zur Gesellschafts-und Kulturgeschichte des Konsums (18. bis 20. Jahrhundert)*, ed. Hannes Siegrist, Hartmut Kaelble, and Jürgen Kocka (Frankfurt: Campus, 1997), 114–23.

16. McGovern, *Sold American*, 23–61; Marchand, *Advertising the American Dream*, 217–22.

17. Paul M. Mazur, *Der Reichtum Amerikas: Seine Ursachen und Folgen*, trans. Rose Hilferding (Berlin: Fischer, 1928).

modern advertising, as the bedrock for the prosperity of his country.[18] In the following year, *The Road to Plenty*, a work by American economists William Trufant Foster and Waddill Catchings, was translated into German.[19] Foster and Catchings were proponents of "under-consumption theory," which blamed economic stagnation primarily on a lack of consumer spending and propagated higher wages to stimulate demand.[20] The work of John Maynard Keynes, who was influenced by under-consumption theory, was also already widely received in Germany by this time.[21] The thriving marketing industry and the professionalization of market research in the US also raised awareness in Germany of the important role of "the consumer" in the economy: while American advertising firms started to make inroads into the German market after the war, many German businesses, inspired by the American example, established their own marketing and market research departments to better address or even stimulate the demand of their customers.[22] The publication that arguably did most for the popularization of the idea of a consumer-driven economy was Henry Ford's autobiography, published in Germany in 1923, in which he promoted the idea of virtually unlimited mass consumption fueled by high wages as the way to prosperity for all.[23]

To be sure, the promise embodied by the American "people of plenty" was

---

18. Paul M. Mazur, *American Prosperity: Its Causes and Consequences* (New York: Viking, 1928), 262.

19. William Trufant Foster and Waddill Catchings, *Der Weg zum Überfluss. Grundlinien für den Wohlstand Aller*, trans. Curt Thesing (Leipzig: List, 1929).

20. For under-consumption theory, see Michael Bleaney, *Under-Consumption Theories: A History and Critical Analysis* (London: Lawrence & Wishart, 1976).

21. Roman Köster, "Vor der Krise. Die Keynes-Rezeption in der Weimarer Republik," *Mittelweg 36* 22, no. 3 (2013): 32–46; Ursula Büttner, "Politische Alternativen zum Brüningschen Deflationskurs. Ein Beitrag zur Diskussion über 'ökonomische Zwangslagen' in der Endphase von Weimar," *Vierteljahrshefte für Zeitgeschichte* 37, no. 2 (1989): 222–23.

22. Peter Borscheid, "Agenten des Konsums. Werbung und Marketing," in Haupt and Torp, *Die Konsumgesellschaft in Deutschland*, 87–92; Corey Ross, "Visions of Prosperity: The Americanization of Advertising in Interwar Germany," in *Selling Modernity: Advertising in Twentieth-Century Germany*, ed. Pamela Swett, S. Jonathan Wiesen, and Jonathan R. Zatlin (Durham, N.C.: Duke University Press, 2007), 61–65; Alexander Schug, "Wegbereiter der modernen Absatzwerbung in Deutschland. Advertising Agencies und die Amerikanisierung der deutschen Werbebranche in der Zwischenkriegszeit," *WerkstattGeschichte* 34 (2003): 29–52.

23. Henry Ford, *Mein Leben und Werk*, trans. Marguerite Thesing and Curt Thesing (Leipzig: List, 1923). For its reception in Germany, see Mary Nolan, *Visions of Modernity: American Business and the Modernization of Germany* (Oxford: Oxford University Press, 1994), 30–57.

by no means uncontroversial or universally welcomed. The traditional bourgeois ideal of rational, frugal consumption heavily influenced consumer politics in the Weimar Republic, with both the left and the right following a paternalistic approach of "reining in" the consumer.[24] Many Weimar intellectuals of all political camps were also critical of the supposed cultural consequences of American-style consumerism.[25] The stance of the SPD was typical in this respect: they welcomed the rise of living standards that the mass production of consumer products promised, but at the same time rejected consumerism. In effect, as Mary Nolan has noted, the SPD "wanted mass consumption, but not a culture of consumption."[26] Ullstein, however, wholeheartedly supported the idea of a German consumer society along the lines of the American model. Despite Ford's well-known anti-Semitism, his ideas undoubtedly were a guiding principle at the Ullstein house. The *Vossische Zeitung* lauded Ford's autobiography as such "an open, manly book" that even words such as "overwhelming" and "astonishing" would not do it justice.[27] In the publication commemorating the company's fiftieth anniversary in 1927, the company's personnel director Georg Sydow expressly subscribed to Fordist ideas of the worker-consumer and the socially stabilizing influence of access to mass consumption:

> [The Ullstein company] believes in the fundamental position that an adequately paid worker will not only be eager to work, but at the same time be a good consumer—which is in the interest of everybody who produces goods.[28]

But Ullstein's most ardent proponent for an American-style consumer society was *Tempo*: the newspaper described the United States as a country of "material blessings, satisfaction, joy of life, and hope for the future," a model that could also be realized on the Old Continent if Europeans would put their conflicts aside and their minds to it.[29] When Ford himself visited Germany in 1930, it ran a hagiographic interview on its front page.[30]

---

24. Torp, "Janusgesicht," 255–63.
25. Torp, *Konsum und Politik*, 165–94, 269–91.
26. Nolan, *Visions of Modernity*, 120.
27. C. A. Bratter, "Henry Ford über sich selbst," *Vossische Zeitung*, 2 December 1923, section Literarische Umschau, 2.
28. Sydow, "Sozialpolitik," 363.
29. "Fragen des Tages: So könnten wir's auch haben, wenn–," *Tempo*, 13 September 1928, 2.
30. G.H., "Deutsches Gespräch mit Henry Ford," *Tempo*, 19 September 1930, 1.

It was no coincidence that the second installment of the "Technology Everybody Needs" series explained what to look for when buying a used car.[31] The automobile was the most powerful symbol of an American-style consumer society, embodied by Ford's basic, mass-produced, "classless" Model T. The vision of American-style mass motorization was a prevalent topic in the Weimar Republic, and from its beginning *Tempo* dedicated much space to every aspect of automobile traffic, from the problems of Berlin's pavement to the introduction of new street signs. True to the paper's service-oriented nature, it launched a special series dedicated to readers' questions about traffic laws, while a twelve-part series on how to become an *Autler* (automobilist) answered the most important question of the aspiring car owner.[32] On 3 October 1928, a photo prominently placed on the last page of the paper showed a traffic jam on Berlin's central Unter den Linden boulevard, a sight normally only to be witnessed in American cities.[33] The decision to print this photo was hardly coincidental: a day later, *Tempo* published an article on the upcoming International Automobile and Motorcycle Exhibition (Internationale Automobil- und Motorradausstellung), the first international motor show in Germany after the war. The return of the trade fair to Berlin was viewed with pride by many Germans and seen as a sign of a resurgent motor industry, revealing "a deep and abiding interest in cars" in the country.[34] *Tempo* predicted falling prices for cars, making the automobile available to the "little man" for the first time.[35] In its coverage of the motor show, *Tempo* emphasized the role of free-market competition in bringing the automobile—described as "the emblem of our time"—within reach of the common man.[36] Accordingly, the takeover of the German car manufacturer Opel by General Motors in 1929 was hailed as an injection of American money and business sense that would bring the country closer to mass motorization.[37]

However, this was not much more than wishful thinking. Owning a car was still an unattainable dream for most Germans—in 1927, there were 196

---

31. "Technik, die jeder braucht," *Tempo*, 12 September 1928, 4.
32. "Im Paragraphendickicht des Verkehrsrechts," *Tempo*, 17 July 1929, 7; ejac, "Wie werde ich Autler?," *Tempo*, 12 October 1928, 7.
33. "Der Verkehr steht—und kein Schupo schimpft," *Tempo*, 3 October 1928, 12.
34. Rudy Koshar, "Cars and Nations: Anglo-German Perspectives on Automobility between the World Wars," *Theory, Culture & Society* 21, nos. 4–5 (2004): 124–39.
35. "Das Auto für den kleinen Mann," *Tempo*, 4 October 1928, 4.
36. "Das Wahrzeichen unser Zeit. Das allermodernste Auto," *Tempo*, 7 November 1928, 3.
37. "Opels Zukunft liegt über dem Wasser," *Tempo*, 18 March 1929, 9.

inhabitants per car in Germany, while in the US there were around five per car—and such promises only highlighted the limitations of a German consumer-driven economy.[38] Even if, as the paper claimed in its report on the Berlin motor show, the cheapest cars would soon be available for as little as 2,000 marks, this price—not to mention the running costs of petrol, repairs, and taxes—put them out of reach of most Germans.[39] In one installment of its automobilist series, *Tempo* listed the running costs of "a decent jalopy" at around 400 marks per month, which was much less, the author claimed, than what many thought it would cost.[40] However, the amount most likely still exceeded the budget of a majority of the paper's audience, as the monthly salary of the average white-collar worker was less than 270 marks.[41] The relatively high taxes on privately owned vehicles—literally a "luxury tax"—were a reflection of the enduring status of the automobile as a nonessential good in Germany.[42] In fact, *Tempo*'s claim of the automobile's affordability was undermined by its own articles written by actual car owners, mostly glamorous people from privileged backgrounds, such as Erika Mann, who regularly reported on her adventures as a female motorist and race-car driver, or Paula von Reznicek, a professional tennis player and author of handbooks on etiquette. This image of the automobile as an exotic novelty was reinforced by *Tempo*'s obsession with motoring records and new inventions such as rocket cars.[43]

However, *Tempo*'s advice columns on road safety, traffic laws, and road etiquette still addressed a very real demand for the virtual consumption of automobiles. Many Germans had an intense interest in issues of personal motorization and automobile traffic, and even if they often could not afford to buy a car, they considered private mobility as an absolutely essential goal.[44] This was reflected in the extraordinarily high number of motorcycles sold in

---

38. James J. Flink, *The Automobile Age* (Cambridge, Mass.: MIT Press, 1988), 129. See also Reiner Flik, *Von Ford lernen? Automobilbau und Motorisierung in Deutschland bis 1933* (Cologne: Böhlau, 2001), 40–52; Kurt Möser, "World War I and the Creation of Desire for Automobiles in Germany," in Strasser, McGovern, and Judt, *Getting and Spending*, 212.

39. "Das Auto für den kleinen Mann," 4. See also Koshar, "Cars and Nations," 138; Flik, *Von Ford lernen?*, 53–61.

40. "Die siebte Autlerstunde," *Tempo*, 2 November 1928, 8.

41. Heinrich Geiger, "Was verdient heute der Angestellte?," *Die Tat*, February 1930, 836–41, at 836. For more detailed data, see also Statistisches Reichsamt, *Statistisches Jahrbuch für das Deutsche Reich 1928* (Berlin: Hobbing, 1928), 373–74.

42. Möser, "Desire for Automobiles," 195–96.

43. See, for example, "Sie versuchen es immer wieder," *Tempo*, 2 January 1929, 12.

44. Alon Confino and Rudy Koshar, "Régimes of Consumer Culture: New Narratives in Twentieth-Century German History," *German History* 19, no. 2 (2001): 156.

Germany in the 1920s, with the more affordable two-wheeled vehicle acting as a "substitute car," bought with the prospect of "upgrading" in the future.[45] The greater individual mobility granted by motor vehicles and their promise of personal freedom and hedonistic fun was especially appealing to young white-collar workers, answering their demand for entertainment and leisure travel.[46] The general enthusiasm for the automobile meant that, as Rudy Koshar put it, "German culture was motorized well before many inhabitants of that nation actually got around in cars."[47] For *Tempo*, the state had a role to play in bringing about American-style mass motorization in Germany. After technological progress had made cheaper cars possible, the paper claimed, the only obstacles to reaching a level of car ownership comparable to the United States or Britain were high taxes, unnecessary regulation, and bureaucracy. It was the government's task to eliminate these obstacles, so the automobile would cease to be a luxury good and become affordable to the common consumer:

> If the Ministry of Transport does not introduce the necessary measures very soon, the automobile will, despite sufficient technological groundwork, remain a privilege of the wealthy classes for years to come, despite the possibility of putting a car in the garage of every small businessman, craftsman and tradesman.[48]

The language used in this paragraph is striking. Essentially, the author defines car ownership as a social right and calls on the state to enforce it. The complaint about high taxes on cars and petrol was common at the time and the high tax rate did indeed stifle the spread of mass motorization in Germany.[49] But while many experts called for lower rates to strengthen the national auto industry and to create new jobs, *Tempo* often argued from the viewpoint of the individual consumer, who had a "right" to have his or her demands fulfilled.

Another important aspect of *Tempo*'s consumerist vision of modern Ger-

---

45. Sasha Disko, *The Devil's Wheels: Men and Motorcycling in the Weimar Republic* (New York: Berghahn, 2016), 2; Frank Steinbeck, *Das Motorrad. Ein deutscher Sonderweg in die automobile Gesellschaft* (Stuttgart: Franz Steiner, 2012), 81–211; Möser, "Desire for Automobiles," 197; Richard J. Overy, "Cars, Roads, and Economic Recovery in Germany, 1932–8," *Economic History Review* 28, no. 3 (1975): 467.
46. Möser, "Desire for Automobiles," 213.
47. Koshar, "Cars and Nations," 122.
48. "Das Auto für den kleinen Mann," 4.
49. Flik, *Von Ford lernen?*, 71–98; Heidrun Edelmann, *Vom Luxusgut zum Gebrauchsgegenstand. Die Geschichte der Verbreitung von Personenkraftwagen in Deutschland* (Frankfurt/Main: Verband der Automobilindustrie, 1989); Overy, "Cars," 467–68.

man society was the promotion of leisure culture and tourism. Weimar had a thriving leisure culture, boosted by social improvements won after the lost war such as shorter working hours and paid holidays.[50] These achievements were small and contentious—the eight-hour day, introduced in 1918, was effectively abolished again in the early 1920s—but the horizon of expectations had changed irreversibly: many people of all walks of life increasingly saw leisure time as a right, rather than a privilege for a select few. In 1928, a guide to the new *Wochenende* (weekend) phenomenon emphasized the recent democratization of leisure time: "The weekend has—almost overnight—become a powerful concept that nobody can ignore. Countless interests, that until now were entertained only by a small and exclusive group, have suddenly become *a necessity for the great masses.*"[51] It was in the Weimar Republic that the idea of free time changed into the idea of "leisure time" (*Freizeit*) that was to be organized and structured.[52] In 1929, the term *Freizeit* entered the German dictionary—a sign that the idea of leisure had become widely accepted. The institution most characteristic for Weimar's mass leisure culture was the free weekend—"*das Wochenende*"—which became a social institution for broad swathes of the population.[53] In the 1920s, the time from Saturday afternoon until Sunday evening came to be seen as a coherent period that could be used for recreation, mostly outside of the city. In Weimar Germany, the weekend was clearly differentiated from conventional leisure time activities, such as the traditional Sunday outing, as a very modern phenomenon. As an import from Anglo-American culture, it had an inherently modern allure, but it was also seen as fitting the demands of a highly industrialized and urbanized society.

---

50. Christine Keitz, "Die Anfänge des modernen Massentourismus in der Weimarer Republik," *Archiv für Sozialgeschichte* 33 (1993): 184–86; Lynn Abrams, "From Control to Commercialisation: The Triumph of Mass Entertainment in Germany, 1900–1925," *German History* 8, no. 3 (1990): 278–93; Reinhard Schmitz-Scherzer and Walter Tokarski, "Zur historischen Entwicklung der Freizeit," in *Freizeit*, ed. Reinhard Schmitz-Scherzer and Walter Tokarski (Stuttgart: Teubner, 1985), 14–57.

51. Edmund Heilpern, "Kaufmännische Reklame und Wochenende," in *Das Wochenende. Anregungen zur praktischen Durchführung*, ed. Karl Tramm and Karl Vetter (Berlin: Mosse, 1928), 199. Emphasis in the original.

52. Adelheid von Saldern, "Die Zeit fährt Auto . . . Zeit-und Raumveränderungen im Zeichen der Moderne," in *Wochenend und schöner Schein. Freizeit und modernes Leben in den Zwanziger Jahren*, ed. Adelheid von Saldern and Sid Auffarth (Berlin: Elephanten Press, 1991), 7–13.

53. Kaspar Maase, *Grenzenloses Vergnügen. Der Aufstieg der Massenkultur 1850–1970* (Frankfurt/Main: Fischer, 1997), 115–38; Abrams, "From Control to Commercialisation," 291–93.

While the retreat into nature still played an important role, Weimar-era weekenders often encountered it in structured, consumerist activities that involved modern sports equipment, such as rowing, sailing, and camping. Despite the fact that thousands pursued these activities, great importance was attached to their individualist character.

Naturally, as a newspaper designed for a young, modern, white-collar audience, *Tempo* embraced the new *Wochenende* phenomenon. It published recipes for weekend snacks, "auto picnics," and hiking foods.[54] The "Technology Everybody Needs" column regularly presented useful gadgets for the weekend break, such as a portable iron, a pocket radio, or a travel gramophone.[55] The newspaper closely followed the activities of the Weekend Committee of Berlin, a pressure group trying to bring together politicians, employers, and unions in order to create a better weekend infrastructure.[56] Mostly, however, *Tempo* reported about life during weekends. The author Ehm Welk, for example, wrote about a drunken group of *Wochenendler* disturbing his weekend break in the countryside, while other articles reported on new campsites and recreational facilities.[57] When Maria Leitner described the weekly pilgrimage of Berlin's workforce to the lakes and forests around the city, she drew a kaleidoscopic picture of a classless weekend society that united golf-playing managers, hiking white-collar couples, and proletarian women exercising with their sports union.[58] But, following them home in the evening, she also clearly expressed the idea that the central function of leisure time was the recuperation of human labor in an industrial society: "And with colorful lights, with a noisy roar, the city welcomes its slaves again."

Besides physical activities in nature, urban amusements and entertainment played an important role in the way people filled their weekends in Weimar Germany. The increasing standardization and rationalization of work, even in white-collar professions, made a clear differentiation between working life

---

54. Dora Sophie, "Kalte Küche fürs Wochenende," *Tempo*, 25 May 1929, 7; Annie Juliane Richert, "Wander-Proviant," *Tempo*, 4 June 1929, 7; Dora Sophie, "Für das Auto-Picknick," *Tempo*, 24 June 1929, 4.

55. "Technik, die jeder braucht," *Tempo*, 15 September 1928, 7; 8 July 1929, 4; 21 September 1929, 4.

56. See, for example, "Wochenende soll organisiert werden," *Tempo*, 2 September 1929, 12.

57. Ehm Welk, "Frontgeist überm Wochenend," *Tempo*, 9 July 1929, 7; "Jungfernheide—Sonntagsparadies," *Tempo*, 8 July 1929, 8; Th. v. P., "Zeltspiele am Werbellin," *Tempo*, 13 July 1929, 3.

58. Maria Leitner, "Eine ganze Stadt erholt sich. Sommer-Sonntag in Berlin," *Tempo*, 1 July 1929, 5.

and leisure time, filled with extraordinary experiences and diversion, a pressing concern. Siegfried Karacauer famously described Weimar's white-collar "cult of distraction," practiced in grand "picture palaces" and the new "pleasure barracks" like the Haus Vaterland, that addressed this need.[59] *Tempo* can be seen as a part of this culture of distraction—an enthusiastic messenger and guide, offering its readers information and orientation for a thrill-filled weekend. Reviews of new films, photos of the latest American stars, and gossip about Berlin's entertainment industry formed a core part of the paper's culture section. The column "The Cheerful Evening" (*Der vergnügte Abend*) provided detailed information and reviews about new shows and revues in Berlin's various nightclubs and music halls, while a long-running illustrated series gave step-by-step instructions to new dance crazes, so *Tempo*'s readers would always be on top of the latest fashion on the dance floor.[60] *Tempo* also often reported on the opening of new entertainment spots: for example, a new bar designed by architect Leo Nachtlicht was celebrated as "non plus ultra of urban life," lauding its light-filled interior that allowed people to "see and be seen," which, according to the author, was so important to modern urbanites.[61] But more than mere information, many articles provided glowing descriptions of a glamorous, cosmopolitan nightlife that *Tempo*'s readers could take part in vicariously by reading *Tempo*. Regular special reports on Berlin's nightlife claimed that the German capital had finally overtaken Paris and London as "the world's most important dance floor."[62] The nightlife of Berlin was often described as a never-ending kaleidoscope of exotic dancers, sweating jazz bands, and wise-cracking comperes:

> Bloody hell! What a tempo. You don't even have time to look left, to look right, to look away; first, a band plays and we laymen dance with a group of angels, then a funny *conferencier* holds court, then the band plays again and an agile couple dance to their music, then the orchestra plays again and we are bopping again . . . , and in the meantime Berlin's youngsters aged eighteen and over show the many out-of-towners how you cut a rug nowadays.[63]

---

59. Siegfried Kracauer, *The Mass Ornament: Weimar Essays*, trans. Thomas Levin (Cambridge: Harvard University Press, 1995), 323–28.
60. Riccardo de Luca, "Jede Woche ein Tanz!," 9 January 1929, 7.
61. "Nachtlichts Nacht-Schöpfung," *Tempo*, 2 February 1929, 9.
62. Gonjac, "Wir haben die besten Tanzbrettl," *Tempo*, 8 December 1928, 5.
63. Jackie, "Der vegnügte Abend: Rings um die Gedächtniskirche rum," *Tempo*, 9 February 1929, 5.

Radio, the most modern form of home recreation, was also given ample room in *Tempo*. While the paper initially only offered a daily listing of broadcasts, it soon featured a whole radio section with reviews by professional critics, letters by readers about their problems with and thoughts on the new technology, previews of upcoming programs, and articles about new transmitters and other technical advancements.[64] The focus on radio is telling of both *Tempo*'s worldview and its audience. As Carsten Lenk has shown, radio was a middle-class medium—in content and in listenership—that disseminated and embodied a "moderate, tempered modernity."[65] Most importantly, by facilitating the consumption of diverse acoustic products, structuring people's leisure time, and as a consumer durable itself, radio acted as a focal point of Weimar's—mostly virtual—consumer society.

The close link between *Tempo* and Weimar's leisure culture was reflected by the fact that advertisements for the latest films, cabaret and theatre shows, and Berlin's popular nightclubs and entertainment complexes, such as Wintergarten, Haus Vaterland, and the Luna-Park fairground, often made up the bulk of all advertising in the paper. This changed somewhat during the summer months, when advertisements for cheap holiday destinations, weekend breaks, and restaurants in the countryside took over. During this time, *Tempo* often offered information about possible destinations, complete with train connections and ticket prices, and devoted many articles to holidays and short weekend trips, presented to its audience—as it had promised in its manifesto—in easily digestible formats. Even more than Berlin's nightlife, the idea of foreign travel served as an aspect of an aspirational lifestyle that reflected *Tempo*'s political mission. Just like the weekend, the development of modern mass tourism in the Weimar Republic was mostly driven by white-collar workers.[66] Clerks, teachers, and other salaried employees now populated the resorts on the Baltic Sea and the spa towns in southern Germany that had been visited primarily by high-ranking military officers, aristocrats, and rich businessmen before the war.[67] The idea of holiday trips as an integral part of a decent standard of living for all was boosted by increased coverage by the media in the 1920s and 1930s.[68] According to *Tempo*, the yearly summer holiday was an

---

64. "Für den Rundfunkhörer," *Tempo*, 13 February 1929, 6.
65. Carsten Lenk, *Die Erscheinung des Rundfunks. Einführung und Nutzung eines neuen Mediums 1923–1932* (Opladen: Westdeutscher Verlag, 1997), 132–35.
66. Hasso Spode, "Der Aufstieg des Massentourismus im 20. Jahrhundert," in Haupt and Torp, *Die Konsumgesellschaft in Deutschland*, 121; Keitz, "Massentourismus," 206–9.
67. Keitz, "Massentourismus," 206–7.
68. Keitz, "Massentourismus," 187.

experience that united all strata of German society, from the manager to the humble typist, including famous Germans such as long-distance runner Otto Peltzer and actor Hans Albers.[69] The costs for vacationing at exotic locations, the newspaper argued, were so affordable nowadays that they should not deter anybody.[70] *Tempo*'s readers could share in this supposedly nationwide experience: on 15 June 1929, the paper announced a photography competition for summer vacationers, calling on them to send in their best holiday snaps. The competition reflected the paper's focus on visual culture, modern technology, and middle-class everyday life. The announcement claimed that a photography competition was a natural fit for *Tempo* and its technophile readers: "*Tempo* is a newspaper of images (*Bilderzeitung*). And who among *Tempo* readers does not have a camera?"[71] According to the rules, only photos from vacations outside the city were accepted, which effectively excluded most working-class readers, who often lacked the funds for expensive holidays. Each submission was to register the location, the name and address of the photographer, and even the camera model used, highlighting the technical aspect of the contest. The competition ran for ten weeks and each week *Tempo* published three of the submitted photos, which were awarded prizes of thirty, twenty, and ten marks, respectively. The subjects of the chosen photos were always the vacationers themselves, relaxing, playing sports, or striking poses in front to the camera, but only three of the thirty submissions were from exotic, international vacation destinations, namely Croatia, Copenhagen, and the Russian countryside. A few readers sent in photos from German holiday destinations such as the Baltic coast or the Bavarian mountains. Rather than expensive holidays, however, the majority of the photos showed people enjoying their free time in much humbler scenery: Berliners relaxing at one of the city's many lakes or even, despite the paper's own rules, in the street, their own back garden, or inner-city locations, such as the Lunabad, the public swimming pool in the Luna-Park. Irrespective of the location, most photos chosen by *Tempo*'s editors had a humorous tone, showing young people fooling around in front of the camera, such as a group of women in swimming costumes at the shores of Crossin Lake at the southeastern corner of Berlin.[72] The photo, titled "Our Young People of 1929," was submitted by "Mrs. Potzenheim," who lived in one of the more well-to-do areas of Neukölln, a traditionally working-class district. This is a fairly repre-

---

69. See, for example, "In welchem Tempo machen Sie Urlaub?," *Tempo*, 18 May 1929, 7; Katta Launisch (i.e., Polly Tieck), "Das Thema der Saison," *Tempo*, 26 June 1929, 3
70. "Was kosten Seereisen?," *Tempo*, 15 January 1929, 7.
71. "Die schönste Ferienaufnahme," *Tempo*, 15 June 1929, 2
72. "Die Preisträger der 3. Woche," *Tempo*, 13 July 1929, 3.

Figure 7. "Preisausschreiben 'Ferienfreude'," *Tempo*, 23 September 1929, 12. © Axel Springer AG. Used with permission.

sentative example: almost as many women as men submitted photos, and most of the submissions came from the lower middle-class areas of the inner-city districts, such as Kreuzberg, Prenzlauer Berg, or Friedrichshain. At the end of the competition, the readers were asked to choose an overall winner among the weekly photos, using a ballot paper printed in the paper. The grand prize was 300 marks, more than the average monthly salary of a German white-collar worker. The winning photo, voted for by 620 readers, showed a humble scene of a couple having a picnic on the banks of a river during their "holiday journey" in a rowing boat (Fig. 7).

There were many reasons for *Tempo* to run such a contest. First, for the Ullstein company, which ran its own chain of travel agencies, the promotion of leisure travel during the summer months made commercial sense. However, images of people enjoying their vacations were also thoroughly political in Weimar Germany. As Shelley Baranowski and Ellen Furlough have argued, tourism is "a quest by commercialized means for experiences and values not necessarily market-based."[73] For many Germans, tourism meant rebuilding a national identity using peaceful means. As Fritzsche has shown, in traveling in their own country, Germans satisfied their "desire to experience the unity of the nation" that had been fundamentally weakened by the lost war.[74] Thus, second, *Tempo*'s photo competition offered its readers a space to share this experience of a national community publicly and for others to take part vicariously. This did not only apply to the few photos taken at German holiday locations but also to the many images of common people humbly enjoying their leisure time, which had come to be seen as a right in Weimar Germany. Third, images of happy vacations, and particularly long-distance holiday trips, created a concrete promise of coming prosperity. As the majority of the actual photos showed, for a large part of *Tempo*'s target audience such journeys remained a dream, but this did not diminish their intense interest in leisure travel. The first holiday prospectuses by professional travel agencies, for example, were collected by many Germans not primarily for their informational value, but as a picture book of exotic locations and a model of future prosperity.[75] The images of exotic locations chosen in *Tempo*'s competition offered the virtual experience of leisure life and, just like its reports on supposedly affordable cars and household appliances, created an inspirational vision of a better future for its readers. This was boosted by many other articles in the paper about exotic holiday experiences. For example, on 13 August 1929, *Tempo* published a photo essay of life on the SS *Bremen*, one of the most modern ocean liners of its day that had crossed the Atlantic in record-breaking speed on its maiden voyage to New York City in July.[76] The newspaper invited its readers to "a free trip over

---

73. Shelley Baranowski and Ellen Furlough, "Introduction," in Being Elsewhere: Tourism, Consumer Culture, and Identity in Modern Europe and North America, ed. Shelley Baranowski and Ellen Furlough (Ann Arbor: University of Michigan Press, 2001), 11.
74. Fritzsche, "Historical Time," 157.
75. Keitz, "Massentourismus," 187.
76. "Auf der 'Bremen,' 1. Klasse," *Tempo*, 13 August 1929, 8.

the ocean—in images," giving them the opportunity to vicariously experience the glamour of drinking cocktails on deck. Finally, there was also an obvious political stance in letting the readership have the final vote over the overall winner of the competition. Using their ballot papers, *Tempo*'s readers recreated the democratic process, which lay at the heart of the new German society they had been a part of since 1919. Thus, combining the increased availability of cheap photography with the democratized desire for leisure travel, *Tempo*'s competitions of holiday snaps provided a forum for the "self-making" aspect of citizenship. Its readers presented themselves and were framed by the newspaper as practicing citizen-consumers, embodying the promise of a democratic German consumer society.

In Weimar Germany, both leisure travel and urban nightlife were seen as the essential practices of the modern, rationalized world the country's white-collar workers inhabited. In his essay "Travel and Dance," published in 1923, Kracauer argued that vacations and jazz music provided "those in the grip of mechanization" with an ersatz experience of the sublime, of what it means to be human.[77] While sharing Kracauer's focus on these practices as an expression of modernity, *Tempo*'s interpretation of their meaning could not be more different. In the newspaper, leisure time was presented as a vision of a more stable society and a better life, and, somewhat paradoxically, consuming leisure time was the way to make this vision a reality. The tensions between *Tempo*'s image of accessible holiday destinations and exciting nightlife on the one hand and the social reality of many of its readers on the other—tensions that also existed in the paper's coverage of the automobile as both a luxury and an affordable consumer good—reflected the dynamism of Weimar society itself. While it was still very much divided along class lines, the Republic embodied the promise of greater social justice and a more equal distribution of prosperity. *Tempo*'s optimistic vision of a lifestyle that defied rigid borders of class, characterized by modern living, leisure travel, and the latest technology at home and at work, was a projection of this promise. Therefore, *Tempo*'s promotion of holidays and largely unattainable products such as automobiles and consumer electronics was more than information for readers indulging in "virtual consumption." It also disseminated a highly political vision of an American-style "democracy of goods" as Germany's future. Thus, it did not matter that most of its audience was—yet—unable to afford a car, a holiday, or a modern fridge, as long as it was conceivable that ownership was an imminent possibility. *Tempo*'s liberal journalists clearly assumed that free-market eco-

---

77. Kracauer, *Mass Ornament*, 71.

nomics and the capitalist order would deliver the desired goods as soon as there was a healthy consumer demand for them. This would lead to a healthy economy and, ultimately, a stable democratic system, softening rigid class differences and integrating all strata of society. However, it is remarkable that when *Tempo*'s readers had a say in how they imagined this future, they chose a decidedly moderate and humble version—rather than exotic holidays in Croatia, they identified with a boating holiday on a local river.

"Every Day a Race against Time!" Technology, Speed, and *Sachlichkeit* in *Tempo*

According to *Tempo*, modern technology would make this peaceful, democratic consumer society a reality. Modern means of transport, for example, had made leisure travel an affordable activity that opened the world to the common man and supported peaceful understanding between the nations:

> Technology has transformed the ways of traveling. While we used to stay inside our country's borders in the past, we are now able to roam the globe and cross the oceans thanks to modern means of transport. Every year thousands of Americans visit the Old World for business and pleasure, while Germans relax in the Mediterranean or Scandinavia, and this brings more people into contact with each other than during the world-shattering events of the Migration Period.[78]

Modern aviation technology was a particular focus of *Tempo*. Planes and airships, Peter Fritzsche has argued, helped Germans "to feel at home in the postwar world" by promising to give their country the ability to project its power beyond its borders and once again play a role in global power politics.[79] *Tempo* actively combatted such militaristic or overly nationalistic notions of technology. It presented the "new Germany" as a peaceful nation, producing internationally acclaimed machinery and consumer goods instead of weapons. When the International Air Show (Internationale Luftfahrtausstellung) was held in Berlin again in 1928 after a twenty-year hiatus, *Tempo* claimed that it was not only the biggest in history but also the first with a strictly civilian char-

---

78. "Was kosten Seereisen?," 5.
79. Fritzsche, "Historical Time," 161.

acter.[80] In an opinion piece on the show, the newspaper celebrated the commercial success of German aircraft, produced only for civilian purposes, over French planes, which were adapted from military models.[81] In Weimar Germany, the L127 *Graf Zeppelin* airship arguably was the most popular aviation technology of the era, put into service a few days after *Tempo*'s launch.[82] The airship's successful journeys around the globe often dominated the headlines of the German press; its landings and even mere flyovers were publicly celebrated mass events.[83] This demonstration of engineering skill was a source of immense pride for many Germans and a symbol of the nation's resurgence after the lost war. While the popularity of the airships before and during the war had had decidedly nationalistic and aggressive undertones, *Tempo* now recruited the *Zeppelin* for the new democratic order. In a leader comment on the *Zeppelin*'s transatlantic voyage to America, it described the airship as a symbol of national unity, peace, and international understanding:

> The *Zeppelin* is a matter of the German people. Even more: it is a matter for all of humanity. The American people are unified with the German people in their anticipation of all news about and in their love for the great work, which shall unify the people as an instrument of peace.[84]

The funds for the construction of the L127 had been raised partly by a nationwide appeal, backed by eminent personalities such as Thomas Mann and Oswald Spengler.[85] This had a long tradition: already in 1908, public donations had saved Count Zeppelin's business after the crash of an earlier model, the LZ4.[86] Twenty years later, *Tempo* interpreted the popular support for the airship as a sign of the people's struggle for freedom. According to the paper, the appeal in 1908 in the face of an indifferent emperor had already been the first spark of a democratic revolution:

---

80. Erich Ottermann, "Was die ILA zeigt," *Tempo*, 6 October 1928, 4.
81. "Fragen des Tages: Zur ILA: Passagiere oder Bomben," *Tempo*, 6 October 1928, 2
82. Hans von Schiller and Hans G. Knäusel, *Zeppelin. Aufbruch ins 20. Jahrhundert* (Bonn: Kirschbaum, 1988), 209.
83. Guillaume de Syon, *Zeppelin! Germany and the Airship, 1900–1939* (Baltimore: Johns Hopkins University Press, 2002), 110–46; Peter Fritzsche, *A Nation of Fliers: German Aviation and the Popular Imagination* (Cambridge: Harvard University Press, 1992), 133–84.
84. Sky, "Fragen des Tages: Zeppelin," *Tempo*, 12 October 1928, 2.
85. Fritzsche, *Nation of Fliers*, 142.
86. Syon, *Zeppelin!*, 40–70; Fritzsche, *Nation of Fliers*, 9–22.

From the beginning, the *Zeppelin* was the business of the German people and not of the former Kaiser. . . . The German people rose up, they gathered the funds, because they believed in Zeppelin and his work. It was more than a collection; it really was a popular uprising, an uprising for Zeppelin and the first great uprising of the people against the Kaiser's regime.[87]

This view of technology as inherently democratic contrasted sharply with the more aggressive and nationalistic portrayal of German engineering in much of the German press.[88] *Tempo* vigorously defended the new airship against its appropriation by right-wing nationalists, who had spread the rumor that the *Zeppelin* had taken a detour over the Netherlands to pay respects to the exiled monarch living in Doorn.[89]

Modern media technology was portrayed as equally emancipatory in *Tempo*. The proliferation of the gramophone, film, and radio had made Germany's provincial towns more "Americanized" than Berlin, Maria Leitner reported, and had expanded the horizons of their inhabitants: teenagers learned English by singing the latest hits and housewives no longer "talk about the neighbor's dress, but about Greta Garbo's or Clara Bow's."[90] The mass media, the American filmmaker Cecil B. DeMille argued in *Tempo*, acted as "democracy's strongest auxiliary forces" by giving all people the same access to knowledge, information, and modern entertainment, no matter where they lived.[91] In its coverage of the International Broadcasting Exhibition (Internationale Funkausstellung) in 1929, the paper stressed the "many foreign delegations of international broadcasting companies" attending the German trade fair.[92] A year later, when Albert Einstein opened the International Broadcasting Exhibition with a live-broadcast speech, *Tempo* quoted the parts in which he connected the new technology with the new political system:

> Remember that it is the engineers who *make real democracy possible* in the first place. They do not only make our daily lives easier, but also make the works of the finest thinkers and artists, whose enjoyment has until

---

87. Sky, "Fragen des Trages: Zeppelin," *Tempo*, 12 October 1928, 2.
88. Bernhard Rieger, *Technology and the Culture of Modernity in Britain and Germany, 1890–1945* (Cambridge: Cambridge University Press, 2005), 243–54.
89. Sky, "Zeppelin," *Tempo*, 12 October 1928, 2.
90. Marie Leitner, "Die Provinz amerikanisierter als Berlin," *Tempo*, 28 May 1929, 2.
91. Cecil B. de Mille, "Der Film—ein Element der Demokratie," *Tempo*, 19 July 1929, 5.
92. C.M.S., "VI. Funk-Ausstellung eröffnet," *Tempo*, 30 August 1929, 3.

recently been a privilege of the favored classes, *accessible for everybody* and thus wake the peoples of the world from sleepy stupor. Broadcasting plays a singular role in the *reconciliation of the peoples*.[93]

In sum, modern technology was nothing to fear, according to *Tempo*'s authors: on the contrary, rather than national competition or dangerous globalization, airplanes and airships embodied international exchange and understanding; rather than the threat of a homogenization of German *Kultur*, Hollywood movies and radio stood for cosmopolitanism and democratization.

An important aspect of *Tempo*'s fascination with modern technology and the hopes it invested in it was an obsession with speed and velocity—expressed most prominently by the paper's own name. In this respect, it was representative of a specific part of Weimar culture: in Germany, the rapid modernization during the late nineteenth century had generated a widespread "sense of general acceleration" of life itself, which intensified after the war.[94] This fascination with speed, extended even to the human body with the popularization of Frederick Winslow Taylor's scientific management, Ford's assembly line, and modern competitive sports, defined the urban culture of the 1920s.[95] For many, the representatives of this accelerated culture—the pilot, the racing-car driver, or even the investigative reporter and the speedy secretary—became role models for modern life.[96] In 1927, the sociologist Werner Sombart described this trend as a consequence of the development of high capitalism, which led to a changed perception of time itself:

> This drive towards acceleration is expressed on the one hand in a feeling of a high importance of time, which is a completely new phenomenon. . . . On the other hand, this drive is reflected in the desire, seizing an ever-greater part of the population, for an acceleration of one's lifestyle. People think it valuable, important, and necessary to walk and travel swiftly—to fly, if possible; to produce, transport and consume quickly; to speak rap-

---

93. "'Das wunderbarste Werkzeug der Mitteilung'," *Tempo*, 22 August 1930, 3.
94. Eley, Jenkins, and Matysik, "Introduction," 4; Hartmut Rosa, *Beschleunigung. Die Veränderung der Zeitstrukturen in der Moderne* (Frankfurt/Main: Suhrkamp, 2005), 71–160.
95. Jensen, *Body by Weimar*, 3–14; Rieger, *Technology*, 116–57; Peter Borscheid, *Das Tempo-Virus. Eine Kulturgeschichte der Beschleunigung* (Frankfurt: Campus, 2004), 186–90; Charles S. Maier, "Between Taylorism and Technocracy: European Ideologies and the Vision of Industrial Productivity in the 1920s," *Journal of Contemporary History* 5, no. 2 (1970): 27–61.
96. Borscheid, *Tempo-Virus*, 213.

idly (acronyms! Telegram style!), to write rapidly (shorthand!). People take great delight in adding the word "express" to all sorts of processes and acts: express train, express liner, express printing, express photography.[97]

Kracauer shared this negative view of the culture of velocity, interpreting the contemporary obsession with speed records as "the final manifestation" of a Weberian disenchantment of the world through modern technology.[98] The press was a crucial element of this accelerated age. Records set by long-distance runners, racing-car drivers, and pilots were not only treated as front-page news: newspapers themselves took part in the race for speed, trying to outdo each other in being the latest and the fastest, to the point that their actual time of publication was sometimes at odds with their very names. In 1920s Berlin, the *12-Uhr-Blatt*, for example, was published at 11 a.m., the *8-Uhr-Abendblatt* at 5 p.m., and the *Welt am Montag* on Sunday evening.[99] In 1931, Rudolf Arnheim sarcastically commented on this race for "up-to-date-ness" and its consequences for contemporary culture:

> The other day, on a midnight walk down one of the busiest streets in Berlin's West End, I saw a paperboy selling the *Mittagszeitung*. . . . Maybe this paperboy felt that the *Mittagszeitung* had crossed an equatorial line: at the stroke of midnight, it reaches the point of the most ridiculous out-of-date-ness and simultaneously acquires an incredible timeliness, setting a new record in promptness of coverage that could never be broken, even if we perfected all means of communication. . . . So was it midday now? Did the newspaper set the time? Who could really know? And who would want to know?[100]

By overtaking themselves, Arnheim argued, the newspapers seemed to unhinge time itself, turning night into day, and the city dweller, walking down the nocturnal boulevard under bright electric lights, began to live not by the natural progression of time but by the fast-running clock of the newspaper.

In contrast to skeptical observers like Sombart, Kracauer, and Arnheim,

---

97. Werner Sombart, *Das Wirtschaftsleben im Zeitalter des Hochkapitalismus*, vol. 1 (Berlin: Duncker & Humblot, 1927), 23–24.
98. Kracauer, *Mass Ornament*, 70.
99. Rudolf Stöber, *Deutsche Pressegeschichte. Einführung, Systematik, Glossar* (Constance: UVK, 2000), 168; Oschilewski, *Zeitungen in Berlin*, 146.
100. Rudolf Arnheim, "Zwölf Uhr nachts," *Die Weltbühne*, 29 December 1931, 969.

Ullstein fully embraced this aspect of modern life and tried to position *Tempo* as the publication that was most in tune with this new spirit of the age. Unlike most newspapers, from the *12-Uhr-Blatt* to the *Welt am Abend*, it was not named after its time of publication, but after speed itself—a programmatic name that turned the frantic chase of the clock hands into a value in itself. For Ullstein, "tempo" was both "the motto of the twentieth century—and its most modern newspaper!"[101] Ullstein was not the only company tapping into the zeitgeist to sell their new product: in March 1927, a short-lived magazine called *Tempo* had been launched in Hamburg, aiming to be a "mirror and brief chronicle of the staggering, real and dizzying tempo that attacks us from all directions and in thousands of ways."[102] In January 1929, *Vereinigte Papierwerke* in Nuremberg introduced the paper handkerchief to the German market under the same name.[103] But more than any other product, *Tempo* seemed to embody that especially hectic part of contemporary culture, the urban Weimar press. In fact, the new publication exactly confirmed Sombart's lament about the contemporary obsession with staccato sentences, abbreviations, and quickly accessible information. Ullstein promoted *Tempo* with the syncopated slogan "Every day a race against time! Every line is news!" (*Täglich Wettlauf mit der Zeit! Jede Zeile Neuigkeit!*).[104] A full-page advertisement in the style of Dadaist collages featured symbols of the new accelerated culture: athletes in action, two disembodied hands punching the keyboard of a typewriter, planes in midair, and a car thundering down a racetrack (Fig. 8). The collage itself advertised *Tempo* as "Germany's most modern newspaper type" and an accompanying article described the paper as offering "the full experience of our time" by giving the reader only the latest and the newest.[105] In the following year, a giant poster was unveiled in Berlin's Kochstraße underground station, close to the Ullstein offices, showing a pack of journalists and photographers running after a hovering terrestrial globe, announcing: "Be up to date by reading *Tempo!*" (*Wer* Tempo *liest, lebt mit der Zeit!*), underlining the paper's international outlook and its focus on a culture of speed.[106] In the newspaper's own terms, laid down in a manifesto-like editorial in its first issue, Sombart's skep-

---

101. "Tempo," *Ullstein-Berichte*, July 1929, 1.
102. Axel Eggebrecht, "Zeitschriftenschau," *Literarische Welt*, 20 May 1927, 6.
103. Florian Langenscheidt, *Deutsche Standards. Marken des Jahrhunderts* (Wiesbaden: Gabler, 2004), 500.
104. *Ullstein-Berichte*, October 1928, 2.
105. "Tempo—die Zeitung der Zeit," *Ullstein-Berichte*, October 1928, 3.
106. *Ullstein-Berichte*, October 1929, 10. See also "Eigenreklame im U-Bahnhof," *Zeitungs-Verlag*, 13 July 1929, 1432.

Figure 8. Advertisement, *Ullstein-Berichte*, October 1928, 2. © Axel Springer AG. Used with permission.

tical remarks appeared as nothing more than the complaints of a bygone generation too old to adapt to the new speed of life:

> What is the meaning, the intellectual purpose of this new paper? The answer lies in our name. We offer information and entertainment succinctly in the tempo of modern life. Only to the ageing this may seem like breathless hurry. For the busy, striving, young person, tempo means the sweep of their ambition, their urge to move forward. Tempo doesn't reside in the legs; it lives in the heart. We address the German generation that no longer groans under the tempo of our lives but sees it as a reflection of their positive outlook on life.[107]

The supposedly accelerated lifestyle of *Tempo*'s target audience of young white-collar workers was catered to by its own use of cutting-edge technology. According to Ullstein, *Tempo* was the first German newspaper using image telegraphy to receive photographs from all over the world in a matter of hours.[108] Its most unique feature, however, was its capacity for a rolling coverage of the day's most important events. *Tempo* was published in three different daily editions, thus giving the newspaper the ability to "renew itself every hour," its manifesto claimed.[109] According to Hans Ullstein's son Karl, the technical director of the company, the editions were printed and distributed in the space of only four hours, between 3 p.m. and 7 p.m.[110] The three time periods in which the different editions were in circulation were defined as "after office hours," "pre-theatre," and "late evening," which points to *Tempo*'s target audience as relatively young, hedonistic white-collar workers.[111] With the newspaper's three editions, Ullstein claimed, the newspaper introduced another Anglo-American trend to the German market: "*Tempo* (following English and American models) is . . . the first German type of newspaper that is printed in several daily editions, which are updated with the latest news."[112] While the publication of several daily editions was nothing new on the German press market, three was a remarkably high number. Most broadsheet newspapers

---

107. "Eine neue Zeitung," *Tempo*, 11 September 1928, 2
108. "Tempo," in *Der Verlag Ullstein zum Weltreklamekongress*, 141; Karl Ullstein, "Unsere Technik," in *Der Verlag Ullstein zum Weltreklamekongress Berlin*, 231.
109. "Eine neue Zeitung," 2
110. Ullstein, "Unsere Technik," 230.
111. *Ullstein-Chronik*, 1928, unpaginated.
112. "Tempo—Die Zeitung der Zeit," 4.

were published twice a day, in the morning and in the evening.[113] But in this case enough time elapsed over the whole day to justify several editions. Evening tabloids such as *Tempo*, however, only had a very short shelf life of a few hours. *Tempo*'s frequency of publication begs the question of whether potential readers really would have wanted to buy a paper that was, by its own design, obsolete after a short while. The editors seem to have anticipated this problem and provided an "operating manual" for their audience in its first issue:

> Naturally, as a new Ullstein paper, we only use the latest printing and illustration technology available. However, some of these innovations are so groundbreaking that some of our readers will need "directions for use." As the first German newspaper, we are published in several daily editions—and some readers might ask themselves: which one should I buy, which is the "right one"? The answer: the edition that is offered to you whenever you leave your apartment, the office or the shops and step into the street is always the right one, because it is always the latest one.[114]

Invoking Ullstein's reputation as the country's foremost publishing house and emphasizing the use of the "very latest" technology hitherto unseen in Germany, *Tempo* was characterized not only as the mouthpiece of a record-breaking age, but as a record breaker itself. The unique technology employed by *Tempo*, the editorial argued further, made it immune to the passage of time itself:

> Because we use the most modern newspaper technology, our coverage does not end with going to press. It allows a continuous updating even while the current edition is being printed. Newspapers are sold on the street for three, four, five hours, becoming outdated over this period. *Tempo* is the first exception to this rule: it does not age, because it renews itself every hour.[115]

According to Ullstein, *Tempo* was perfectly adapted to a world dominated by technology and speed, and thus the ideal companion for life in modern Germany, as envisioned by the newspaper.

Tempo's optimistic view of modern technology reflected a broader current

---

113. Stöber, *Pressegeschichte*, 168–69.
114. "Eine neue Zeitung," 2.
115. "Eine neue Zeitung," 2.

in German interwar culture that Helmuth Lethen has described as "embracing alienation" (*Einverständis mit der Entfremdung*).[116] The key concept of this affirmative stance toward modernization was *Sachlichkeit* ("objectivity" or "rational-ness"). The term had entered the public discourse during Germany's rapid modernization in the late nineteenth century, gaining further significance during the First World War, as a stoic reaction to the uncontrollable processes that seemed to rule the modern world.[117] In the Weimar Republic, it manifested itself not only in the cultural movement of Neue Sachlichkeit but also in political manifestos and philosophical essays by members of the whole intellectual spectrum, from liberal politicians such as Hans Luther and Walther Rathenau to sociologists like Sombart and Karl Mannheim, to exponents of the "Conservative Revolution" such as Ernst Jünger and Carl Schmitt.[118] These people defined the term in very different ways, but it was generally used to describe an unemotional stocktaking of the present and the dismissal of nostalgia, which fit the *Machbarkeitswahn*—the obsession with shaping the future—of the Weimar era.[119] The parts of the German middle class and white-collar workers that took this positive stance toward modernization adopted *Sachlichkeit* as a worldview that embraced modern technology, but did not look to use it to fundamentally change society.[120] In this sense, *Sachlichkeit* was firmly rooted in the broader idea of a "moderate modernity," a rationally managed modern world without extremes. Frank Trommler has argued that, politically, this interpretation of modern technology was an ideological compromise that was aimed at "taking the wind out of the sails of anti-modern cultural and leftist social revolutionaries."[121] This is also reflected in Karl Mannheim's definition of

---

116. Helmut Lethen, "Freiheit von Angst. Über einen entlastenden Aspekt der Technik-Moden in den Jahrzehnten der historischen Avantgarde 1910–1930," in *Literatur in einer industriellen Kultur*, ed. Götz Grossklaus and Eberhard Lämmert (Stuttgart: Cotta, 1989), 72.

117. For a historical discussion of the term, see Hans-Eduard Hengstenberg, "Sachlichkeit," in *Historisches Wörterbuch der Philosophie*, ed. Joachim Ritter and Rudolf Eisler (Darmstadt: Wissenschaftliche Buchgesellschaft, 2004), 8:1100–1102.

118. Willibald Steinmetz, "Anbetung und Dämonisierung des 'Sachzwangs'. Zur Archäologie einer deutschen Redefigur," in *Obsessionen. Beherrschende Gedanken im wissenschaftlichen Zeitalter*, ed. Michael Jeismann (Frankfurt/Main: Suhrkamp, 1995), 293–333.

119. Graf, *Zukunft*, 84; Peukert, *Weimar Republic*, 110.

120. Frank Trommler, "Technik, Avantgarde, Sachlichkeit," in Grossklaus and Lämmert, *Literatur in einer industriellen Kultur*, 66.

121. Trommler, "Technik, Avantgarde, Sachlichkeit," 61.

Sachlichkeit in his work *Ideologie und Utopie*, published in 1929.[122] For Mannheim, the term denoted a certain state of "tensionless-ness" that characterized his time, meaning a dissolution of grand ideologies and a concentration on the here and now. Only left-wing and right-wing camps still harbored utopian, overarching world views, Mannheim argued, while the "centrist wing" (*Flügel der Mitte*) dismissed such concepts and focused on the management of the plurality of processes shaping reality, with the "American consciousness," characterized by the aim of "technical and managerial control of reality" (*organisatorisch-technische Wirklichkeitsbeherrschung*), as a role model.[123] Keeping in mind the extreme ideological polarization that would come to dominate Weimar's political culture shortly after the publication of Mannheim's work, this almost postmodern worldview seems like a spectacular misjudgment. However, it shows that Ullstein's offer of a liberal "moderate modernity" grew out of a broad intellectual current that has been eclipsed in Weimar historiography by the focus on the more extreme visions of Germany's future.

Ullstein went to great lengths to portray itself as a particularly *sachlich* institution, a proponent of this sober, unpartisan spirit unencumbered by ideological in-fighting. According to Paul Schlesinger, the author of the essay about the democratic "Ullstein spirit," *Sachlichkeit* was the company's pervading quality as a new kind of organization characterized by democratic principles and a flat hierarchy.[124] In various publications of the firm, Ullstein's high rate of production, its effective organization, and even its buildings, in particular the vast printing complex erected in the Berlin suburb of Tempelhof in 1927, were described as reflections of the sober, rational, and objective attitude of *Sachlichkeit*.[125]

Forging Rational Citizens: *Tempo*'s Definition of Democracy

According to *Tempo*, *Sachlichkeit* was also the most important characteristic of a German democratic citizen. During the unfolding of the "Sklarek scandal," a corruption affair that brought down Berlin's DDP mayor Gustav Böß before

---

122. For the following, see Karl Mannheim, *Ideologie und Utopie* (Frankfurt/Main: Vittorio Klostermann, 1985), 213–25.
123. For this realist, utopia-critical discourse in the Weimar Republic, see also Graf, *Zukunft*, 329–58.
124. Sling, "Geist des Hauses," 1927, 386.
125. Max Osborn, "Das neue Ullstein-Druckhaus in Berlin-Tempelhof," *Ullstein-Berichte*, April 1927, 1.

the local election in November 1929 and that has been interpreted as an important reason for the Nazis gaining an electoral foothold in Berlin, *Tempo* emphasized the importance of reasonableness and common sense.[126] When Böß was verbally abused by demonstrating mobs, the author "Sky" called for an objective, reasoned debate:

> What happened in the Berlin city council should not be whitewashed, glossed over or brushed under the carpet. . . . We cannot criticize these dealings harshly enough. But we also must always remain objective (*sachlich*). This strict objectivity (*Sachlichkeit*) is severely hindered, or even made impossible, by the abuse we have witnessed at Böß's arrival. Every man of judgment, tact and taste must be disgusted by it.[127]

Sachlichkeit was a core concept of the political culture of the Weimar Republic. In the Reichstag, parliamentarians of all colors used the term to describe a political style that both refrained from personal attacks and discussed the issues at hand in an objective and impartial way.[128] In this rational "mode of arguing," politicians attacked their opponents only on factual rather than ideological grounds, which created a space for deliberation and compromises. For *Tempo*, this democratic culture of *Sachlichkeit* was only really put into practice in Western nations. The newspaper closely followed the US presidential election of 1928, and American political culture, supposedly based on rational arguments and respectful deliberation, was contrasted favorably with the ideological and volatile politics at home.[129] When Herbert Hoover eventually won in a landslide, the newspaper described the new American leader as a cosmopolitan, rational statesman.[130] According to "Sky," it was not surprising that German political culture was still imperfect: in only ten years, and under such harsh circumstances, it was impossible to develop a system as stable as in Britain or France. But sooner or later, Germany would catch up with its West-

---

126. For the "Sklarek scandal," see Cordula Ludwig, *Korruption und Nationalsozialismus in Berlin, 1924–1934* (Frankfurt/Main: Lang, 1998), 133–81. For the role of the media in the scandal, see Fulda, *Press and Politics*, 146–49.
127. Sky, "Die widerlichen Straßen-Szenen," *Tempo*, 1 November 1929, 2.
128. Thomas Mergel, *Parlamentarische Kultur im Reichstag der Weimarer Republik. Politische Kommunikation, symbolische Politik und Öffentlichkeit im Reichstag* (Düsseldorf: Droste, 2002), 252–59.
129. Sky, "Fragen des Tages: Amerika, du hast es besser," *Tempo*, 6 November 1928, 2.
130. "Der neue Mann, der Amerika regiert," *Tempo*, 7 November 1928, 2

ern neighbors in terms of democratic experience.[131] This plea for patience was echoed by Roda Roda, who admired the levelheadedness of British political culture, but reminded his readers that the Germans had only just begun to take control of their own fate and thus occasional problems were to be expected.[132]

Ullstein made a point of the fact that *Tempo* did not pursue its "great political mission" of promoting a sense of democratic citizenship among the nation's youth in the old-fashioned style of pompous editorials, but rather in short, clear columns that fitted the lifestyle of its target audience, concentrating on facts and avoiding political preaching.[133] However, this did not mean that *Tempo* refrained from taking a clear political stance and only expressed its support for the new order through consumerist fantasies. The newspaper was outspoken in its pro-democratic ethos and in its rejection of the old order. *Tempo*'s most vocal support for the Republic came only a few weeks after its launch, celebrating the tenth anniversary of the proclamation of the Republic on 9 November 1918. *Tempo* published a paean on the "new Germany," while its direct competitors *Welt am Abend* and *Nachtausgabe* openly rejected the new state.[134] Other pro-democratic papers, such as the *Vossische Zeitung* or the *8-Uhr-Abendblatt*, also celebrated the anniversary, but remained rather reserved and muted, a fact that the Communist newspaper *Welt am Abend* interpreted as a creeping disenchantment of the bourgeoisie with the Republic.[135] *Tempo*, in contrast, was positively exuberant. It praised the founding of Germany's first unified, democratic state as a miracle, a deed more heroic and astonishing than anything that had happened in the past few centuries of German history. It alluded to Weimar's political martyrs, such as finance minister Matthias Erzberger and foreign minister Walther Rathenau, who were both assassinated. The real heroes, however, were not politicians, but the German people, who had created a stable, functioning democracy:

> Our new *Reich* is not the work of a single man. There certainly were men who laid the foundations, men who have been paid for this work with ingratitude, persecution in their time, even death, and who will only be

---

131. Sky, "Fragen des Tages: Politische Lehrjahre," *Tempo*, 5 March 1929, 2

132. Roda Roda, "Fragen des Tages: Die weite Sicht, die lange Hand," *Tempo*, 9 April 1929, 2

133. "Tempo—Die Zeitung der Zeit," 4.

134. Sky, "Fragen des Tages: Zehn Jahre Frieden," *Tempo*, 9 November 1928, 2; Otto Heller, "Der Anfang," *Welt am Abend*, 9 November 1928, 1–2; Kgk., "Zehn Jahre Volk in Not," *Nachtausgabe*, 8 November 1928, 2.

135. Heller, "Anfang," 1.

judged justly by history. But the finished building of the new Germany has been *the ingenious work of the whole people*. Never before has the genius of the German people proven more brilliant. In merely ten years, the German people have achieved what eluded them for centuries after the Thirty Years' War and what took more than two generations after the Napoleonic revolution. In merely ten years—that is German tempo, in the best sense of the word.[136]

By combining an emphasis on newness and speed—the characteristics it also attributed to itself—with notions of national unity and plebiscitary cooperation, *Tempo* constructed the image of a progressive, dynamic, and modern Germany, built by a unified people working together. However, rather than spending much time talking about lofty ideals of equality and freedom, the paper tried to connect the readers' everyday experiences with the Weimar state. In particular, the stable currency and rising standards of living were highlighted as the most important achievements of the Republic:

> And what about the little—but all the more important—things of everyday life? The *Mark* is a *Mark* again and not just a bunch of dirty paper that is not worth its printing costs in the morning. Do you still have to queue for hours for fifty grams of butter of bad quality? Are you still dependent on the good will of a civil servant when you want to buy a shirt? Do you still praise the day when a tiny bit of stringy meat finds its way into your soup?[137]

In characteristic fashion, *Tempo* provided a consumerist perspective on the foundation of the Republic and linked its success to the material well-being of its citizens.

On this significant day, *Tempo*'s front page carried an excerpt of an article by Gustav Stresemann, the nation's foremost statesman, foreign minister, and chairman of the liberal-conservative German People's Party (Deutsche Volkspartei, DVP).[138] In his article, he defended the DVP's democratic credentials and directly attacked his critics in the DDP. Stresemann's party always saw the German revolution and the collapse of the monarchy as a tragedy for the nation

---

136. Sky, "Zehn Jahre Frieden," 2.
137. Sky, "Zehn Jahre Frieden," 2.
138. "Stresemann zum 9. November: Aufstieg in der Republik," *Tempo*, 9 November 1928, 1.

and it had only accepted the Republic on pragmatic grounds.[139] Most significantly, it had voted against the Weimar Constitution in 1919, and in 1920 it had sympathized with the reactionary forces of the Kapp Putsch.[140] In the text printed in *Tempo*, Stresemann took a swipe at his "more-republican-than-thou" critics (*Überrepublikaner*), who demanded his party pay lip service to the new order when it had already proven its allegiance through its actions. He argued that the DVP's cooperation in running the affairs of the state implied an affirmation of the Republic and the Constitution and thus an explicit, outspoken commitment was not needed. The fact that Stresemann, and not a DDP representative, was given such prominence on *Tempo*'s front page on this day is a telling sign of the change of political allegiance at the Ullstein house in 1928. The results of the general election in May 1928 had led to a significant break in the relationship between the DDP and the liberal press, including Ullstein. Surprisingly, the party had slumped under 5 percent, despite the relative economic and political stability the voters had enjoyed during the previous four years. This result had come as a shock to many Democrats, who had assumed that the stability of the Republic would pay off in increased votes, and prompted the liberal press to look for strategic alternatives.[141] Stresemann emerged as a promising figurehead, who seemed the only man capable of uniting German liberalism in order to save it from obscurity.[142] Despite Stresemann's age and nationalistic past, *Tempo* built him up as an embodiment of its ethos of youthful, modern democratic citizenship. On New Year's Eve in 1928, the last day of its first year of publication, the paper published another appeal by the statesman under the title "To the German Youth!," in which he urged all politically active young people to join the work on the new German state:

> One of the most welcome developments in politics is the increasingly enthusiastic, even boisterous engagement of young people, because it shows that a new generation feels ready to offer the state not only their hands, but their ideas. The state and the parties cannot possibly do without them. All of you who feel young: into the state, into the parties![143]

---

139. "Grundsätze der Deutschen Volkspartei, Leipzig, 19. Oktober 1919," in *Deutsche Parteiprogramme seit 1861*, ed. Wolfgang Treue (Göttingen: Musterschmidt, 1968), 127–35. See also Childers, "Languages," 331–38; Jones, *Liberalism*, 44–54.
140. Jones, *Liberalism*, 47, 63.
141. Sösemann, *Ende*, 60–62; Bosch, *Liberale Presse*, 77–81; Eksteins, *Limits*, 141.
142. Jones, *Liberalism*, 309–22; Sösemann, *Ende*, 97–98; Eksteins, *Limits*, 142–47.
143. Gustav Stresemann, "Der deutschen Jugend!," *Tempo*, 31 December 1928, 2.

Stresemann defined youth not in terms of age, but as an enthusiastic attitude of vitality, a constructive position aimed against extremist or reactionary concepts of the state. This political energy of Weimar's young people had to be channeled into the parliamentary system and used to strengthen the democratic foundation of the new state.

In the following months, the idea of a merger of the DDP with Stresemann's DVP gained currency at the Ullstein house. In 1929, Franz Ullstein approached the DDP's regional leaders and tried to convince them to cooperate with the DVP in the upcoming local elections, which brought him into conflict with Georg Bernhard and DDP chairman Erich Koch-Weser.[144] In *Tempo*, Stresemann enjoyed full support. His speeches addressing parliament and his own party were regularly reprinted on the front page, analyzed over several pages, and routinely judged as "strong," "powerful" or "great."[145]

Apert from building up Stresemann, *Tempo* loudly rejected the representatives and proponents of the old order to defend Germany's young democracy. The paper often poked fun at the former kaiser and the various princes and princesses, counts and duchesses that still played an important part in Germany's social life.[146] It was critical of the leaders of Germany's heavy industry when they locked out hundreds of thousands of workers during the Ruhreisenstreit in November and December 1928, calling it a blatant attack on the government and the new democratic order.[147] Its principal political target during the first years of the paper's existence, however, was the staunchly monarchist German National People's Party (Deutschnationale Volkspartei, DNVP). After Alfred Hugenberg became chairman of the party in October 1928, *Tempo* regularly ridiculed him as a self-important would-be dictator and attacked his policies as amateurish scheming against Germany's best interests.[148] Another focus

---

144. Franz Ullstein to Erich Koch-Weser, 15 October 1929, in Bundesarchiv Berlin-Lichterfelde (BArchL), N2193 Carl Misch, Nr. 14, fol. 29.

145. Roda Roda, "Fragen des Tages: Gustavs Vernunftehen," *Tempo*, 26 November 1928, 2; "Stresemann-Rede über die große deutsche Krise," *Tempo*, 26 February 1929, 1–2; Sky, "Fragen des Tages: Der tiefe Eindruck," *Tempo*, 27 February 1929, 2; "Stresemann Sieger über Westarp und Hugenberg," *Tempo*, 24 June 1929, 2; "Stresemann über Europas Einigung," *Tempo*, 9 September 1929, 1–2.

146. See, for example, Roda Roda, "Fragen des Tages: Apropos Jutta," *Tempo*, 19 December 1928, 2; Stefan Großmann, "Fragen des Tages: Spalierstehen," *Tempo*, 10 June 1929, 2; Heaven, "Fragen des Tages: Eine Lippe," *Tempo*, 3 July 1929, 2.

147. "Die Ruhr-Industrie versucht Regierungskrise anzuzetteln," *Tempo*, 2 November 1928, 1.

148. See, for example, Roda Roda, "Fragen des Tages: 13 Republiken, 13 Königreiche," *Tempo*, 22 October 1928, 2; "Hugenbergs Amerika-Brief und seine Diktaturpläne," *Tempo*,

of the paper's political coverage was the upstart Nazi Party (Nationalsozialistische Deutsche Arbeiterpartei, NSDAP). The paper reported on the movement for the first time on 23 November 1928, after the authorities banned a planned funeral procession by the "swastika-ers" for Hans Kütemeyer, a NSDAP member who had drowned in Berlin's Landwehr Canal.[149] Although the official report into Kütemeyer's death concluded that he had died in an accident, the Nazis tried to frame it as politically motivated murder and called for the institution of a self-defense unit for right-wing organizations. *Tempo* condemned this initiative in no uncertain words: "There is no doubt that this is an attempt to create, on the flimsiest pretext, a fascist hit squad to be used, like in Munich in 1923, for an 'action'."[150] From this point onward, *Tempo* put a spotlight on Nazi activities, from listing minor assaults to launching full-scale reporting into National Socialist plans to overthrow the Republic.[151] However, in the paper's humorous review of the past year on New Year's Eve 1928, Hitler was mocked as being full of hot air: "The swastika's premier force, this man's an impressive chap. When all else fails, he can rely on his great big trap."[152] This two-sided approach of raising alarm about Nazi extremism on the one hand and ridiculing the movement's populism and nationalistic affectations on the other characterized much of *Tempo*'s coverage of the party before 1930.

At the tenth anniversary of the signing of the Constitution on 11 August 1929, *Tempo* showed the same enthusiasm it had exhibited on the Republic's decennial in 1928. Constitution Day was Weimar's official national day and the accompanying festivities played a central role in its political culture. The parades and mass plays organized by the Reichsbanner organization and Edwin Redslob, the state secretary for culture (*Reichskunstwart*), were demonstrations of national unity and inclusiveness aimed at fostering a new sense of republican community among the population.[153] The celebrations of the tenth

---

25 March 1929, 2; "Die Hugenberg-Hetze gegen Deutschlands Kredit," *Tempo*, 28 March 1929, 2; Roda Roda, "Fragen des Tages: Hugenbergs Prozente," *Tempo*, 10 June 1929, 2; C. Enseo, "Fragen des Tages: Politische Vernebelung," *Tempo*, 17 June 1929, 2; Roda Roda, "Fragen des Tages: Hugenbergs Utopia," *Tempo*, 14 October 1929, 2.

149. "Der Begräbnisumzug der Hakenkreuzler verboten," *Tempo*, 23 November 1928, 1.

150. "Der Begräbnisumzug," 1.

151. "Die Militärübungen der Hakenkreuzler," *Tempo*, 29 November 1928, 1; "Hakenkreuzler verprügeln Konsul," *Tempo*, 29 November 1928, 2; "Der Hakenkreuzlerskandal in Hessen-Kassel," *Tempo*, 5 December 1928, 1; "Verdächtig des Reichstags-Attentats: Nat.-soz. Terrorgruppe," *Tempo*, 2 September 1929, 1–2.

152. "Silvester-Knallbonbons," *Tempo*, 31 December 1928, 2.

153. Nadine Rossol, *Performing the Nation in Interwar Germany: Sport, Spectacle and Political Symbolism 1926–36* (Basingstoke: Palgrave Macmillan, 2010), 58–79.

Constitution Day in Berlin in 1929 were on an unprecedented scale, taking over urban spaces all over the city, and despite minor disruptions by antirepublican groups like the Stahlhelm, Nazis, and Communists, the liberal press uniformly interpreted the anniversary as a resounding success and as a true expression of the people's support for the new state.[154] *Tempo* was no exception, enthusiastically describing the festivities as "an overwhelming victory" for the young Republic, bridging class differences, uniting the nation, and even converting skeptical bystanders:

> There was not one wrong note disrupting the enormous all-day festivities that unified the capital's people in all of the city's districts beyond all class differences. There were no rows, no riots. This great national holiday concluded in rare peacefulness and harmony and will undoubtedly become a milestone in the development of the republican idea and the consolidation of the German Constitution. . . . We heard some and talked to some who have not yet found the right combination of honoring the past and the devotion to the new—people who came to the celebrations as critics. But in the end even they had to confess that here we felt the pulse of the whole nation.[155]

Tempo contrasted the inclusive festivities, open to everyone and actively encouraging popular participation, with the remote demonstrations of power of the official celebrations in the Kaiserreich, when the state and the people were separated by a gulf of hierarchies and protocol. In the new democratic Germany, the paper argued, the head of the state was not a bearded monarch, or even a person at all, but the Constitution itself:

> Constitution Day necessarily is the highest public holiday of the democratic Republic. Because everything is based on the Constitution: the President as well as the lowliest civil servant swear their oath of allegiance to it, it regulates the life of the state. In terms of the depth of its spiritual significance, the birthday of any personality, even the most admired one, does not come close to these celebrations of the birth of the Constitution.[156]

---

154. Rossol, *Performing the Nation*, 68–69.
155. "Tag der deutschen Nation," *Tempo*, 12 August 1929, 3.
156. "Gedanken zum Festtage," *Tempo*, 10 August 1929, 1.

Despite *Tempo*'s support for Stresemann, the belief in the Constitution and the unity of the people, rather than an individual politician, was the real focus of the newspaper. This sentiment was also reflected in its daily political coverage. Rather than drumming up support for any particular political party, *Tempo* often tried to bring the democratic process itself—and its representatives—closer to its audience. One significant example is a cartoon series by political caricaturist Emery Kelen, titled "The Party's Tenors" and "The Party's Sopranos," introducing leading male and female politicians of all major parties to the readership, much in the same way *Tempo* regularly presented famous sports teams (Fig. 9).[157] This educational approach had an important reason: apart from the DDP's abysmal results, the election in 1928 had also seen the lowest voter turnout in the history of the Republic and the centrist parties had suffered the most from it.[158] Thus, *Tempo* placed great importance on mobilizing and educating the electorate. *Tempo*'s authors often warned their readers of the dire consequences of their political passivity. Roda Roda bemoaned the inactivity of the European electorate, who did not use the democratic rights the outcome of the war had brought them, leading to a return of tyranny in many European states.[159] "Sky" warned that apathetic voters would never build a better future.[160] The paper called on its readers to act as rational, responsible, and active democratic citizens instead, with the supposedly rational and respectful political culture of the United States as their model.[161]

A similar sentiment pervaded *Tempo*'s coverage of the renegotiation of the German reparations payments, the so-called Young Plan, during the first half of 1929. After a meeting of the Young Committee in Paris had run into repeated difficulties, *Tempo* was confident that "the last and very last hurdles" in the long and arduous steeplechase of the reparations negotiations would be overcome.[162] In times of absolutism, the article argued, political conferences might have run more smoothly, because they were conducted in a small circle of monarchs instead of a many-voiced arena of politicians answerable to their electorate at home. However, this was a small price to pay for democracy, the

---

157. "Die Partei-Tenore," *Tempo*, 16 November 1928, 2; 17 November 1928, 2; 19 November 1928, 2; 22 November 1928, 2; 23 November 1928, 2; 27 November 1928, 2; 29 November 1928, 2; "Die Parteisoprane," 20 November 1928, 2; 3 December 1928, 2.

158. Alfred Milatz, *Wähler und Wahlen in der Weimarer Republik (Bonn: Bundeszentrale für politische Bildung, 1968)*, 129.

159. Roda Roda, "Fragen des Tages: Die Kette," *Tempo*, 4 January 1929, 2.

160. Sky, "Fragen des Tages: Apathie," *Tempo*, 26 February 1929, 2.

161. Sky, "Fragen des Tages: Amerika, du hast es besser," *Tempo*, 6 November 1928, 2.

162. Sky, "Fragen des Tages: Wie sage ich es meinem Volk?," *Tempo*, 23 May 1929, 2.

Figure 9. Emery Kelen, "Die Partei-Tenore," *Tempo*, 16 November 1928, 2. © Axel Springer AG. Used with permission.

article concluded. The campaign for the Young referendum, a *Volksentscheid* initiated by right-wing forces against the German government's acceptance of the Young Plan, prompted "Sky" to ponder the question of whether the German people were ready for democracy.[163] His conclusion was optimistic: the Germans had the right political instincts, he argued, they just needed more time to fully develop them.

Despite their belief in the democratic instincts of the German people, Stresemann's sudden death on 3 October 1929, which dashed Ullstein's hopes for a gathering of liberal forces, deeply affected the newspaper's editors and the rest of the liberal press. *Tempo* dedicated the first four pages to his memory, and in the culture section his impact on German intellectual life was celebrated over another two pages.[164] Stresemann's death is a telling example for the discursive cohesion of the Weimar press over and beyond party-political fault lines. The Communist *Welt am Abend* called him "one of the cleverest and most able strategists" of the ruling class, dedicating the front pages of two successive days to the late statesman.[165] Even Hugenberg's papers paid their

---

163. Sky, "Fragen des Tages: Politische Lektion," *Tempo*, 24 October 1929, 4. For the Young referendum, see Otmar Jung, *Direkte Demokratie in der Weimarer Republik. Die Fälle "Aufwertung," "Fürstenenteignung," "Panzerkreuzerverbot" und "Youngplan"* (Frankfurt/Main: Campus, 1989), 67–146.

164. *Tempo*, 3 October 1929, 1–4, 5, 7.

165. Paul Friedländer, "Gustav Stresemann," *Welt am Abend*, 3 October 1929, 1. See also "Staatsbegräbnis für Stresemann," *Welt am Abend*, 4 October 1929, 1–2.

respects to Stresemann, which *Tempo* in turn interpreted as sickening hypocrisy.[166] However, by that time, *Tempo*'s main political focus of attention started to shift from Hugenberg and the German National People's Party. This was not only a reaction to the slow rise of the NSDAP, but also because Ullstein saw parts of the party as possible allies. On 17 November 1929, an internal memo advised Ullstein's editors-in-chief, including Gustav Kauder, that in light of recent Nazi successes, several high-ranking National Conservatives planned to oust Hugenberg and put the party on a prorepublican track. These politicians were seen as compatible with the company's own liberal ethos: "There are men in these circles, who, despite their conservative attitude regarding questions of social and foreign policy, do not stand too far away from us."[167] Thus, the memo continued, the editors should take care that this "transformation" was not interrupted by unnecessary attacks on the party.

The memo seems to have been a reaction to the election to the Berlin city council on the same day that had resulted in the Nazis entering the local parliament for the first time, while the German National People's Party lost seven seats. The city council election was the first major party-political event *Tempo* covered. In the run-up to the election, the paper gave much room to representatives of its target audience, such as functionaries of white-collar unions and female politicians.[168] However, *Tempo*'s support for the new democratic system did not mean it shied away from criticism. On the eve of the election, "Heaven" directly addressed the voters, urging them to make use of their democratic right, but also bemoaned the fact that a total of twenty-one parties were vying for their votes.[169] There was no need for such fragmentation, he argued, because despite their different political ideologies all Berliners had the same interests as citizens (*Bürger*)—a term that should not be confused with "bourgeois," he pointed out.

During the local election campaign and the German referendum against the Young Plan a month later, *Tempo* reported extensively on politically motivated clashes, mostly between Communists and Nazis, portraying the perpetrators as a violent minority terrorizing the majority of upright citizens by making the streets unsafe, ruining the Christmas trade, and plotting to overthrow the

---

166. "Staatsbegräbnis für Stresemann," 1–2; "Fragen des Tages: Ehrfurcht vor dem Schicksal . . . ," *Tempo*, 7 October 1929, 4.

167. *Hausmitteilung*, 17 November 1929, in BArchL, N2193 Misch, Nr. 13, fol. 49.

168. "Was Berlins Bürgerschaft von den Stadtwahlen erwartet," *Tempo*, 22 October 1929, 3; 28 October 1929, 3.

169. Heaven, "Sie gegen 21 . . . Die Qual der Wahl," *Tempo*, 16 November 1929, 3.

government.[170] *Tempo* paid particular attention to new trends in populist campaign methods, such as mass rallies and the use of film and recorded speech.[171] These new approaches to political propaganda were mostly related to the political right and left and were contrasted with the rational (*sachlich*) methods of the liberal parties of the center, who were trying to convince voters with rational arguments rather than firing up their emotions.

The image of democracy that was constructed through *Tempo*'s political coverage before 1930 is not easy to pin down. On the one hand, the paper was a staunch supporter of the status quo and of popular government in particular. The Western parliamentary democracies in the US, France, and the UK were its models and the paper's emphasis on a *sachlich* mind-set of citizenship, supposedly shared by the whole population across party-political divides, was clearly meant to support the current political system. On the other hand, the paper made a clear distinction between the rational, democratically minded citizens that made up the people (*Volk*) and their elected representatives. While it lauded capable leaders like Stresemann and other political "tenors" and "sopranos," *Tempo* was vague in its support of individual politicians and parties. The electorate was imbued with an infallible democratic instinct, which was often imperfectly put into practice by Weimar's politicians—a view that reflected the essentialist role of the *Volk* in the Constitution. Like its construction of a consumerist paradise, *Tempo*'s view of a unified, rational body politic was founded less on a serious engagement with Weimar's realities than it was meant as an optimistic vision that would have an educational effect on its readers.

Young Germans as Consumer-Citizens: Representations of Modern Masculinity and Femininity

According to *Tempo*, the embodiment of the rational citizen and the modern consumer was the young generation—the people who had experienced the war as children on the home front and had grown up under the new democratic regime.[172] They seemed to be at ease with the new, faster pace of life of Weimar

---

170. "Putschplan in Holstein," *Tempo*, 13 November 1929, 1; "Wahlauftakt: Wilde Schießereien," *Tempo*, 16 November 1929, 1–2; "Neue Krawall-Pläne für heute abend," *Tempo*, 21 December 1929, 1; "Roter Aufruf zur Revolution entdeckt," *Tempo*, 28 December 1929, 1.

171. "Die Kampfpropaganda in den Straßen," *Tempo*, 16 November 1929, 2.

172. Parts of this subchapter have been published as Jochen Hung, "The Modernized Gretchen: Transformations of the 'New Woman' in the Late Weimar Republic," *German History* 33, no. 1 (2015): 52–79.

Germany and unencumbered by traditional class-based patterns of consumption.[173] *Tempo* interpreted young people as a force of the future and an embodiment of optimism and progress: only the youth of today could change the present, the newspaper argued, while clinging to the past was a sign of weakness.[174] The relationship between young and old was extraordinarily contentious in Weimar Germany: the lost war had pitted generations against each other and gave a boost to a specific youth culture, while the lowering of the voting age by five years to age twenty significantly broadened the political influence of young people. However, the fierceness and the ubiquity of the debate about the political and cultural role of young people in Weimar society was not only motivated by recent events. It was also a reflection of a long intellectual and social process: since the late eighteenth century, generational conflict and the idea of a generation as an independent political and cultural entity had played a central role in European culture, gaining importance during the emerging Industrial Revolution and the political upheavals in America and France.[175] In Germany, this had found an expression in the Jugendbewegung that sprang up before the war, a cultural and educational movement of mainly male middle-class youths centered around outdoor activities.[176] After the First World War, generational thinking—meaning a "generational mode of interpreting and organising social reality"—experienced a surge in popularity in many European countries, at least among the middle class.[177] The customs and traditions of the older generations, who had led the world into a disastrous global conflict, seemed to belong to a bygone age, whereas the new lifestyle and attitudes

---

173. For the link between youth and consumer culture in Weimar Germany, see Detlev J. K. Peukert, *Jugend zwischen Krieg und Krise. Lebenswelten von Arbeiterjungen in der Weimarer Republik* (Cologne: Bund, 1987), 190–244.

174. Sky, "Das Stadtgespräch: Der heilige Mantel," *Tempo*, 10 March 1929, 3.

175. Michael Wildt, "Generation als Anfang und Beschleunigung," in *Generationen. Zur Relevanz eines wissenschaftlichen Grundbegriffs*, ed. Ulrike Jureit and Michael Wildt (Hamburg: Hamburger Edition, 2005), 160–79; Pierre Nora, "Generation," in *Realms of Memory: Rethinking the French Past*, ed. Pierre Nora, trans. Arthur Goldhammer, vol. 1, 3 vols. (New York: Columbia University Press, 1996), 499–612; John R. Gillis, *Youth and History: Tradition and Change in European Age Relations, 1770-Present* (New York: Academic, 1981); Manfred Riedel, "Generation," in *Historisches Wörterbuch der Philosophie*, ed. Joachim Ritter and Rudolf Eisler, vol. 1, 12 vols. (Darmstadt: Wissenschaftliche Buchgesellschaft, 1974).

176. For the history of the Jugendbewegung, see Peter D. Stachura, *The German Youth Movement 1900–1945: An Interpretative and Documentary History* (London: Macmillan, 1981); Walter Laqueur, *Young Germany: A History of the German Youth Movement* (London: Routledge & Kegan Paul, 1962).

177. Robert Wohl, *The Generation of 1914* (London: Weidenfeld & Nicolson, 1980), 82.

of the youth represented the young twentieth century.[178] The importance of the generational conflict in the public discourse of the Weimar Republic is reflected in the plethora of publications on the topic: fierce declarations of youthful self-determination, from political pamphlets such as Gregor Strasser's *Macht Platz, ihr Alten!* (1927) to literary interpretations like Ernst Glaeser's *Jahrgang 1902* (1928), that in turn provoked concerned observations by representatives of older age groups such as Heinrich Mann.[179]

Tempo embraced this generational conflict and attempted to channel it. It was the only German mass-market newspaper that directly and outspokenly addressed young people as a new consumer group and a new political force. Their most significant characteristic, according to Ullstein's promotional material, was *Sachlichkeit*, developed as a reaction to their traumatic experiences during the war and the following economic turmoil, and defined as soberness, cool detachment, an affinity for technology, and the ability to navigate their way through modern life:

> The modern male and female youth, whose education has been limited or even wholly disrupted by the war and the inflationary breakdown, have been pushed into professional life prematurely. In this sudden and tough struggle, they have become modern and objective (*neuzeitlich-sachlich*), maybe even a little too soberly materialistic and technical, but also very clear-thinking and perceptive.[180]

To cater to these new young and *sachlich* citizens and consumers, the paper's point of reference was less rooted in Germany's past than it was in the present of the new democratic order of the Weimar Republic and the prosperous future this order promised. Accordingly, it painted an optimistic image of the new state as a place full of consumerist opportunities and focused on contemporary popular culture and the social issues of its time: sport, cinema, fashion, changing gender relationships, female independence, and the social and political status of young people. This did not mean that *Tempo* only reported on

---

178. Graf, *Zukunft*, 238–42; Stambolis, *Mythos Jugend*, 75–88; Frank Trommler, "Mission ohne Ziel. Über den Kult der Jugend im modernen Deutschland," in Koebner, Janz, and Trommler, *"Mit uns zieht die neue Zeit,"* 14–49.

179. Gregor Strasser, "Macht Platz, Ihr Alten! (8. Mai 1927)," in *Kampf um Deutschland*, ed. Gregor Strasser (Munich: Franz Eher, 1932), 171–74; Ernst Glaeser, *Jahrgang 1902* (Berlin: Kiepenheuer, 1928); Heinrich Mann, "Jugend früher und jetzt," *Die Literarische Welt*, November 9, 1928.

180. *"Tempo*—Die Zeitung der Zeit," 3.

the latest movies, cabaret premieres, and popular music, and completely shunned "high" culture, such as fine art exhibitions, classical concerts, and opera. However, these traditional art forms had to meet the new taste of a younger audience. According to a programmatic article demanding the introduction of "short operas" (*Kurzopern*), "high art" had to adapt to the demands of the new, unceremonious times and tastes of today's youth: "The people of today are rational, unceremonious, full of an urgent desire for a colorful, exiting and fulfilled life and expect the same from the theatre and their evening entertainment."[181] Opera in particular, the author claimed, was guilty of adhering to outdated traditions of opulence and ornament. Despite the successful experiments by modern composers and conductors such as Kurt Weill, Paul Hindemith, and Otto Klemperer, most opera houses, especially outside of Berlin, still offered only pompous, overlong productions of classical operas such as Wagner's *Walküre*, the article continued. Such backwardness ran counter to the lifestyle and the taste of young people of today:

> The naked, trained, slim, young form cannot grow in such an atmosphere. It needs small bays in the hustle and bustle of the inner city, where you can easily dock for an hour; theatres that offer two or three shows a day, not run by professional businessmen, but by someone like the people of the *Threepenny Opera*, who know how to draw up something completely new and make the people in front of the stage happy. . . . No, we do not want to escape anymore to the bearded, sword-rattling gods of the past. We want the people of today, their character, their life, their art.[182]

To address the modern demand for brief and succinct plays such as Bertolt Brecht and Kurt Weill's *Threepenny Opera*, *Tempo* introduced short "sample reviews" (*Stichprobenkritiken*) for theatregoers with little time to read extensive reports on a play. These reviews were not based on the premiere, which, as Manfred Georg argued, only a small elite circle of critics and aficionados saw anyway, but on a later performance aimed at the lay audience—and thus the majority of the people buying a theatre ticket.[183]

As was expected for a paper that put so much emphasis on visual content, *Tempo* also used photographs and illustrations to address its young audience. A long-running series of photographs of young artists and actresses representing

---

181. E. K., "Wir wollen Kurzopern!," *Tempo*, 23 November 1928, 6.
182. E. K., "Wir wollen Kurzopern!," 6.
183. M. G. (i.e., Manfred Georg), "Die zweite Besetzung," *Tempo*, 28 September 1928, 7.

"the face of the young generation" provided role models for *Tempo*'s readers by explicitly presenting their subjects as the personification of the new rationality and *Sachlichkeit* of the modern youth. The first "face" was Maria Solveg, a twenty-one-year-old Jewish actress working in film and theatre, who often played the role of "the modern and natural" girl.[184] These images did not differ much from the photos of film stars that other newspapers printed regularly, but *Tempo* explicitly presented them as representatives of German youth. Many of its editors and regular writers, such as Billy Wilder, Charlotte Pol, Ruth Landshoff, and Hanns G. Lustig, were in the same age group as *Tempo*'s core target audience. Some of them were even well-known representatives of their generation, such as Marga von Etzdorf, born in 1907, who was one of the first female pilots in Germany and who reported for *Tempo* from her record flight from Berlin to Tokyo.[185] Arguably one of *Tempo*'s most notable representatives of the young generation was Erika Mann, not only because of her famous father but also because of her involvement in the controversial plays *Anja und Esther* (1925) and *Revue zu Vieren* (1927), written by her brother Klaus, which examined the attitudes of Germany's youth.[186] For *Tempo*, she wrote about her colorful life as a member of Germany's artistic haut monde, recounting, for example, a world trip she had recently completed with her brother, giving insights into her work as an actress, describing meetings with celebrities and artists, and reporting from a 10,000-mile car race through Europe she took part in and ended up winning.[187] In *Tempo*, these writers represented a youth at ease with the speed of modern life and modern technology, their role in society, and the democratic state they were living in.

It is remarkable that Ullstein explicitly included "male and female youth" in the generational definition of *Tempo*'s intended audience.[188] This went

---

184. "Das Gesicht der jungen Generation," *Tempo*, 19 October 1928, 5. For Solveg, see Kay Weniger, *"Es wird im Leben dir mehr genommen als gegeben . . .". Lexikon der aus Deutschland und Österreich emigrierten Filmschaffenden 1933 bis 1945* (Hamburg: Acabus, 2011), 466–67.

185. For Marga von Etzdorf and the significance of pilots as a symbol of youth and modernity in German culture, see Evelyn Zegenhagen, *"Schneidige deutsche Mädel." Fliegerinnen zwischen 1918 und 1945* (Göttingen: Wallstein, 2007), 166–76; Rieger, *Technology*, 119–57; Fritzsche, *Nation of Fliers*, 153–70.

186. Klaus Mann, *Anja und Esther. Ein romantisches Stück in sieben Bildern* (Berlin: Oesterheld, 1925); Klaus Mann, *Revue zu Vieren. Eine Komödie in drei Akten* (Berlin: Oesterheld, 1926).

187. Some of Mann's articles for *Tempo* were later published in Erika Mann and Klaus Mann, *Rundherum* (Berlin: Fischer, 1929).

188. For *Tempo*'s generational concept, see Jochen Hung, "'Der Deutschen Jugend!' The

against the contemporary usage of the term "young generation": despite its classless and gender-neutral nature, in Weimar Germany it was often used to refer to young middle-class men.[189] However, in practice, *Tempo*'s authors were not entirely free of such preconceptions and frequently used it as a synonym for the nation's male white-collar workers, whose situation was of particular interest to the newspaper. Their often precarious situation, working in a field that was on the receiving end of processes of rationalization, experienced an influx of female labor, and often offered few career prospects, made this group a symbol for the interwar crisis of masculine identity. As Richard McCormick has argued, it was not only the disastrous experience of a lost war that had undermined traditional masculinity in Germany, but the disconcerting experience of modernization in general.[190] In the Weimar Republic, the relatively unambiguous image of masculinity of the nineteenth century had been shattered and many concepts of male identity competed with each other.[191] Historians have often focused on concepts that tried to reassert a soldierly authority to a damaged male identity, ideas that gained significance during the late Weimar Republic and that have been interpreted as a breeding ground for antidemocratic sentiment.[192] One of the groups that has received most attention

---

Newspaper *Tempo* and the Generational Discourse of the Weimar Republic," in Hung, Weiss-Sussex, and Wilkes, *Beyond Glitter and Doom*, 105–18.

189. For the androcentric character of generational concepts in the Weimar Republic, see Daniel Siemens, "Kühle Romantiker. Zum Geschichtsverständnis der 'jungen Generation' in der Weimarer Republik," in *Die Kunst der Geschichte. Historiographie, Ästhetik, Erzählung*, ed. Martin Baumeister, Moritz Föllmer, and Philipp Müller (Göttingen: Vandenhoeck & Ruprecht, 2009), 189–90; Christina Benninghaus, "Das Geschlecht der Generation. Zum Zusammenhang von Generationalität und Männlichkeit um 1930," in *Generationen. Zur Relevanz eines wissenschaftlichen Grundbegriffs*, ed. Ulrike Jureit and Michael Wildt (Hamburg: Hamburger Edition, 2005), 127–58; Jürgen Reulecke, "Neuer Mensch und neue Männlichkeit. Die 'junge Generation' im ersten Drittel des 20. Jahrhunderts," in *Jahrbuch des Historischen Kollegs 2001* (Munich: Oldenbourg, 2002), 109–38.

190. Richard McCormick, *Gender and Sexuality in Weimar Modernity: Film, Literature and "New Objectivity"* (New York: Palgrave Macmillan, 2001), 3.

191. For the changed image of masculinity in the Weimar Republic, see McCormick, *Gender and Sexuality*, 59–98; Jens Schmidt, *"Sich hart machen, wenn es gilt." Männlichkeitskonzeptionen in Illustrierten der Weimarer Republik* (Münster: Lit, 2000); George L. Mosse, *The Image of Man: The Creation of Modern Masculinity* (Oxford: Oxford University Press, 1996), 133–54; Ute Frevert, *"Mann und Weib, und Weib und Mann." Geschlechter-Differenzen in der Moderne* (Munich: Beck, 1995), 34–35.

192. Klaus Theweleit's pathbreaking study *Male Fantasies* (Minneapolis: University of Minnesota Press, 1987) set the tone that has guided research on this topic since then, particularly in the field of *Generationengeschichte* (generation history); see, for example, Siemens, "Kühle Romantiker," 194–202; Bernd A. Rusinek, "Krieg als Sehnsucht. Militärischer Stil

in this respect is the Tatkreis, a small circle of young national-conservative radicals loosely connected with the intellectual journal *Die Tat*.[193] In this publication, which had criticized *Tempo*'s mass-market orientation when the paper was launched in 1928, the courting of the youth by the established political forces was commented on frequently. At first glance, *Die Tat* addressed a far more exclusive audience than the mainstream tabloid *Tempo*. However, since the days of the Youth Movement, *Die Tat* had acted as a forum for young middle-class readers.[194] At least to some extent, *Tempo* must have seemed like an unwelcome competitor, even more so as *Die Tat*'s publisher, Eugen Diederichs, had recently begun to bring in new writers to reach a wider audience, including the young Ullstein journalists Hans Zehrer and, a few years later, *Tempo*'s economics editor, Ferdinand Friedrich Zimmermann.[195] Zehrer, Zimmermann, and the rest of the Tatkreis were all well-educated sons of the traditional *Bildungsbürgertum*, who in prewar Germany would have followed a career as civil servants, lawyers, or academics. In the Weimar Republic, they faced financial insecurity and diminished social prestige. For them, the new democratic state was the work of the older generations who had bankrupted the country and a symbol of the general decline of the German nation. The pivotal personality of this group was Zehrer: born in 1899, he had been an editor for Ullstein's *Vossische Zeitung* since 1923 and, most likely with the knowledge of his employers, had written regularly for *Die Tat* since April 1928, finally taking over its editorial control in October 1929.[196] In his first articles for *Die Tat*, Zehrer had prophesied the decisive role of the youth—read: young men—in the Reichstag elections in May 1928.[197] He argued that the established parties,

---

und 'junge Generation' in der Weimarer Republik," in *Generationalität und Lebensgeschichte im 20. Jahrhundert*, ed. Jürgen Reulecke (Munich: Oldenbourg, 2003), 127–44; Andreas Schulz and Gundula Grebner, "Generation und Geschichte. Zur Renaissance eines umstrittenen Forschungskonzepts," *Historische Zeitschrift Beiheft* 36 (2003): 1–23; Mommsen, "Generationskonflikt und Jugendrevolte," 59–60; Reulecke, "Neuer Mensch"; Wildt, *Generation des Unbedingten*. See also Hung, "Der Deutschen Jugend!," 105–9.

193. Klaus Fritzsche, *Politische Romantik und Gegenrevolution. Fluchtwege in der Krise der bürgerlichen Gesellschaft: Das Beispiel des Tat-Kreises* (Frankfurt/Main: Suhrkamp, 1976); Kurt Sontheimer, "Der Tatkreis," *Vierteljahrshefte Für Zeitgeschichte* 7, no. 3 (1959): 229–60.

194. Klaus Werner Schmidt, "Die Tat (1909–1939)," in *Deutsche Zeitschriften des 17. bis 20. Jahrhunderts*, ed. Heinz Dietrich Fischer (Pullach: Verlag Dokumentation, 1973), 353.

195. Fritzsche, *Politische Romantik*, 47; Ebbo Demant, *Hans Zehrer als politischer Publizist. Von Schleicher zu Springer* (Mainz: Hase & Koehler, 1971), 57–62.

196. Demant, *Zehrer*, 13–35.

197. Hans Zehrer, "Parole für die Wahlen," *Die Tat*, April 1928, 60; Hans Zehrer, "Ein Vorschlag an die Verbände," *Die Tat*, May 1928, 122–28.

dominated by the older generations, were finally waking up to the important role of the youth in the rejuvenation of the country.[198] However, according to Zehrer, the political youth should dismiss their advances and boycott the elections altogether. In April 1929, Zehrer again urged the "Young Front" (Junge Front), a term he used for the politically active nationalist youth, to withstand the advances of the established parties and to resist the urge to take part in the traditional political process:

> Should we rush to support the state and work for it? Everybody who knows the Young Front, who knows its sense of responsibility, also knows the moral conflict it finds itself in at the moment. Thus, nobody can accuse us of being irresponsible when we fight for our rallying cry: stay out![199]

Zehrer was worried to see that despite his calls, many politically active young men seemed prepared to contribute to the constructive rebuilding of the country. Supporting the Weimar state, he argued, would only prolong the flawed and moribund compromise of ineffectual parliamentarianism, private economic interests, and old-boy networks that represented postwar Germany. To be able to build a genuinely new society it was necessary to stand back and let it all go to pieces.[200] Zehrer, who had seen active duty during the war, was especially critical of *Tempo*'s target audience: people born after 1900, who had not served at the front. For him, they were "baby-faced nobodies," without real convictions and driven only by ambition.[201] By January 1930, Zehrer had completely lost faith in the postwar generation, denouncing Weimar's *sachlich* young men as the new enemy, who had surrendered in the fight of the youth against the establishment:

> These boys gave up without a fight. . . . And once you receive the first salary, smoke cigars in a holder and start to grunt when sitting down, then it is time to share a smile about the stupid fights of your youth.[202]

---

198. Zehrer, "Vorschlag," 124.
199. Hans Zehrer, "Achtung, junge Front! Draußenbleiben!," *Die Tat*, April 1929, 25–40, at 33. For Zehrer's general ideology, see Demant, *Zehrer*, 29–56; Walter Struve, "Hans Zehrer as a Neoconservative Elite Theorist," *American Historical Review* 70, no. 4 (1965): 1035–57.
200. Zehrer, "Achtung," 40.
201. Zehrer, "Achtung," 36.
202. Hans Thomas (i.e., Hans Zehrer), "Absage an den Jahrgang 1902," *Die Tat*, January 1930, 744–46. The title is a reference to Ernst Glaeser's novel *Jahrgang 1902*, see n179.

The image of masculinity constructed in *Tempo* could not be different from Zehrer's, while addressing the same problems young middle-class men faced in the Weimar Republic. In direct contrast to Zehrer and the *Tatkreis*, *Tempo* urged young middle-class men to work for the new state. *Tempo* frequently demanded a greater role for young people in the political process, it argued for giving young representatives more time to speak in parliament, and it blamed the introduction of proportional representation for keeping young men and their ideas out of politics.[203] *Tempo*'s image of masculinity was characterized by cool *Sachlichkeit*, common sense, and cautious optimism in the face of the demands of modernity. According to the newspaper, the young, modern German man had to navigate a rocky career path, but instead of reacting with pessimism or hotheaded protest he sought to make the best of his difficult situation; he was a pacifist not by conviction, but because war had been proven a folly; he did not suffer under adolescent *Weltschmerz* but focused on the here and now. Politics did not feature prominently in this image, but by immersing himself in Weimar's modest consumer culture, *Tempo*'s man of today clearly supported the present order. *Tempo* regularly defended the male youth of today against accusations by older generations, arguing that young people—read: young, middle-class men—were "clear, natural, and know what they want" and much more rational than the young people thirty or forty years ago.[204] This attitude was expressed most poignantly by Hanns G. Lustig's review of Heinrich Mann's *Bibi, Jugend 1928*, a musical comedy about the life of a young profiteer during the hyperinflation of the early 1920s, which premiered in Berlin's Theater am Palmenhaus in Berlin on 22 October 1928. Lustig, born in 1902, criticized the fifty-seven-year-old Mann's image of today's youth as a detached and hedonistic generation:

> But isn't it honorable that he shows interest in the subject of "the youth"? Yes, but we, the young people, are not interested in this subject anymore! That's a melody of yesterday. We do not have the time anymore to give or listen to speeches about ourselves, we do not have the time anymore for narcissistic joy or despair. . . . There finally is something more important than the subject of "youth," namely: to be young.[205]

---

203. Sky, "Männer oder Parteien?," *Tempo*, 20 November 1928, 2; g., "Als ich so alt war wie sie . . . ," *Tempo*, 25 April 1929, 2; Lu., "Verwendet junge Gehirne," *Tempo*, 2 January 1933, 6; C. Enseo, "Der teure Name," *Tempo*, 18 February 1929, 2.
204. Sky, "'Verlotterte Jugend'," *Tempo*, 9 February 1929, 3.
205. Hanns G. Lustig, "Jugend 1928?," *Tempo*, 23 October 1928, 6.

Weimar's young men, Lustig argued, were tired of the overly emotional debate about their place in society that had characterized the prewar Youth Movement. He stressed the unsentimental attitude and rationality of his generation and dismissed the idea of youth as a time of agitated emotions and romantic idealism. His description of young people as characterized by maturity and a sense of responsibility for their own actions painted the image of a generation ready and willing to play a constructive role in society.

According to *Tempo*, this new *sachlich* attitude included the dismissal of the romantic idea of youthful rebellion of sons against their fathers. Young people, the paper claimed in an interview with the popular writer Jakob Wassermann, had more pressing concerns on their minds than quarrelling with their elders.[206] The fifty-six-year-old Wassermann had just published his novel *Der Fall Maurizius* about a young aristocratic student who rebels against his authoritarian father.[207] However, *Tempo*'s interviewer suggested that Wassermann's protagonist and the novel's romantic image of male youth revolting against the older generation were outdated. *Tempo*'s dismissal of the romanticized image of youth as a time of confusion and rebellion had a special significance against the background of two recent scandals, the so-called Steglitzer Schülermordprozess and the Fall Hußmann. In both cases, young, male, well-educated middle-class students were accused of cruelly murdering their friends in a fit of emotional fervor.[208] Paul Krantz, in particular, the main offender in the Schülermordprozess, whose cruelty, detachment, and inhumanity baffled and downright frightened adult observers, was seen by many as representative of the neglected postwar generation. The court case in February 1928 was a media sensation and the young defendant was often described as cold and calculating, showing no signs of remorse or pity.[209] *Tempo*, however, drew very different conclusions from the two cases. In an editorial, Hußmann and Krantz were described as exceptions, who did not represent the rational and grounded youth of today:

---

206. Go., "Auf welche Jugend kommt es an?," *Tempo*, 7 March 1929, 5. See also Victor Zuckerkandl, "Der Dichter stellt sich der Jugend," *Tempo*, 10 March 1929, 8.

207. Jakob Wassermann, *Der Fall Maurizius* (Berlin: Fischer, 1928).

208. For the *Schülermordprozess*, see Heidi Sack, *Moderne Jugend vor Gericht. Sensationsprozesse, "Sexualtragödien" und die Krise der Jugend in der Weimarer Republik* (Bielefeld: transcript, 2016), 123–393; Thomas Lange, "Der 'Steglitzer Schülermordprozess' 1928," in Koebner, Janz, and Trommler, "Mit uns zieht die neue Zeit," 412–37; for the Hußmann case, see Sack, *Moderne Jugend*, 366–72; Sabine Kettler, Eva-Maria Stuckel, and Franz Wegener, *Wer tötete Helmut Daube? Der bestialische Sexualmord an dem Schüler Helmut Daube im Ruhrgebiet 1928* (Gladbeck: Kulturförderverein Ruhrgebiet, 2000).

209. Lange, "Schülermordprozess," 415–16.

Don't let anybody tell you the Hußmann case is typical for the youth of today! It is just as unrepresentative as the Krantz trial. Both cases were exceptions.... The young people of today are completely different. They are neither romantic, nor dulled or melancholic. Rather, they are clear and sober, often alarmingly so—but that is better than the opposite.[210]

According to *Tempo*, Weimar's young men revolted by focusing on the future. Today's students at institutions of higher education, "Heaven" argued, did not passively accept the traditions and knowledge of their parents anymore, but rejected outdated subjects like Latin and ancient Greek in favor of more useful classes in English, Russian, and business administration.[211] As an alternative to the stereotype of a wasted youth embodied by Paul Krantz, *Tempo* presented the positive image of young people as an avant-garde of Weimar's new consumer society. It often reported on a new, "Americanized" urban youth culture developing in Berlin that differed greatly from the nature-loving Youth Movement. These young people, which *Tempo* dubbed "ice-cream-parlor youth" (*Eisdielenjugend*), met in local establishments, where male and female teenagers mixed, gender roles were tested out, and even first sexual experiences occurred—all, however, in a decidedly casual and unceremonious fashion.[212] Adult observers were outraged by the apparently unsupervised gatherings, the financial independence of the young clients, their extravagant clothes, and the sexually charged atmosphere, but *Tempo* interpreted this as an "understandable wish of young people to be able to act like 'grown-ups,' to be taken seriously for once."[213]

The war, the great generational dividing line between fathers and sons in Weimar Germany, was interpreted by these young men only as a pacifist lesson for the future. According to *Tempo*, Weimar's rational youth had seen through the lies of war propaganda and hero worship that had seduced the idealistic young people of 1914 and was now staunchly opposed to violent conflicts. In

---

210. Sky, "Fragen des Tages: Älteste Jugend," *Tempo*, 18 October 1928, 2.
211. Heaven, "Das Stadtgespräch: 'Eine abgeschlossene Bildung'," *Tempo*, 26 February 1929, 3.
212. See, for example, H. R–z., "Die Bar der Halbwüchsigen," *Tempo*, 6 July 1929, 4; L. F., "Die Eisdiele," *Tempo*, 23 August 1930, 3.
213. H. R–z., "Bar der Halbwüchsigen," 4. For the "Americanization" of European youth culture in the 1920s, see Jon Savage, *Teenage: The Creation of Youth Culture* (New York: Viking, 2007), 235–51; for adult reactions in Germany, see Detlev J. K. Peukert, "Das Mädchen mit dem 'wahrlich metaphysikfreien Bubikopf'. Jugend und Freizeit im Berlin der zwanziger Jahre," in *Im Banne der Metropolen. Berlin und London in den zwanziger Jahren*, ed. Peter Alter (Göttingen: Vandenhoeck & Ruprecht, 1993), 157–75.

1928–1929: Banging the Drum for Democracy   93

Figure 10. Advertisement, *Ullstein-Berichte*, January 1930, 7. © Axel Springer AG. Used with permission.

1928, Manfred Georg praised the antiwar play *U-Boot S4* by the young author Günther Weisenborn as a sign of the pacifist attitude of Weimar's young generation.[214] A young reader, whose review of the play was published in *Tempo*'s column for lay critics a day later, even argued that a pacifist stance was now a matter of course, and that the youth of today was tired of hearing about the war at all: "I already read enough about battleships in the papers. Soulful war poets must accept the fact that we live in times of peace. It has been proven that waging war is madness."[215]

This sensible, positive, and constructive masculinity championed by *Tempo* was embodied in an advertisement in the *Ullstein-Berichte* depicting a sharply dressed young man in a café or gentlemen's club, eagerly reading *Tempo* (Fig. 10).

---

214. Manfred Georg, "Ein junger Mensch schreit gegen den Krieg," *Tempo*, 17 October 1928, 5.
215. "Das Urteil des Parketts," *Tempo*, 18 October 1928, 5–6.

He has devoured all other newspapers already and, in his hunger for news and entertainment, is oblivious to the disapproving stares of the older men in the background. The message of the advertisement is clear: the male *Tempo* reader was a young, inquisitive, and dynamic professional with an affirmative attitude toward the modern world—represented by the newspaper itself. This, and his unceremonious, informal style, set him apart from the older generation, who can only look on while young people like him take control.

Despite growing up under the extraordinary circumstances of war, revolution, and economic chaos, Ullstein implied with such articles and images, the *sachlich* young men of the Weimar Republic focused on the opportunities the new democratic state offered them, and looked to the future, not to the past. In this perspective, Weimar's young men embodied the "moderate modernity" that *Tempo* tried to establish as a constructive, positive vision for Germany's future.

However, while Ullstein's newspaper enthusiastically painted a picture of a rational and constructive German youth, Manfred Georg, in an article for *Die Weltbühne*, warned of an increasing radicalization of young men in Germany and their attraction to authoritarian ideologies.[216] Georg's fears were not exaggerated: around 1928, a radically nationalist and authoritarian interpretation of the war became increasingly significant in the public discourse, particularly as a guiding idea and mode of identification for the male youth of the Weimar Republic.[217] In particular, many of Weimar's supposed future leaders—young educated middle-class men born around 1900—seemed to be disillusioned with the new state and in thrall of nihilistic or radical ideologies, something that was reflected in the ideology of the Tatkreis.[218] The extraordinarily successful semiautobiographical novel *Jahrgang 1902* by Ernst Glaeser, about the disconcerting experiences of a teenage boy in Germany before and during the war, provided the catchphrase for this "lost generation."[219] When the book was published in 1928, this "cohort of 1902," which under prewar circumstances would have started careers as civil servants, academics, officers, or businessmen, faced an unstable job market with diminished employment prospects.

In a special report about "the private life of the young salesman of today," *Tempo* shed light on the precarious situation of this generation of young male

---

216. Georg, "Der jüdische Revolutionär," *Die Weltbühne*, 25 February 1930, 314.
217. Rusinek, "Krieg," 139; Reulecke, "Neuer Mensch," 131.
218. Stambolis, *Mythos*, 118–26; Siemens, "Kühle Romantiker."
219. Jürgen Reulecke, *"Ich möchte einer werden so wie die . . .": Männerbünde im 20. Jahrhundert* (Campus, 2001), 35–46. For Glaeser, see n179.

white-collar workers.[220] The times of the generous expense accounts of previous generations were over, the paper reported, and Berlin's modern young salesmen were diligent workers who worried about increasing unemployment and threatening rationalization. With a monthly salary between 120 and 220 marks, most of them still lived with their parents. These circumstances forced many of them into singlehood, and the ones that had a partner could often not afford to marry or start a family. Most partners of the interviewed employees worked themselves and one currently unemployed salesman was even supported by his girlfriend, a *Fremdsprachenkorrespondentin* (foreign language correspondence clerk) earning 300 marks a month. Although the young salesmen often spent around half of their salary on entertainment, this still did not allow them any costly indulgences. Their usual weekend activities consisted of going to the cinema, followed by a dance in a cheap *Tanzdiele* (dance hall), with any female companions having to pay for their own drinks. One interviewee, a twenty-four-year-old sales assistant in a grocery shop, forewent all such pleasures, including female company, and spent his whole entertainment budget on sports. Most university students of the same age, *Tempo* reported in another article, only had an income of around 120 marks a month.[221] With dwindling opportunities for part-time work, the romantic days of jolly student life were over, the paper concluded. However, while the young men portrayed in such articles struggled to establish themselves under the burden of Weimar's shaky economy, they managed their situation with a *sachlich*, commonsense approach that awarded them with small consumer pleasures in the form of popular entertainment or sporting equipment. Furthermore, the rather bleak reports on the realities of white-collar careers were balanced by more optimistic articles that supplied *Tempo*'s male audience with information about the opportunities the job market continued to offer, such as working for the industrial giant Siemens.[222]

The *sachlich* attitude of modern young men included a new view of male-female relationships, which was reflected in the idea of companionate marriage, a topic that was given much room in *Tempo*. The concept had been introduced to the German public by the translation of Benjamin Barr Lindsey's publications in late 1920s.[223] As Thomas Kühne has argued, the German term

---

220. Dr. O. H., "Es gibt keine Portokassen-Kavaliere mehr," *Tempo*, 28 February 1929, 4.
221. Ben., "Werkstudent und Arbeitslosigkeit," *Tempo*, 26 July 1930, 3.
222. Dr. O. H., "Kann man im Großbetrieb noch Karriere machen?," *Tempo*, 20 November 1928, 10.
223. Benjamin Barr Lindsey, *Die Kameradschaftsehe*, trans. Rudolf Nutt (Stuttgart: Deutsche Verlagsanstalt, 1928); Benjamin Barr Lindsey, *Die Revolution der modernen Ju-*

Kameradschaftsehe carried a very masculine connotation in the context of postwar Germany. It was defined not by romantic love, but by common suffering and emotional discipline—a soldierly companionship against economic hardship and social and cultural change, which integrated it into the contemporary "cult of *Sachlichkeit*."[224] *Tempo* frequently printed photos of supposed companionate couples; in one of them, the man tended to the stove in a sparse flat, while the woman was doing gymnastics (Fig. 11). The modern German man, *Tempo*'s female authors contended, should be an equal partner who respects women's independence. In a four-part series published in December 1928, the journalist Charlotte Pol went undercover as a female tourist traveling alone in Berlin, a phenomenon that, according to Pol, was still rare in Germany, where society was still "far more conservative than commonly thought."[225] However, in the final installment of her reportage, she concluded that Berlin men were now so cosmopolitan and "*sachlich*" that a single woman traveling on her own could not only go about her business in peace, but could initiate a flirt with them if she wanted to:

> If said female tourist wants to make an "acquaintance" or not is up to her entirely, because her wish to be on her own will always be respected if it is sincere. And if she does make an "acquaintance" (why not?), the progress of the relationship will be determined by her inclination alone. After all, today's women are no longer "poor victims" who get "molested."[226]

A few days after Pol's report, following the publication of the German translation of Anita Loos's bestseller *Gentlemen Prefer Blondes*, *Tempo* "turned the tables" and asked several young female celebrities, including Josephine Baker, the actress Carola Neher, the novelist Gina Kaus, and tennis player Paula von Reznicek, if women in turn preferred blond men. The answers illustrate a new view of the man as equal partner. Kaus, for example, declared old-style seducers and lady-killers to be out of fashion:

---

gend, trans. Toni Harten-Hoencke and Friedrich Schönemann (Stuttgart: Deutsche Verlagsanstalt, 1927).

224. Thomas Kühne, *Kameradschaft. Die Soldaten des nationalsozialistischen Krieges und das 20. Jahrhundert* (Göttingen: Vandenhoeck & Ruprecht, 2006), 93.

225. Charlotte Pol, "Eine Dame allein in Berlin," *Tempo*, 18 December 1928, 7. For Pol, see Kirsten Steffen, *"Haben Sie mich gehasst?" Antworten für Martin Beradt (1881–1949). Schriftsteller, Rechtsanwalt, Berliner jüdischen Glaubens* (Oldenburg: Igel, 1999), 309–15.

226. Pol, "Eine Dame allein in Berlin," 8.

Kameradschaftsehe

Figure 11. "Kameradschaftsehe," *Tempo*, **20 October 1928, 8. © Axel Springer AG. Used with permission.**

We neither need the dashing, mysterious daredevil, nor the sensitive seducer, who tries to sneak into our bedroom via the labyrinth of the soul. Both types have become a bit ridiculous today. We neither need to be conquered nor seduced, because we only want one thing—a partner for work, sport, playing Bridge and for love.[227]

However, when it came to sexuality, *Tempo*—or, at least, the paper's male authors—insisted on traditional gender roles, in which the man played the active part. In a series on the "proper strategies" for love-making, the popular physician and author Joseph Löbel described sexual intercourse as something that could and should be trained following scientific principles.[228] Such texts were part of a rationalization of sexuality, which the publication of the immensely popular sex education manual *Het volkomen Huwelijk* (The Perfect Marriage) by the Dutch gynecologist Theodor van de Velde had introduced to Germany in the 1920s.[229] However, while the book aimed at the sexual satis-

---

227. "Auch der blonde Mann bevorzugt? Das Ergebnis einer Umfrage," *Tempo*, 24 December 1928, 9.
228. Joseph Löbel, "Muss man Liebe lernen?," *Tempo*, 22 January 1929, 7.
229. Published in Germany as Theodor van de Velde, *Die vollkommene Ehe. Eine Studie über ihre Physiologie und Technik* (Leipzig: Konegen, 1926). See also Tilla Siegel, "It's Only Rational: An Essay on the Logic of Social Rationalization," *International Journal of Political Economy* 24, no. 4 (1994): 41–43.

faction of both partners, it still allocated to the man the role of the "leader" and "eternal seducer" in sexual relationships.[230] Löbel echoed this definition: in an extraordinary description full of military analogies, he explained that the man, driven by "erotic imperialism" and "bodily munitions factories," was naturally inclined to attack the "barbed wire of shame" and "trenches full of social prejudices" the woman put in his way.[231] Her job was restricted to "parrying" his advances, even if she secretly welcomed them.[232]

Löbel's militaristic language points toward the pathological aspects of the cool persona that the ideal of *Sachlichkeit* demanded of Weimar's men. As Helmut Lethen has argued, the "armoring" of the ego that he diagnosed in Weimar white-collar culture as a reaction to modernization was driven by a deep-seated fear of the female, "which stimulates a compulsive attempt to contain phenomena suggestive of chaos or fluidity."[233] Richard McCormick and Änne Söll have further analyzed the tension that lay at the heart of the *sachlich* masculinity by interpreting "New Objectivity" films and paintings as reflecting male strategies to adapt to the modern world, while defending traditional male authority at the same time.[234] Thus, the figure of the modern man, as constructed by *Tempo*, was a conflicted one. The ideal of *Sachlichkeit* commanded that he accept and actively adapt to fundamentally changed professional and private worlds, while it reinforced the archetype of the active, energetic, and dominant man. This tense mixture of progressive and traditional elements reflected the situation in the wider society. On the one hand, many young couples increasingly saw companionship as their ideal, rather than the imposed polarity of the sexes that had defined prewar relationships.[235] On the other

---

230. van de Velde, *Die vollkommende Ehe*, 8–9.

231. Joseph Löbel, "Muss man Liebe Lernen? Die Strategie des Mannes," *Tempo*, 25 January 1929, 7. For Löbel, see also Patrice Petro, *Joyless Streets: Women and Melodramatic Representation in Weimar Germany* (Princeton: Princeton University Press, 1989), 119–27.

232. Joseph Löbel, "Muss man Liebe Lernen? Die weibliche Parade," *Tempo*, 29 January 1929, 7.

233. Helmut Lethen, *Cool Conduct: The Culture of Distance in Weimar Germany* (Berkeley: University of California Press, 2002), 47.

234. Änne Söll, *Der neue Mann? Männerporträts von Otto Dix, Christian Schad und Anton Räderscheidt 1914–1930* (Paderborn: Wilhelm Fink, 2016); McCormick, *Gender and Sexuality*.

235. Helen Boak, *Women in the Weimar Republic* (Manchester: Manchester University Press, 2013), 205–7; Kessemeier, *Sportlich, sachlich, männlich. Das Bild der "Neuen Frau" in den zwanziger Jahren. Zur Konstruktion geschlechtsspezifischer Körperbilder in der Mode der Jahre 1920 bis 1929* (Dortmund: Ebersbach, 2000), 79–81; Ute Frevert, *Frauen-Geschichte. Zwischen bürgerlicher Verbesserung und neuer Weiblichkeit* (Frankfurt/Main: Suhrkamp, 1986), 197–99.

hand, traditional concepts of marriage, with the husband as sole provider, were still the societal norm, and by the end of the 1920s, married women were increasingly discouraged from working as "double earners," who were supposedly taking jobs from unemployed men.[236]

In 1927, shortly before he left the *8-Uhr-Abendblatt* to join *Tempo*, Manfred Georg published an article on the variety of female types existing in Germany at the time, differentiating between "Gretchens," "Girls," and "Garçonnes."[237] Such female typologies played an important role in Weimar culture: Lynne Frame has pointed out the significance of these classifications "as tools for negotiating the challenges of interpersonal contact" between men and women in German postwar society.[238] The "Garçonne" type, Georg argued, personified the modern, masculinized, rational, and independent female, embodying women's supposed intrusion into formerly male-dominated spheres such as sport, technology, intellectual debate, and sexual agency, challenging men on their own territory.[239] At the same time, however, this figure—named after a novel by Victor Margueritte translated into German in 1923—also embodied male fears of female dominance, reflected in Georg's warning that the "Garçonne," once she enters the playing field on the same terms as men, often beats them at their own game and thus becomes a source of conflict.[240] The "Garçonne" type played an important role in the image of modern femininity constructed in *Tempo*, where young women were often depicted behind the steering wheel of fast cars or operating airplanes, at the workplace, or as successful athletes.[241] When Erika Mann started writing for *Tempo*, she was

---

236. Boak, *Women*, 164; Frevert, *Frauen-Geschichte*, 192–94; Renate Bridenthal, "Beyond 'Kinder, Küche, Kirche:' Weimar Women at Work," *Central European History* 6, no. 2 (1973): 156–57.

237. M. G. (i.e., Manfred Georg), "Drei Frauen stehen heute vor uns. Die drei Typen: Gretchen, Girl, Garçonne," *8-Uhr-Abendblatt*, 4 June 1927, unpaginated. This article has become a touchstone for research on the "New Woman" in Weimar Germany, see Julia Bertschik, *Mode und Moderne. Kleidung als Spiegel des Zeitgeistes in der deutschsprachigen Literatur (1770–1945)* (Cologne: Böhlau, 2005), 181; Kessemeier, *Sportlich*, 50–82; Lynne Frame, "Gretchen, Girl, Garçonne? Weimar Science and Popular Culture in Search of the Ideal New Woman," in *Women in the Metropolis: Gender and Modernity in Weimar Culture*, ed. Katharina von Ankum (Berkeley: University of California Press, 1997), 12–40.

238. Frame, "Gretchen," 14.

239. For the "Garçonne," see Katie Sutton, *The Masculine Woman in Weimar Germany* (New York: Berghahn, 2011), 25–65; Kessemeier, *Sportlich*, 50–62; Sabine Hake, "In the Mirror of Fashion," in von Ankum, *Women in the Metropolis*, 195–96.

240. Victor Margueritte, *La Garçonne: Sittenroman aus dem heutigen Paris*, trans. Edmund Edel (Berlin: Ehrlich, 1923). See also Frame, "Gretchen," 12.

241. See, for example, "Bogenschießen, ein idealer Frauensport," *Tempo*, 5 December 1929, 11.

introduced with a photo showing her wearing the "Garçonne" attire of a man's shirt and tie.[242] The young female pilot Marga von Etzdorf, who wrote in *Tempo* about her adventures traveling the globe, could also be seen as a representative of this type.[243] But even beyond such direct allusions to the "Garçonne," *Tempo* put extraordinary emphasis on portraying women as a politically, socially, and economically significant members of society. According to the newspaper, the process that most vividly reflected the speed and scale of women's emancipation was their entry into professional life, where they often outshone their male colleagues. Regular series on the topic painted a picture of women claiming new fields of employment for themselves and advancing into formerly exclusively male domains.[244] An article on female bosses even claimed that in many cases women had not only caught up with men professionally, but had overtaken them.[245] *Tempo* emphasized the international nature of this trend: the paper regularly published photos of emancipated female role models from all over the world, such as the director of a Japanese travel agency, a senior official of the US Post Office, female British inventors, and Parisian students of electrical engineering.[246] The guiding ideal was again the United States, where women worked in professions, such as stylist, radio director, and estate agent, which supposedly did not even exist for women in Germany.[247] These accounts of new opportunities for women were accompanied with informative tables and articles advising its female readers how to succeed in professional life, suggesting that every woman could have a fulfilling, well-paid career in the white-collar sector of Weimar Germany.[248]

This view of female emancipation even extended to *Tempo*'s fashion col-

---

242. Erika Mann, "Kinder-Theater," *Tempo*, 28 September 1928, 5.
243. St., "Marga von Etzdorf. Werdegang der ersten Verkehrs-, Kunst-und Sportfliegerin," *Tempo*, 11 December 1930, 10.
244. Charlotte Pol, "Der Vormarsch der Frau in neue Berufe," *Tempo*, 11 November 1929, 3; 12 November 1929, 7; 15 November 1929, 3; 18 November 1929, 7; 22 November 1929, 3; 27 November 1929, 3; 2 December 1929, 3.
245. "Die Frau als Vorgesetzte," *Tempo*, 7 June 1930, 5.
246. "Sie leitet das größte Reisbüro Japans," *Tempo*, 16 October 1928, 7; "Eine tüchtige Frau," 14 November 1928, 7; "Frauen konkurrieren mit Männern um Erfindungen," 12 October 1928, 8; "Immer mehr Frauen in Männerberufen," 21 January 1929, 7.
247. Arthur Rundt, "Amerikanische Frauenberufe, die es bei uns nicht gibt," *Tempo*, 26 June 1930, 7; 1 July 1930, 7; 7 July 1930, 7.
248. Cecil B. de Mille, "Filmgold verdienen, ohne zu filmen. Neue Stellungen für Frauen," *Tempo*, 12 September 1928, 6; Dr. O. H., "Wie man Verkäuferinnen schult," *Tempo*, 2 November 1928, 4; "Die Schule des Lächelns," *Tempo*, 20 August 1929, 3; "Berufsaussichten für Frauen," *Tempo*, 15 November 1929, 3; 22 November 1929, 3.

umns: in one example, the anonymous columnist criticized the German term *Bubikopf* (literally, little boy's head) for the bob haircut most closely associated with modern femininity at the time. Women, the author argued, appreciated the practicality and hygienic qualities of short hair just like men did, yet the derogatory, infantilizing name was keeping many from getting it cut. Gender equality should include the same rights to short hair: "If we have to work like men, we want to be as comfortable as men. Short hair (don't say *Bubikopf!*) is not a fashion statement—it is a question of progress."[249] Female emancipation since 1918, *Tempo* argued with such articles, had fundamentally changed gender relations and put men and women on a more equal footing. Women were now accepted as full members of society and thus could choose if they wanted to marry or not, as they no longer had to rely on men for social status:

> It is safe to say that today women will only marry if they want to have children. If they don't, they won't. Because there can hardly be any doubt that, despite all, they have taken an enormous step forward, especially regarding love and marriage. And men will need to hurry up or be left behind.[250]

There was a limit, however, to *Tempo*'s celebration of the "Garçonne" type. Four weeks after the paper's launch, it published a photo of Mary Allen, the commandant of the Women's Auxiliary Service, a British organization of volunteer policewomen. The image showed Allen, who lived in a homosexual relationship, in full uniform next to an assistant in similar dress and was captioned "the exaggeration of woman's masculinization."[251] The supposed "masculinization" of women was a much-discussed topic in Weimar Germany.[252] As long as this meant women's entrance into supposedly masculine fields of work, leisure, and consumption, *Tempo* was a vocal supporter of this process. However, when it came to women's sexuality, the paper rejected the challenge to strictly heterosexual gender norms the "Garçonne" type embodied.

The "Gretchen" type was the polar opposite of the "Garçonne": according to Georg, she embodied the antiquated ideal of the obedient wife and caring

---

249. "Das gute Aussehen, die gute Haltung," *Tempo*, 29 October 1928, 7. The author was Lucy von Jacobi, who was responsible for *Tempo*'s fashion columns, see Below, "Wege der Professionalisierung," 64.
250. Dr. Nanette, "Warum noch heiraten? Was 'moderne' Frauenköpfe beschäftigt," *Tempo*, 13 September 1928, 7.
251. "Übertreibung der Vermännlichung der Frau," *Tempo*, 12 October 1928, 7.
252. Sutton, *Masculine Woman*, 1–24.

young mother, which had recently been pushed into public discourse again by Weimar's resurgent far-right forces. However, it was not only the far right, as Georg claimed, that supported the restriction of women to their role as mothers in the Weimar Republic. There was a wide societal consensus, ranging from criminologists like Erich Wulffen to left-liberal publicists like Stefan Großmann and even female Social Democrats like Clara Bohm-Schuch, about women's regenerative duty and its importance for the fate of the nation.[253] In fact, Georg himself had argued for restricting women's political rights to areas they were "responsible" for, namely motherhood and child-rearing.[254] The state also generally continued to espouse the idea of motherhood as a woman's "real" role in society, which was reflected in the heated debate about Article 218 of the German penal code that harshly punished abortion.[255] Tellingly, state-controlled radio, arguably with the exception of *Deutsche Welle*'s program "The Young Girls' Hour," also focused on reinforcing traditional women's roles such as the housewife.[256] The discussion about women's role as mothers highlighted the continuity of traditional ideas about gender roles in the Weimar Republic and the fears about a supposed moral and physical decline of the German nation that the image of the masculine "Garçonne" evoked.[257] At least in the first years of its existence, the "Gretchen" type obviously played no prominent role in a newspaper such as *Tempo* that styled itself as exceedingly modern. However, aspects of the idea of the woman as caring mother and housewife were also reflected in the paper's image of modern femininity. True to its service-oriented nature, *Tempo* often printed short poems and excerpts of popular children's books for mothers

---

253. Boak, *Women*, 207–11; Moritz Föllmer, "Auf der Suche nach dem eigenen Leben. Junge Frauen und Individualität in der Weimarer Republik," in *Die "Krise" der Weimarer Republik. Zur Kritik eines Deutungsmusters*, ed. Moritz Föllmer and Rüdiger Graf (Frankfurt: Campus, 2005), 288; Ingrid Sharp, "Riding the Tiger: Ambivalent Images of the New Woman in the Popular Press of the Weimar Republic," in *New Woman Hybridities: Femininity, Feminism and International Consumer Culture, 1880–1930*, ed. Margaret Beetham and Ann Heilmann (London: Routledge, 2004), 121–22; Cornelie Usborne, *The Politics of the Body in Weimar Germany: Women's Reproductive Rights and Duties* (Basingstoke: Macmillan, 1992), 53–68; Frevert, *Frauen-Geschichte*, 194.

254. Manfred Georg, "Das Recht auf Abtreibung," *Die Weltbühne*, 5 January 1922, 7–9.

255. Usborne, *Politics of the Body*, 156–81.

256. Kate Lacey, *Feminine Frequencies: Gender, German Radio, and the Public Sphere, 1923–1945* (Ann Arbor: University of Michigan Press, 1996), 57–95. See also, in more detail, Angela Dinghaus, "Frauenfunk und Jungmädchenstunde. Ein Beitrag zur Programmgeschichte des Weimarer Rundfunks" (PhD diss., University of Hannover, 2002). The one-sided focus of state radio was raised by one of *Tempo*'s readers, see "Der Radiohörer hat das Wort: Rundfunk und berufstätige Frau," *Tempo*, 8 December 1928, 6.

257. Katharina von Ankum, "Introduction," in von Ankum, *Women in the Metropolis*, 5.

to read to their offspring.[258] One characteristic example was a poem about the Zeppelin airship, which encouraged the child to imagine flying to America.[259] These short texts were always positioned next to the fashion and beauty columns, addressing a modern mother who supposedly cared both for her looks and her children. In one of these columns, between advice on the right eye cream and the importance of *"sachlich"* stationary, Lucy von Jacobi gave pointers on how to raise children without disturbing one's husband.[260] In Weimar Germany, this idea of a "moderately modern" woman, combining traditional and progressive elements, was also embodied in the figure of the efficient housewife, who used modern technology and modernist design to create a home fit for the changed times.[261] Like most aspects of the "New Woman," the figure of the modern housewife had its roots in American culture.[262] *Tempo* gave this an ironic spin: a cartoon depicted female athletes performing their domestic tasks as sport, boxing the dough in the kitchen, playing tennis with the carpet-beater, and teaching the children competitive swimming in the bathtub (Fig. 12). The title of the strip—"the perfect sportswoman as the perfect housewife"—referred to van de Velde's marriage manual and, through its association with spectator sports, it framed housewifery as distinctly modern, while its humor still acknowledged the drudgery it entailed.

Finally, the "Girl" type was the epitome of American-style consumerism, superficial glamour, and sanitized sexuality, embodied by dancing troupes such as the "Tiller Girls."[263] While this type had an American shape, it embod-

---

258. See, for example, "Dem Kinde vorzulesen: Pinocchios Abenteuer," *Tempo*, 16 November 1928, 11.

259. "Dem Kinde vorzulesen: Zeppelin, Zeppelin," *Tempo*, 1 November 1928, 11.

260. Billie (i.e., Lucy von Jacobi), "Das gute Aussehen, die gute Haltung," *Tempo*, 20 September 2918, 10.

261. Peukert, *Weimar Republic*, 105.

262. Nancy F. Cott, "The Modern Woman of the 1920s, American Style," in *A History of Women in the West*, ed. Françoise Thébaud, vol. 5 (Cambridge: Harvard University Press, 1994), 86–87.

263. For the link between consumerism and the "Girl" type, see Alys Eve Weinbaum et al., "The Modern Girl as Heuristic Device: Collaboration, Connective Comparison, Multidirectional Citation," in *The Modern Girl Around the World: Consumption, Modernity, and Globalization*, ed. Alys Eve Weinbaum et al. (Durham, N.C.: Duke University Press, 2008), 20–22; Lisa Jaye Young, "Girls and Goods: Amerikanismus and the Tiller-Effekt," in *The New Woman International: Representations in Photography and Film from the 1870s through the 1960s*, ed. Elizabeth Otto and Vanessa Rocco (Ann Arbor: University of Michigan Press, 2012), 252–69; Bertschik, *Mode und Moderne*, 198–207; Atina Grossmann, "Girlkultur or Thoroughly Rationalized Female: A New Woman in Weimar Germany?," in *Women in Culture and Politics: A Century of Change*, ed. Judith Friedlander, Alice Kessler-Harris, Carroll Smith-Rosenberg, and Blanche Wiesen Cook (Bloomington: Indiana University Press, 1986), 67–70.

Figure 12. "Die vollkommene Sportsfrau als vollkommene Hausfrau," *Tempo*, 2 October 1928, 3. © Axel Springer AG. Used with permission.

ied the narrative of a feminized modernity that had linked consumerism with passivity, desire, and irrationality in Europe since the turn of the twentieth century.[264] *Das Girl* was closely associated with young, female, single white-collar workers—the secretary, the telephonist, the salesgirl. This was in part because white-collar work was bound up with notions of an emerging mass culture that was often interpreted as female.[265] The social process behind the "Girl" phenomenon was the explosive rise of female employment in this field, as the expansion of white-collar work discussed above was in large part fueled by women entering the job market. Between 1907 and 1925, the number of female clerks tripled, and in 1925 40 percent of all commercial clerks were female.[266] At the same time, the percentage of women working in manual labour in agriculture, factories, and domestic services declined, and in 1930 a study by the socialist white-collar union Zentralverband der Angestellten concluded that white-collar work was increasingly becoming the typical form of female employment.[267] In Weimar Germany, where female white-collar

---

264. Bernd Widdig, *Culture and Inflation in Weimar Germany* (Berkeley: University of California Press, 2001), 197.

265. Irmgard Roebling, "'Haarschnitt ist noch nicht Freiheit'. Das Ringen um Bilder der Neuen Frau in Texten von Autorinnen und Autoren der Weimarer Republik," *Jahrbuch zur Literatur der Weimarer Republik* 5 (1999/2000): 17; Luisa Passerini, "The Ambivalent Image of Woman in Mass Culture," in *A History of Women in the West*, ed. Françoise Thébaud, trans. Joan Bond Sax, vol. 5 (Cambridge: Harvard University Press, 1994), 328–36; Andreas Huyssen, *After the Great Divide: Modernism, Mass Culture, Postmodernism* (Basingstoke: Macmillan, 1986), 44–62.

266. Boak, *Women*, 150–54; Frevert, *Frauen-Geschichte*, 172; Ute Frevert, "Traditionelle Weiblichkeit und moderne Interessenorganisation: Frauen im Angestelltenberuf 1918–1933," *Geschichte und Gesellschaft* 7 (1981): 507–33, at 511.

267. Susanne Suhr, *Die weiblichen Angestellten. Arbeits-und Lebensverhältnisse. Eine Umfrage des Zentralverbandes der Angestellten* (Berlin: Zentralverband der Angestellten, 1930), 2–6. See also Benninghaus, *Die anderen Jugendlichen*, 125–33.

employees had far fewer children than women of the working class or the traditional bourgeoisie, the frivolous "Girl" stood in obvious opposition to images of the woman as mother.[268] However, the naïveté and unthreatening eroticism that was part of this figure also set it apart from the "Garçonne."

The rise of beauty contests in Germany, an obvious adoption of American traditions and perceived as part of a new republican culture, was a reflection of the popularity of this "Americanized" type of femininity. The candidates, with bob haircuts and dressed in the latest fashion, personified a new Germany, voted for by a representative jury of Weimar's celebrated artists, such as Heinrich Mann, Richard Tauber, and Fritz Lang.[269] For many educated Germans, however, the embodiment of the American "Girl" was Lorelei Lee, the pleasure-seeking, flighty, uneducated, yet brashly self-confident protagonist of *Gentlemen Prefer Blondes*.[270] After its great success in the United States, the novel was published in serialized form by Ullstein's biweekly women's magazine *Die Dame* in 1925 and as a book, translated by *Tempo*'s future editor-in-chief Gustav Kauder, in the following year. *Die Dame* was a glossy, expensively produced publication for an affluent and well-educated readership that appreciated both high culture and modern mass entertainment.[271] Thus, it is not surprising that Anita Loos's frivolous tale appeared alongside Arthur Schnitzler's *Traumnovelle*, serialized in *Die Dame* at the same time. However, as Lethen has pointed out, it is highly significant that the installments of *Gentlemen Prefer Blondes* were dotted with advertisements, while Schnitzler's work was left untouched by such invasive commercialism, a fact that highlights the inextricable link of the "Girl" with consumer culture in the minds of Weimar contemporaries.[272] Many male observers, such as Siegfried Kracauer, Fritz Giese, and

---

268. Reinhard Spree, "Angestellte als Modernisierungsagenten. Indikatoren und Thesen zum reproduktiven Verhalten von Angestellten im späten 19. und frühen 20. Jahrhundert," *Geschichte und Gesellschaft. Sonderheft* 7 (1981): 293–304.

269. Veit Didczuneit, *Miss Germany. Eine schöne Geschichte* (Bonn: Haus der Geschichte der Bundesrepublik Deutschland, 2000), 6–7; Coleen Cohen, Richard Wilk, and Beverly Stoeltje, "Introduction," in *Beauty Queens on the Global Stage: Gender, Contests, and Power*, ed. Coleen Cohen, Richard Wilk, and Beverly Stoeltje (New York: Routledge, 1996), 3.

270. Roebling, "Haarschnitt," 18–24. For the American influence on German notions of the "Girl," see also Nina Sylvester, "Das Girl: Crossing Spaces and Spheres: The Function of the Girl in the Weimar Republic" (PhD diss., University of California, 2006), 11–14; Nolan, *Visions of Modernity*, 120–27; Cott, "Modern Woman," 76–91.

271. Kessemeier, *Sportlich*, 275–76. See also Christian Ferber, *Die Dame. Ein deutsches Journal für den verwöhnten Geschmack, 1912–1943* (Berlin: Ullstein, 1980).

272. Helmut Lethen, *Neue Sachlichkeit 1924–32. Studien zur Literatur des "Weißen Sozialismus"* (Stuttgart: Metzler, 1970), 35.

Alfred Polgar, saw the "Girl" as a sign of a dumbed-down mass culture and the encroachment of Fordist principles of standardization on German ideas of character and identity (*Persönlichkeit*).[273] However, the "Girl" type also had a political aspect in Weimar culture: as described above, the introduction of a democratic system in Germany coincided with the emergence of a—largely virtual—consumer culture, and the act of voting, by women in particular, became associated with shopping. The consumerist choice between different products was not only equated with the democratic process but also with the economic stability of a nation just emerging from grueling crises, and thus women, as the "wielders of the shopping basket," were perceived as the vanguard of the new notion of the citizen-consumer.[274]

Keeping in mind *Tempo*'s white-collar target audience and its obsession with all things "American," it is not surprising that the image of modern German femininity constructed in the paper largely centered around the "Girl" type. Photos of glamorous, young American film stars embodying this stereotype, such as Louise Brooks, Anna May Wong, and Clara Bow, were a regular staple of the entertainment section, as were uncredited models striking frivolous poses in other parts of the newspaper: next to the serious female athletes, the sports section also regularly printed photos of "Sport-Girls," usually scantily dressed young women occupied with various athletic disciplines.[275] One representative example is the photo of a young woman hanging in the ropes of a boxing ring, looking into the camera, with the caption "Do you want to box with me?" (Fig. 13)[276] A few weeks after *Tempo*'s launch, a comic strip gave a lighthearted, yet somewhat programmatic, view of its own readership: Brigittchen, daughter of Brigitte, a young woman dressed in "Girl" attire, beats the competition with the help of *Tempo*'s fashion columns and lands a rich man, giving her access to a glamorous lifestyle, complete with a fast sports car (Fig. 14). The cartoon was an obvious nod to similar characters in American "girl strips" of the 1920s, such as Joseph P. McEvoy's *Dixie Dugan* or Chic Young's

---

273. Kracauer, *Mass Ornament*, 75–85; Alfred Polgar, "Girls," *Die Dame*, April 1926, 2–3; Fritz Giese, *Girlkultur. Vergleiche zwischen amerikanischem und europäischem Rhythmus und Lebensgefühl* (Munich: Delphin, 1925).

274. Victoria de Grazia, "Empowering Women as Citizen-Consumers," in *The Sex of Things: Gender and Consumption in Historical Perspective*, ed. Victoria de Grazia and Ellen Furlough (Berkeley: University of California Press, 1996), 275–86; Cott, "Modern Woman," 89–91.

275. See, for example, "Gymnastik daheim," *Tempo*, 17 October 1928, 11; "Auch eine Wintersportlerin," *Tempo*, 11; "Sie ist nicht zimperlich," *Tempo*, 17 January 1929, 11.

276. The uncredited photo in fact depicted the American actress Audrey Ferris. I am indebted to Pamela Hutchinson for identifying her.

Figure 13. "Möchten Sie mit mir boxen?," *Tempo*, 21 September 1928, 11. ©Axel Springer AG. Used with permission.

Figure 14. Hans Boht, "Brigittchen," *Tempo*, 16 October 1928, 8. © Axel Springer AG. Used with permission.

Dumb Dora, a forerunner of his famous flapper character *Blondie*.[277] These cartoons "featured an attractive and fashionably dressed young single woman with a spunky, optimistic outlook" as the main character.[278]

But Brigittchen was more than just a Germanized version of such American cartoon girls: Ullstein's established women's magazine, *Blatt der Hausfrau*, which was aimed at an older readership, had long introduced a "Brigitte" character as an embodiment of the modern housewife. She appeared in advertisements for the company's sewing patterns with the catchphrase "Be thrifty, Brigitte, take Ullstein patterns," and Ullstein held regular "Brigitte Days," events offering lectures by nutrition experts, demonstrations of new household appliances, and revue-style entertainment.[279] *Tempo*'s targeted readership grew up with Brigitte, seeing their mothers read the *Blatt der Hausfrau*, and the flapper Brigittchen was obviously created as a generational foil for her more conventional "mother"—and as an embodiment of *Tempo*'s youthful spirit. This notion is reinforced by the cartoon's sense of beauty as fabricated and constructed that allows Brigittchen to change her "type" by following *Tempo*'s advice, an allusion to a modern femininity available to all.[280] The fact that Brigittchen still needs a rich man to achieve social status grated with the claims

---

277. For Chic Young, see Moira Davidson Reynolds, *Comic Strip Artists in American Newspapers, 1945–1980* (Jefferson, N.C.: McFarland, 2003), 75–77.

278. Barbara Erdman, "See You in the Funnies! An Analysis of Representation," *Journal of Visual Literacy* 13, no. 2 (January 1, 1993): 51.

279. Volker Ilgen, "Sei sparsam Brigitte, nimm Ullstein-Schnitte!," in *125 Jahre Ullstein. Presse-und Verlagsgeschichte im Zeichen der Eule* (Berlin: Axel Springer, 2002), 54–61. See also Nina Sylvester, "Before *Cosmopolitan*: The Girl in German Women's Magazines in the 1920s," *Journalism Studies* 8, no. 4 (2007): 553.

280. For the idea of "democratized" beauty in the Weimar Republic, see Annelie Ramsbrock, *The Science of Beauty: Culture and Cosmetics in Modern Germany, 1750–1930* (Basingstoke: Palgrave Macmillan, 2015), 109–55.

of female emancipation and empowerment made elsewhere in the paper, but the cartoon still portrayed her as a free-spirited and sexually powerful young woman, who ultimately controls the men around her as well as her own car—an offering to younger women looking for new role models independent from their mothers' generation.

A few weeks later, Joseph P. McEvoy's novel *Show Girl*, a lighthearted comedy about a young American woman joining the famous Ziegfeld Follies as a revue dancer, was serialized in *Tempo* under the title *"Revue-Girl."*[281] In Weimar Germany, serialized novels played an important part in a newspaper's circulation and popularity, so the choice of author and material is highly significant.[282] The novel had been published in *Liberty* magazine during the first half of the year and had been a great success in the US, providing the inspiration for the *Dixie Dugan* cartoon.[283] It is not hard to see why McEvoy's story was included in *Tempo*: the central character, Dixie Dugan, embodied the breathless modernity, American materialism, and carefree femininity the newspaper often promoted. Dixie, obviously modeled after Loos's Lorelei Lee, was advertised in *Tempo* as "the cool gal who knows how to warm up young and old men," with an accompanying illustration that bore an uncanny resemblance to Louise Brooks (Fig. 15). In the days before the start of the series, *Tempo* ran regular advertisements for its new story and even orchestrated a publicity photo shoot with dancers from Berlin's equivalent of the Ziegfeld Follies, the Haller-Revue. Ullstein newsstands, if *Tempo*'s own photographers were to be believed, were plastered with posters of Dixie's face (Fig. 16).[284] In an introductory article, the story's German translator, Arthur Rundt, defined the protagonist as the quintessential "Girl" type, with an explicit reference to the protagonist's physical traits—even her body weight—and to Loos's famous character:

> Dixie . . . strikes it big under the depraved neon lights of Broadway and becomes a star. Her shapely legs and the natural agility of her delicate body (51 kilograms!) certainly helped, but she would have never hit the big time without today's great, naïve, modern lack of restraint. She is the even more modern perfection of Lorelei, the blonde preferred by the gentlemen.[285]

---

281. J. P. McEvoy, "Revue-Girl," *Tempo*, 23 November 1928, 7
282. Fulda, *Press and Politics*, 29, 34.
283. Joseph P. McEvoy, *Showgirl* (New York: Simon & Schuster, 1928).
284. *Tempo*, 24 November 1928, 3.
285. Arthur Rundt, "Zu unserem Roman 'Revue-Girl'," *Tempo*, 22 November 1928, 7.

Figure 15. "Revue-Girl," *Tempo*, 19 November 1928, 8. © Axel Springer AG. Used with permission.

Revue-Girl/Roman eines kühlen Mädels, das jungen und älteren Herren warm zu machen weiß **beginnt demnächst im Tempo**

Revue-Girl, Rundt argued, provided an almost sociological glimpse into the worldwide "Girl" phenomenon and, despite its frivolous subject matter, offered a serious analysis of its time. He described the story and its protagonist as manifestations of the utmost modernity, and its immediacy and "today-ness" was expressed, according to Rundt, in the story's collage-like style that "was more succinct, acute and realistic than similar novels"—which of course meant Loos's book.

The glamour of real and fictional "Girls" such as Dixie Dugan, Louise Brooks, and Brigittchen presented on *Tempo*'s pages did not have much in common with the lives of its female audience. The shift from manual to white-collar work in Germany had not led to a higher social status for working women. Female employees earned 10 to 25 percent less than men for the same work, a fact that was generally accepted in Weimar society and even enshrined

Die Premiere des „Revuegirls" bei den Revuegirls
Hallers Revuegirls benötigten gestern einen eigenen „Tempo"-Verkäufer, weil sie schon in der Proben-Pause die Lektüre von Dixies Lebensroman beginnen wollten

Figure 16. "Die Premiere des 'Revuegirls' bei den Revuegirls," *Tempo*, 24 November 1928, 3. © Axel Springer AG. Used with permission.

in the collective labor agreements between white-collar unions and employers.[286] This inequality had its roots partly in the persistence of traditional bourgeois ideas of gender roles in white-collar work: female nonmanual labor was widely perceived as a temporary phase between education and marriage, even by the women themselves.[287] Thus, the majority of female white-collar employees were under twenty-five, the average marrying age for women at the time, while the female proportion of the white-collar labor force declined rapidly after that age.[288] And even this short phase of employment was hardly a time of independence and emancipation. Most unmarried female white-collar workers

---

286. Boak, *Women*, 153; Frevert, "Traditionelle Weiblichkeit," 513; Ute Frevert, "Vom Klavier zur Schreibmaschine. Weiblicher Arbeitsmarkt und Rollenzuweisung am Beispiel der weiblichen Angestellten der Weimarer Republik," in *Frauen in der Geschichte. Frauenrechte und die gesellschaftliche Arbeit der Frauen im Wandel*, ed. Annette Kuhn and Gerhard Schneider (Düsseldorf: Schwann, 1979), 87–91; Bridenthal, "Weimar Women," 156. See also Suhr, *Angestellten*, 31.

287. Frevert, "Klavier," 90–91.

288. Frevert, "Traditionelle Weiblichkeit," 514; Suhr, *Angestellten*, 8–9.

still shared a flat with their parents, where they often had to pay rent and help with the housework in their free time.[289] After living costs and food, the highest expenses of female white-collar workers were for clothes and personal hygiene, according to the Zentralverband der Angestellten.[290] But even these small private expenses have been interpreted as an attempt to raise women's chances of "marrying up" by meeting an eligible husband of a higher socioeconomic status at the workplace.[291] Ultimately, the life of a married housewife was still the only viable existence for most middle-class women in the Weimar Republic.[292] Thus, the female *Angestellte* embodied the "dialectics of emancipation" of women in the Weimar Republic, reflecting newfound political, economic, and sexual freedom, but also highlighting old and new pressures regarding social hierarchies and body image.[293]

The fact that the many articles in *Tempo* about a glamorous and carefree lifestyle, female equality, and the professional opportunities for women were describing an ideal rather than the reality of Weimar Germany was illustrated best by the experience of Lucy von Jacobi, the paper's only female editor. A financially independent, well-educated, and emancipated woman, she had to take a significant pay cut after her male colleagues on the culture desk, Manfred Georg and Hanns G. Lustig, had complained about her relatively high salary.[294] However, while discrimination against females was accepted in its own offices, on its pages *Tempo* fought to change the precarious situation that many German women faced in the Weimar Republic. Weimar's legal framework, the paper argued in many articles, did not adequately reflect the social changes in Germany.[295] *Tempo* was an outspoken advocate of the right to abortion and regularly demanded a reform of the infamous Article 218 of the penal code that severely punished terminations of pregnancy. When Hans José Rehfisch's play *Der Frauenarzt* premiered in Berlin in November 1928, *Tempo* gave the author a forum to explain his beliefs about women's right to control

---

289. Suhr, *Angestellten*, 38–39. See also Boak, *Women*, 153; Frevert, "Traditionelle Weiblichkeit," 516.

290. Suhr, *Angestellten*, 44–45.

291. Frevert, "Traditionelle Weiblichkeit," 517; Frevert, "Klavier," 96; Bridenthal, "Weimar Women," 162.

292. Frevert, *Frauen-Geschichte*, 174–75; Bridenthal, "Weimar Women," 162. See also Suhr, *Angestellten*, 9.

293. Roebling, "'Haarschnitt'," 17; Frevert, *Frauen-Geschichte*, 171–72.

294. Jacobi diary, January 1929, unpaginated, in Akademie der Künste Berlin (AdK), Lucy-von-Jacobi-Archiv, Nr. 16, fols. 54–55. See also Below, "Professionalisierung," 61.

295. Adsum, "Moderne Ehe-und Scheidungsurteile," *Tempo*, 24 October 1929, 3; "Der Mann stimmt für die Frau," *Tempo*, 14 December 1929, 9.

their own bodies, and published a discussion about the legal situation.[296] In a review of the play, Manfred Georg lambasted the law for "immorally and inhumanely ruining thousands of people."[297] The controversial play *Cyankali (§218)* by medical practitioner and playwright Friedrich Wolf was also reviewed prominently.[298]

In a regular column called "From the Woman's Complaints Book," the paper drew attention to other continuing inequalities and injustices. One telling example is the case of a successful director of a beauty salon who still needed her husband's authorization to open a bank account.[299] Her story elicited a sympathetic response from a female reader, who decried the fact that, even in the "age of female equality," the laws were still made by men.[300] In her reportage on the working life of German women, Maria Leitner showed the downsides they faced working in demanding, low-paid jobs in retail and administration. For example, a female clerk working in a department store gave a vivid insight into her life full of long hours at work, housework at home, and without any prospect of improvement.[301] Even the representatives of the glamorous "Girl" type, such as show dancers, actresses, and models, did not have it much better:

> The "Girl" is supposed to be the queen of modern womanhood, but the reporter looking for the truth will find that the reality is quite different. These girls, whose work is not as easy as it looks, are paid 3.5 marks per night by the elegant revues. . . . For "sculptures"—the technical term for naked show performances—they get two to three marks, depending on the venue. . . . Beauty—at least the honest, hard-working beauty—is not valued very highly in Berlin.[302]

---

296. Hans J. Rehfisch, "Schutz der persönlichen Freiheit," *Tempo*, 2 November 1928, 5; Dr. F. S. Bader, "Finden Sie, dass sich der 'Frauenarzt' richtig verhält?," 16 November 1928, 7.

297. Manfred Georg, "H. J. Rehfisch: Der Frauenarzt," *Tempo*, 3 November 1928, 5.

298. Alfred Trostler, "Friedrich Wolf klopft an . . . ," *Tempo*, 6 September 1929, 5; "Cyankali (§218)," *Tempo*, 7 September 1929, 5.

299. Dora Sophie, "Aus dem Beschwerdebuch der Frau," *Tempo*, 18 February 1929, 3. The column's author was probably Walter Benjamin's wife, Dora Sophie, who worked for Ullstein's women's magazine *Die praktische Berlinerin*, see Below, "Wege der Professionalisierung," 69.

300. "Tribüne für Alle: Aus dem Beschwerdebuch der Frau," *Tempo*, 25 February 1929, 5.

301. Marie Leitner, "Das Warenhaus-Fräulein erzählt mir," *Tempo*, 22 December 1928, 3–4.

302. Marie Leitner, "Wie hoch im Kurs stehen Berliner Schönheiten?," *Tempo*, 20 No-

Tempo's peculiar mixture of idealistic celebrations of female empowerment, the sexualized depictions of "Girls," and realistic reporting on the enduring discrimination against women was a result of the paper's need, as a mass-market publication, to address a relatively diverse audience of both female and male readers with different interests, political allegiances, and social backgrounds. It also reflected the conflicting situation of many women at the end of the 1920s, when the hope for social change after 1918 had been dampened by continuing inequalities. The lack of clarity surrounding the new role of women in society became a battleground for the wider debate about the form of a German modernity: the way women behaved, consumed, dressed, and voted was interpreted as a signifier for the shape German society was to take.[303] In this debate, *Tempo* offered the model of a "moderately modern" woman: an Americanized, athletic, emancipated, and heterosexual female, who uses lipstick and earns her own salary, but still reads bedtime stories to her children and provides a good home for her husband.

During the first months of the paper's existence, this *Tempo* type—a mixture of the three female types Georg had described—was only constructed implicitly through the coexistence of optimistic articles celebrating women's new freedom and reports on the harsh living conditions of female employees. Soon, however, *Tempo* found a face for its "moderately modern" female type. On 19 January 1929, the paper announced "The Beauty of the Working Woman," a beauty contest aiming to show the "real face" of modern femininity. On the front page of that day, an illustration promoting the contest in the masthead of the newspaper showed the embodiment of this type: bob-haired young women wearing lipstick. The contest was part of a general pursuit in the late 1920s for a definitive female type, reflected in competitions such as the first "Miss Germany" pageant in 1927 or, a year later, the widely publicized art contest Das schönste Frauenporträt.[304] In contrast to these initiatives, however, *Tempo*'s pageant was outspokenly political, aiming to show women as an inte-

---

vember 1928, 3. See also "Junge Schauspielerin klagt," *Tempo*, 26 September 1928, 5; "Tauentzien-Girls," *Tempo*, 1 November 1928, 4.

303. Sutton, *Masculine Woman*, 29; Canning, "Claiming Citizenship," 130–32; Rüdiger Graf, "Anticipating the Future in the Present: 'New Women' and Other Beings of the Future in Weimar Germany," *Central European History* 42, no. 4 (2009): 661–72; Mila Ganeva, *Women in Weimar Fashion: Discourses and Displays in German Culture, 1918–1933* (Rochester, N.Y.: Boydell & Brewer, 2008), 3–4; Bertschik, *Mode und Moderne*, 180–82; Sneeringer, "The Shopper as Voter," 476–501.

304. For the first "Miss Germany," see Didczuneit, *Miss Germany*, 6–7; for Das schönste Frauenporträt, see Susanne Meyer-Büser, *Bubikopf und Gretchenzopf. Die Frau der 20er Jahre* (Hamburg: Edition Braus, 1995), 28–33.

gral part of the democratic society of Weimar Germany. The competition was explicitly directed against critics of women's new role in professional life, by proving that working did not negatively affect female beauty or threaten German society and culture:

> The mistake of most beauty pageants is the fact that nearly all of them are only open to professional beauties of film or fashion. But the characteristic female type of today is not the professional beauty, but the working woman, the working girl. This type, characterized by intelligence, independence, and a free mindset, defines the face of the female generation. Yet this dominant type is never represented in beauty pageants. Maybe their organizers still believe that working compromises a woman's beauty. We want to refute, with physical evidence, this often-voiced claim that modern female labor leads to racial decadence.[305]

Professional models, actresses, and showgirls were barred from entering the competition, while the eligible groups were divided into eight categories: office workers, sales clerks, telephonists and other technical professions, teachers and nurses, hospitality workers, factory workers, academic professions and students, and domestic workers including housewives. To be considered for the contest, the participants had to send in at least one full-length photo; an internal jury then chose three winners in every category, who were awarded with sixty, forty, and twenty-five marks, respectively. Just as in *Tempo*'s holiday photography competition, the overall winner of the grand prize of 1,000 marks—nearly half a year's salary for a female office worker—was not chosen by a select few, but by the audience, using a ballot paper published with an overview of the twenty-four final contenders that the readers had to cut out and send in to the Ullstein offices (Fig. 17).

Despite the sincere tone of the introduction of the contest, which equated a beauty contest with the promotion of modern women's independence, Ullstein did not launch "The Beauty of the Working Woman" only to empower women, but also to attract readers—not only an interested female audience, but also men who might buy the paper to ogle some pretty "girls next door." In fact, following the publication of the final group of contenders, *Tempo* published a photo of a group of men excitedly gathered around a copy of the paper.[306] Thus, we should treat the submissions for the contest not as a direct expression of

---

305. "Die Schönheit der berufstätigen Frau," *Tempo*, 19 January 1929, 5.
306. "Wer die Wahl hat, hat die Qual," *Tempo*, 19 March 1929, 12.

Figure 17. "Welcher die 1000 M.?," *Tempo*, 16 March 1929, 5. © Axel Springer AG. Used with permission.

Tempo's readership, but as part of the editorial content. The choice of published photos and their presentation were guided by commercial decisions and executed by paid editors, who depended on advertising revenue. However, even in the context of a commercial publication, *Tempo*'s beauty pageant was exceptional. American and French newspapers and magazines had organized similar photographic beauty contests already since the turn of the century to boost their circulation. However, these contests often presented a rather conservative feminine ideal, focusing on the "virtue" of the contestants and their potential as future mothers.[307] In the 1920s, they were often positioned against the threatening new female ideals of the flapper or the "Garçonne." The contestants of the first Miss America pageant in 1921, for example, were not allowed to wear bobbed hair or makeup.[308] *Tempo*'s beauty contest differed markedly from these traditions by explicitly focusing on women as modern professionals. The allusion to right-wing claims of "racial decadence" in the introduction to the contest also shows how thoroughly political it was, despite its commercial setting in a mainstream medium. The fact that this ideal of women as professionals was presented through a beauty contest decided by a popular vote among its readers is highly significant, as it connected *Tempo*'s initiative to the new democratic order of the Weimar Republic. In a country in which women's active and passive suffrage, and the democratic process per se, were still contested topics, this cannot be interpreted purely as a marketing stunt. As with its earlier holiday photo competition, *Tempo* offered a playful rehearsal of still relatively unfamiliar political processes. This time, however, the candidates up for the vote were exclusively women, underlining their new status as full citizens.

According to *Tempo*, several thousand women participated in the pageant as contestants, of which 111 were shown over a ten-week period, expressly chosen to reflect as many different professions and characters as possible.[309] The average age of these participants was twenty-four and while the majority were from Berlin, there were also submissions from, among others, Hamburg, Cologne, Heidelberg, and Dresden, underlining *Tempo*'s nationwide reception. Many posed in a style that imitated the "Girl" type, wearing fashionable dresses, stockings, makeup, and a bob haircut. Some even sent in photos show-

---

307. Holly Grout, "Between Venus and Mercury: The 1920s Beauty Contest in France and America," *French Politics, Culture & Society* 31, no. 1 (2013): 48–49.
308. Grout, "Between Venus and Mercury," 55.
309. "Unser 2000-Mark-Wettbewerb," *Tempo*, 16 February 1929, 8.

ing them in bathing costumes or similarly revealing outfits. More importantly, however, *Tempo* also showed women dressed in their work clothes, such as Hanna Preußer-Schmidt, a thirty-year-old medical doctor working in a Berlin hospital and winner of the academic professions category, who was depicted in her white lab coat, or Hertha Diedicke, a nurse from Danzig and winner of the education and care category.[310] Another notable example was Lore Feininger, daughter of modernist painter Lyonel Feininger, who worked as a professional photographer and won in the category of technical professions.[311]

The audience clearly favored these successful professional women over the other contestants. The overall winner, Erna Koch, a twenty-one-year-old confectioner working in Roberts, an American-style fast food restaurant in Berlin, had been shown in a photograph that was not erotic or glamorous at all, but rather formal and professional, wearing a prim, yet modern uniform with shirt, tie, and cap, serving a confectionary (Fig. 18). An interview with the happy winner revealed a life that was most probably closer to the experiences of *Tempo*'s female audience than Brigittchen's glamorous exploits. The journalist sent from *Tempo*'s offices to announce the good news described the small, orderly flat Erna shared with her petit-bourgeois parents, noted her low salary, but also the enthusiasm for her job and her successful career. She had, the article continued, been divorced after a short, unhappy marriage, and had a young child to look after. Asked how she would spend the prize money, she showed modest, yet typically white-collar, middle-class preferences, planning to spend a holiday at the Baltic Sea, buy some new dresses, and save the rest.[312] When the winner was presented to the public at the "Brigitte Days," the regular revue-style event for Ullstein's female audience, she appeared in her work uniform, but was accompanied by glamorously dressed show dancers called *Tempo*-Girls (Fig. 19).

"The Beauty of the Working Woman" is an illustrative example of the way tabloid newspapers like *Tempo* helped women of the Weimar Republic to reconcile old and new norms of femininity and thus to negotiate the pitfalls of modern life.[313] It combined current social issues, in this case women's entry into more publicly visible jobs, with the commercial mass-market

---

310. *Tempo*, 6 March 1929, 8; 10 March 1929, 8.
311. *Tempo*, 5 March 1929, 8.
312. See bh, "Erna Koch bei sich zu Hause," *Tempo*, 30 March 1929, 4. For white-collar lifestyles in the Weimar Republic, see Spree, "Modernisierungsagenten," 279–308; Sandra Coyner, "Class Consciousness and Consumption: The New Middle Class during the Weimar Republic," *Journal of Social History* 10, no. 3 (1977): 310–31.
313. Föllmer, "Junge Frauen," 302–14.

Figure 18. Erna Koch, *Tempo*, 21 February 1929, 4. © Axel Springer AG. Used with permission.

Figure 19. "*Tempo*-Girls und die Schönheits-Siegerin Erna Koch," *Tempo*, 6 April 1929, 8. © Axel Springer AG. Used with permission.

appeal of a beauty pageant to endorse the social and political changes associated with the new democratic regime. With this, it addressed the experiences of young women in the Weimar Republic and offered them a way to connect their own life with the role model of the "Girl," the "Garçonne," and the "Gretchen" disseminated in other parts of the paper, but also in films, novels, and magazines. If Erna Koch is taken as its embodiment, the result of this negotiating process was a selective, moderately modern mixture of all three of Georg's types: an independent working woman and wholesome mother wearing the emblems of modern womanhood—the bob haircut and professional working clothes—without possessing any of the subversive features of the "Girl" or the "Garçonne." This sober female type undermined the dominant narrative of a feminized, threatening modernity embodied by these types. By combining politics and popular culture, *Tempo*'s contest also helped reinforce the notion of women as citizen-consumers, a fact highlighted by the comment accompanying the announcement of the final results of 30 March 1929: "The count of the valid ballot papers resulted in 23,440 votes cast by our readers. (So here, too, the great 'voter fatigue' of the public was also evident and here, too, the non-voters formed the overwhelming majority.)"[314] The placing of the announcement on the paper's front page and the use of such formal language put the pageant in the context of high politics; the critical, pedagogical undertone, referring to the relatively low voter participation in the national elections of May 1928, linked it to the actual democratic election process. Using the topicality of female suffrage to attract readers was not an unusual practice: Weimar's advertising industry frequently used electoral imagery to sell everyday products from soap to shoes.[315] However, with its beauty pageant, *Tempo* aimed at more than shifting copies: rather than selling its product, it tried to sell the democratic process itself by linking it to popular culture. The implicit political message of the ideal of the citizen-consumer was clear: only the new democratic system reflected the unstoppable social process that had swept aside old traditions and morals, had liberated women, and had brought German society closer to gender equality. Women, who finally got the right to vote in the Weimar Republic, were presented in *Tempo* as the new state's natural representatives. The close relationship between women and democracy was reflected, the paper argued, in their voting behavior. In the election to the Berlin city council in 1929 a majority of women had voted for pro-democratic parties and

---

314. "1000 Mark Siegerin," *Tempo*, 30 March 1929, 1.
315. Sneeringer, "The Shopper as Voter," 476–501.

had shunned the Communists and the NSDAP.[316] *Tempo*'s use of a beauty contest to promote women's role in democratic politics illustrates the fact, pointed out by Kathleen Canning, that female citizenship was not negotiated only in the "official" forums of public life such as the Reichstag.[317] Popular culture also played a role in establishing women as vital actors in the democratic process.

---

316. "Wie die Frauen wählen," *Tempo*, 3 December 1929, 4.
317. Canning, "Claiming Citizenship," 119–25.

CHAPTER 2

1930–1931
Adapting to the Crisis

The year 1930 was a dramatic turning point for the Weimar Republic and the Ullstein house, which had a profound influence on *Tempo*'s vision of a modern Germany. At the beginning of the year, the global economic crisis, which had already caused great turmoil in the US since late 1929, reached Germany.[1] In September, the explosive gains of the Nazis in the general election delivered a shock to Weimar's political system. Between these historical milestones, Ullstein was gripped by an internal dispute that paralyzed the company during these times of fundamental changes and hobbled *Tempo*'s effectiveness in reaching the goals the company had set itself with its new publication.

Already in 1929, the German economy had shown signs of weakness, such as falling consumer spending. The diversity and scale of the Ullstein enterprise initially made it relatively resilient to the economic collapse: in 1930, sales suffered only slightly and the incurred losses were balanced by cost cuts.[2] But by the end of 1931, yearly profits had dropped by 50 percent to 660,000 marks and first layoffs were looming.[3] In 1932, at the height of the economic crisis, the company recorded its first overall loss of around 14,000 marks, ballooning to over 577,000 marks in 1933.[4] The mood at the company's headquarters on Berlin's Kochstraße was characterized by tensions and disorientation. In the quickly deteriorating economy, the Ullstein management tried to broaden the appeal of the company's newspapers, while many editors aimed to use them as a tool to influence the increasingly partisan political climate. In

---

1. Ursula Büttner, *Weimar. Die überforderte Republik 1918–1933* (Stuttgart: Klett-Cotta, 2008), 401–5.
2. *Ullstein-Geschäftsbericht* 1930, unpaginated.
3. *Ullstein-Geschäftsbericht* 1931, unpaginated.
4. *Ullstein-Geschäftsbericht* 1932–33; "Meldungen," *Zeitungs-Verlag*, 15 October 1932, 734. See also Eksteins, *Limits*, 231–32.

October 1929, the manager of the Ullstein branch in Wilmersdorfer Straße reported that many longtime readers of the *Vossische Zeitung* had canceled their subscription because of its increasingly partisan tone.[5] One reader was quoted as saying that the paper "now agitates like the *Lokal-Anzeiger*," the far-right tabloid controlled by DNVP chairman Alfred Hugenberg, by trying to "impose its political opinion on the reader." Antagonizing the audience in such a way was not acceptable for management, and in this struggle between commercial considerations and political agitation, the long-standing antagonism between editors and publishers that exists at most newspaper offices quickly developed into an outright power struggle.

Besides these internal tensions and the worsening economic crisis, a family dispute among the owners, the so-called Ullstein affair, perceived by the public as one of "the biggest scandals of the Weimar era," only added to the low morale of the employees.[6] Since the company's conversion into a listed company in 1921, tension over the future of the enterprise had been brewing between Franz Ullstein, the director of the firm's newspapers and de facto chief executive, and his brother Louis, the financial director.[7] Shortly after Franz remarried in 1929, allegations arose that his new wife, Rosie Gräfenberg, acted as a double agent for France and Germany. Joining forces with Georg Bernhard, Louis and several younger family members used these rumors to oust Franz. In a bitter legal battle that unfolded over the course of 1930, the allegations proved to be unfounded, but the feud, waged publicly in *Das Tage-Buch*, *Die Weltbühne*, *Montag Morgen*, and *Vossische Zeitung*, seriously damaged the Ullsteins' reputation and hobbled the company's performance at a politically and economically difficult time.[8] Franz was forced to leave his post on 28 January and Georg Bernhard, the company's political figurehead, resigned from his position as editor-in-chief of the *Vossische Zeitung* in August 1930. Ullstein now effectively operated without a political compass at a time when Weimar's political landscape changed dramatically.

5. Monthly branches report, 31 October 1929, BArchL, NL Misch, f. 128.
6. Arthur Koestler, *Arrow in the Blue: An Autobiography* (London: Readers Union, 1954), 166. For a detailed account of the family feud, see Eksteins, *Limits*, 180–93; Koszyk, *Deutsche Presse 1914–1945*, 253–55.
7. Eksteins, *Limits*, 115; Ullstein, *Rise and Fall*, 185–86.
8. Josef Bornstein, "Ullstein-Roman," *Das Tage-Buch*, 28 June 1930, 1020–33; Georg Bernhard, "Erklärung," *Vossische Zeitung*, 10 July 1930, 3; Franz Ullstein, "Die Autoren des Ullstein-Romans," *Das Tage-Buch*, 12 July 1930, 1109–13; Josef Bornstein, "Neues zum Ullstein-Roman. Zu einer Erklärung Georg Bernhards," *Montag Morgen*, 14 July 1930, 2; Georg Bernhard, "Verlegertragödie," *Die Weltbühne*, 15 July 1930, 82–86; Hellmuth von Gerlach, "Redakteur-Tragödie," *Das Tage-Buch*, 19 July 1930, 1149–52; Josef Bornstein, "Zum Fall Ullstein," *Das Tage-Buch*, 19 July 1930, 1152.

With its politicized overtones, the affair reflected the febrile atmosphere of the late 1920s and early 1930s in Germany. Contemporary observers were quick to interpret the family feud as a symbol of the crisis of the Weimar Republic and evidence of a general deterioration in public life, political decency, and liberal unity.[9] *Tempo*'s economics editor, Ferdinand Friedrich Zimmermann, argued in *Die Tat* that the affair played out Weimar's generational conflict between the older generation and the cynical, careerist part of the youth, eager to take over positions of power in society.[10] The left-liberal publisher Leopold Schwarzschild later called the Ullstein affair "an extraordinary manifestation of the general decay in Germany."[11] This crisis of leadership, compounded by unprecedented economic woes, made the company even more politically cautious and risk-averse than it had been before. While the Ullsteins continued to support the liberal cause privately, they were more anxious than ever not to lose any readers and advertising clients for their newspapers, leading to a more conservative corporate policy.[12] The affair also had direct consequences for the DDP. A special party committee reprimanded their Reichstag deputy Georg Bernhard for his role in the intrigue and he lost his place on the party list of candidates for the coming general election after the Democrats had transformed into the German State Party (Deutsche Staatspartei, DStP) in July.[13]

The founding of the DStP was the political sensation of the run-up to the Reichstag election in September. On 27 July, the DDP announced its fusion with the People's National Reich Association (Volksnationale Reichsvereinigung), the political arm of the Jungdeutscher Orden (JuDo), under the new name.[14] This surprising move seemed to confirm Zehrer's worries that the younger generation had turned toward the democratic establishment he had always attacked. The collaboration of the JuDo, which just two years earlier had dismissed *Tempo* as a "flower of the concrete" and, regarding its ideology and political aims, had much in common with the Tatkreis, shows that *Tempo*'s call for a constructive role for young people was not a fringe opinion, but reflected a broad political current. It also underlined the importance that liberal forces attached to the youth vote, which had already been reflected in the foundation of *Tempo* itself. However, the maneuver was met with skepticism by

---

9. Bornstein, "Ullstein-Roman," 1031.
10. Ferdinand Fried (i.e., Ferdinand Friedrich Zimmermann), "Höhengewitter," *Die Tat*, April 1930, 340–42.
11. Leopold Schwarzschild, "The Ullstein Papers," *Nation*, 4 October 1943, 529.
12. Eksteins, *Limits*, 200.
13. Eksteins, *Limits*, 186–88; Koszyk, *Deutsche Presse 1914–1945*, 255.
14. Frye, *Democrats*, 155–67.

some parts of the liberal-democratic establishment, namely the *Berliner Tageblatt*.[15] The political language used by the new party differed significantly from the DDP, which had always adhered to the political culture of *Sachlichkeit*, championing notions of responsible citizenship and democratic consensus, while the JuDo's antiparliamentarianism and militarism clearly had influenced the DStP's program.[16] Most significantly, it heralded a discursive shift from the DDP's emphasis on democratic education of the electorate toward ideas of an organic "people's community" (*Volksgemeinschaft*).[17] In the new party's manifesto, the Republic was described as a "fake democracy" (*Scheindemokratie*) and the idea of citizenship based on the Constitution was replaced by the more conservative and confrontational notion of "a civic attitude informed by the idea of the people's community of all Germans."[18] The polemics in the DStP's manifesto heralded a partisan entrenchment in Weimar's political culture, away from rational deliberation and cooperation, that was also felt in parliament after 1930.[19] The JuDo leader Artur Maraun saw the DStP less as a new political party than as a vehicle to reform the parliamentary system. The name of the new party reflected his criticism of *Parteiismus*, the view that the state stood above political parties, which only distorted the real will of the people.[20] Effectively, as Dieter Langewiesche has remarked, the DDP shed its liberal tradition with this merger in the hope for better election results: "The DDP's escape into cooperation with the *Jungdeutschen* was an escape from liberalism."[21]

Despite this troubling shift—and the JuDo's well-known anti-Semitism—Ullstein supported the DStP. The company even made a sizeable donation of 10,000 marks to the new party, which faced its first political litmus test in the upcoming general election.[22] The *Vossische Zeitung* described it as Stresemann's legacy and a "renewal of centrist politics," a standard-bearer for "all liberal and democratic circles in our nation" and particularly for Weimar's youth.[23] *Tempo*, as the self-fashioned voice of Germany's young people, greeted the new party's founding with enthusiasm. It welcomed the DStP as a

---

15. Sösemann, *Ende*, 108; Bosch, *Presse*, 71.
16. Sösemann, *Ende*, 101.
17. Childers, "Languages," 349–51.
18. *Das Manifest der Deutschen Staatspartei* (Berlin: Jungdeutscher Verlag, 1930), 1, 5.
19. Mergel, *Parlamentarische Kultur*, 428–65.
20. Mergel, *Parlamentarische Kultur*, 399–408.
21. Langewiesche, *Liberalismus*, 251.
22. Bundesarchiv Koblenz (BArchK), N1012 Koch-Weser, fol. 239, cited in Eksteins, *Limits*, 200.
23. "Erneuerung der Mitte," *Vossische Zeitung*, 28 July 1930, 1–2.

wind of change in the fossilized political landscape and lauded its promise to give a voice to the young generation.[24] While it still had to be seen how the new party would fare in day-to-day politics, *Tempo* argued, its manifesto promised a solution for the problematic division of Germany's pro-democratic forces and was thus an embodiment of the late Stresemann's ideas.

Ironically, considering the DStP's rejection of the liberal tradition, one of the reasons the founding of the new party generated such enthusiasm at the Ullstein house was the fact that it provided a glimmer of hope for the upcoming general election, which was widely seen as make-or-break time for German liberalism.[25] The government formed by Heinrich Brüning in March effectively operated by grace of President Paul von Hindenburg and constituted an affront to liberal notions of parliamentary democracy. This "shift of power away from Parliament and the parties, in favor of the President's ever-expanding authority" had become exceedingly clear in July, when Hindenburg dissolved the Reichstag after a majority had overturned one of his emergency decrees.[26] For the liberal press, the continuing reliance on the notorious Article 48 in running the affairs of the state, the ever-increasing volatility and extremism of the political climate, as well as the deepening economic crisis, called for a clear decision by the electorate in the next election scheduled for September.[27] A strong, democratic, and operable Reichstag was needed to prevent further descent into an authoritarian dictatorship.

Under these influences, the image of democracy constructed in *Tempo* began to change. Increasingly, the paper voiced criticism of a perceived *Parteiismus* and focused on the directly elected President Hindenburg as the real representative of the will of the people. The Constitution Day celebrations in August 1930, coming just weeks after the dissolution of the parliament, were a much more subdued affair than a year earlier.[28] Still, *Tempo* stressed the "enormous interest" of the population flocking "in bright droves" to the Reichstag building—not to take part in the celebrations, however, but mainly to welcome the president.[29] Hindenburg was portrayed as a benevolent sovereign, smiling down graciously on the people waiting in front of the Reichstag, while the members of the dissolved parliament were criticized for their absence from the

---

24. "Die neue Staatspartei der jungen Generation," *Tempo*, 28 July 1930, 1–2.
25. Sösemann, *Ende*, 76. Other liberal publishers also supported the new party for similar reasons, see Eksteins, "Frankfurter Zeitung," 23.
26. Kolb, *Weimar Republic*, 117.
27. Bosch, *Presse*, 160–207; Eksteins, *Limits*, 197–98.
28. Rossol, *Performing the Nation*, 80–84.
29. "Feststunde im Reichstag," *Tempo*, 11 August 1930, 1–2.

official celebration. The difference from *Tempo*'s earlier emphasis on inclusiveness and involvement a year ago is striking. The mass play with 7,000 participating schoolchildren, which Edwin Redslob had staged in Berlin's main stadium a day earlier and that had been visited by 40,000 to 50,000 people, was not mentioned in the paper at all.[30] Instead, *Tempo* focused on Hindenburg's remote representation, which was not very different from the former emperor's public appearances that the paper had criticized so harshly before. While *Tempo* had hailed the Constitution as the bedrock of the Weimar state in 1929, now the personality of Hindenburg embodied the foundation of the Republic. This shift was noticeable in the whole of the liberal press: in light of the spreading economic and political crises, Hindenburg, who had been severely criticized before, was now widely seen as an important sheet anchor for Weimar democracy and, over the following years, was turned into an *Ersatzkaiser*—an almost godlike paternal figure watching over the nation.[31]

By this time, political commentary, one of *Tempo*'s unique selling points, had lost its usual place in the paper. During continuous layout changes over the course of 1929, the column "Questions of the Day" on the second page, which usually carried the daily leader comment on current politics, had been relegated to the back pages in July and was discontinued altogether by the end of the year.[32] This did not mean that *Tempo* refrained from political commentary—far from it. Its coverage of Nazi activities, for example, was broadened and became more confrontational as the general election drew closer. In July, *Tempo* criticized the *Koblenzer Nationalblatt*, a paper founded by the future head of the German Labor Front, Robert Ley, for using a tragic accident during the official celebrations marking the end of the French occupation of the Rhineland to attack the government.[33] The Nazi paper in turn accused *Tempo* of misrepresenting its coverage, which *Tempo* countered by reprinting the incriminating passages.[34] In the weeks immediately before Election Day, the paper for the first time attempted to seriously analyze the movement. Stefan Großmann compared the Hitler cult with organized religion and Roda Roda portrayed the NSDAP as "the party of the drunks."[35] Both authors explained

---

30. For the play, see Rossol, *Performing the Nation*, 93.
31. Anna von der Goltz, *Hindenburg: Power, Myth, and the Rise of the Nazis* (Oxford: Oxford University Press, 2009), 142–43; Bosch, *Presse*, 229–35; Eksteins, *Limits*, 219–22.
32. The last column appeared on 28 November 1929.
33. "Die Koblenzer Katastrophe," *Tempo*, 23 July 1930, 1–2: "Die Bergungsarbeiten in Koblenz," *Tempo*, 24 July 1930, 2.
34. "Das Totenlied des Nazi-Blattes," *Tempo*, 29 July 1930, 3.
35. St. Gr. (i.e., Stefan Großmann), "Christus-Hitler," *Tempo*, 27 August 1930, 3; Roda Roda, "Die Partei der Betrunkenen," *Tempo*, 29 August 1930, 3.

the popularity of the movement with a mass hypnosis it had cast on a downtrodden population.

In the run-up to the 1930 general election, the paper intensified its focus on the campaign methods of the different parties. In a prominently placed series of articles, it presented the expensive, "American-style" campaigns of the SPD and the DNVP, which used special films shown in mobile cinemas all over the nation, colorful demonstrations and rallies, speeches on gramophone records, and custom-made neon signs in city centers.[36] However, in the case of the DNVP, these examples of modern campaigning were also described as an illustration of how money could buy political influence beyond the actual size of the party. In contrast, *Tempo* argued, the centrist parties such as the DVP, the Centre Party, and above all the DStP appealed to the voters' intelligence and sense of *Sachlichkeit*. In the coverage of the tactics of the German Communist Party and the Nazis, the use of illegal or violent means such as pasting over other parties' posters and the disruption of political events were highlighted.[37] Although the series was presented as an objective analysis and a service for the readers, *Tempo*'s political affiliation was evident. It gave much room to a selection of DStP and DVP campaign posters and poked fun at the extremist parties by using photos of Communist graffiti full of spelling mistakes and of a Nazi campaigner enjoying a nap (Fig. 20).

Sachlichkeit remained a central value in *Tempo*'s worldview, particularly when it came to politics. As a contrast to the supposedly hysterical followers of the Nazis, *Tempo* constructed the image of the responsible voter, the complementary audience of the supposedly rational campaign of the DStP. In a series that ran from August until a few weeks after the election, "Heaven" took on the personality of "the voter," commenting on the political campaigns and party politics in general. On the eve of Election Day, he reminded his readers to find out about the location of their polling station and to vote early in order to beat the rush around noon.[38] The whole spectacle of modern campaigning, "the voter" argued, was not worth the effort, as only sound reasoning and common sense could convince him:

> You don't have to bring out the big guns. Screaming is always wrong. Give me your argument calmly and rationally (*sachlich*), don't promise me any miracles or scare me with coming catastrophes. That won't

---

36. "Wie und womit die Parteien agitieren," *Tempo*, 8 September 1930, 2; 10 September 1930, 3.

37. "Wie und womit die Parteien agitieren," *Tempo*, 12 September 1930, 2. See also "Ein Reichstag von über 600 Abgeordneten?," *Tempo*, 12 September 1930, 1.

38. Heaven, "Der Wähler denkt," *Tempo*, 13 September 1930, 3.

Figure 20. Detail from "Wie und womit die Parteien agitieren," *Tempo*, 10 September 1930, 3. © Axel Springer AG. Used with permission.

wash. . . . Only the party that speaks with the voice of civic reason (*staatsbürgerliche Vernunft*) gets my vote.[39]

Particularly when it came to extremists of the left and right, *Tempo* constructed a distinct separation between egoistic, self-serving politicians trying to

---

39. Heaven, "Der Wähler denkt," *Tempo*, 8 September 1930, 3.

fire up the masses for their own benefit, on the one hand, and the wider population of hard-working, honest citizens, on the other, who wanted nothing more than to live a decent life in peace and harmony. In his guise of "the voter," "Heaven" repeatedly described politicians as promising the electorate the moon as long as voters ticked their box on the ballot. After Election Day, they then were quickly forgotten: "I know that, come next Sunday, I'm not a big man anymore, but a small, insignificant object that nobody pays attention to. I will have cast my vote, and without a vote I will return to being a mere shadow, only to be resurrected in time for the next election."[40] With this pronounced image, *Tempo* differentiated between detached and calculating parliamentarians and the German people, who embodied the real democratic instincts of the country. "The voter," as a representative of the rational electorate, was confident in his political convictions, unmoved by modern propaganda methods and immune to the sound of extremist Pied Pipers: "Don't think you can catch me with catchphrases. Don't think you can influence or even change what I think and feel by screaming at me or by chalking up the walls."[41] On the day before the election, "Heaven" included the whole population in this distinction between self-interested, rabble-rousing functionaries and the stoic, level-headed population: "They have underrated us voters. Did they think we are asleep and it would be necessary to wake us up by making a violent racket? It is childlike and childish to think a party would get even one vote more by chalking up the walls and disrupting traffic."[42] For the contemporary reader, the reference to illegal campaign methods and particularly to the slogan "Germany, wake up!" (*Deutschland erwache!*) were a thinly veiled swipe at the Nazis.

Women and young men in particular were described as part of this reasonable electorate. In an article on women's politics of the far-right parties, Charlotte Pol mocked the Nazis' reactionary ideology as a crude mixture of anti-Semitic and misogynistic fairy tales.[43] On the same page was an article about a speech by Katharina von Kardorff, a prominent DVP politician and feminist, laying out "the women's politics of the liberal center."[44] The intent of these articles and their placement was evident: to show *Tempo*'s female readers that

---

40. Heaven, "Der Wähler denkt," *Tempo*, 8 September 1930, 3. See also Heaven, "Der Wähler denkt," *Tempo*, 2 August 1930, 3; 5 September 1930, 3; 7 September 1930, 3.
41. Heaven, "Der Wähler denkt," *Tempo*, 2 August 1930, 3.
42. Heaven, "Der Wähler denkt," *Tempo*, 13 September 1930, 3.
43. Charlotte Pol, "'Nur die entsittliche Frau kämpft um Frauenrechte'," *Tempo*, 11 September 1930, 3.
44. G. W., "Katharina von Kardorff spricht," *Tempo*, 11 September 1930, 3.

the centrist parties were the only real choice for them. The youth was addressed in a similar fashion. A few days before Election Day, *Tempo* again called for a greater role for young people in politics.[45] The majority of Weimar's youth, the article implied, were firmly integrated into German postwar society and eager to contribute to it.

Tempo's optimism and its hope for the voters' support for reason and democracy were dealt a serious blow by the results of 14 September 1930. The NSDAP emerged as the strongest political force after the Social Democrats and, while Brüning stayed in power, political liberalism was roundly rejected by the voters: the DStP only gained a disappointing twenty seats in the new Reichstag, five less than the DDP's abject result in 1928; the DVP even lost fifteen seats.[46] The *Vossische Zeitung* interpreted this outcome as a "debacle of the center" that should worry "the whole of Germany's middle class."[47] Though *Tempo* was more optimistic, announcing a victory for Brüning on its front page, the shock and disappointment about the Nazis' gains was palpable in the rest of the issue.[48] In a report on the feverous atmosphere of election Sunday the National Socialist victory was called "a rude 'awakening'" for Germany and the author marveled about the fact that people just went to work on Monday despite the nation having turned radical seemingly overnight.[49] The idea of a unified liberal movement as a bulwark against rising extremism had also been discredited by the poor results in southwest Germany, where the DVP and the DStP had run on a collective list.[50] The only good news was the high circulation of 250,000 copies *Tempo* enjoyed on the day after the election, its highest-ever daily print run, a fact the paper advertised in bold letters on the inside pages.[51] While this sudden jump in printed copies was restricted to this day, the heated political climate continued to boost *Tempo*'s popularity, and by the end of 1930, its circulation reached an average of 145,450 copies printed each day between October and December.[52]

---

45. C. Enseo, "Schrei der Jugend," *Tempo*, 10 September 1930, 3.
46. Milatz, *Wähler und Wahlen*, 126–35.
47. M. R. (i.e., Max Reiner), "Sieg des Radikalismus," *Vossische Zeitung*, 15 September 1930, 1.
48. "Regierung bleibt!," *Tempo*, 15 September 1930, 1.
49. "Die Nacht nach der Wahl," *Tempo*, 15 September 1930, 3.
50. "Gewinne und Verluste," *Tempo*, 15 September 1930, 1–2.
51. "*Tempo* heute ¼ Million Auflage," *Tempo*, 15 September 1930, 4.
52. *Ullstein-Berichte*, January 1931, 4. The average circulation was always calculated for the past three months, so Eksteins is wrong in stating that *Tempo* reached this number in early 1931, see Eksteins, *Limits*, 122. The *Ullstein-Chronik* reported *Tempo*'s highest-ever monthly circulation of 153,011 in October 1930.

In the immediate aftermath of the election, Weimar's liberal establishment interpreted the shocking result as a protest vote, a desperate reaction by the population to economic hardship and a criticism of traditional parliamentarianism.[53] While Hitler and his movement had mostly been dismissed and belittled before 1930, the liberal press now engaged in an intensive exploration of this political phenomenon.[54] In an effort to make sense of the results, many liberal observers blamed young people, women, and white-collar workers for the swing to the right. For example, in his analysis of the election the sociologist Theodor Geiger saw the "ideological confusion" of the new middle class and "the stronger emotionality of the woman" as the most important factors that contributed to the Nazis' success.[55] Subsequent research has cast doubt on this contemporary assessment, but *Tempo* accepted it as fact: the paper noted that particularly women and the youth, the groups the paper had put most faith in and that it had been courting since its foundation, had supported extremist parties.[56] The paper further explained the NSDAP's astonishing success and the disastrous performance of the DStP with a demoralized middle class clinging to false promises.[57] For the anonymous author of the article, the high number of middle-class Nazi supporters was a worrying sign of the dissolution of the German bourgeoisie, the traditional seat of liberal values of citizenship and rationality. The despair of the ideologically and financially bankrupt petty bourgeoisie, the article argued, had made them susceptible to the Nazis' grand promises and their mass hypnosis:

> In their desperation, the petty bourgeoisie—crushed and pulverized economically, with their spirit broken and not really interested in politics—ran to the people who promised them a miracle, the miracle of the "Third Reich" or any other empty catchphrase. . . . It was a late consequence of the war, of the inflation, of the development of the social order in general: to be neither hammer nor anvil, but the piece of iron between them, being

---

53. Eksteins, *Limits*, 238–46.
54. Fulda, *Press*, 163–66; Eksteins, *Limits*, 203–05.
55. Theodor Geiger, "Panik im Mittelstand," *Die Arbeit* 7, no. 10 (1930): 647–52.
56. "Die Frauen radikal," *Tempo*, 15 September 1930, 2, "Hoffnung auf Wunder," *Tempo*, 15 September 1930, 3. For the voting behavior of women, young people, and white-collar workers, see Jürgen W. Falter, *Hitlers Wähler* (Munich: C.H. Beck, 1991), 136–37, 146–54, 230–42. See also Jürgen W. Falter, "'Anfälligkeit' der Angestellten—'Immunität' der Arbeiter? Mythen über die Wähler der NSDAP," in *Die Schatten der Vergangenheit. Impulse zur Historisierung des Nationalsozialismus*, ed. Uwe Backes, Eckhard Jesse, and Rainer Zitelmann (Berlin: Ullstein, 1992), 265–90.
57. "Hoffnung auf Wunder," *Tempo*, 15 September 1930, 3.

pounded flat. It has to be said, the National Socialists knew how to mold them.[58]

The significance of the September election as a watershed moment for the political culture of the Weimar Republic can hardly be overstated. After the shocking results, most liberal newspapers underwent a major swing in editorial policy: an increasingly ineffectual Reichstag led many liberal journalists to abandon their vision of a democracy built around a strong parliament, favoring a more centralized rule that would replace the Western-style "party state" (*Parteienstaat*) with a form of plebiscitary dictatorship.[59] Most papers grudgingly lent their support to Brüning and even accepted the rule by emergency decrees as a necessary evil that might override parliament, but still reflected the democratic will of the people in the person of the directly elected president. *Tempo* was no exception: in multiple articles, the paper expressed its support for Brüning, interpreting the chancellor's continuing reliance on Article 48 as necessary in order to finally introduce a better voting system that would stop the parliamentary fragmentation and make majority governments possible again.[60]

After the shocking results of the election, *Tempo* began to have doubts about an overtly rational style of politics. Weimar's weak republican culture, the paper claimed, lacked the emotional punch offered in other democratic nations such as France and the USA.[61] The symbolic significance of the storming of the Bastille, celebrated by the French every year on 14 July, was much more powerful than Weimar's Constitution Day, it conceded. The reason lay in the utter hopelessness that had sparked Germany's revolution: there had been nothing left to be stormed in Germany in 1918, *Tempo* claimed. The monarchy had made itself redundant and the nation had to be rebuilt from the ground up, starting with the Constitution. The paper also pondered the claim that Weimar was a "republic without republicans," that parts of the German population still had not warmed to the new state and supported it for purely rational rather than emotional reasons.[62] It might be true that Weimar's founding fathers and mothers had been too idealistic in shunning the emotionality and grandiosity culti-

---

58. "Hoffnung auf Wunder," *Tempo*, 15 September 1930, 3.
59. Sösemann, *Ende*, 66–91; Eksteins, *Limits*, 216–18.
60. C. Enseo, "Worte statt Männer," *Tempo*, 16 September 1930, 3; C. Enseo, "Nun gerade, Herr Brüning!," *Tempo*, 19 September 1930, 3; C. Enseo, "Ohne Reichstag regieren?," *Tempo*, 24 September 1930, 3.
61. P.f.v., "Unser Pech mit Nationalfesten," *Tempo*, 18 January 1931, 3.
62. C. Enseo, "Vernunft-Republikaner und Gefühls-Monarchisten," *Tempo*, 18 February 1931, 3.

vated under the monarchy, *Tempo* argued. The efficiency, competence, and *Sachlichkeit* that characterized Weimar's democratic institutions rarely provoked strong emotions, but the promise of the new state could still win people over. If the republic managed to bring about social unity in Germany, something the monarchy had never been able to do, then it would also win the people's hearts, the paper concluded.

Two weeks after the election, *Tempo* had recovered its optimism and, in an emotional call to all parties in Brüning's coalition to bury the hatchet and save the country from its turmoil, it stressed that the time had come to act decisively:

> We do not want to exaggerate things and to join the chorus of those who see nothing but the end. That does not help us to make progress. Calling SOS will not save us in such a situation. There is nothing to do but grit one's teeth and get going. It is always *doing* that will save us, not just good will.[63]

The anniversary of Stresemann's death in October was a welcome opportunity for *Tempo* to reiterate its support for the Republic. Stresemann's foreign policy successes, the paper claimed, had always been based in his strong belief in the democratic experiment at home:

> The victory of the democratic idea in Europe means progress and peace for Europe. The precondition for this state is democracy in your own country—nobody was more aware of this than Stresemann. Never was the need greater to profess to this faith and to live by it than today, a year after his death.[64]

However, *Tempo*'s hopes that Brüning would fill Stresemann's boots were soon disappointed. At the end of the year, the government launched a sustained attack on the freedom of the press, which included putting increasing pressure on Ullstein—and *Tempo* was the government's main target. The paper had long been a nuisance to the chancellor, and in a cabinet meeting on 3 September 1930, he bitterly complained about press reports on internal government messages that had been leaked to Ullstein papers.[65] One of the articles that espe-

---

63. C. Enseo, "Fünf vor zwölf!," *Tempo*, 29 September 1930, 3.
64. "Stresemann," *Tempo*, 3 October 1930, 3.
65. BArchL, R 43 I, 1446, fols. 199–208.

cially enraged Brüning was a report in *Tempo* about a conflict between ministers Julius Curtius and Gottfried Treviranus.[66] A few weeks later, the defense ministry filed a lawsuit for treason against *Tempo*'s editor-in-chief, Gustav Kauder, and its political editor, Josef Reiner. According to the ministerial correspondence, *Tempo* had published inside information about the so-called Amlinger case leaked to Kauder by retired high-ranking officers.[67] The young officer Amlinger had been killed on 20 August 1930 in a plane crash in Russia, bringing to light a secret collaboration between the Reichswehr and the Red Army.[68] The defense ministry first insisted that Amlinger had died in an accident during a horse race, but the affair took a dramatic turn after his widow killed herself by jumping out of a flying plane shortly after Amlinger's death, citing in her suicide note her wish to die like her husband. Only twelve years after the end of the First World War, these revelations about German military operations in cooperation with the new Bolshevik state attracted considerable attention in the international press, which explains the heavy-handed reaction by the German government.[69] According to the defense ministry, the information revealed by *Tempo* was also used as a reason for "anti-German attacks" in the French Chamber of Deputies.[70] The lawsuit against *Tempo* would have been very inconvenient for Ullstein at this time of economic crisis and the company's internal chaos. But after the September election and the momentous shift in Weimar's political landscape, it became a serious liability.

In the power vacuum left by Franz Ullstein and Bernhard in the aftermath of the "Ullstein affair," new people moved into positions of influence at the company. Julius Elbau, Bernhard's long-standing, unobtrusive deputy, became editor-in-chief of the *Vossische Zeitung*, while Louis Ullstein's son Heinz, a man far less sympathetic to the liberal ideals of the older generation and who even sympathized with Otto Strasser's leftist variety of National Socialism,

---

66. "Konflikt Curtius—Treviranus," *Tempo*, 2 September 1930, 2.
67. BArchL, R 43 I, 688, fols. 246–50. The files refer to an article headed "Fragen an die Reichswehr," published on 14 September 1930, see BArchL, R 43 I, 688, fol. 249. However, *Tempo* was not published that day, as this was a Sunday. There are no articles with this title in any of the surviving *Tempo* issues. However, the paper did publish long front-page reports on the Amlinger case, see "Russland und Reichswehr. Zur Tragödie Amlinger," *Tempo*, 29 August 1930, 1; Georg von der Lippe, "Reichswehr und Russland," *Tempo*, 30 August 1930, 1.
68. Manfred Zeidler, *Reichswehr und Rote Armee, 1920–1933. Wege und Stationen einer ungewöhnlichen Zusammenarbeit* (Munich: Oldenbourg, 1993), 171–207.
69. Zeidler, *Reichswehr und Rote Armee*, 278–82.
70. "Gutachten," 11 February 1931, in BArchL, R 901/27361, fols. 13–14.

gained more influence over editorial policy at the company.[71] In October, former DDP finance minister Peter Reinhold joined the Ullstein supervisory board.[72] Reinhold was a well-known Democrat and an experienced newspaperman. Before his political career, he acted as publishing director and editor-in-chief of the *Leipziger Tageblatt* and had cofounded the publishing house Neuer Geist, a home for pacifist writers like Kurt Hiller and Friedrich Wilhelm Foerster.[73] After he resigned from his post in 1927, he had spent some time teaching at American colleges.[74] In short, he fit perfectly into the liberal tradition and Americanophile spirit of the Ullstein house. Still, under these men, commercial considerations finally gained the upper hand over editorial independence at the company. Critical or unruly editors were bullied by the new management: in November 1930, Heinz Ullstein relieved *Tempo*'s well-respected film critic Hanns G. Lustig from his duties after Germany's biggest film production company, Universum Film AG (Ufa), had complained about his articles, a decision that caused outrage among German journalists.[75] In December, the SPD journalist Eugen Prager decried the depoliticization of the Ullstein press: "They are getting rid of every opinion that could hurt the sales of the company's publications."[76]

Despite the dispiriting developments on the national stage and behind the scenes of the Ullstein house, *Tempo* provided an optimistic outlook on the coming year at the end of 1930. It printed excerpts from Brüning's official New Year's message to the nation, in which he called on the German people to join the constructive development of the new state, alongside interviews with Henry Ford and Carl Duisberg, chairman of the Reich Association of German Industry, who both painted a cautiously optimistic picture of a coming recovery.[77] An accompanying cartoon provided a—tongue-in-cheek, yet hopeful—script for 1931:

> The big turnaround has happened. . . . Taxes are refunded retrospectively from 1897. Peace has returned to Parliament. Hitler gives [SPD leader

---

71. Eksteins, *Limits*, 191; Koszyk, *Deutsche Presse 1914–1945*, 254; Heinz Ullstein, *Spielplatz meines Lebens. Erinnerungen* (Munich: Kindler, 1961), 282–93, 314–19. For Heinz Ullstein's meeting with Otto Strasser, see Schäffer diary, 15 August 1932, in LBI, AR 7177/MF 512, 10, Nr. 3, fols. 748–57.
72. See the note in *Zeitungs-Verlag*, 11 October 1930, 10.
73. "Reinhold, Peter," in *Reichshandbuch*, 2:1505.
74. "Reinhold, Peter," *Reichshandbuch*, 2:1505.
75. Heinz Pol, "Ullstein und Ufa," *Die Weltbühne*, 29 September 1931, 477.
76. Eugen Prager, "Zusammenfassung der Arbeit!," *Mitteilungen des Vereins Arbeiterpresse*, 1 December 1930, 2.
77. "Und 1931 . . . wird es besser?," *Tempo*, 31 December 1930, 1–2.

Carl] Severing a tender kiss. Goebbels is awarded the Nobel Prize for Humility. . . . The Nazis roam the streets handing out donuts and a giant loudspeaker shouts from the Radio Tower: Happy New Year!!![78]

However, the hopes *Tempo* invested in 1931 were not rewarded, as the new year brought new problems for the Ullstein house and the Weimar Republic. Shortly after he had taken up his new duties at the company, Reinhold was approached by the government and asked to rein in the Ullstein papers.[79] According to Hermann Pünder, state secretary and head of the Chancellery, he bowed to the pressure. On 2 January 1931, Pünder wrote to Defense Minister Wilhelm Groener to inform him that Reinhold had repeatedly lobbied Brüning to withdraw the pending lawsuit against *Tempo*. The chancellor was in favor of granting the former minister's wish, Pünder explained, as his new employers were now backing the government: "We have to admit that the Ullstein company is more and more supportive of the current government and will remain that way in the future, thanks to Minister Reinhold's influence."[80] However, both Groener and the éminence grise of the Reichswehr, General Kurt von Schleicher, were unwilling to let *Tempo* off the hook. On 8 January, Pünder reported to Brüning that both men feared being attacked by the Nazis for meddling in a pending lawsuit in favor of a defendant accused of treason, which otherwise would surely end in a conviction. The defense minister had been under pressure himself since the Ulm Reichswehr trial in September 1930, a high-profile court case involving three young officers accused of treason for spreading National Socialist propaganda and plotting to overthrow the Republic.[81] During the trial, the officers had accused Groener of following a "leftist course."[82] In a carefully worded reply to Groener, Pünder again stressed the recent compliance of the Ullstein papers and suggested, as long as the company promised continued support, postponing or prolonging the judicial proceedings, so the damning verdict would not hit Ullstein "at this politically very unfortunate moment."

The *Tempo* case shows how deeply the Nazi gains had unsettled Weimar's

---

78. Charlie Roellinghoff and Ferdinand Barlog, "Drehbuch zum großen Tonfilm 1931," *Tempo*, 31 December 1930, 5.
79. Eksteins, *Limits*, 233–34.
80. For the following, see BArchL, R 43 I, 688, fols. 220–47.
81. For a detailed account, see Peter Bucher, *Der Reichswehrprozess. Der Hochverrat der Ulmer Reichswehroffiziere, 1929–1930* (Boppard: Boldt, 1967).
82. William Mulligan, "The Reichswehr and the Weimar Republic," in *Weimar Germany*, ed. Anthony McElligott (Oxford: Oxford University Press, 2009), 97.

political establishment. The Ullstein management was prepared to abandon editorial independence to prevent a conviction for treason that would reflect badly on the company in a political climate that was increasingly characterized by fervent nationalism, while the defense ministry and the Reichswehr were at pains not to appear negligent toward such an apparently unpatriotic publication. Thus, even Pünder's suggested compromise fell on deaf ears. On 17 January, Groener refused to withdraw the lawsuit for "legal and national-political (*staatspolitische*) reasons." Furthermore, the defense minister explained, he did not have the feeling that *Tempo* was really toeing the government line as Pünder had suggested and the Ullstein management had promised. In the court hearing on 6 January, Kauder had stated that the paper's coverage of the Amlinger case was rooted in his personal political convictions and that he considered "even a merely strategic cooperation with Bolshevism" as political suicide. This, Groener remarked, did not sound like support for government and Reichswehr policies. On the contrary, Kauder's defiant stance, he argued, characterized *Tempo*'s coverage as a whole. In an earlier note to foreign minister Curtius, Groener had already explained what he thought of Kauder and his ilk. Dropping the charges in connection with the Amlinger case against *Tempo*, the *Berliner Tageblatt*, and other papers, he argued, would without doubt be very harmful for Germany's national defense interests. The ruthless application of the criminal law was the only effective means in the fight against such "deserters and traitors."[83]

While Ullstein was entangled in the *Tempo* lawsuit, Germany was struck by an unprecedented economic disaster. In July, the deepening crisis turned into an acute financial breakdown, when the Danat-Bank, the nation's second largest credit institution, went bankrupt. For *Tempo*, the event was one of the three great crises, after the military collapse in 1918 and the hyperinflation of 1923, that had rocked Germany since the end of the war.[84] The paper's coverage of the Constitution Day celebrations in August 1931 reflected the tense mood. There were no jubilant articles on the front page, only a photo of Hindenburg in the president's box in the Reichstag, among the members of the cabinet.[85] In an accompanying op-ed on the inside pages, *Tempo* discussed the Constitution and Weimar's republican culture.[86] A legal text might be a rather abstract symbol that did not easily rouse people's emotions, the paper con-

---

83. Groener to Curtius, 16 January 1931, in BArchL, R 43 I, 688, fol. 249.
84. "Die Art der Krise und woher sie kam," *Tempo*, 13 July 1931, 2
85. "Verfassungsfeier im Reichstags-Plenarsaal," *Tempo*, 11 August 1931, 1.
86. C. Enseo, "Reform zu noch besserer Verfassung," *Tempo*, 11 August 1931, 3.

ceded. Furthermore, the abuse of the Constitution's elements of direct democracy by extremists of the left and the right had shown that it was too idealistic in places.[87] Thus, the Constitution had to be reformed to become "even better." Particularly after 1930, the issue of "constitutional reform" was a keyword of antidemocratic forces from the left and the right, used to attack the foundations of the Republic.[88] Their aim was to transform Weimar's crisis-ridden democratic system, and overcoming the "obstacle" of the Constitution was to be the first step. In contrast to *Tempo*'s vehement defense of the Constitution before, the paper now cautiously acknowledged some of the criticism.

While the nation was rocked by economic disaster, things had quieted down at the Ullstein house. On 30 March 1931, the Ullstein brothers had formally reconciled and Franz had been reinstated as chairman of the board.[89] However, the economic and political situation had changed fundamentally since the affair had unfolded and the management continued to put pressure on editors who seemed to harm Ullstein's commercial interests. This simmering power struggle between the editors and the management quickly came to a head: after Lustig's demotion in the previous year, the *Vossische Zeitung*'s left-leaning film critic Heinz Pol left the company in September after he had been asked by Elbau to tone down his reviews in order to appease Ufa.[90] Controlled by DNVP chairman Alfred Hugenberg, the film company had canceled its advertisements in the *Vossische Zeitung* as a reaction to Pol's polemical tone. The government also continued to put pressure on Ulstein: although Brüning, with the emergency decrees issued over the course of 1931, had considerably expanded his power to impose costly bans on recalcitrant publications, the company's papers still were a constant source of annoyance to the chancellor.[91] In particular, the regular publication of classified material and secret cabinet meetings were, in Brüning's view, undermining government attempts to steer the country into safer waters. On his behalf, Hans Schäffer, state secretary at the finance ministry, contacted several Ullstein editors, including Elbau, Otto

---

87. In 1928, the German Communist Party had initiated a referendum against the construction of a new battleship and in 1929 right-wing forces, including the DNVP and the NSDAP, had initiated a referendum against the Young Plan; see Jung, *Direkte Demokratie*, 67–146.

88. Christoph Gusy, "Selbstmord oder Tod? Die Verfassungsreformdiskussion der Jahre 1930–1932," *Zeitschrift für Politik* 40, no. 4 (1993): 393–417.

89. "Erklärung," *Vossische Zeitung*, 30 March 1931, 1.

90. "Skandal bei Ullstein," *Welt am Abend*, 12 September 1931, unpaginated; Pol, "Ullstein und Ufa," 482.

91. For Brüning's press laws, see Fulda, *Press*, 169–202.

Robolsky, editor-in-chief of Ullstein's *Berliner Morgenpost*, Franz Höllering, editor-in-chief of the *B.Z.*, and Josef Reiner, *Tempo*'s political editor, in order "to find a way to avoid the publication of incorrect reports and news about secret matters in the future."[92] While the editors agreed to consult the government before the publication of politically sensitive material in the future, Schäffer was not able to bring them behind government policy:

> It was not exactly easy to make these gentlemen commit to the general accord to confer with me before they print such news in their papers in the future. Even after I promised to be available day and night, there were still some who were skeptical if such an agreement could be put into a workable practice. They feared to lose out against other newspapers, with which such a gentlemen's agreement did not exist, and that their freedom of speech will be compromised.[93]

While Elbau quickly agreed to act as "the government's paladin" at the Ullstein house, Höllering proved more difficult.[94] It was the job of the press to control government, he told Schäffer, and it was not at all clear if Brüning would not soon be forced by Hindenburg and others to follow a line his paper could not support. While some of the company's journalists put up a fight against government interference, the Ullstein management continued to exert pressure on its own editorial staff. On 8 December 1931, an internal circular advised Ullstein's senior editors, including Elbau, Robolsky, Höllering, Reiner, and the *Vossische Zeitung*'s political editor, Carl Misch, that "economic hardship and political tension" increased the danger of damaging backlashes to any "errors of judgment" on their side.[95] Thus, the memo continued, the editors should advise their staff that the newspapers had to be kept out of the political fray and to focus on objective information for a wide audience:

---

92. Schäffer to Brüning, 14 November 1931, reprinted in *Quellen zur Geschichte des Parlamentarismus und der politischen Parteien*, ed. Karl Dietrich Bracher et al. (Düsseldorf: Droste, 1959–), third series: the Weimar Republic (1980), 4/2:1097. In a cabinet meeting on 11 November 1931, Brüning had complained about the ongoing coverage of false or classified information, see R 43 I, 1166, fols. 124–29. See also Schäffer diary, 10–12 November 1931, in LBI, AR 7177/MF 512, 9, Nr. 17, fols. 1009–17.

93. Schäffer to Brüning, 14 November 1931, 1097–98.

94. Schäffer diary, 11–12 November 1931, in LBI, AR 7177/MF 512, 9, Nr. 17, fols. 1014–17.

95. Dr. Wolf to Robolsky, Höllering, Elbau, Misch, Goetz, Josef Reiner, Dr. v. Müller, 8 December 1931, in BArchL, N2193 Misch, Nr. 13, fol. 70.

It is not the job of *B.Z.*, *Tempo* or *Montagspost* to actively take part in the political struggle. . . . Their coverage is supposed to inform the audience about political programs and events objectively and in accordance with the republican and social principles of our house. The coverage must not be of aggressive or hurtful character or attempt to support any parties or groups. These papers are meant to offer a broad audience the opportunity to inform themselves objectively about the latest events.[96]

When individuals or companies were the subject of any critical articles, the memo concluded, they should be published only after the attacked parties had time to reply, and under no circumstance should the overall character of the Ullstein papers be defined by negative stories about crime and similar "affairs." In the case of tabloid papers sold on the street, such as *Tempo* and *B.Z.*, sensationalist and tendentious headlines were also discouraged, even if they boosted sales.[97] Ullstein now went so far as to incur losses in sales in order to avoid fanning the flames of political conflict. However, this call for a more restrained and optimistic tone did not seem to have much impact: a few days later, another circular was sent to all senior editors, urging them again to rein in their staff and to tone down their papers' coverage.[98] This time, the reason for the calls for more restraint was spelled out: according to the memo, the economic threat of newspaper bans by the government put the whole company in grave danger.

With these circulars, the management had drawn a line in the sand. Only a few days later, they showed that they were prepared to sacrifice anyone who crossed it. On 14 December 1931, *Tempo* and *B.Z.* published reports on Hitler's secret plans to form a Nazi aviation corps. In its investigative report, *Tempo* warned of the establishment of a private air force by the Nazis and the undermining of national aviation organizations.[99] The *B.Z.* article implied that the Defense Ministry condoned the Nazis' plans.[100] Such an attack on the government, at a time when one of the company's publications was involved in an ongoing lawsuit for high treason, proved to be a step too far. According to Höllering, Groener was furious and "a high official of the publishing house"

---

96. Wolf to Robolsky et al., 8 December 1931, in BArchL, N2193 Misch, Nr. 13, fol. 70.
97. *Ullstein-Chronik*, 1931, unpaginated; Wolf to Robolsky et al., 8 December 1931, in BArchL, N2193 Misch, Nr. 13, fol. 71.
98. Unsigned circular, 12 December 1931, in BArchL, N2193 Misch, Nr. 13, fols. 106–8.
99. "Wozu braucht Hitler Flugzeuge?," *Tempo*, 14 December 1931, 1. For the following, see also Fulda, *Press*, 189–90; Eksteins, *Limits*, 236–38.
100. "Hitler organisiert ein Fliegerkorps," *B.Z. am Mittag*, 14 December 1931, 1.

warned him that he had to "learn how to make compromises."[101] After Höllering refused, he was removed as editor-in-chief. His successor at the *B.Z.*, Fritz Stein, was appointed only after consultation with the government, and in a letter to Brüning, Stein promised to redirect the Ullstein papers to the path of "responsible political thought and action."[102]

After Höllering's dismissal, Carl von Ossietzky, the highly regarded *Weltbühne* editor, launched a blistering attack against Ullstein: "The Höllering case is another sad milestone in the demise of a great liberal-democratic publishing house."[103] Ossietzky seemed to be well informed about the internal dispute at the Ullstein house, and he argued that the circulars that the management had sent to the editorial staff in December were a farewell to the company's traditional liberal course. Instead of using their newspapers to put up a robust fight against the antidemocratic forces undermining the Republic, Ullstein tried to please everybody, from the Nazis to the Communists, for fear of losing readers and revenue. Under the rule of Heinz Ullstein—"[a] blasé young man without respect for people, ideas, hard work or accomplishments"—the *Vossische Zeitung* had shed its international reputation, the *B.Z.* had lost its attitude and colorfulness, and *Tempo* was threatened with being discontinued completely, Ossietzky warned.[104] To him, it was clear who benefited most from this situation: Ullstein's purge of any overtly political content was "the most scandalous capitulation to National Socialism" of Weimar's liberal press yet.[105]

The question of how to deal with the Nazi phenomenon had indeed caused intensive soul-searching among the company's leaders after 1930. *Tempo* had increased its coverage of Nazi activities even further after September, not only owing to the party's success in the election but also to a number of high-profile court cases that made headlines in the following weeks and which Hitler used with great effect to attract attention. On 25 September 1930, the Nazi leader appeared as an expert witness in the Ulm Reichswehr trial, in which he infamously promised that "heads will roll" when the Nazis were in power; a day later, the murderers of the late Sturmabteilung (SA, stormtroopers) member Horst Wessel were sentenced to six years in prison in a separate case. *Tempo* attacked Hitler vigorously, following the proceedings closely and spiking its

---

101. Franz Höllering, "I Was an Editor in Germany," *Nation*, 5 February 1936, 152.
102. Fritz Stein to Brüning, 19 December 1931, in BArchL, R 43 I, 2480, fol. 106.
103. Ossietzky, "Der Fall Höllering," Die Weltbühne, 5 January 1932, 1.
104. Ossietzky, "Der Fall Höllering," 5.
105. Ossietzky, "Der Fall Höllering," 5.

reports with barbs against him and his followers.[106] The paper also began a long-lasting feud with Joseph Goebbels, the party's regional leader in Berlin at the time. In November, some of the paper's informants infiltrated a secret party meeting in Berlin and reported about Goebbels's promises of a coming Nazi-led government. As interior minister, *Tempo* quoted him, he would send the SA to torture editors of critical newspapers, while drivers of foreign-made cars would be beaten up.[107] When one of the paper's contributors, the left-liberal journalist Walter Oehme, published a study of the Nazi movement, *Tempo* quoted on its front page the parts in which Goebbels was described as a disfigured "Mephistopheles of the party."[108] Goebbels was furious about the paper's sustained attacks. In his diary, he recounted a meeting on 13 January 1931 with Oehme, who had been sent to interview him for *Tempo*.[109] However, Goebbels had only agreed to the meeting to lure the journalist into a trap. Once Oehme was inside the party headquarters, the Nazi leader proceeded to shout at him until stormtroopers threw him out on the street again. In the meantime, the windows of Oehme's car had been smashed. The attack was not mentioned in *Tempo*, but the paper directly took on Goebbels in June, when it reported on a Nazi solstice ceremony planned at the city's Grunewald racetrack.[110] According to the paper's investigation, any outside party using the stadium had to commit to raising the Republic's flag, a condition the Nazis had accepted by signing a contract with the authorities. The event was subsequently canceled and Goebbels denied ever committing to such an agreement, a claim *Tempo* countered by reprinting the signed contract on its front page.[111] When the SA opened a new tavern called "Tempo" in Berlin's Schöneberg district in August, the paper did not miss the opportunity for a dig at Goebbels, wondering if reading *Tempo* would now become compulsory for Nazis in the capital.[112]

For the company management, the popularity of National Socialism was no laughing matter, however. It had become increasingly clear that many of Ullstein's readers sympathized with the Nazis despite the traditional liberal-

---

106. See, for example, "Hitler: 'Köpfe werden rollen.'," *Tempo*, 25 September 1930, 1–2; C. Enseo, "Hitlers Eid," *Tempo*, 26 September 1931, 3.

107. "Goebbels in Geheimsitzung," *Tempo*, 4 November 1930, 1. Goebbels denied the claims, see "'Aus dem Zusammenhang gerissen.' Dr. Goebbels berichtigt," *Tempo*, 5 November 1930, 2.

108. "Goebbels-Biographie," *Tempo*, 13 December 1930, 2.

109. Joseph Goebbels, *Die Tagebücher*, ed. Elke Fröhlich (Munich: Sauer, 1998–2008), vol. 2, pt. 2 (2005), 321–24.

110. "Nazi-Sportfest unter Reichsflagge," *Tempo*, 19 June 1933, 1.

111. *Tempo*, 23 June 1931, 1.

112. "Tempo ist Nazi-Pflicht," *Tempo*, 12 August 1931, 3.

democratic ethos of the company's papers.[113] Losing a sizeable portion of its audience in the midst of the most severe economic downturn in modern history only to retain the moral high ground by continuing to ridicule and attack Nazi voters did not seem to be a plausible option. For a company that had always considered the will of the people as the most important reflection of democracy and had seen as its calling serving the demands of the widest possible audience, this was also a complicated moral conundrum. Ullstein had always stressed national unity, tolerance, and peaceful coexistence as the bedrock of democracy and prosperity, and the increasing radicalization, shrillness, and violence that characterized Weimar's political culture was a grave threat to this vision. Joining the political in-fighting would not only hurt the company commercially but also pour oil onto the fire of political conflict, national disunity, and ideological hatred that seemed to rage on Germany's streets.

The Ullstein management did not seem to have a straightforward solution for this problem, urging their editors both to take National Socialism seriously as a political movement and not to overstate its real strength, while retaining as much of Ullstein's liberal tradition as possible. In the general confusion about the nature and the real aims of the movement, Hermann Ullstein even considered a return of the monarchy as the best way to counter the Nazis' popularity.[114] In the immediate aftermath of Höllering's dismissal, an internal memo warned that overly zealous or sensationalist coverage of Nazi activities played into Hitler's hands.[115] A call by the Nazi leader for trained pilots among his party faithful did not amount to the creation of a private air force, the memo explained. On the contrary, such supposedly secret files were often leaked on purpose to boost coverage, creating a distorted view of the real strength of the Nazis: "By focusing on such news, the politically inexperienced reader will easily be led to the conclusion that the Hitler movement is growing every day and that the leader of the National Socialist party is the next big thing."[116]

However, not just Ullstein, but the whole of the liberal press was on the back foot and many newspapers also struggled with the problem of readers sympathizing with the Nazis. Thus, the gradual erosion of civil liberties, including the severe curtailment of press freedom that had set in with Brüning's minority government and intensified after its resignation in May 1932, was by and large accepted without much resistance.[117] In part, this was owed to the

113. Ullstein, *Rise and Fall*, 183.
114. Schäffer diary, 28 June 1931, in LBI, AR 7177/MF 512, 10, Nr. 13, fol. 620.
115. Unsigned memo, 18 December 1931, in BArchL, N2193 Misch, Nr. 13, fols. 74–76.
116. Unsigned memo, 18 December 1931, in BArchL, N2193 Misch, Nr. 13, fol. 75.
117. Eksteins, *Limits*, 241.

fact that the alternative, a Nazi-led government, promised even harsher retrenchments, but such authoritarian policies also seemed to be supported by a majority of the readership. The strain of a rapidly deteriorating economic climate had started to force many newspapers to gradually abandon their traditional educational mission in order to placate their readers, who seemed to increasingly favor more conservative politics and an authoritarian style of government.[118]

Consuming against the Crisis: *Tempo*'s Vision of a German Consumer Society after 1930

At the same time, *Tempo* stepped up its positive spin on the Republic's economic performance. In the week before the general election in September 1930, *Tempo* ran a series of articles on Germany's economic crisis by eminent scholars, politicians, and businessmen titled "When Will It Get Better?"[119] Each article took up nearly the whole business section and was announced prominently on the front page. All experts believed that, despite the hardship, the end of the crisis was near and that the nation had the strength to pull through. As the title implied, for *Tempo* it was not a question of whether or not things would ever get better, but when. With its timing, just days before the election, the series was an unmistakable pledge for the Republic and the status quo. The nation's most pressing problem, rising unemployment, was addressed with a short series of articles that focused on the problems of white-collar workers, *Tempo*'s targeted readership.[120] The liberal value of individual responsibility and the optimistic idea of the possibility of changing one's fate were fundamental to *Tempo*'s worldview: the paper believed that unemployment was not primarily a problem of political or economic processes, but of individual agency. In contrast to many contemporary observers, *Tempo* did not blame rationalization for the high unemployment in this sector, but the inability or unwillingness of individual workers to keep up with modern times. Assembly line work or the handling of complicated business machines was only exhausting and degrading if employees kept to their traditional work patterns and ignored new, more modern modes of work, the author argued. There

---

118. Bosch, *Presse*, 35; Eksteins, *Limits*, 247–58.
119. "Wann wird es besser?," *Tempo*, 6 September 1930, 4; 8 September 1930, 6; 10 September 1930, 6; 13 September 1930, 6.
120. "Unser größtes Problem: Die Arbeitslosigkeit," *Tempo*, 18 July 1930, 3.

were still plenty of jobs for flexible workers willing to learn a new language or how to drive a car.[121] Furthermore, the increasing popularity of credit purchase and paying by installments boosted the demand for clerks with experience in debt collection, the series concluded cheerily.[122] With the right attitude, the paper implied, every citizen could do his or her bit to counter economic hardship.

More than through hard work and a go-getter attitude, however, Germans could solve the crisis through being good consumers, *Tempo* contended. To drive home this point, the newspaper's touting of a modest consumer society and of consuming as a value grew more urgent during the crisis. The "Technology Everybody Needs" series, although appearing less frequently, kept promoting the purchase of electrical appliances and other consumer products, stressing their continued affordability. In an installment presenting new film projectors for home use, *Tempo* hailed the new product as making the expensive technology "attainable for the smaller budget."[123] Whenever an electrical appliance was introduced, the column now mentioned its low power consumption. For example, a new bug zapper, lauded as introducing a new, modern way of killing insects with the hygienic force of electricity, was described as using only "undetectably small amounts of energy."[124] The way *Tempo* described even appliances as mundane as an electric insect killer both as symbols of a modern lifestyle and affordable purchases sent the clear message that Weimar's promise of prosperity survived even during the economic crisis. In its coverage of the 1931 International Broadcasting Exhibition in August, the paper focused on new, even more affordable radio sets that promised better technology at half the price.[125] The car remained the most important symbol for prosperity in *Tempo*. In April 1930, the paper introduced a weekly, full-page motoring section that loudly advertised the automobile as an attainable consumer good. In the first installment, an article argued that the view of the automobile as a luxury was "completely wrong."[126] On 6 June 1930, an article broke down the considerable costs of buying and maintaining even a compact car in a way that showed that it only cost 2.5 pfennings per passenger per kilometer a year—

---

121. "Arbeiter noch gesucht—aber ein neuer Typ," *Tempo*, 21 July 1920, 3.
122. "Die Angestellten—am schwersten getroffen," *Tempo*, 23 July 1930, 3.
123. "Technik, die jeder braucht," *Tempo*, 14 January 1930, 4.
124. "Technik, die jeder braucht," *Tempo*, 18 July 1931, 3.
125. Eduard Rhein, "Empfangs-Geräte billiger!," *Tempo*, 1 August 1931, 6; Eduard Rhein, "Kleiner, billiger—aber noch verbessert," *Tempo*, 21 August 1931, 2.
126. "Motorrad oder Kleinauto," *Tempo*, 26 April 1930, 4.

arguing that having a car was "absolutely not a luxury."[127] In fact, the author claimed, owning a car was akin to a civic duty:

> From a macroeconomic perspective, the automobile supports goods turnover, profit, and progress in every respect. The more automobiles a country has, the faster is its turnover of goods and the lower are costs of transportation—thus, the more competitive the country will be on the world markets. The owner of an automobile does more for this raising of general prosperity than the one who does not use an automobile.

The shocking results of the election in September only intensified this. In October, an article in the new section predicted the imminent introduction of a "people's car" (*Volksauto*), an affordable compact car for everybody.[128] The only obstacles, the author argued, were still overregulation and high taxes.

Tempo's optimistic outlook was not justified at all. At the end of the year, the number of unemployed stood at over three million and the average salary had started falling, while the German auto industry experienced a serious slump, with overall production and sales of private cars dropping significantly from its high point in 1929.[129] However, *Tempo* was not interested in such facts, but in raising its readers' consumer morale. In fact, the paper's editors clearly believed that generating optimism among their audience by putting a positive spin on economic reality was the only way to solve the crisis. For *Tempo*, consumers played a central role in stimulating the economy and creating jobs. When the Brüning government urged the population to tighten their belts in these austere times, *Tempo* reacted furiously, arguing that abstinence from worldly pleasures would create even more unemployment: "If the people who have money to spend cut back even more than they are doing already, other people will earn even less."[130] In December, *Tempo* warned its readers of the dangers of an overly pessimistic outlook, which would only deepen the crisis. The basis of any economic improvement, the paper argued, was optimism:

> We must make optimism fashionable as soon as possible. . . . It is wrong to assume that the economy only consists of or is even created by numbers. Rather, the whole economy rests on incalculable causes that have no

---

127. Walter Dette, "Der Kleinwagen—das Auto für alle," *Tempo*, 6 June 1930, 7.
128. K. J-z, "Statt Führerschein—Fahrschein!," *Tempo*, 23 October 1930, 4.
129. Hans-Ulrich Wehler, *Deutsche Gesellschaftsgeschichte* (Munich: Beck, 1987–2008), 4:260; Edelmann, *Luxusgut*, 129–30; Overy, "Economic Recovery," 468–75.
130. P.f.v., "'Übermaß' an Vergnügen?," *Tempo*, 30 October 1930, 3.

real names, but only a collective term: mood. The numbers we deal with in economics are just the ultimate summary of this moving force. They are its expression, but not its root. The root is always the mood.[131]

A few weeks later, the paper again urged its audience to focus more on the little pleasures of life, such as "a stimulating evening in the theater, a more or less funny joke, a book that distracts us from our worries for a few hours."[132] Such positive thinking, *Tempo* argued, was something that could—and should—be learned, even in the face of economic crisis and escalating political violence.

Tempo's insistence on an upbeat, optimistic tone as the solution to the downturn was grounded in the economic theory guiding the political principles of the Ullstein house. When the Great Depression hit Germany in 1930, two approaches to consumer culture—the traditional paternalistic view of reining in consumption and the American-inspired vision of a consumer-driven economy—informed opposing plans of how to counter the crisis.[133] The Brüning government followed strict austerity policies that included severe cuts in salaries and wages and higher taxes on many consumer products such as cars, tobacco, and beer to drive down Germany's deficit and boost exports.[134] Others, like Anton Erkelenz, one of the DDP's founders, who had left the party after its fusion with the Jungdeutscher Orden, called for stimulating consumer spending to support the ailing economy.[135] This debate, which foreshadowed today's discussions about austerity politics, was not confined to Germany. It was waged in most countries suffering from the Depression, with John Maynard Keynes emerging as the most prominent advocate of countercyclical spending. Ullstein was a vocal representative of the Keynesian camp. The management strongly believed that the blame for the economic slump lay in part with scared investors and consumers. In the *Ullstein-Berichte*, the company repeatedly appealed to businesses to be optimistic and start investing again. Some of Ullstein's high-profile journalists, such as Otto Robolsky, the editor-in-chief of the *Berliner Morgenpost*, took to the pages of the public relations publication to call on managers not to rely on the government or American loans for a resuscitation of the economy, but to create demand for their products themselves.[136]

Naturally, Ullstein's appeals to kick-start the economy were also moti-

---

131. C. Enseo, "Die Gefahr der schlechten Stimmung," *Tempo*, 5 December 1930, 3.
132. Heaven, "Nachtseiten des Lebens," *Tempo*, 28 January 1931, 3.
133. Torp, "Janusgesicht," 263–66.
134. Büttner, "Alternativen," 211–17.
135. Torp, "Janusgesicht," 264; Büttner, "Alternativen," 235–38.
136. Otto Alfred Robolsky, "Kurble selber!," *Ullstein-Berichte*, July 1931, 1–2.

vated by self-interest. Just like the rest of the press, Ullstein's publications were dependent on advertisements, and by 1931 these revenues had declined by 50 percent compared with the industry's high point in 1928.[137] However, *Tempo*'s continued advertising of a consumerist lifestyle even in times of severe economic crisis also sprang from a concern for the survival of Germany's liberal democracy. Its editors believed that stimulating private spending would lead the ailing Republic out of its crisis. At the end of 1930, *Tempo* published an excerpt of an article by Keynes, in which the economist explained the importance of consumer spending in combatting the worldwide crisis and warned of the political consequences of austerity measures, leading to "agitation, unrest and revolution."[138] For German liberals, who had only recently lived through a revolution sparked by widespread destitution during the war, this prospect was alarming. For people at the Ullstein company, who had experienced firsthand the consequences of civic unrest when their headquarters were occupied by Spartacist forces in January 1919, the specter of another revolution was particularly menacing. Using *Tempo* as their bullhorn, they spread the message that consumption was fundamentally political and an integral part of democratic citizenship.

A few weeks later, in January 1931, *Tempo* explained how its readers could act as good citizens and help with the stimulation of the economy and thus the stabilizing of the state—they had to spend their savings.[139] After the hyperinflation of 1923 had wiped out their savings, the paper claimed, all Germans had become cautious spenders. Now over ten billion marks had accumulated in their savings accounts, while five million people were unemployed in the country. Thus, everybody had to start spending to create jobs for their fellow citizens, the paper concluded. To make its audience spend their money, *Tempo* intensified its advertisement of consumption over the course of the year, with the car still as the central symbol of consumer modernity. Weeks before the annual motor show in Berlin, *Tempo* again alluded to the coming "people's car," this time singling out the costly driving license as an obstacle to mass motorization.[140] In its coverage of the exhibition itself, it declared that the car had finally evolved from luxury good to basic commodity.[141] At the sight of these affordable automobiles, *Tempo* claimed, Berliners

---

137. Eksteins, *Limits*, 222.
138. "Wir haben einen Maschinendefekt. Worte zur Krise von John Maynard Keynes," *Tempo*, 22 December 1930, 6.
139. Ludwig Eberlein, "Soll man jetzt sparen?," *Tempo*, 28 January 1931, 3.
140. G.G., "Dem Volksauto den billigen Führerschein," *Tempo*, 5 February 1931, 4.
141. Stephan von Szénásy, "Zwei Hallen voll Autos in der eröffneten Schau am Kaiserdamm," *Tempo*, 19 February 1931, 4.

went "car-hungry" or even fell into the grip of a "car virus"—in short, the whole city was "car-crazy:"

> As soon as the common man arrives at Kaiserdamm, he is under the spell of the exhibition, he catches the fever, runs like a madman from booth to booth, eagerly collects and hoards prospectuses that will later rob him of his sleep, wants to know about everything, from the six-cylinder engine to the cigarette lighter.[142]

Even President Hindenburg, the paper contended, admired the new compact cars on his official visit to the exhibition, and would have taken one for a spin if only his entourage would not have kept such a watchful eye on him. The common people, on the other hand, threw all financial caution overboard. One particularly beleaguered seller even had to be sent to a mental hospital at the day's end because of the stress of fielding overly eager buyers, the article continued. *Tempo* quoted one exalted car salesman who claimed that the motor show had finally set free the restrained power of the consumer:

> At long last, we have our self-confidence again. The whole vitality of all classes, producers and consumers, which has been stockpiled and held back in an unnatural fashion, is now breaking free. We might get ahead of ourselves here, but only optimism can save us. Hopefully, the auto industry will have given the push in the right direction.

Even if there were people who could not yet afford a car, it was only a matter of time, *Tempo* concluded, because every visitor to the motor show had caught the "car-bug." The paper also lauded the increased attention paid to women this year, as their influence on the purchase of cars was supposedly becoming ever greater.[143] In the following months, in the many anecdotes and short stories usually scattered across the paper, the car featured as a desirable investment despite the economic downturn. In one example, the author's grandfather defies all her warnings about the insecure times and rushes off to buy a used car; in another one, the author openly confesses her "car-envy."[144] The writer Eva Boy assured her readers that "a car doesn't really cost that much," while regular contributor Polly Tieck wrote a poem on the "elated feeling" of driving

---

142. B.R., "Berlin ist auto-wahnsinnig," *Tempo*, 23 February 1931, 4. The quotes in the following paragraph are all from this article.
143. "Frauen in der Ausstellung," *Tempo*, 19 February 1931, 4.
144. Yvonne Kraehe, "Auto-Neid," *Tempo*, 11 May 1931, 8; Mala, "Ausgerechnet heute?," *Tempo*, 29 July 1931, 2.

an automobile.[145] In advertisements by car manufacturers appearing in *Tempo*, the automobile's status of a luxury item was now suppressed, while the durability and economic fuel consumption of their products were stressed.[146] Women were often portrayed as the pioneers of consumption. In an article about the upcoming summer sales, Lucy von Jacobi described how women "will do their utmost" to find ways to spend their family's money—not irrationally and on useless junk, but methodologically and with a plan.[147] The yearly sales were presented as "women's days of battle" (*Kampftage der Frau*), the time when they could do their bit for society. For example, a used compact car—which "almost belongs to the prerequisites of life"—was had for as little as 200 marks, according to Jacobi.

The other aspects of *Tempo*'s vision of prosperity—leisure culture, weekend life, and vacations—also still featured prominently in the paper despite the economic crisis. Berlin's entertainment industry was an early victim of the economic downturn, after many people had cut down on their leisure expenses. *Tempo* followed the crisis of Berlin's nightlife with upbeat articles about its resilience, reporting on plans for new establishments that proved that "Berlin as an entertainment city is alive!"[148] It vigorously defended the city's entertainment industry when the Brüning government criticized people spending money on supposedly nonessential leisure: "Outside of the city, they talk of Berlin and its amusements with that sort of envy that cloaks itself in moral outrage. . . . [But] cheerfulness is an essential part of life, just as food and clothing."[149] In a special report, the newspaper painted an image of an irrepressible industry weathering the storm through "the extraordinary optimism of its leaders, their vigorous language, their rational (*sachlich*) demands."[150] Despite this crisis, *Tempo* continued to portray dancing and nightlife as a central element of Berlin's leisure culture, for example with a long-running series introducing the latest ballroom dances.[151]

The same was true for holidays and weekend breaks. Just as in the years

---

145. Eva Boy, "Der Deckel vom Benzintank," *Tempo*, 27 May 1931, 7; Katta Launisch (i.e., Polly Tieck), "Autofahren," *Tempo*, 23 June 1931, 7.
146. See the advertisements in *Tempo*, 18 September 1930, 3; 11 May 1931, 9; 27 August 1932, 3.
147. Billie (i.e., Lucy von Jacobi), "'Preis-Sturz.' Vorschau auf den Ausverkauf—Die Kampftage der Frau," *Tempo*, 31 July 1931, 4.
148. P.S., "Berlin wieder Vergnügngsstadt," *Tempo*, 29 August 1930, 6.
149. P.f.v., "'Übermaß' an Vergnügen?," *Tempo*, 30 October 1930, 3.
150. "Die Not bedrängt das Vergnügen," *Tempo*, 29 January 1931, 5.
151. Riccardo de Luca, "Tanzen Sie mit!," *Tempo*, 30 January 1931, 5.

before, there were various articles in the paper that simply described weekend and holiday life, painting an idyllic picture of white-collar leisure undeterred by current events, political turmoil, or economic crisis. Polly Tieck contributed a poem in which the secretary "Lieschen Lassdas," a prototype of Weimar's female white-collar work force who appeared regularly in her texts, enjoys a day sailing in her humble skiff, only shortly dreaming of owning a luxury yacht before realizing that real happiness is only found in the simple pleasures of life.[152] In an ironic report about a weekend on the shores of one of Berlin's many lakes, not even a grim Nazi arriving in his kayak—"like Lohengrin on the swan"—is able to put a damper on the sun-filled scene.[153] This idyllic image was underpinned by many photographs of happy scenes of leisure and recreation, mostly of young, healthy, female holidaymakers (Fig. 21).

During the Easter weekend of 1930, *Tempo* reported the numbers of vacationers leaving Berlin and out-of-towners visiting the city as front-page news, reporting on an allegedly "giant stream to and from Berlin."[154] During the summer months, the paper ran many articles with handy suggestions of possible destinations, complete with train connections and ticket prices. However, the destinations had become humbler: instead of exotic spots on the Mediterranean, *Tempo* now advertised holiday locations in Germany, such as the Riesengebirge or the forests of Brandenburg.[155] At the same time, the advertisements of the Ullstein travel agency that often accompanied *Tempo*'s articles on holiday destinations now stressed its reduced prices.[156] *Tempo* reprised its holiday snap competition in 1930 and 1931, albeit in a humbler format. The amount of the cash prizes was reduced, and the overall prize was scrapped. The technical details of the used camera type and, most importantly, the democratic element of readers choosing their favorite photo were dropped. There were still photos from exotic locations, such as Morocco and the exclusive French spa Juan-les-pins, and from holiday spots all over Germany, but photographs of people enjoying their free time at home and in the city's green belt dominated. In contrast to 1929, most people submitting a photograph were located in the more well-to-do parts of Berlin, such as Halensee, Steglitz, and Grunewald, which suggests that many readers living in less affluent districts could not afford to go on holidays or even to maintain camera equipment any longer.

---

152. Lieschen Lassdas (i.e., Polly Tieck), "Kleiner Kahn," *Tempo*, 8 July 1931, 5.
153. G.W., "Wo die Badehose herrscht," *Tempo*, 1 July 1931, 3.
154. "Reisestrom aus und nach Berlin," *Tempo*, 19 April 1930, 1.
155. See, for example, "Wanderung durch den Blumenthal," *Tempo*, 4 July 1931, 3; "Wochenende im Riesengebirge," *Tempo*, 22 July 1931, 3.
156. See the advertisement in *Tempo*, 12 June 1931, 6.

Figure 21. "Sonne, See, Sand und Schweben," *Tempo*, 6 September 1930, 4. © Axel Springer AG. Used with permission.

Figure 22. "Kamera-Glück in den Ferien," *Tempo*, 15 August 1931, 6. © Axel Springer AG. Used with permission.

Most of the subjects were still young, happy Berliners, but some showed a certain defiance in enjoying the summer holidays despite the hard times. For example, a photo chosen as the weekly winner in August 1931 showed a couple lying in a small tent, with the caption "There is room even in the smallest weekend chalet" (Fig. 22). However, the overall tone of the winning photos expressed joy and the happiness of life during the summer months.

These articles often blurred the boundaries between editorial content and advertisement—not for a particular company or product, but for consumption itself. They sent a clear message: a prosperous lifestyle was still attainable in Weimar Germany, even under harsher conditions. Furthermore, by spending their savings, Germans could make an active contribution to the long-term stability of the economy, and thus of the new state itself. Yet *Tempo* could not ignore the fact that the economic downturn had made most durable consumer products and organized leisure even less affordable for many Germans. The paper sometimes directly addressed the strained situation of its readers, which had put the promises of consumer society even further out of reach. However, such articles often put an optimistic spin on this cut in living standards, such as the upbeat tale of two young sisters who, after their father announces that their summer holiday had to be canceled, go on a hiking tour through Germany instead, with a daily budget of fifty pfennigs, defying the tough times with pluckiness and youthful ingenuity.[157] *Tempo* also began to paint an even more conciliatory picture of white-collar life. One of the most remarkable examples is an anecdote told by Tieck's "Lieschen" character. When she notices her boss's mended socks while taking a dictation, the revelation that her superior is not above such frugality seems to level the social gulf between them and make him more humane:

> He had a wonderful car, a beautiful house, two very well-behaved children and a pretty wife. But all of this was very far from my own life. I didn't have any of this and would never have it. But mended socks I had. . . . With these mended socks I suddenly shared something with my boss. He was like you and me, accessible, understandable; he had the same worries as us.[158]

A few days later, another text painted a happy ending for "Lieschen" herself. Just a while ago, the character mused in the article, she had been working long hours as a shop assistant in a big department store, but now she was a married woman who could afford to shop in the very same places she used to work in.[159] With such romanticized versions of white-collar life, *Tempo* offered a vision of modest prosperity and happiness even in times of crisis and, most importantly, of peaceful coexistence of people of all classes.

---

157. A. and F. Basolt, "Ferien-Reise für 50 Pf. täglich," *Tempo*, 13 July 1931, 7.
158. Katta Launisch (i.e., Polly Tieck), "Lieschens versöhnliche Geschichte," 12 June 1931, 7.
159. Lieschen Lassdas (i.e., Polly Tieck), "Lieschen und der Lauf der Welt," *Tempo*, 16 June 1931, 7.

However, despite its enduring optimism, *Tempo*'s vision of a prosperous German democracy changed after 1930, most significantly in regard to its American model. For many Germans, the deep economic crisis that had gripped the United States and that had swept over the Atlantic seemed to expose the country's prosperity and modernity as nothing but a myth—an "*Amerikalegende*."[160] In a well-received book published shortly before he left *Tempo* and Ullstein for *Die Tat*, Ferdinand Friedrich Zimmermann even predicted the "End of Capitalism," which was foreshadowed in the economic crisis of the United States.[161] American economic principles, he argued, were not suited to German traditions. The disappointment with the American dream was also evident in *Tempo*. While the newspaper still displayed much interest in the "American way of life," its reporting now also featured hordes of unemployed people roaming the streets.[162] Texts such as the letter of a German emigrant who complained about the "prosperity scam" in the United States or the excerpt from a new study on "the exposed paradise" of the US economy illustrate the newspaper's bitter disillusionment with the American dream.[163] Manfred Georg even called for an end to the "Americanization" of German culture:

> We aped the Americans in many things: we had competitions for the fastest-drinking babies, records in pole-sitting and the whole fuss about any kind of "celebrity." ... We have to put an end to this inflation of the so-called "celebrities," which is an inflation of the mind itself.[164]

The American economy, Georg argued in another article, was based on an "unproductive, predatory capitalism" that had finally been exposed as "the most dangerous and craziest form of economic anarchy."[165] Even Arthur Rundt, the translator of the American novel *Show Girl* that had been serialized in *Tempo* in 1928, had lost his enthusiasm for the United States. In his introduction to the flapper girl Dixie Dugan, Rundt had sung the praises of modern American womanhood; now, he railed against America's economic model that

---

160. Klautke, *Unbegrenzte Möglichkeiten*, 315–24.
161. Ferdinand Fried (i.e., Ferdinand Friedrich Zimmermann), *Das Ende des Kapitalismus* (Jena: Diederichs, 1931). See also Klautke, *Unbegrenzte Möglichkeiten*, 320–21.
162. Yosa Morgan, "Die Melodie von New York," *Tempo*, 8 July 1931, 7.
163. A.W.L., "Brief eines U.S.A.-Arbeitslosen," *Tempo*, 27 May 1931, 2; A. E. Johann, "Das entlarvte Paradies," *Tempo*, 27 June 1932, 6.
164. M.g. (i.e., Manfred Georg), "Falsche Prominenz," *Tempo*, 19 June 1931, 5.
165. Manfred Georg, "Untergang am Überfluss," *Tempo*, 2 August 1932, 6.

seemed like a bad example for Germany, characterized by rampant capitalism, excessive rationalization, and an overly specialized population.[166]

Technology vs. the Soul: *Tempo*'s Discourse of Technology and Speed after 1930

Despite the fall from grace of its American model of prosperity, *Tempo* still believed that modern technology would be the decisive means to achieve a German consumer society. However, the paper no longer saw technological progress as an absolutely positive force, but as something that had be tempered and kept in check. In sharp contrast to its earlier obsession with speed and modern technology, *Tempo* argued that exaggerated mechanization threatened the needs of the individual both as worker and consumer.[167] The paper even warned that "technology (meaning civilization) has left our soul (where culture is rooted) so far behind that we can only hobble helplessly after it."[168] The opposition of "Western" civilization and organic "German" culture had traditionally been espoused by German conservatives to underline their country's incompatibility with the supposed materialism and rationalism of France, Britain, and the United States.[169] During the First World War, this view of an alien "West" came to include the institution of liberal democracy.[170] The fact that *Tempo* now employed such views was not only a striking shift away from the paper's earlier vision of utmost modernity toward an ideal of a reconciliation of progress with tradition, but also a subtle distancing from a "Western" understanding of democracy. In contrast to its earlier image of technological progress as the driving force for individual comfort and international understanding, *Tempo* now linked it to national unity. In its coverage of the International Broadcasting Exhibition in 1931, which took place only days after Constitution Day, the radio was hailed for bringing the German people together during the dark times of the German banking crisis:

---

166. Arthur Rundt, "Die Wahrheit über Amerikas Krise," *Tempo*, 25 July 1932, 5.
167. "Aufstieg des Tüchtigen. Eine Warnung vor übertriebener Mechanisierung," *Tempo*, 19 January 1931, 6.
168. Rao, "Überspitzung der Technik," *Tempo*, 30 July 1931, 3.
169. Mark Hewitson, "The Kaiserreich and the Kulturländer: Conceptions of the West in Wilhelmine Germany, 1890–1914," in *Germany and "the West": The History of a Modern Concept*, ed. Riccardo Bavaj and Martina Steber (New York: Berghahn, 2015), 58–61.
170. Riccardo Bavaj and Martina Steber, "Introduction: Germany and 'the West': The Vagaries of a Modern Relationship," in Bavaj and Steber, *Germany and "the West"*, 17–20.

During those difficult days of July the radio fulfilled its most important mission. It unified the worried, long-suffering people into an alert parish and made us realize that nobody can stand apart in such an hour, that we are all bound in a community of fate (*Schicksalsgemeinschaft*).[171]

This shift in *Tempo*'s framing of technology was also reflected in a changing view of the speed of modern life. While the topic of an accelerated urban lifestyle was still discussed regularly in the paper, it was now frequently seen critically and contrasted with a more wholesome pace of life. More and more frequently, the paper published nostalgic photographs of scenes of supposedly idyllic village life surviving in the middle of metropolitan Berlin. One example, captioned "small town idyll on Potsdamer Platz," showed a brewer's drayman rolling a barrel over the nearly deserted intersection in front of the iconic traffic light (Fig. 23). In an article about anglers on Berlin's riverbanks, the author juxtaposed their patience with Berlin's hectic traffic:

All around cars are honking, brakes screeching, buses grinding, trams ringing, trains rolling.... Traffic of the metropolis. Tempo! Impatience! No time! The four men sitting on the banks of the Spree do not hear any of this. They are fishing. Unhurried, they pull up their rods from time to time, dip it in the water again, let the lines drift.[172]

At regular intervals, the author reported, the heavy traffic spits out an impatient urbanite, who watches them for a few moments until impatience with the lack of immediate results drives them on again. In the end, even the author cannot bear it any longer, as the fast pace of the city catches up with him: "I need to see results. The madhouse of the traffic, the tempo, the haste all around tests my patience.... I romp away."

Over the course of 1930 and 1931, under the pressure of political and economic crisis, *Tempo*'s vision of a German consumer modernity endured, but only in changed form. The ideal, embodied by the US, of the unity of prosperity, high technology, and Western democracy, slowly faded. It was gradually superseded by the image of a humbler, moderate, somehow more "German" consumer society—in other words, a consumer *Gemeinschaft*—that still promised a high standard of living, but was not individualistic, soulless, and overly rationalized. *Tempo*'s image of the agents of a German consumer modernity

---

171. "'Akropolis des Funks'," *Tempo*, 21 August 1931, 1–2.
172. Henio, "Angeln mitten in Berlin," *Tempo*, 30 June 1931, 3.

160　Moderate Modernity

Figure 23. "Kleinstadtidyll auf dem Potsdamer Platz," *Tempo*, 18 August 1931, 3. © Axel Springer AG. Used with permission.

changed accordingly. To German liberals, both young men and young women had lost much of their appeal as embodiments of progress after 1930, as both groups seemed to be in thrall to the Nazis. *Tempo* adapted the way it addressed these groups to reflect the transformed political landscape, but overall German youth played a diminished role in the newspaper's vision of Germany's future.

Citizen-Consumers during a Time of Crisis: *Tempo*'s Construction of Modern Masculinity and Femininity after 1930

With the results of the 1930 election, the hopes of many liberals of winning over Weimar's young middle class for their cause had been disappointed.[173] The experiment of the DStP, conceived as a rejuvenation of liberal politics and as a pro-democratic platform for the young generation, had failed spectacu-

---

173. Parts of this section have been published in Jochen Hung, "The Modernized Gretchen: Transformations of the 'New Woman' in the Late Weimar Republic," *German History* 33, no. 1 (2015): 52–79.

larly. On 7 October 1930, only a few weeks after the election, the Jungdeutscher Orden left the new party. In contrast, the NSDAP seemed to have attracted large parts of the youth: the party had benefitted especially from the high voter turnout of 82 percent, suggesting that many first-time voters had supported the party.[174] Research into historical voting patterns has challenged this analysis: not only was the overall amount of young voters too small to account for the enormous increase in votes for the NSDAP, but a comparison by age group even suggests that it was rather older voters who helped the party to its high gains.[175] Still, most contemporary observers—including *Tempo*—supported the view of a radicalization of the youth. Apart from the disillusioned middle class, *Tempo* argued a day after the election, "our young people, who were voting for the first time," had fueled the astonishing gains of the Nazis.[176] *Tempo*'s changed image of the youth was expressed most clearly in a quote by British novelist St. John Erskine, which the paper published, without further comment, under the heading "What Are Young People Really Like?":

> The most dangerous person in every society is the young man and the young girl bent on ignoring everything that happened in the world before their own birth. Indeed, there are many young people of both sexes who think the world was only created in 1918.... It is about time to talk about youth in a more sensible way. Nothing is more foolish than always talking about the kindness and noble-mindedness of youth. Young people are mean, cruel, and petty.[177]

This outspoken rejection of the idolization of young people that *Tempo* had practiced just a year before underlines the transformative effect of the election of September 1930. However, the way the newspaper adapted its image of Weimar's young white-collar workers differed remarkably between the two genders.

The idea of young men as a positive force for the future had lost much appeal for *Tempo* after September 1930. Increasingly, they appeared in the paper as adolescent radicals, dangerous louts, and a threat to Weimar democracy. When Chancellor Brüning was harassed by an angry mob on a visit to Chemnitz in January 1931, *Tempo* described the perpetrators as "very young

---

174. Büttner, *Weimar*, 265.
175. Falter, *Hitlers Wähler*, 146–54.
176. "Hoffnung auf Wunder," *Tempo*, 15 September 1930, 3.
177. "Wie ist die Jugend wirklich? Von St. John Erskine," *Tempo*, 18 August 1931, 3.

Nazis" and "unemployed Communists" acting in an "extraordinarily rude" manner.[178] These adolescent extremists, the paper warned, were "possessed by the same spirit that has brought misery upon Germany" once already by starting a disastrous war.[179] In August, after Communist demonstrations for the dissolution of the Prussian parliament led to riots, *Tempo* published a large photo of broken shop windows on its front page, captioned with the headline "This Is How Radical Adolescents Do Politics."[180] Even Berlin's teenagers, the "ice cream parlor youth" *Tempo* had defended so enthusiastically before 1930, were now described as threatening rowdies:

> Outside on the street, in front of the ice cream parlor, there is a pack of young people with their bikes, mocking passers-by and laughing when the victims reprimand them. They use dirty words of such a drastic quality that all pedagogues and teachers would be dumbfounded and have to admit the inadequacy of all educative paragraphs.[181]

Another shocking sign for the supposed seduction of Weimar's young middle-class men by the Nazis was the above-mentioned Ulm Reichswehr trial. The young officers in the dock all belonged to the age group born after 1900, who Zehrer had once labeled "baby-faced nobodies"; they had begun their military careers after the war and had been noted as exceptionally talented and ambitious, but were soon disillusioned by ossified hierarchies and the diminished role of the military in German society.[182] During the negotiations over the Young Plan in 1929, they turned to National Socialist organizations and, in the following months, developed plans to unseat the democratically elected parliament by "freeing the national spirit" of the Reichswehr. For *Tempo*, these young officers personified the threat of a radicalized young postwar generation, who were aiming for "the paralysis of the state as such."[183] The paper reported in detail on the case, quoting the statements of the defendants and prosecution each day of the proceedings over several pages.[184] *Tempo* pointed out that the officers showed no remorse and saw their actions as part of

---

178. "Brüning-Krawall in Chemnitz," *Tempo*, 23 January 1931, 1.
179. C. Enseo, "Ehre für Brüning," *Tempo*, 24 January 1931, 3.
180. "So machen jugendliche Radikale Politik," *Tempo*, 8 August 1931, 1.
181. Lizzy Fritz, "Vorgeschrittene Jugend . . . ," *Tempo*, 24 September 1930, 3.
182. Bucher, *Der Reichswehrprozess*, 15–37.
183. P.f.v., "Die Gefahr in der Reichswehr," *Tempo*, 25 September 1930, 3.
184. The coverage ran from 23 September to 4 November, with a front-page article nearly every day.

a war of liberation waged by the youth against a system dominated by the older generation that had squandered the nation's glory.[185] For "Heaven," this uncompromising radicalism did not represent "real" youth, but belonged to a bygone age that had been made obsolete by the course of history, and the officers' youthful inexperience had made them blind to their backwardness.[186] At the end of the year, *Tempo* published an article by Arnold Brecht, a former official in the Interior Ministry and highly respected defender of Weimar democracy, calling for a renewed attempt to win over the youth to the cause of the Republic. Young educated men had been excluded from public life and from careers in politics or administration, he warned, and it was no wonder they rejected the state their fathers had rebuilt after the war.[187] The *Reichswehrprozess* (Reichswehr trial) had shone a light on the deep rift between the prewar and postwar generations, he argued, and to secure Weimar's continued existence, a bridge had to be built between the two. However, a reply to Brecht's article from a young reader showed that *Tempo*'s initial vision of a modern, metropolitan, Westernized Germany was rejected at least by a part of its audience: "The German youth rejects America, its 'Girl' culture and the homogenization of life. The new forms of life that young people are striving for will be very down-to-earth and will be found outside the big cities."[188]

Such self-definitions by bourgeois, intellectual male youth became a prominent object of discussion after the election. While self-appointed spokesmen of the front generation such as Zehrer had dominated the debate before, now actual members of the postwar youth spoke up. These authors, who had not seen any active duty during the war themselves, constructed a military masculinity in peacetime that rejected liberal democracy and the liberal values of personal responsibility and individualism that *Tempo* had always touted as the foremost characteristics of the modern youth. In 1930, twenty-seven-year-old journalist Frank Matzke published a pseudo-philosophical manifesto in Reclam's *Junge Deutsche* series in which he defined the members of his generation as drawn toward collectivism, abandoning liberal notions of personal freedom:

> We see individualism ... neither as the goal of Creation, nor as progress, nor as the necessary foundation of every "culture and civilization." Rather,

---

185. "Die Angeklagten haben das Wort," *Tempo*, 2 November 1930, 2.
186. Heaven, "Der Offiziers-Prozess," *Tempo*, 30 September 1930, 12.
187. Arnold Brecht, "Was trennt junge und alte Generationen?," *Tempo*, 27 December 1930, 1–2.
188. Fritz Taeuber, "Eine Antwort der jungen Generation an Min.-Dir. Brecht," *Tempo*, 29 December 1930, 7.

we long for community, submission, and bonds.... We are prepared to be in submission to leaders. We feel only contempt for the small-minded nursing of the many vanities of the ego, so typical for the past, which made you believe that it was wrong to obey orders.[189]

His generation, Matzke claimed, fought against the relativism of the modern world and cultivated "an ethics of the soldier," who willingly subordinated himself to a greater good.[190] According to Matzke, one of the representatives of his generation was Paul Krantz, the young offender whom *Tempo* had dismissed in 1929 as an exception among male German youth.[191] A year later, twenty-seven-year-old sociologist Ernst Wilhelm Eschmann published a polemic about the role of the young generation in society, in which he directly rejected political liberalism and the idea of liberal democracy.[192] The institution of parliament, founded on liberal principles, no longer reflected the reality of German society, he claimed. Thus, middle-class (*bürgerlich*) youth had found other values: "The young generation has made the experience that authority, orders, loyalty and devotion can be sources of personal and social renewal."[193] In 1932, Ernst Günther Gründel, born in 1903, published his 460-page manifesto *The Mission of the Young Generation*.[194] In his much-discussed book, Gründel, who quoted extensively from Matzke's and Eschmann's publications, defined his "war youth generation," the age group born between 1900 and 1910 that had experienced the war only at the home front, as the pivotal group that was destined to overcome Germany's crisis, while Zehrer's "front generation," despite all their undeniable sacrifices, could only pave the way.[195] Gründel made it clear that only men were part of the "war youth generation," while women should only strive for fertility and motherhood. He dismissed Weimar's modern women as "emancipated viragos" and rejected the changed gender relationship in German society, holding up the conservative ideal of the "soulfully devoted woman" instead.[196]

---

189. Frank Matzke, *Jugend bekennt: So sind wir!* (Leipzig: Reclam, 1930), 80–83. For Matzke, see Siemens, "Kühle Romantiker," 193.

190. Matzke, *Jugend*, 95.

191. Matzke, *Jugend*, 48.

192. Leopold Dingräve (i.e., Ernst Wilhelm Eschmann), *Wo steht die junge Generation?* (Jena: Eugen Diederichs, 1931), 30–34.

193. Dingräve, *Wo steht die junge Generation?*, 30.

194. E. Günther Gründel, *Die Sendung der jungen Generation. Versuch einer umfassenden revolutionären Sinndeutung der Krise*, (Munich: Beck, 1933), 22–63. For Gründel, see Siemens, "Kühle Romantiker," 193.

195. Gründel, *Sendung*, 60.

196. Gründel, *Sendung*,136.

While the military masculinity constructed by these authors differed markedly from the modern man that appeared in *Tempo*, they too cited *Sachlichkeit* as the overarching characteristic of their male age cohort. They interpreted this trait mainly as a reaction to their cataclysmic experience of the destruction of the old bourgeois order during the war and the following chaos of revolution and inflation.[197] This materialistic *Sachlichkeit* manifested itself, according to the authors, in an affinity for technology and sports. Gründel, using almost the same terms as *Tempo* in its own manifesto from 1928, defined his generation as sober, unsentimental, flexible, and quick-witted, with a "pronounced sense for rational methods and for economic principles in general."[198] Despite speaking in generational terms, all three writers saw themselves as part of a small elite. They echoed Zehrer's argument that the majority of Weimar's young men was either willingly collaborating with the political establishment or belonged to the depoliticized masses, obsessed with American pop music, the latest dance craze, cars, and other consumer products. Such people, they argued, played into the hands of the older generations determined to hold on to the seats of power.[199] In contrast to Zehrer, however, who often characterized himself as spokesmen of his generation, the representatives of the younger national-conservative generation were acutely aware that they were only speaking for, and to, their own peer group. Eschmann was very outspoken about this fact:

> The people calling themselves the "young generation" today are from a very small circle among the still (relatively!) well-off upper middle class, whose normal career path in the political and economic institutions, predestined by their background, has been cut short for various reasons.[200]

A unified youth with a common political goal was, according to Eschmann, still wishful thinking and not an existing social entity yet.[201] They dismissed National Socialism as a political alternative, but all members of this circle nurtured the hope that the common experiences of deprivation, chaos, and national humiliation would transcend class barriers and unite the youth under their own leadership.[202] Zehrer's contradictory position as a paid employee of the liberal Ullstein house and an outspoken opponent of the Weimar state in *Die Tat* natu-

---

197. Gründel, *Sendung*,22, 81–85; Dingräve, *Generation*, 14–21; Matzke, *Jugend*, 41, 126–83.
198. Gründel, *Sendung*,85.
199. Dingräve, *Generation*, 53; Gründel, *Sendung*, 91.
200. Dingräve, *Generation*, 9.
201. Dingräve, *Generation*, 5.
202. Dingräve, *Generation*, 16; Gründel, *Sendung*, 40; Zehrer, "Ein Vorschlag," 125.

rally brought him into conflict with his superiors. In September 1931, he left Ullstein and fully dedicated himself to working for the journal.[203] In December, Ferdinand Friedrich Zimmermann followed, having been replaced by Alfred Oesterheld as *Tempo*'s economics editor.[204]

The ideas of the "war youth generation" and *Tempo*'s representation of the modern male as prudent, common-sense, optimistic, and respectful toward women were clearly aimed at the same audience, in a struggle to bring them into their respective political camp. However, after September 1930, *Tempo* retreated from this fight for Weimar's young middle-class men. Their situation was discussed less often, and when they were directly addressed it was often as representatives of the crisis that had engulfed the country. For example, starting on 1 December 1930, *Tempo* serialized the novel *Chronicles of a Gigolo* by British writer Arthur Applin. The story of Julian, a young paralegal who loses his job and is forced to earn his keep as a taxi dancer in glamorous clubs and bars, was advertised in the newspaper as "a very modern novel" that chronicled the life of a "rootless, modern youth."[205] The figure of the *Eintänzer*, the paid male dancer, played an important role in Weimar-era masculinities as a male counterpart to the ubiquitous showgirl character, embodying a "groomed and cosmetics-friendly" masculinity.[206] While the *Eintänzer* was often portrayed as being more aware of his exploited position than the "Girl," they equally represented, in their status as a commodity, the helpless situation of the modern individual in a cutthroat capitalist world. The fact that women exert power over him by paying for his dances—and, occasionally, sexual favors—also reflected male fears of an ambivalent gender relationship during the Weimar era. In this sense, the *Eintänzer* character, holding up the façade of male bourgeois respectability while being crushed by economic forces and social changes, embodied Weimar's young middle-class men's fears about a loss of social status. While Applin's story approached the topic in a humorous and romantic way, the central character still has to suffer multiple humiliations at the hands of predatory women. The fact that *Tempo* chose to serialize the novel in such a prominent spot shows that the newspaper's editors were well aware of these fears, but the

---

203. Demant, *Zehrer*, 24–27.

204. "Hausmitteilung," 15 March 1932, in BArchL, N2193 Misch, Nr. 13, fol. 72. Oesterheld's name appeared in the imprint on 17 November 1931. He was replaced by Kuno Ockhardt in 1932, see *Handbuch der deutschen Tagespresse*, 116.

205. "Allzu hübscher Junge. Tagebuch-Roman eines Gigolo," *Tempo*, 29 November 1930, 8.

206. Mihaela Petrescu, "Billy Wilder's Work as *Eintänzer* in Weimar Berlin," *New German Critique* 40, no. 3 (2013): 68.

story hardly provided any consolation or a counterweight to the military masculinity of the "war youth generation."

There were still voices in the newspaper defending the male youth against unfair generalizations about their radicalization, such as the reader who responded to *Tempo*'s damning article about the "ice cream parlor youth," arguing that the deterioration of traditional family life was to blame for this new phenomenon.[207] However, *Tempo*'s discourse of a rational, sober, constructive male youth had been replaced by a more suspicious stance toward young men, as they seemed to reject vehemently the paper's original vision of modernity as Western parliamentarianism, social equality, and urban cosmopolitanism. The paper did not make much of an effort to adapt its content to address this radicalized part of the male youth. However, it did change its strategy when it came to young female readers.

Tempo's image of women also changed significantly after 1930. After the September election, there was widespread prejudice among male observers that women, owing to their supposed emotionality and inexperience in politics, had overwhelmingly voted for the NSDAP.[208] Jürgen Falter has shown that the opposite was true: while the movement quickly gained popularity among female voters after 1930, many women had actually rejected the Nazis' violent campaign methods before then.[209] Nevertheless, the stereotype of fanatic female Nazi supporters, "acting almost hysterically to see 'their Adolf'" or disrupting prodemocratic meetings as "shriek troopers" (*Keif-Abteilungen*), instantly entered *Tempo*'s discourse about women in politics.[210] The change in the paper's depiction of femininity was expressed most strikingly in an article attacking the role of several female censors in a recent clampdown on antiwar films:

> This newspaper has always fought for the liberation of women and for women's rights.... However, what we fight against—together with every woman who really feels as such—are the recent beginnings of a "ladies' regiment."... We do not want older ladies to tell us what morals and good manners are, we want to decide it for ourselves. Nobody will understand that better than the millions of women, be they earning their own living or working in the one profession that every woman aspires to.[211]

---

207. Ejo, "Verteidigung der Eisdielenjugend," *Tempo*, 26 September 1930, 3.
208. Falter, *Hitlers Wähler*, 136–37.
209. Falter, *Hitlers Wähler*, 145–46.
210. "Hitler: 'Köpfe werden rollen.'," 1; Charlotte Pol, "Nazi-Frauen," *Tempo*, 5 February 1931, 3.
211. C. Enseo, "Damen-Regiment in Deutschland?," *Tempo*, 6 January 1931, 3.

The article is exemplary of *Tempo*'s conflicting approach to women after 1930. It clearly shows the rising fear of reactionary tendencies among them, which the male author tried to address—in a similar way to the paper's characterization of youth as a mindset—by effectively defining "real" womanhood as a political conviction. Most significantly, however, the article declared motherhood as the only female profession worth aspiring to—a definitive break from *Tempo*'s earlier focus on working women and glamorous "Girls."

Tempo's beauty contest of 1929 had already introduced a more moderately modern female type, and with the economic crisis this became the dominant image of femininity in the paper. By 1930, the glamorous "Girl" type had all but disappeared from *Tempo*'s pages. To be sure, the paper still rarely missed an opportunity to show photos of young, pretty women, but their presentation had changed considerably. Film stars such as Marlene Dietrich, Raquel Torres, and Camilla Horn were increasingly depicted not as independent, glamorous "Girls," but as caring mothers and housewives.[212] For example, Anita Page, one of the most famous film stars of the time, was shown sewing clothes, with a caption describing her "simple life" at home after work, sewing, washing, and cooking dinner (Fig. 24). If "Girl" archetypes, such as show dancers and models, appeared in the paper at all, they did so only as victims of the changed times. In Hollywood, *Tempo* reported, the introduction of sound film and changed tastes had left 5,000 "dance girls" jobless; in Berlin, hundreds of them were unemployed. The situation of the ones who still had a job was not much better, as the "oversupply" depressed wages and forced them to accept long hours with little pay.[213] The example of a former showgirl, whose skin and health had been ruined by cheap makeup and punishing working hours, exposed the dream of a glamourous career on stage as a fraud.[214] While the "Girl" had represented the promise of American-style consumer society before 1930, now it became a symbol for the economic crisis that seemed to engulf Germany and the rest of the world.

While the optimistic tone of 1928—when total gender equality seemed to be just around the corner and women were described as set to overtake men in all parts of life—had disappeared from the paper's image of feminin-

---

212. See, for example, "Zwischen zwei Aufnahmen," *Tempo*, 12 February 1929, 5; "Der langhaarige Filmstar: Camilla Horn," *Tempo*, 20 February 1929, 6; "Der Morgengruß," *Tempo*, 11 May 1931, 5; "Mutter und Kind," *Tempo*, 24 July 1931, 5.

213. See, for example, ps., "SOS: Girls in Not!," *Tempo*, 8 October 1930, 5; "8 Girls 15 Mark," *Tempo*, 22 October 1930, 5; "Elendes Leben oder: Krach in der Damenkapelle," *Tempo*, 1 August 1931, 5.

214. E. Th., "Nummernmädchen-Tragödie," *Tempo*, 8 November 1930, 3.

Figure 24. "Anita Page näht . . . ," *Tempo*, 9 January 1931, 5. © Axel Springer AG. Used with permission.

ity, *Tempo* still tried to present female role models that combined the fundamental achievements of the Republic in terms of women's rights with the more somber, austere mood of the early 1930s. The paper continued to criticize the attacks on female "double earners," defending women's work as a vital part of the economic process and trying to disprove the arguments against it as baseless.[215] Furthermore, abortion rights continued to play a prominent role in the paper. When Friedrich Wolf was accused of illegally administering abortions, *Tempo* called his arrest a scandal in a bold-lettered headline on its front page.[216] While the "Girl" might have been retired as *Tempo*'s role model, the paper's new image of femininity still retained modern features: the *Tempo* woman still went to the office and was still interested in buying cars, but now *Tempo* also included her role as mother, loving partner, and housewife. While Charlotte Pol had portrayed the young single women of 1928 as self-assured, independent urban travelers making "acquaintances" with men on their own terms, they were now described as "weekend brides," who organized their cautious contacts with men around their busy working life and their sincere interest in nature:

> "Weekend brides" are ordinary girls, who seek the company of an agreeable person of the same age. They enjoy Sunday trips to the countryside, because this meets their love of nature and the demands of their weekly working life. . . . A big part of our female youth is—fortunately!—very serious about their love of nature. To them, nature is often as important as their companion, and the "weekend" is more important to them than the state of being a "bride."[217]

In contrast to Pol's article, *Tempo* now mentioned the danger of pregnancy and urged women to take all precautions not to ruin their lives for such short-lived romances. Most significantly, despite the disappointment with an alleged radicalization of women, the paper continued to emphasize the central role of working women in society. One representative example was a series on craftswomen, in which Charlotte Pol described female glaziers, carpenters, butchers, and plumbers as determined pioneers slowly making inroads into traditionally male-dominated spheres, "taciturn, yet self-assured; simple, yet confident."[218]

---

215. "'Hinaus mit dem Doppelverdiener'," *Tempo*, 22 January 1931, 3; Charlotte Pol, "Doppelverdienerin—oder Doppelarbeiterin?," *Tempo*, 10 February 1931, 7.
216. "Der Skandal der §218-Verhaftung," *Tempo*, 21 February 1931, 1–2.
217. Jean, "Wie kommt man zu einer Wochenend-Braut?," *Tempo*, 28 August 1931, 3.
218. Charlotte Pol, "Weibliche Handwerker," *Tempo*, 27 October 1930, 3. For the rest of

The emergence of this image of modest, yet self-confident women, which had been introduced to *Tempo*'s visual vocabulary with Erna Koch, the winner of its beauty contest, was part of an international trend. Kristen Lubben has shown, for example, how the wholesome Amelia Earhart was built up by American media as the female type for the 1930s.[219]

As the popular vote for Erna Koch indicated, the paper's evolved image of the "modernized Gretchen" was arguably much closer to the everyday experiences of the majority of Germans than the glamorous "Girl" or the intellectual "Garçonne" had ever been, incorporating as it did both women's changed political and social status as well as persisting traditional values. A telling indicator for the contemporary negotiation process about the meaning of modern femininity that stood behind *Tempo*'s gradual change in its image of women is the column "Ask Frau Christine." Introduced on 2 August 1930, nine months after the Wall Street Crash of 1929 and six weeks before the general election in September, it offered advice on matters of the heart, professional life, and general problems of a personal nature under the name of the eponymous counselor "Frau Christine." Prewar women's magazines had featured similar sections called "letter box," acting as a forum for its readers, but *Tempo* was the first daily newspaper to introduce such a column and none of its competitors offered anything comparable.[220] The introduction to the series explicitly pointed out the continuing struggle over women's place in society in the late Weimar Republic:

> Letters regarding *the emotional turmoil of today's women and young girls* are particularly frequent among the replies we receive from our readers. This is easily understandable, considering how much the world has changed for women in particular. Old, established morals or prejudices have fallen victim to social change. New ones have developed but are still contested. This often leads to confusion. This is why we have asked Frau Christine, a colleague with much experience in life and knowledge of human nature, to give advice in such cases.[221]

Instead of painting the changes to women's role in Weimar Germany exclusively in a positive light as before, *Tempo* now acknowledged the conflicts they

---

the series, see *Tempo*, 1 November 1930, 3; 7 November 1930, 3; 11 November 1930, 3; 17 November 1930, 3; 26 November 1930, 3; 9 December 1930, 2.

219. Kristen Lubben, "A New American Ideal: Photography and Amelia Earhart," in Otto and Rocco, *New Woman International*, 291–9.

220. Föllmer, "Junge Frauen," 310.

221. "Fragen Sie Frau Christine," *Tempo*, 2 August 1930, 7.

caused in the daily lives of many women. While the new column was mainly aimed at a female audience, men were also expressly invited to write in about their problems. "Ask Frau Christine" was one of the most successful series in *Tempo*, regularly running every week and always taking over at least half a page. Soon, *Tempo* was advertised with explicit reference to the weekly column.[222] It is impossible to say whether "Frau Christine" was an individual person or a fictitious entity used by different editors answering the letters. However, *Tempo* supplied a photo of a younger woman working at a desk that led its readers to believe that this was no old-fashioned agony aunt, but a professional who knew about the problems of today's young women and men (Fig. 25). The 545 queries answered by "Frau Christine" over 153 weeks were sent in from all over the nation and even from Switzerland, Sweden, and Argentina. To be sure, these were only the letters published in the paper; regular announcements urging readers not to forget to add a return address for an individual written answer and notes calling on the writers' patience, as "the overwhelming flood of inquiries" made it impossible to answer immediately, suggest that the number of people who sought advice from "Frau Christine" was much greater.[223] To be sure, just like *Tempo*'s beauty contest, the weekly column was designed to attract readers to a commercial medium. Through the advertisements placed next to it, for services such as hairdressers and matchmaking agencies, as well as products such as slimming tea, vacuum cleaners, and "*Zuckooh* face crème for all young girls," it targeted women as a specific consumer group. The advertisers even explicitly used "Frau Christine" as a spokesperson for their products. For example, Nilfisk, a Danish producer of vacuum cleaners, claimed that "Frau Christine" was a "proud" owner of their product.[224] However, to some extent, the chosen letters had to be of interest for the widest audience possible to make the column interesting for advertising clients, and it thus gives a representative insight into the most common problems and opinions of *Tempo*'s female readership.

Most readers—over 70 percent—writing in to "Frau Christine" were unmarried or divorced, but other personal information, such as exact age, occupation, and social background, was often only hinted at in the letters. While the writers were mainly female, there was also a sizeable number of men among

---

222. See, for example, "Wir könnten eigentlich Frau Christine fragen," *Tempo*, 9 September 1930, 8; "Lesen Sie *Tempo* täglich," *Tempo*, 14 March 1932, 2.
223. "Fragen Sie Frau Christine," *Tempo*, 8 November 1930, 10; 1 October 1932, 8.
224. *Tempo*, 29 October 1932, 8.

Figure 25. "Frau Christine," *Tempo*, 6 September 1930, 10. © Axel Springer AG. Used with permission.

them: 219 male readers, around 40 percent of all published letters, asked for advice. Just half of all letters explicitly mentioned the age of the writer, but of these, over 50 percent were written by readers under thirty years of age, reflecting *Tempo*'s focus on Weimar's young working population. However, this also means that at least nearly as many were well outside this age group, and there were in fact letters from people up to the age of sixty—a surprising age for a reader of such a self-consciously youthful publication. Only eighty-nine of the 326 female enquirers expressly mentioned they were working outside the home at all, while many seemed to rely on their family or men for financial support, suggesting that even among *Tempo*'s readership, financially independent women were still a minority. The social background is the most difficult to gauge from the published letters, but there were many writers who clearly belonged to a white-collar environment, characterizing themselves as office workers or "lowly clerks." However, they did not form an overwhelming majority. Rather, most people were middle class in the widest sense: shopkeepers, housewives, entrepreneurs, academics, artisans and craftspeople, students and civil servants. There were also letters by working-class people and even upper-class and aristocratic readers, but these were exceptions.

Reflecting the relatively diverse background of the letter writers, the questions posed to "Frau Christine" were very wide ranging in their subjects. Apart from relationship guidance, people looked for advice on smoking etiquette, a neutral arbitrator to solve arguments about marital sleeping arrangements, or just a forum to share their exasperation about their partner's extreme enthusiasm for sports.[225] However, despite this variety, there are several overarching topics that can be gleaned from the letters. First, they reveal a deep uncertainty over the shifting gender relations of the time. Many letter writers experimented with new forms of relationships, such as cohabitation, dating, and "companionate marriage." The exact meaning of this concept did not seem entirely clear to *Tempo*'s readers: some interpreted it as a sexless marriage, some as strictly platonic friendships. But mostly this term was used for long-term relationships outside marriage or engagement, an arrangement some readers also called a "marriage of conscience" (*Gewissensehe*).

These new concepts of gender relations granted women a more active role and put the romantic partners on a more equal footing, but it is clear from the letters that these new forms were still far from socially accepted. Having a boyfriend—a long-term partner outside officially sanctioned relationships—seemed to be a common experience among *Tempo*'s female audience, but this was often a source of generational conflict. For example, a reader complained that her long-term partner was not invited to a family gathering, blaming the snub on her parents' "old bourgeois mindset" (*altbürgerliche Anschauung*) that clashed with her "modern opinions."[226] "Modern-ness" was used by many readers as an umbrella term for new ideas about gender relations, a phrase associated most with the young women who grew up unencumbered by prewar sentiments, such as an eighteen-year-old white-collar employee who regularly spent time with different men.[227] As Detlev Peukert has shown, this relative freedom and carefreeness among young people

---

225. "Fragen Sie Frau Christine: Liebe oder Sport," *Tempo*, 9 August 1930, 7; "Fragen Sie Frau Christine: Die Frau des Fußball-Enthusiasten," 27 December 1930, 10; "Fragen Sie Frau Christine: Das Ehebett," 5 September 1931, 6; "Fragen Sie Frau Christine: 'Bitte, ein wenig Feuer!'," 9 January 1932, 8.

226. "Fragen Sie Frau Christine: Abgelehnte Patenschaft," *Tempo*, 13 December 1930, 10.

227. "Fragen Sie Frau Christine: Viele Freunde—oder einen 'Freund'," *Tempo*, 9 August 1930, 7.

regarding relations with the opposite sex was relatively common in the urban centers of Weimar Germany, but it is clear from her letter that this still caused controversy and threatened a woman's respectability.[228] However, more often than not these new forms of relationships were an economic necessity rather than a question of morals. Many couples willing to marry could not afford the costs of a shared household that was considered a prerequisite for matrimony at the time, while some women simply had to move in with a man and rely on his financial support because they lacked the proper education to find a job.[229]

The erosion of traditional gender roles, especially in courting, reflected in the "modern opinions" of young women, also generated anxiety among their peers. For example, a thirty-two-year-old divorcee, characterizing herself as a typical "intermediate product" (*Zwischenprodukt*) shaped by both the prewar and the postwar eras and eager not to appear "unmodern," asked "Frau Christine" if it was now necessary for women "to make the first move."[230] In direct contrast to Charlotte Pol's earlier article about female tourists in Berlin, *Tempo*'s counselor dismissed this idea. Such an active role in courtship, she argued, was not yet common for women. A frequent complaint by female readers was the fact that men used this insecurity about the "modern" way of doing things to pressure women into sexual relationships by accusing them of backwardness and staid morals when they rejected their advances.[231] In an environment that frequently held up the promiscuous "Girl" and the sexually independent "Garçonne" as role models, this was considered a serious slight, a conundrum Erika Mann explored in one of her articles for *Tempo*.[232] Even the idea of equal, companionate marriage, "Frau Christine" argued, was used to exploit women sexually:

> Unfortunately, the word "companionate marriage" is frequently being misused these days. This innocent sounding term is very often used to trick women into relationships they would never consent to if they were called by their real names, i.e., cohabitation or concubinage.[233]

---

228. Peukert, "Das Mädchen," 164–65.
229. See, for example, "Fragen Sie Frau Christine: Heiraten ohne Geld," 30 August 1930, 10; "Fragen Sie Frau Christine: Stubenmalerin möchte ich werden," *Tempo*, 20 December 1930, 10; "Fragen Sie Frau Christine: Zwickmühle der Zeit," 30 January 1932, 8.
230. "Fragen Sie Frau Christine: Soll ich ihm den Hof machen?," *Tempo*, 30 August 1930, 10.
231. "Fragen Sie Frau Christine: Bin ich Freiwild?," *Tempo*, 7 March 1931, 10; "Fragen Sie Frau Christine: Die Unschuld," 9 January 1932, 8; "Fragen Sie Frau Christine: Das Freiwild," 14 May 1932, 8.
232. Erika Mann, "Verführer am Nebentisch," *Tempo*, 13 August, 1929, 7.
233. "Fragen Sie Frau Christine: Kameradschaftsehe—ein Notbehelf," *Tempo*, 17 January 1931, 10.

Thus, it seems that the Weimar-era discourse on the "modern," more active female role in heterosexual relationships could at times actually disadvantage women. It made them more vulnerable to sexual exploitation, while they had to exclusively bear the danger of pregnancy in unmarried relationships—a situation frequently alluded to in the letters and the answers offered by "Frau Christine."[234]

Second, despite the apparently more open attitude toward sexuality in "modern" relationships, the letters reveal the persistence of traditional bourgeois sexual morals. For many men, virginity still seemed to be an important quality in their prospective spouses. This was doubly hard on women, as men still demanded sexual intercourse in a "modern" relationship, even if it was clear that it would not end in marriage. A fairly typical case was the letter of a twenty-five-year-old man, who was shocked to learn that his twenty-year-old girlfriend, with whom he had an "excellent" relationship, was not an "innocent woman."[235] Deeply disappointed, he asks "Frau Christine" if his insistence on female virginity was wrong, whereupon she promptly reprimanded him: *Tempo*'s counselor did not see anything wrong with his wishes, but with the fact that he entered into the relationship without any serious intention of marrying her, as this behavior caused the "problem" of "devalued" women in the first place.

Thus, it is not surprising that, third, despite all the interest in new forms of relationships, the letters also show the persistent dominance of the traditional ideal of marriage, with the man as sole provider, as the only accepted or sometimes even the only practically feasible way for women to live independently from their families. In a society with a shortage of eligible men, and where women were disadvantaged in professional life, this posed a serious problem even for women with their own income, such as the thirty-two-year-old office worker who felt she was forever stuck in an unsatisfying and underpaid job because she could not find a husband.[236] In another case, an ambitious female laboratory technician, who had put every effort into her education and into maintaining her independence, but as a woman was unable to further her career

---

234. "Fragen Sie Frau Christine: Fräulein mit Kind," 28 February 1931, 10; "Fragen Sie Frau Christine: Die zerbrochene Kameradschaftsehe," 4 July 1931, 6; "Fragen Sie Frau Christine: Einblick in eine Kameradschaftsehe," 29 August 1931, 6; "Fragen Sie Frau Christine: Wieder einmal die Kameradschaftsehe," 16 January 1932, 8.
235. "Fragen Sie Frau Christine: Ihre Vergangenheit," *Tempo*, 11 June 1932, 8.
236. "Fragen Sie Frau Christine: Qualvolles Warten," *Tempo*, 11 June 1932, 8.

in her profession, felt that marriage ultimately was the only way to financial security.[237]

The "Ask Frau Christine" column offered female readers another forum for "self-making" as citizens, not only by discussing modern forms of relationships generally associated with the new democratic regime but also by giving room to explicitly political topics. For example, in September 1930, just days before the general election, "Frau Christine" advised the reader to keep politics out of her marriage, but urged her to make use of her civil right to vote:

> Don't talk politics—he will just force his opinions on you. (Men are less willing to compromise when it comes to politics, while women "don't care that much.") But you have the right to your own political opinion and also to cast your vote according to your own mind.[238]

As *Tempo*'s official voice in relationship matters, "Frau Christine" embodied a further shift in the paper's image of femininity. As mentioned above, *Tempo*'s counselor was far from an unequivocal defender of "modern" gender relations; rather, she took a position that contrasted starkly with earlier articles in the paper. While she praised the more informal courtship between younger people, she still held up matrimony as the only real union of man and woman and described the "modern" forms of relationships as mere makeshift options.[239] To be sure, her reasons were not primarily of a moral nature, but based in the above-mentioned economic disadvantages and legal inequality women faced in such unofficial relationships:

> The woman will always be at a disadvantage in a companionate marriage. She loses all benefits of a wife (entitlement to an inheritance and a pension, etc.) when the man dies, if he hasn't provided for her support in his will. And not to mention the question of children—the weakest spot of such companionate marriages. . . . If one day the companion doesn't want to be a good companion any longer, if the so-called marriage ends, the

---

237. "Fragen Sie Frau Christine: Fatum und Versorgungsheirat," *Tempo*, 28 November 1931, 8.
238. "Fragen Sie Frau Christine: Das Ehepaar vor dem Wahltag," *Tempo*, 6 September 1930, 10.
239. "Fragen Sie Frau Christine: Verlobung noch nötig?," *Tempo*, 6 September 1930, 10; "Fragen Sie Frau Christine: Kameradschaftsehe—ein Notbehelf," 17 January 1931, 10.

abandoned woman is dependent on alimony just like an illegitimate mother.[240]

This rejection reflected the disillusionment of many women with the less formal gender relations that Charlotte Pol had celebrated in her article on female tourists in 1928, after it had become clear that women had to shoulder the downsides of such "acquaintances" alone.[241] However, instead of calling for more legal equality, "Frau Christine" urged women not to "sell" themselves below value and to insist on the legal security of marriage.

Furthermore, "Frau Christine" also espoused relatively conservative marital roles. While she urged single women to find work, she discouraged married women from keeping their jobs or starting to earn money. In the very first letter published in the new column in August 1930, a thirty-two-year-old woman complained about her husband, who did not allow her to find a paid job, even though their family struggled financially.[242] *Tempo*'s counselor advised her to accept her fate to keep marital harmony—a programmatic first answer. Similarly, a housewife and trained medical doctor, who felt her husband—who was also a physician—did not take her seriously as a professional, was told to be happy with the fact that her partner saw her primarily as a wife and not as a colleague.[243] This stance reflected the growing backlash against married working women as so-called double earners (*Doppelverdiener*) after the rising unemployment made it harder for men to find jobs, and directly contradicted articles in other parts of the paper.[244]

The change in *Tempo*'s image of femininity was part of a general shift in the political culture of the Weimar Republic in the early Depression years. Julia Sneeringer has shown that, from 1930 onward, the image of women in the political discourse was dominated by the idea of devoted motherhood, not only in Nazi propaganda, but even in the campaigns of supposedly centrist middle-class parties such as the DStP.[245] *Tempo*, in the embodiment of "Frau Christine," did indeed espouse a much more conservative and traditional role for

---

240. "Kameradschaftsehe—ein Notbehelf," 10.
241. Ankum, *Women in the Metropolis*, 2–4; Frevert, *Frauen-Geschichte*, 187.
242. "Fragen Sie Frau Christine: Geld und Eheglück," *Tempo*, 2 August 1930, 7.
243. "Fragen Sie Frau Christine: Berufskollegen," *Tempo*, 16 August 1930, 7.
244. For the *Doppelverdiener* debate, see Boak, *Women*, 164; Frevert, *Frauen-Geschichte*, 192–94.
245. Julia Sneeringer, *Winning Women's Votes: Propaganda and Politics in Weimar Germany* (Chapel Hill: University of North Carolina Press, 2002), 169–218.

women than the paper had done in 1928. However, this was not a radical about-face, but a recalibration of the different aspects of the moderate modernity that had always characterized its image of femininity. The result was not simply a reactionary view of passive motherhood, but a more conservative idea of modern womanhood. Despite her relatively old-fashioned morals, "Frau Christine" nevertheless consistently supported the idea of female individuality and emotional self-reliance: *Tempo*'s counselor called on her readers to remain independent even in the narrower confines of the more traditional role model she supported.[246] This moderately modern perspective seemed to reflect the actual experiences of *Tempo*'s readers, as the motherly woman constructed in political campaigns of the early 1930s was as much an ideal as the "Girl" had been before, and it again had to be reconciled by female readers with their own particular economic and social situation, which often seriously restricted any plans of starting a family. The letters written to "Frau Christine" suggest that the result of this negotiating process was, similar to the case of *Tempo*'s beauty pageant, an often pragmatic mixture of old and new norms.

The "Ask Frau Christine" column as a whole—the letters by readers and *Tempo*'s replies—is a complex picture of modern womanhood at the end of the Weimar Republic that comprised contested gender relations and new ideas about sexual relationships as well as persisting legal and political inequalities, traditional ideas of femininity, and the effects of economic hardship. The letters published in the column give an insight into the ways in which a moderate modernity was negotiated in practice in the critical political and economic situation of the early 1930s. While "modern" ideas about relationships were put into practice by men and women, these progressive tendencies were often frustrated by persisting social norms. Furthermore, the onset of the economic depression revealed the precariousness of the situation of women who had to balance new ideas about their social role with more traditional goals, such as financial security and romantic love, in a society that seriously disadvantaged them legally and economically. For these women, cohabitation outside of marriage or working outside the home was often neither a moral choice nor the result of female emancipation, but rather an economic necessity. The advice that "Frau Christine" gave *Tempo*'s readers about negotiating these issues reflected a shift in the paper's vision of women's roles in modern society: the earlier optimism about gender equality had been replaced by a rather conservative, subdued perspective.

---

246. Föllmer, "Junge Frauen," 310–17.

In sum, *Tempo*'s vision of a modern Germany changed considerably under the pressure of political radicalization and a global economic downturn. Instead of a Western-oriented, cosmopolitan, progressive, and liberal state on a trajectory toward "American" prosperity, the paper now constructed a more modest image of a troubled yet dedicated nation defiantly standing its ground in the global crisis. The idea of a consumer society remained vital in the paper's worldview, but it was less and less connected to the ideal of the United States, a country that now stood for the pitfalls of excess. Instead, *Tempo* constructed a Germanized version of modest, rational prosperity that unified a fractured society, a vision that manifested itself in the idea of the affordable *Volksauto*. The loss of the American ideal as a model for the future was reflected in *Tempo*'s increasing references to Germany's past, most significantly to the country's own democratic tradition of the nineteenth century. According to *Tempo*, events such as "the first flowering of a noble longing" for democracy at the Hambach Festival in 1832 and the revolution of 1848 had regained an "urgent timeliness" by the early 1930s.[247] However, instead of Western parliamentarianism, *Tempo* now voiced cautious support for a more direct or "organic" version of democracy, embodied by the *Ersatzkaiser* Hindenburg and expressed in the manifesto of the DStP. While young men did not play a central role as representatives of this ideal of a moderate modernity anymore, *Tempo*'s adapted image of femininity clearly reflected this vision.

The liberal idea of the rational individual—not the irrational collective—as the center of all political and societal processes still remained one of *Tempo*'s core values. This was embodied in the figure of the responsible voter, who had it in his or her hands to save the Republic. Not only the paper's belief in the power of the individual to change the future prevailed but also its unwavering optimism. At the end of 1931, *Tempo* urged its readers to enjoy themselves on New Year's Eve despite the desperate situation. Not only because the barkeepers and waiters would miss out on an important part of their income if people stayed at home, but because optimism was especially needed during such difficult times:

> Our dark future will not change if we don't keep a light that shines even for the most disheartened among us. Didn't we just put a year full of sorrow behind us? That is already progress! So: Happy New Year 1932—it'll be all right![248]

---

247. P.f.v., "Die gestohlene Erinnerung," *Tempo*, 3 November 1930, 3; –e., "Eine Erinnerung. Das Hambacher Nationalfest," *Tempo*, 24 May 1932, 6.
248. T., "Zwiespältige Jahreswende," *Tempo*, 31 December 1931, 3.

Despite this outward cheerfulness, however, *Tempo*—and Ullstein as a whole—had gone on the defensive behind the scenes. Over the course of 1931, *Tempo*'s daily circulation had dropped from its high point of 153,000 in October 1930 to around 122,000. While the paper's overall yearly running costs in 1931 of 602,744 marks were relatively low, the continuing economic crisis forced the company to scrap the paper's most unique feature, its multiple daily editions.[249] From 31 August 1931, *Tempo* was published only once a day.[250]

---

249. "Gehälter/Gesamtkosten," unpaginated, in UAS, Ullstein files. In comparison, the running costs for the *Vossische Zeitung*, which had a circulation of only 69,000 daily copies in 1931, are listed as RM 1,503,755 in the same document. The scrapping of *Tempo*'s multiple daily editions cut the running costs to RM 468,978 in the following year.

250. In the *Ullstein-Chronik*, this change is dated 19 January 1931. However, until 30 August, *Tempo*'s imprint still spoke of "several daily editions."

CHAPTER 3

1932–1933

"Nobody but Ourselves Can Save Us"

In June 1932, *Tempo* reported that sparrows were finally returning to Berlin. The birds had deserted the city after the automobile had replaced the horse as the major means of transport and thus eliminated the birds' most important food source. In characteristically optimistic fashion, the newspaper interpreted the birds' adaptation to the modern world as an example for crisis-ridden Germans: "If the sparrows can manage to adapt, perhaps we—stupid and clumsy humans that we are—will also be able to make it, even if it will take us longer? In the end, nobody but ourselves can save us from this global crisis."[1] The scale of the economic slump that plagued the country and the misery it brought to its population were indeed daunting. At the beginning of the year, more than six million people—a third of the German workforce—were unemployed. Yet *Tempo*'s pages were full of uplifting stories that put a positive spin on this seemingly hopeless situation. For example, two old beggars who earned a paltry keep by dancing in backyards and proclaiming proverbs in a park were portrayed as "standard-bearers of optimism" and "soldiers of life, who fight the heroic battle against the gray tide of misery and worry in our city, one day at a time."[2] Lucy von Jacobi praised a housing development for families with multiple children, in some cases up to eighteen, as a "colony of optimists."[3] Over the summer months, *Tempo* presented examples of "people who refuse to give up," a series of success stories about jobless Berliners who had found new work by exhibiting a spirit of self-help and entrepreneurship—a sailor who put

---

1. Lobti, "Berlin hat wieder Spatzen!," *Tempo*, 25 June 1932, 3. Parts of this chapter have been published as Jochen Hung, "The 'Ullstein Spirit': The Ullstein Publishing House, the End of the Weimar Republic and the Making of Cold War German Identity, 1925–77," *Journal of Contemporary History* 53, no. 1 (2018): 158–84.

2. Elkoe, "Das sind Optimisten!," *Tempo*, 14 May 1932, 3.

3. Lot (i.e., Lucy von Jacobi), "Kolonie der Kinderreichen," *Tempo*, 12 August 1932, 3.

his knowledge of exotic plants to use as a gardener, a humble worker who landed a job as an assistant editor at a newspaper after learning to touch-type and to write shorthand in the evenings, a housewife who set up a business selling her own chocolate desserts.[4] According to the introduction to the series, this kind of flexibility used to be common in America before the economic crisis but now it was hard to find new jobs even there—and even harder in crisis-ridden Germany. And yet, "despite all these difficulties, some of us have succeeded in adapting. . . . They have made a career in fields they did not know before and are happy and content, because their talents do not go to waste."[5]

Tempo's continuing unbridled optimism and its full-throated claims about individual agency and the possibility of changing your own fate seemed increasingly tone-deaf in the context of the widespread misery of the early 1930s. However, it followed a broader strategy at the Ullstein house of keeping the vision of a prosperous democratic Germany alive during an escalating political crisis that accompanied the country's economic woes. During the year 1932, Weimar's political system went through several critical developments that seriously undermined its democratic foundations. While Hindenburg prevailed against Hitler to win his second term as president, the Nazis emerged as the strongest party in both the Prussian state election in April and the general election in July. Between these dates, Chancellor Brüning was deposed by Hindenburg and replaced by Franz van Papen, a relatively unknown conservative politician and aristocrat. Political violence reached a climax in the infamous Altonaer Blutsonntag (Altona Bloody Sunday), leading to the removal of Prussia's SPD-led government, widely seen as Weimar's last bulwark for democracy. By then, the plan of Weimar's antidemocratic elites, namely Hindenburg, his camarilla, and the generals of the Reichswehr, to "transform the parliamentary democracy into an authoritarian state governed by the political right" had been all but completed.[6] The only hope of many liberal journalists was a "hibernation" of parliamentarianism during the rule of an authoritarian government that would preserve Germany's democratic roots until the economic and political crises had passed.[7] The liberal press did voice severe criticism about Brüning's fall and protested when the new Chancellor Papen forced out the Prussian government, but it generally tried to calm its readers instead of rally-

---

4. "Menschen, die nicht verzweifeln," *Tempo*, 26 June 1932, 3; 4 July 1932, 6; 13 July 1932, 4.
5. "Menschen, die nicht verzweifeln," *Tempo*, 26 June 1932, 3.
6. Kolb, *Weimar Republic*, 116.
7. Eksteins, *Limits*, 222–24, 48–49.

ing forces to the defense of democracy.[8] By that time, the notion of parliamentary democracy had effectively been dropped from the political discourse. In the feverish atmosphere of the election year 1932, the liberal press could not call on the voters to show their support for liberal democracy as it had done two years earlier, because parliament had been sidelined and hardly even worked anymore: the number of plenary sessions of the Reichstag had decreased significantly since 1930.[9] Instead, liberal journalists appealed for a defense of fundamental values such as individual freedom and the rule of law against impending state terrorism.[10] The central point of reference remained the Constitution. For the liberal press, it was the embodiment of Weimar's democratic spirit and the last bastion of the Republic.[11] As long as the Constitution survived, many liberal journalists believed, Germany could handle a temporary retrenchment of democracy.

Ullstein, still the country's biggest liberal publishing house, was a central proponent of this approach. This included a changed view of National Socialism: by mid-1932, Ullstein's approach to the Nazis had evolved from a tone of mockery and warnings of the party's seductive extremism to a view of the movement as a legitimate expression of a part of the German population, making a strict distinction between Nazi leaders and their followers. This change of course reflected a generational rift among the company's owners. Franz Ullstein, who had personally observed Hitler on an overnight train ride through Bavaria, saw the Nazi leader as "a poor fanatic, a pitiful man" and said he thus could not take the movement seriously.[12] Louis Ullstein's son Heinz, however, personally reprimanded the editorial office over the mocking tone of an article in the *Vossische Zeitung* on the supposed ideological confusion of the NSDAP.[13] Taking the Nazis seriously was also the core demand of a strategy paper written a few days later by Carl Jödicke, an assistant to Ullstein's general manager, Richard A. Müller.[14] It is not clear how much influence this paper really had on the company's politics, but it is a telling sign of the struggle at the Ullstein house to come to terms with the movement that had so quickly become the dominant political force in

---

8. Sösemann, *Ende*, 75.
9. Mergel, *Parlamentarische Kultur*, 180.
10. Sösemann, *Ende*, 156.
11. Bosch, *Presse*, 30–36.
12. Schäffer diary, 8 August 1932, in LBI, AR 7177/MF 512, 10, Nr. 3, fol. 722.
13. Heinz Ullstein to Dr. Wolf, 4 May 1932, in BArchL, N2193 Misch, Nr. 13, fol. 57. The article in question was "Maifeier und Hohenzollern," *Vossische Zeitung*, 3 May 1932, 3.
14. "Taktische Skizze," 9 May 1932, in Munich, Institut für Zeitgeschichte, F110 Carl Jödicke, fols. 2–5.

Germany. National Socialism, Jödicke argued, had to be accepted as a "movement for political freedom and economic justice." Ullstein had to attack its political enemies on these fundamental terms, he continued, and not get caught up in a "politics of petty details" of reporting only "assaults of 'evil' Nazis on peaceful *Reichsbanner* groups." To be able to compete with Nazi propaganda, the Ullstein papers had to change their tune, Jödicke claimed. Instead of touting lofty ideals of individual freedom and democracy they had to follow a resurgent patriotism, which strongly emphasized the "welfare of the whole community" instead of the individual and worked with emotions instead of reason and skepticism, as this was the only way to gain influence with the masses. The temporary curtailing of civil rights and democracy was inevitable in this time of crisis, he argued. Shouldered with their daily struggle, the people did not care much for the "'luxury' of freedom" at the moment anyway. As he showed in a later memorandum, Jödicke was clearly fascinated by the Nazis. The core principle of the movement, he argued, was a "return to universally accepted, non-debatable, unchangeable forms of life instead of general relativity."[15] According to Jödicke, this "simplicity" gave the movement the ability to lead the masses with uncomplicated, highly simplified, primitive slogans, which stood in sharp contrast to the DStP's ineffective "intellectualism."

These appeals by the management seemed to have an effect on the editorial policy of the Ullstein papers. On 16 May, the *Vossische Zeitung*'s court reporter Moritz Goldstein complained bitterly about the toning down of one of his articles, in which he had claimed that Nazi voters approved of crimes committed by NSDAP representatives.[16] Goldstein had reported about the ongoing trial of NSDAP deputy Robert Ley, who had attacked and severely beaten SPD chairman Otto Wels.[17] Carl Misch replied that it was necessary to distinguish between voters and functionaries.[18] While criticizing politicians was fair, abusing voters, Misch explained, was not helpful for Ullstein's agenda. Not all readers, however, agreed with the company's new course. In May 1932, the Jewish intellectual Gershom Scholem privately criticized the Ullstein press as "one of the most dishonest and misleading there is," because he felt the company's papers turned a blind eye to Nazi atrocities.[19]

---

15. "Die Ideologie des Nationalsozialismus: Soldatentum in der Politik," 20 April 1933, in Munich, Institut für Zeitgeschichte, F110 Jödicke, fols. 8–9.
16. Goldstein to Misch, 16 May 1932, in BArchL, N2193 Misch, Nr. 13, fols. 62–64.
17. "Sühne für den Überfall auf Wels," *Vossische Zeitung*, 15 May 1932, 1.
18. Misch to Goldstein, 17 May 1932, in BArchL, N2193 Misch, Nr. 13, fols. 62–64.
19. Gershom Scholem to Betty Scholem, 1 May 1932, in Gershom Scholem, *Mutter und Sohn im Briefwechsel 1917–1946*, ed. Itta Shedletzky (Munich: Beck, 1989), 265–66.

Ullstein's continuing struggle with the Nazi phenomenon happened before the backdrop of ongoing family troubles. Despite their official reconciliation, the previously effective cooperation between the Ullstein brothers had been replaced by an atmosphere of mutual distrust.[20] Quarrels about the ownership of the company continued to poison their relationship and made concerted efforts to find an answer to Weimar's changed political landscape impossible. State secretary Hans Schäffer, who had tried to bring the company's papers behind Brüning's policies in November 1931, was called upon as an outside moderator in the continuing family feud. On 6 June 1932, after resigning from his position, he joined the company as director general.[21] With Schäffer, Ullstein finally had found a replacement for Georg Bernhard as the company's political helmsman, who could navigate its cautious course through the stormy years ahead. Schäffer had excellent connections to all major political players in Weimar Germany, from Schleicher, Papen, Hans Luther, Otto Braun, and Rudolf Hilferding to international observers such as John Foster Dulles, and met them regularly for informal conversations and off-the-record exchanges even after he had relinquished his position in the civil service.[22] At Ullstein, he set the general political agenda and often personally oversaw the final makeup of the newspapers.[23] Schäffer was paid a handsome salary for his expertise: he received a monthly salary of 66,000 marks, with an additional 12,000 marks expense allowance, and a share of the company's profits.[24] As a state secretary, he had only earned around 24,000 marks.[25]

For Ullstein, this seemed money well spent. One obvious reason to employ such a well-connected man was to shield the company from further government attacks: the pending *Tempo* court case still loomed large during the troubled year of 1932. According to Carl von Ossietzky, it had been one of the reasons why the company had come down so hard on Höllering after the *B.Z.*'s attack on the Defense Ministry at the end of 1931, and his successor as the

---

20. Eksteins, *Limits*, 232–33.
21. Schäffer diary, 20 November 1931, in LBI, AR 7177/MF 512, 9, Nr. 17, fols. 1046–49; 6 June 1932, in LBI, AR 7177/MF 512, 10, Nr. 2, fols. 562–63.
22. Schäffer diary, 1924–33, in LBI, AR 7177/MF 512, 9–10. See also Eckhard Wandel, *Hans Schäffer: Steuermann in wirtschaftlichen und politischen Krisen* (Stuttgart: Deutsche Verlagsanstalt, 1974), 67.
23. Schäffer's contract with Ullstein, Hans Schäffer-Eckhard Wandel Collection, in LBI, AR 7023/MF 511, Nr. 16, fols. 3–5. See also Schäffer diary, 3–4 July 1932, in LBI, AR 7177/MF 512, 10, Nr. 2, fol. 634.
24. Schäffer contract, LBI, AR 7023/MF 511, Nr. 16, fol. 4.
25. See "Reichsbesoldungsordnung," in Reichsministerium des Innern, *Deutsches Reichsgesetzblatt* (Berlin: Verlag des Gesetzsammlungsamts, 1927), 1:388.

paper's editor-in-chief immediately tried to shut down the ongoing lawsuit.[26] On 29 January, Fritz Stein approached the Foreign Ministry, arguing that *Tempo*'s report about the Amlinger case and the collaboration of the Reichswehr with the Red Army had not been news but in fact had long been public knowledge abroad.[27] Ullstein also hired Erich Koch-Weser, the former chairman of the DDP, as their lawyer for the case. Koch-Weser compiled a lengthy dossier with clippings from the foreign press to show that *Tempo* had not divulged any previously unknown information in the article in question. He also met with Georg Martius, a high official in the Foreign Ministry and long-time DDP member, to convince the government that convicting the Ullstein house for treason would have "catastrophic" consequences and would be "grist to the mill for the opposition against President Hindenburg in the presidential election" in March.[28] This made an impression, and in a meeting with representatives of the Defense Ministry and the Justice Ministry, Martius asked his colleagues to present this argument to their superiors.[29] In a brief submitted to the court and forwarded to Martius, Koch-Weser and Max Alsberg, one of Germany's most famous defense lawyers, argued that Ullstein had always taken "a patriotic standpoint that is friendly towards the military."[30] The fact that Ullstein now fashioned itself as Hindenburg's mouthpiece and the company's need to distance itself from its liberal and antimilitarist reputation show the owners' precarious situation in the 1930s after the weak result of the DStP had left them without a political representative they could throw their weight behind. It also reflects the widespread feeling that the very existence of the political system was in grave danger, and that Hindenburg was the only bulwark against its takeover by extremists on the left and right.

In August, once he had settled in his new position, Schäffer made another push to bring the ongoing court case against *Tempo* to an end. He met with Bernhard Wilhelm von Bülow, the highest-ranking civil servant in the Foreign Ministry, and convinced him to meet with Koch-Weser again.[31] The Foreign Ministry had been asked by the court to act as expert witness regarding the question of whether the *Tempo* article about the collaboration between the Reichswehr and the Red Army had put the country's interests in danger. Koch-

26. Carl von Ossietzky, "Der Fall Höllering," *Die Weltbühne*, 5 January 1932.
27. "Vermerk," 29 January 1932, in BArchL, R 901/27361, fol. 43.
28. "Vermerk," 24 February 1932, in BArchL, R 901/27361, fols. 37–38.
29. "Aufzeichnung," 29 February 1932, in BArchL, R 901/27361, fols. 39–40.
30. Erich Koch-Weser and Max Alsberg to District Court III Berlin, 4 March 1932, in R 901/27361, fols. 43–53.
31. "Vermerk," 18 August 1932, in BArchL, R 901/27361, fol. 88.

Weser wanted to make sure that the ministry followed his argument that the information had already been known abroad. However, his efforts were fruitless: on 21 September 1932, Koch-Weser was informed that the ministry had judged the article in *Tempo* a divulgence of official secrets.[32]

Despite this setback, Schäffer seemed to be the ideal man for the delicate position Ullstein found itself in 1932. He was a very different character from the flamboyant Bernhard and had been part of Weimar's efficient bureaucracy, which gave the new state stability despite its frequent crises and changing governments.[33] A lawyer by trade, he had joined the civil service after the war and had enjoyed a long and successful career, gaining a reputation as an expert on reparation laws. Although he had briefly been a DDP member shortly after its foundation and had close ties to the SPD, Schäffer did not belong to any party. He considered himself as being above party lines, falling to the left of the DDP and the right of the SPD, preferring to stay out of the limelight and pulling strings in secret. Yet Schäffer was not without clear political beliefs. One of the reasons why he had accepted Ullstein's offer was the opportunity to forge the company's papers into an efficient weapon against the Nazis. The liberal press, he complained, had for a long time not taken the Nazi movement seriously and had treated it with ridicule or dismissed it as a rabble-rousing gang of louts.[34] When Brüning asked him why he had taken up the post at Ullstein, he argued that the high circulation of *Morgenpost* and *Tempo*, together with the *Vossische Zeitung*'s prestige, could be used to form a "really serious ideological stance against National Socialism," something the company had failed to do until now.[35] Schäffer's antipathy against the Nazis was not only based in his belief in democracy and the Constitution, which he regularly held up as guiding principles in the weekly political conferences with the editors, but also in his Jewish faith.[36] His aim was the neutralization of the Nazis' political influence by forcing them into a responsible role in a legal government and thus removing their aura of a mass movement that supposedly transcended narrow party politics. For Schäffer, a majority government with Hitler as minister or even chancellor was preferable to a continuation of the presidential cabinets that had

---

32. "Aufzeichnung," 21 September 1932, in BArchL, R 901/27361, fol. 89.
33. For Schäffer's biography, see Wandel, *Schäffer*, 17–129.
34. Schäffer diary, 20 November 1931, in LBI, AR 7177/MF 512, 9, Nr. 17, fol. 1038. See also Fulda, *Press*, 159–62; Eksteins, *Limits*, 241–46; Koszyk, *Geschichte*, 3:347.
35. Schäffer diary, 20 November 1931, in LBI, AR 7177/MF 512, 9, Nr. 17, fol. 1048.
36. Schäffer diary, 9 August 1932, 15 August 1932, 29 August 1932, 4 October 1932, 25 October 1932, in LBI, AR 7177/MF 512, 10, Nr. 3, fols. 724–931. See also Wandel, *Schäffer*, 17–23.

ruled Germany since Brüning, because this promised to "wear out" the Nazi leader as a potential candidate for the next presidential election.[37] The threat of a Reich president Hitler had become worryingly real only in April, when the Nazi leader gained nearly 40 percent of the vote against Hindenburg. To this end, Schäffer cautiously supported the government's attempts, pursued by both Papen and his successor Kurt von Schleicher, to involve the NSDAP in a coalition government with a "loyal, but critical opposition" by the Ullstein papers.[38]

Schäffer's cautious course was also a reaction to the absence of a viable political party to which the company could lend its direct support. The formation of the DStP had proven to be a poor solution for the rapid loss of influence of the Democrats, and after gaining only twenty seats in the general election in 1930, the DStP fraction shrunk again to just four seats after the election in July 1932. Under Schäffer, Ullstein withdrew its support for the party except in constituencies where it had a realistic chance of winning a seat.[39] However, he also opposed the founding of yet another party to avoid further fragmentation of the already weakened liberal spectrum.[40] After the inevitable implosion of the Nazi movement, he reasoned, the masses would come flooding back to the moderate liberal center. This hope might have been the reason why direct support for the SPD, the only remaining political force still defending Weimar's status quo, never seems to have been seriously considered at the Ullstein house.

Without a liberal-democratic voice in parliament for the time being, Schäffer instead set a course of a rather abstract support for a general liberal *Weltanschauung* without an attachment to an individual party.[41] Rather than attacking the Nazis directly, he aimed at strengthening the liberal tradition of individual freedom and citizenship as an ideological alternative. For Schäffer and the Ullsteins, a greater threat for the Republic than Hitler was a disillusionment of the working class with the new state.[42] The fear of civil war and a violent uprising of the workers against a government led by aristocrats such as Papen held the whole of the liberal press in thrall.[43] Thus, apart from containing the Nazis' rise, Schäffer's principal aim was to calm Ullstein's readership

---

37. Schäffer diary, 30 August 1932, 9 September 1932, in LBI, AR 7177/MF 512, 10, Nr. 3, fols. 813–42.
38. Schäffer diary, 2 September 1932, in LBI, AR 7177/MF 512, 10, Nr. 3, fol. 832.
39. Schäffer diary, 8 July 1932, 19 July 1932, in LBI, AR 7177/MF 512, 10, Nr. 2, fols. 650, 666.
40. Schäffer diary, 14 June 1932, in LBI, AR 7177/MF 512, 10, Nr. 2, fol. 581.
41. Schäffer diary, 7 November 1932, in LBI, AR 7177/MF 512, 10, Nr. 3, fol. 959.
42. Schäffer diary, 21 July 1932, in LBI, AR 7177/MF 512, 10, Nr. 2, fols. 671–72.
43. Fulda, *Press*, 169–202.

and to inject reason and common sense into the political discussion.[44] However, in practice, this led to overly positive coverage of Papen's authoritarian politics, something even the government press office acknowledged with surprise.[45]

Under Schäffer, *Tempo* underwent some far-reaching changes in content and structure that reflected Ullstein's new course. Over the course of 1932, it dedicated more and more space to reports about street fighting, assaults, and supposed illegal activities of Nazis and Communists in all corners of the Reich.[46] During the first half of the year, this turned into a daily numeration of casualties, arrests, and property damage that painted the picture of a country on the brink of civil war. However, the most striking aspect of *Tempo*'s political coverage in 1932 compared to the 1930 campaign is the lack of its long-established commentators Roda Roda, "C. Enseo," "Heaven," and "Sky." The paper certainly did not become depoliticized; it was still unmistakably prorepublican and pro-democratic, but it had lost the distinctive voices that had personified its spirit of optimism and progressivism. The fact that the focus on violence on the streets went hand in hand with a cut of genuine commentary was clearly a consequence of Ullstein's attempt to find a compromise between objectively informing its readers without giving up the company's liberal stance, as demanded in the management's internal memos. However, while the Communist Party and the NSDAP were vigorously attacked in the remaining commentary pieces, the government was spared almost any criticism. Even when Papen presented an explicitly antidemocratic manifesto, directly attacking the institutions of parliament and the Constitution, *Tempo* only pointed out that he had borrowed these ideas from the far right.[47] Schäffer's arrival at Ullstein also led to a shake-up among *Tempo*'s editorial staff. Fritz Lachmann took over from Manfred Georg as managing editor, while Kauder was replaced by Ernst Wallenberg as *Tempo*'s editor-in-chief.[48] Schäffer did not think much of Kauder's work, frequently changing his dispatches when he reported from the

---

44. Schäffer diary, 20 July 1932, in LBI, AR 7177/MF 512, 10, Nr. 2, fol. 669.
45. Schäffer diary, 2 September 1932, in LBI, AR 7177/MF 512, 10, Nr. 3, fol. 832.
46. See, for example, "Blutat in Breslau," *Tempo*, 9 March 1932, 1; "Die Nazi-Führer als Landesverräter," *Tempo*, 4 April 1932, 1; "Nazi-Überfälle in ganz Preußen," *Tempo*, 23 April 1932, 10; "Die Bilanz des Berliner Wahlkampfes," *Tempo*, 23 April 1932, 2; "Ein Todesopfer der nächtlichen Zusammenstöße," *Tempo*, 26 July 1932, 10; "Große Waffenfunde bei Nationalsozialisten," *Tempo*, 3 August 1932, 1.
47. "Erklärung oder Wahlaufruf?," *Tempo*, 4 June 1932, 2.
48. *Handbuch der deutschen Tagespresse*, 116. See also "Personalien," *Der Spiegel*, 28 August 1948, 17.

Lausanne Conference of 1932 and bemoaning his unreliability and tendentiousness.[49] Wallenberg, a trained dentist, had been the *B.Z. am Mittag*'s editor-in-chief before Höllering, where he earned a reputation for modernizing its typography, but was otherwise not known for his strong political views or convictions.[50]

In its coverage of the various elections in 1932, *Tempo* rarely made a distinction between individual parties anymore, but described the voters' alternatives as a stark choice between democracy or tyranny. Hindenburg was now the unchallenged symbol of the Weimar state. When the president announced his renewed candidacy, *Tempo* described the coming election as a choice between "the man who wants to serve the fatherland beyond all party lines and the man who wants to turn the fatherland into a servant of the party."[51] During the two rounds of the presidential election on 13 March and 10 April 1932, *Tempo* portrayed Hindenburg as a stately and dignified leader, even discarding its usual antimilitarism when it reported glowingly on the president's inspection of the Berlin guards regiment, calling it a "military spectacle."[52] Nearly every issue carried a large Hindenburg-related photo on the front page, either Hindenburg himself meeting his fellow citizens or a reprint of the president's campaign posters.[53] On the front page of the last issue before the final ballot, *Tempo* urged its readers to cast their vote for the acting president.[54] On the eve of the first round of the election, *Tempo* expressed its continuing faith in the German people's sense of responsibility even in troubled times:

> Even if she is struggling and has been weakened by many hard and painful measures, Germany could be in rude health, if she only wants to. We will not give up this sincere hope for the reawakening of the people's healthy energy and intentions.[55]

This time, *Tempo*'s hope was rewarded, and Hindenburg prevailed. But the gains of the Nazis in the Prussian state election on 24 April and the appointment of Franz von Papen as chancellor on 1 July did not bode well for Wei-

---

49. Schäffer diary, 2–4 July 1932, in LBI, AR 7177/MF 512, 10, Nr. 2, fols. 630–34.
50. "Bitterer Lorbeer," *Der Spiegel*, 30 September 1953, 14.
51. M.m., "Hindenburg und die anderen," *Tempo*, 16 February 1932, 3.
52. "Hindenburg-Parade des Wachregiments," *Tempo*, 4 March 1932, 1.
53. *Tempo*, 4 March 1932, 1; 7 March 1932, 1; 9 March 1932, 1; 10 March 1932, 1; 12 March 1932, 1–3; 4 April 1932, 1; 6 April 1932, 1; 7 April 1932, 1; 8 April 1932, 2.
54. "Morgen Wahl-Sonntag," *Tempo*, 9 April 1932, 1.
55. M. m., "Der gesunde Sinn," *Tempo*, 12 March 1932, 3.

mar's future. In the run-up to the Reichstag election on 31 July, *Tempo* tried to construct the image of a silent majority of commonsense, levelheaded citizens that stood apart from the violent minority of extremists in the streets. While his own paper was filled with reports of bloody clashes between Nazis and Communists all over Germany, Gustav Kauder traveled to political trouble spots in the provinces with the explicit aim of proving the headlines of the press wrong and to show that the silent majority had no interest in political violence: "Murder, bloody hatred, even party uniforms, badges and flags—this is the exception in Germany. The mass of the people is having none of that."[56] Most Germans, he reported, were acting like good citizen-consumers, calmly going about their business and living "their perfectly normal everyday lives," ignoring the campaign posters, the speeches, and propaganda and going shopping or on holiday instead. This would be reflected in the coming election, he believed:

> We will again witness a very high turnout; 40 million people in Germany are incredibly interested in the election on the 31st of July. But of these 40 million only 200,000 at best take part, actively and passively, in the mindless hatred, the provocations and the bloody murder. 99½ per cent of all Germans are as passionate about politics as anywhere else in the world—and as civilized.[57]

However, the image of a rational, civilized, and sober majority ignoring the political violence around them contrasted sharply with the paper's ever more urgent and insistent calls for the defense of the Republic. During the campaign for the general election in July, Schäffer's presence made itself felt in *Tempo*'s coverage. A day before the election, *Tempo* issued one of its strongest calls yet to support the Republic, with almost the whole paper dedicated to the activation of the voters. The front page featured a big headline announcing a choice between "freedom or dictatorship," with a paragraph in bold letters stressing that what was at stake was nothing less than Germany's soul:

> Tomorrow is the day the German people take charge of their destiny at the ballot boxes of the general election. Never before has their choice been more important: at stake are all matters of public and personal life, Germany's unity, German culture and individual freedom. Germans: do your

---

56. Gustav Kauder, "Mordland?," *Tempo*, 21 July 1932, 3.
57. Kauder, "Mordland?," 3.

duty tomorrow, visit your polling station in time and help bring victory to Germany's freedom.[58]

In contrast to 1930, *Tempo* did not call on its readers to support parliamentarianism, the democratic system, or even the Republic, but much more basic values, such as personal freedom and German culture itself. The belief in the rational voter and in individual agency remained central, however. According to *Tempo*, every German ultimately had it in their hands to determine the nation's future. The call to arms continued on the inside pages. The democratic Republic, a commentary warned, had given the people the opportunity to determine their own fate, but the voters were about to use that power against it and thus themselves:

> For years, the battle raged for the preservation and consolidation of the democratic Republic against the destructive forces that attacked it tirelessly. It gave the German people the freedom to unleash these forces against themselves, but also the freedom to bind them with the force of their political will, to oppose the spirit of destruction with the spirit of loyalty—the loyalty to the freedom of the Republic, won with blood and suffering.[59]

Under these circumstances, Kauder observed in the same issue, the character and meaning of democracy changed.[60] Faced with such a fundamental choice, he argued, the electorate underwent a process of "massification," shunning the small parties of the center and their *sachlich* politics for the mass propaganda of the SPD, the Communists, and the NSDAP. However, Kauder prophesied, this was by no means a permanent change. After the all-or-nothing vote in July, the voters would return to their "old love" of the bourgeois center, he argued. A positive consequence of the modern mass campaigns, he added, was the primacy of the democratic idea itself. The "spiritual revolution" in Germany, meaning the success of the idea of free democratic elections, had been ingrained so deeply in the minds of the population that it could not be ignored even by the extremists.[61]

---

58. "Wahlkampf um Freiheit oder Diktatur," *Tempo*, 30 July 1932, 1.
59. M. m., "Sieg der Treue," *Tempo*, 30 July 1932, 6.
60. Gustav Kauder, "Stadion und Lautsprecher," *Tempo*, 30 July 1932, 5.
61. Kauder, "Stadion und Lautsprecher," 5.

Tempo's belief in the responsible voter was, once again, disappointed. The NSDAP emerged as the strongest party from the election, winning nearly fourteen million votes and spectacularly disproving Kauder's optimistic predictions of merely 200,000 "active and passive" supporters of its politics. *Tempo* reacted in an astounding fashion. In contrast to other papers, such as the *Vossische Zeitung*, it did not report on the election results on its front page, but solely on Nazi assaults during the night, drawing attention to the brutality with which the party hunted its political enemies in the provinces.[62] In its analysis of the results on the inside pages, *Tempo* still found a silver lining. Although they had used "all means of American advertising methods," the Nazis had only gained slightly compared to the presidential elections a few months earlier.[63] The fact that American political culture was now used as a shorthand for destructive populism shows how *Tempo*'s perspective on the US had changed since 1930.

However, despite this positive outlook, *Tempo*'s seemingly unwavering faith in the future seemed to fade after July 1932. There were no uplifting articles anymore on the resilience of ordinary citizens after this point and the paper reported with great alarm on the ceremony for Weimar's last Constitution Day, used by the Papen government as a platform to attack the Constitution and the Republic itself.[64] When parliament was dissolved again a few months later and another election was called for November, *Tempo*'s editors seemed to revert to earlier ideals regarding the best way to govern the country. The paper delivered an urgent plea to its readers to support parliamentary democracy as the only real reflection of the will of the people. It again stressed the responsibility that came with the democratic right to vote:

> You are voting for the German Parliament, according to the Constitution established through the will of the people. This is why you will not vote for those who disregard the Parliament and attack the Constitution, and who want to bring down the will of the people together with the Parliament and the Constitution. The German voters can only protect the Parliament and the Constitution with their vote—a democratic Parliament and a democratic Constitution, expressing the democratic will of the people that has to be free to be effective and creative. This is why you can only vote

---

62. "In Königsberg, Braunschweig und Schlesien. Unerhörte Terror-Akte," *Tempo*, 1 August 1932, 1–2.
63. "Die Bilanz des 31. Juli 1932," *Tempo*, 1 August 1932, 3.
64. "Weimar-Feier der Reichsregierung," *Tempo*, 11 August 1932, 1–2.

for those parties that honor and respect democracy and the foundation of all public life on the will of the people—no other parties![65]

This anxious appeal, desperately trying to hammer home its message, was *Tempo*'s last direct message of support for the democratic system of the Republic, despite the first encouraging signs for its future. The NSDAP lost thirty-four seats in the election in November and, in December, Franz von Papen was replaced by Kurt von Schleicher, who, as *Tempo* remarked, renounced any experiments with the Constitution.[66] Still, the paper's outlook at the end of the year was relatively bleak. Instead of the encouraging words *Tempo* usually had for its readers on New Year's Eve, this year only an illustration of a haggard woman, symbolizing "Mother Germany," proclaimed the hope that her "problem children"—the paramilitary organizations of the Stahlhelm, the Iron Front, the Communists, and the Nazis—would get along next year (Fig. 26). Despite its somber tone, however, the illustration suggested that all of these groups—including the Nazis—were part of the same national family, and had enough in common to find common ground in the future.

"We Vow to Be Happy!" Consumption as Duty in 1932

In 1932, at the height of the economic crisis, *Tempo*'s editors seemed to have doubts about their message of unrestricted consumer spending as the antidote to the economic slump. In the ideological debate about the best way to restart the economy, the paper argued, the economists and experts were always changing their minds: one day people were told to hold on to their money and to spend it the next.[67] Surely, the article concluded, striking a balance between excessive saving and reckless spending was the order of the day. However, this nod to the dire situation of many readers was offset on the same page by an article about the laudable initiative of American businessmen aimed at "cranking up" (*ankurbeln*) the economy by signing a public oath to spend their savings on consumer products.[68]

Despite its wariness of the US model, it was evident from the pages of the *Ullstein-Berichte* that the company still believed that the example of the Amer-

---

65. "Jeder wähle!," *Tempo*, 5 November 1932, 2.
66. "Das neue Regierungs-Programm," *Tempo*, 2 December 1932, 2. For the results of the November 1932 election, see Milatz, *Wähler und Wahlen*, 112.
67. "Sparen? Nicht sparen?!," *Tempo*, 18 July 1932, 3.
68. F.Z., "Die Ankurbler," *Tempo*, 18 July 1932, 3.

Figure 26. "Mutter Deutschland und ihre Sorgenkinder," *Tempo*, 31 December 1932, 1. © Axel Springer AG. Used with permission.

ican businessmen should be followed. In the July issue of the promotional publication, *Tempo*'s regular columnist "C. Enseo" praised the untapped potential of the developing tourism industry and urged the government to extend the school holidays in summer to give it a further boost.[69] The header of each issue of the promotional magazine usually carried short aphorisms or motivational sayings, and this issue declared that "everybody has to buy as much as they can afford!"—an appeal that turned consumption almost into a national duty. When the Papen government announced an investment program to inject life into the stagnating economy in 1932, Paul Elsberg, editor-in-chief of Ullstein's central business desk, lauded the move and prophesied a considerable strengthening of purchasing power in the near future.[70] But Ullstein did not rely on the government alone to make consumers spend again. The same issue featured tear-out flyers for readers to send to their own clients, urging them to build a "front of all optimists fighting against the fear of consumption (*Kaufangst*)."[71] In the accompanying instructions on how to use these leaflets, the readers were called upon to set an example by increasing their own expenditure: "Spending creates jobs! Jobs create income, which will be spent on your products. So fight with us for a healthy consumer optimism (*Kaufoptimismus*) and start—in your own interest—with yourself!"[72]

Thus, it is not surprising that *Tempo*'s emphasis on consumer products and idyllic scenes of leisure—and on spending money on them—did not change over the course of 1932, even when its consumerist vision was undermined by the ongoing crisis. The "Technology Everybody Needs" column continued to introduce readers to electric shavers, vacuum cleaners, and new photography equipment. However, the dire situation of the country also left its mark on this series dedicated to conspicuous consumption. One installment presented a novel concealed truncheon as a defensive weapon in case *Tempo*'s readers found themselves in a street robbery, while another one introduced new motorized gardening tools for *Kleinsiedler*, people living in suburban emergency housing for the unemployed.[73] Despite the depressing fact that its read-

---

69. C. Enseo, "Es gibt keine tote Saison!," *Ullstein-Berichte*, July 1932, 1–2.
70. Paul Elsberg, "Die Kauflust ist erwacht," *Ullstein-Berichte*, October 1932, 1–2.
71. *Ullstein-Berichte*, October 1932, unpaginated.
72. *Ullstein-Berichte*, unpaginated.
73. "Technik, die jeder braucht," 11 May 1932, 2; 7 September 1932, 4. For the history of "Kleinsiedlungen" in the Weimar Republic, see Susan R. Henderson, "Self-Help Housing in the Weimar Republic: The Work of Ernst May," *Housing Studies* 14, no. 3 (May 1999): 311–28; Tilman Harlander, Katrin Hater, and Franz Meiers, *Siedeln in der Not. Umbruch von Wohnungspolitik und Siedlungsbau am Ende der Weimarer Republik* (Hamburg: Christians, 1988).

ers might be in need of such gadgets, the newspaper still advertised them in the same enthusiastic tone it used when introducing common consumer durables.

Women were called upon once again to act as the vanguard of consumption. At the start of the traditional sales weeks in January, *Tempo* painted an image of female consumers storming the shops and frantically spending their money despite their limited means, because "after all, there is but one way to fight the crisis: buying!"[74] Housewives were reminded again of their important role as wielders of the shopping basket: "You can go shopping even with limited means and that is why it is important—very important, even—to appeal to the proven economic power of the housewife."[75] The fall sales at the end of the year were also a major news item in *Tempo*, with prominently placed photos showing crowds of shoppers thronging the stores. The sales had started a day after the parliamentary elections on 31 July 1932, and *Tempo* explicitly linked the act of shopping to the democratic process by captioning one of the photos with the line "Women must continue voting (*wählen*)" (Fig. 27).

According to *Tempo*, the worse the times got, the more fervently people engaged in entertainment and leisure culture. There was a supposed "bull market for dancing" in Berlin, despite the mass unemployment of musicians and dance orchestras, the paper claimed.[76] People either danced at home or in cheap bars, with music provided by the radio or the gramophone, but the "joy in dancing" (*Tanzlust*) was unprecedented. The institution of the free weekend also still featured prominently in *Tempo*. However, the image of Berlin's green periphery changed from an integral part of the urban experience, where humble white-collar workers and senior managers alike came together to enjoy their leisure time, to an escape from the desolation of the city. A new illustrated series published every Thursday presenting routes for day trips to the countryside described the weekend as a time to escape from the worries of the crisis-ridden metropolis.[77] When the city administration put on an informational fair about ways to spend the weekend, from working an allotment to camping, *Tempo* lauded the initiative for "showing the way toward the courage to face life and a love of life."[78] While the newspaper had earlier framed the weekend as a necessary way to recuperate one's work capacity in an industrial society, it now focused on the way it enabled people to form "a bond with our native soil." At the beginning of the Whitsun holiday, *Tempo* reported about a sudden

---

74. "Ausverkauf—trotz allem," *Tempo*, 3 January 1932, 3.
75. "Die Hausfrau soll wieder kaufen!," *Tempo*, 5 October 1932, 6.
76. "Tanzlust wie noch nie," *Tempo*, 6 January 1932, 5.
77. "Der Zeichner führt ins Wochenende," *Tempo*, 12 May 1932, 3.
78. "Sommerschau vor der Eröffnung," *Tempo*, 29 April 1932, 3.

Figure 27. "Herbst-Ausverkauf beginnt," *Tempo*, 1 August 1932, 3. © Axel Springer AG. Used with permission.

interest in trips to the countryside, leading to an "almost life-threatening rush" on Berlin's railway stations.[79] The article, printed on the front page next to a report about Robert Ley's attack on SPD chairman Otto Wels, was headed with a line from a Stefan George poem from 1896 as a motto: "We vow to be happy!" (*Geloben wir, glücklich zu sein!*). Again, happiness through consumption was framed as a national duty that had to be performed in the face of widespread destitution, pessimism, and political violence. At the start of the summer season, *Tempo* reported on the supposedly fully booked chartered trains to Bavaria and the Baltic Sea that showed that "despite everything" people were still eagerly booking their holidays.[80] Considering the sharp fall in revenues of Ger-

---

79. "Hinaus ins Grüne! Großer Pfingstverkehr. Die Pfingst-Parole: 'Geloben wir, glücklich zu sein!'," *Tempo*, 14 May 1932, 1–2.
80. "Trotz allem Ferienreisen!," *Tempo*, 28 June 1932, 10.

many's biggest travel agency, the Mitteleuropäisches Reisebüro, this has to be considered a very optimistic, if not deliberately falsified, account of the situation.[81] A day later, *Tempo* reported on its front page that sunny weather was predicted in the whole of Europe for the coming weeks and that "the summer holiday we yearned for for so long can now be started with the greatest optimism."[82] In the same issue, "Hans Einfach," *Tempo*'s voice of the common man, weighed up the question of going on a holiday in the middle of the deepest economic crisis in modern history. The character, a sensible, salt-of-the-earth fellow, had been introduced at the beginning of the year with his own column. True to his name, this "John Simple" made unpretentious remarks about the folly of political violence, gave his two pennies' worth about the appointment of Franz von Papen, and poked fun at the Nazis.[83] He described the decision to spend money on a holiday, despite not being able to afford it, as a necessary defiance of the economic situation: "Finally it's summer. Many people are sitting at home at the moment, contemplating if they can afford a few days of holiday. I have come to the conclusion that I can't afford it. And that's exactly why I will go on a holiday! . . . We just *have* to afford it."[84] Even *Tempo*'s voice of common sense framed vacationing as a duty rather than a luxury. However, the fact that *Tempo*'s traditional competition for readers' holiday snaps was quietly discontinued this year suggests that the majority of its audience could not afford such a luxury, even if they had the utmost conviction to do so.

Even when the paper addressed the precarious situation of many of its readers, it continued to put a positive spin on it. An article described life in the many permanent campsites that had emerged in Berlin's countryside as "tent city magic," painting a romantic image of places that in fact often served as makeshift homes for tenants who had been evicted from their houses in the city.[85] People who only a few years ago had spent their weekends in their cramped apartments or loitering in the streets, the author claimed, now enjoyed

---

81. Keitz, "Massentourismus," 192.

82. "Mit Sonne in die Ferien!," *Tempo*, 27 June 1932, 1.

83. "Hans Einfach denkt ganz einfach," *Tempo*, 1 June 1932, 10; 15 June 1932, 10; 28 June 1932, 10.

84. "Hans Einfach denkt ganz einfach," *Tempo*, 29 June 1932, 10.

85. Evmari, "Zeltstadtzauber," *Tempo*, 18 May 1932, 3. See Eve Rosenhaft, "The Unemployed in the Neighbourhood: Social Dislocation and Political Mobilisation in Germany 1929–33," in *The German Unemployed. Experiences and Consequences of Mass Unemployment from the Weimar Republic to the Third Reich*, ed. Richard J. Evans and Dick Geary (London: Routledge, 2015), 194–227.

healthy activities such as swimming and sailing in the fresh air and were able to forget their daily strife. Similarly, the public summer camps for underprivileged and malnourished children offered by Berlin's city council were described as a "holiday paradise."[86] According to *Tempo*, young people fled the daily struggle of unemployment and destitution to cheery work camps in the countryside.[87]

The Political Appeal of Slowness: Technology and Speed during the Crisis

While the image of nature as an antidote to the modern malaise grew ever more important in *Tempo*, the paper became even more suspicious of modern technology over the course of 1932. Gustav Kauder now identified it as a problematic influence on politics: modern loudspeakers flattened all nuances in political speeches and contributed to a "massification" of politics that replaced face-to-face deliberation.[88] While *Tempo* had described radio's ability to unite the nation in its coverage of the International Broadcasting Exhibition only a year earlier, there was no hope for it this year. On the contrary, as *Tempo* reported, the exhibition's opening was repeatedly interrupted by groups of Communists and Nazis.[89] Even here, a location that the paper had always portrayed as a place of national unity and a showcase for the Republic's strength and ingenuity, Germany's domestic fragmentation made itself felt. *Tempo* also did not glorify speed and the modern culture of velocity any longer. When a new record was established for the flight from Berlin to New York, "Hans Einfach" asked if it really was so desirable if the world was growing smaller all the time: "How about somebody trying to go from Berlin to Potsdam in the slowest way possible?"[90] In contrast to its earlier obsession with speed and technology as a necessary aspect of modern society that reflected the spirit of youth, *Tempo* now embraced a deceleration of life. The slowness and steadiness of life had also finally become *Tempo*'s aim in politics. On the eve of the first round of the presidential election, *Tempo* stressed what was at stake: "[The German people] have to choose between slow and steady reconstruction or quick destruction,

---

86. L.B., "Im Paradies der Ferienkinder," *Tempo*, 19 July 1932, 3.
87. Renée Christian, "Jugend findet Arbeit," *Tempo*, 29 June 1932, 3.
88. Gustav Kauder, "Stadion und Lautsprecher," *Tempo*, 30 July 1932, 5.
89. "Funk-Ausstellung eröffnet," *Tempo*, 19 August 1932, 1–2.
90. "Hans Einfach denkt ganz einfach," *Tempo*, 7 July 1932, 12.

between hard work or risky venture, between Hindenburg or Hitler."[91] In stark contrast to 1928, *Tempo* now no longer linked speed to democracy and progress, but to destructive politics, while Hindenburg's old age, dependability, and deliberateness stood for the country's future.

In a similar fashion, *Tempo*'s embrace of *Sachlichkeit* changed. In politics, *Tempo* continued to espouse the ideal of the rational, commonsense, levelheaded citizen. Instead of the figure of "the voter," who had embodied this ideal in 1930, this time "Hans Einfach" took over this role. *Tempo*'s voice of the common man often compared the hostile climate of Weimar's political sphere to everyday situations, such as a squabbling family or life in a tenement house, with the extremists being portrayed as wayward sons or annoying neighbors, but ultimately part of the community, who could be tamed and integrated.[92] Clearly, the aim of such articles was to create a sense of normality in uncertain times among *Tempo*'s audience and to give them a model to follow. In other parts of the paper, however, the value of rationality had lost its allure. The lax morals of the "rational girls" (*sachliche Mädchen*) of the 1920s, "Frau Christine" argued in one of her columns, had given men a twisted idea of sexuality and had ultimately lowered their respect for women.[93] *Sachlichkeit* had changed its meaning in *Tempo* from a progressive, affirmative approach to the modern world to an ambivalent quality of a commonsense conservatism in politics on the one hand and a soulless materialism in culture on the other.

The Oldest Guard Leads the Way:
Constructions of Modern Masculinity and Femininity in 1932

Tempo's conflicting approach to Weimar's young people continued in 1932. By that time, young men played only a marginal role in *Tempo* and the paper did not go to great lengths to construct an adapted ideal of modern masculinity as it did with its image of women. One of the few instances in which *Tempo* engaged in a definition of the modern man was an article that urged men to share the burden of domestic work. Since the economic crisis had forced many married women to work and to "leave the house as early as him, just to return as tired as him," the female author argued, it was unacceptable that many men still refused to take up cooking. This was not only a question of equality, but of common sense, because sharing these chores saved time, money, and energy:

---

91. M. m., "Der gesunde Sinn," *Tempo*, 12 March 1932, 3.
92. "Hans Einfach denkt ganz einfach," *Tempo*, 31 May 1932, 10; 2 June 1932, 10.
93. "Fragen Sie Frau Christine: Tolpatsch der Liebe," *Tempo*, 10 December 1932, 8.

A real woman does not lose any of her femininity because she holds down a job during the day and real masculinity is not compromised by using logic and care in the household for a change. On the contrary, a man who knows how to prepare a good *omlette* has real "sex appeal!"[94]

A similar tone was struck in a collectible series of German and international film stars that ran over the second half of the year. Many of the male actors presented in the series were described as coming from humble origins, having worked their way up to stardom while retaining their down-to-earth nature. According to *Tempo*, Willy Fritsch, one of the most popular German actors at the time, "has always remained the natural, humble, nice person he was when he started out," which was the source of his "likable, fresh masculinity."[95] Conrad Veidt, an actor famous for his haunting portrayals of dark characters, was portrayed as a doting father of "his little daughter Vera-Viola."[96] Even international film stars such as Gary Cooper and Harold Lloyd were described, respectively, as "a bloke (*Kerl*) through and through, who never relies on his stardom in his films, but convinces through his magnificent naturalness" and as a "loving father."[97] Rather than extravagance, fame, and exoticism, the masculinity these men represented, according to *Tempo*, was domesticated, relatable, and entailed the hope of hard work paying off—a masculinity fit for the crisis year of 1932. Even in the construction of the modern man, a return to nature and an unpretentious "naturalness" (*Natürlichkeit*) had become a desirable quality in *Tempo*, a trend that was also visible in men's fashion.[98] Consequently, Luis Trenker, the South Tyrolean alpinist turned film star, was presented as "the most manly type in German film" by the paper.[99]

Politically, however, modern young men had become even more suspect than in 1930. In fact, a large part of the liberal spectrum had given up winning over young people for their cause. The pedagogue and publisher Peter Suhrkamp explained young people's rejection of all liberal parties as a longing for economic security, ideological simplicity, and intellectual uniformity in a complex, complicated, and relativist world—something Weimar's liberal

---

94. Hedwig Hirschbach, "Männer, lernt kochen!," *Tempo*, 22 January 1932, 5.
95. "Ist das ihr Film-Typ?," *Tempo*, 3 June 1932, 6.
96. "Ist das ihr Film-Typ?," *Tempo*, 3 May 1932, 6.
97. "Ist das ihr Film-Typ," *Tempo*, 19 May 1932, 6; 13 June 1932, 6.
98. Katie Sutton, "From Dandies to Naturburschen: The Gendering of Men's Fashions in Weimar Germany," *Edinburgh German Yearbook* 2 (2008): 130–48; Petro, *Joyless Streets*, 124.
99. "Ist das ihr Film-Typ?," *Tempo*, 20 June 1932, 6.

forces were not able to offer.[100] Similarly, the economist Moritz Julius Bonn argued that postwar Germany had no place for young, educated, middle-class men.[101] In an article for *Das Tage-Buch*, Manfred Georg wrote an epitaph for Weimar's democratic youth. The Weimar Republic, he argued, had been built on the "Ebert line," a compromise between the people and the state based on the realistic attainability of an adequate standard of living.[102] Now that it had become clear that young men had no realistic chance of achieving this standard anymore, they were fighting against a state that did not seem to offer them any opportunities to lead a decent life. Georg put the blame firmly on the liberal establishment. With the young generation, he claimed, Weimar's political leaders had squandered the Republic's best and most promising asset. In *Tempo*, it was the old generation that now stood for the political future of the Republic. Instead of the "face of the young generation," its 1928 series of young actors and actresses, the paper now presented "Berlin's oldest guard"—long-serving chauffeurs, well-known waiters in famous restaurants, and other semipublic figures—as a symbol of perseverance and reliability in troubled times and as an inspiration for young men.[103] The most important representative of these weathered pillars of society was President Hindenburg. After he had announced his renewed candidacy for the presidential election in 1932, *Tempo* lauded him as a shining example for the nation's youth.[104] His decision to stand again, the paper argued, came at an important moment:

> This happens at a time that has created a veritable cult around youth and worships immaturity. It almost seems as if youth is not an enviable age, but something of a personal achievement; as if young people, just because they haven't achieved anything yet, are destined for the greatest achievements; as if a lack of experience is a blessing, youthful rashness is real drive, uncritical enthusiasm is the only judgment that counts. Our political parties, particularly the demagogues of all colors, can't get enough of this glorification of youth.[105]

---

100. Peter Suhrkamp, "Söhne ohne Väter und Lehrer. Die Situation der bürgerlichen Jugend," *Neue Rundschau*, January 1932, 695–96.
101. Moritz Julius Bonn, "Die intellektuelle Jugend," *Das Tage-Buch*, 16 July 1932, 1105–9.
102. Manfred Georg, "Wo blieb die Jugend der Republik?," *Das Tage-Buch*, 30 January 1932, 190–91.
103. E–i., "Berlins älteste Garde," *Tempo*, 29 February 1932, 3. The series ran over the whole year in over twenty installments.
104. M.m., "Der Alte und die Jungen," *Tempo*, 17 February 1932, 3.
105. M.m., "Der Alte und die Jungen," 3.

With this rejection of the "cult of youth," *Tempo* distanced itself completely from its own role as an advocate of young people it had claimed in 1928 and even condemned the political mobilization of the youth that Ullstein had presented as one of the central aims of the new paper.

By 1932, *Tempo* had also completely turned away from the "Girl" and the "Garçonne" and distanced itself even further from its feminine ideal of 1928. In one of the poems that regularly appeared on *Tempo*'s entertainment pages, Polly Tieck described an intellectual, bob-haired, urban woman, spending her time in bohemian cafés, as "the woman of yesterday."

> That's the type of yesterday,
> which has almost gone extinct.
> She is not very popular
> with her younger sisters.
> . . .
> She sits at coffee tables
> in many coffee houses,
> and rarely ever sees
> the dewy forest.[106]

The difference between this negative image of the "New Woman" and the paper's own positive promotion of a "modern" type of femininity in 1928 could not be greater. The cosmopolitan "Girl" type now stood for a bygone age, while naturalness and closeness to nature were framed as "modern" instead. A serialized report about the life of silent film star and variety show dancer Lya de Putti was a veritable swan song for the "Girl" type. The Hungarian actress, born Amália Putti, had enjoyed phenomenal success in Germany in the early 1920s with roles as a seductive flapper, but she died alone in 1931 in a New York hospital after her attempts to make it in Hollywood had been unsuccessful. *Tempo*'s sensationalized account of her life described her as a reflection of "the spirit of the inflation years, which turned everything upside down, and in which she led her whole life."[107] In the same space in which *Tempo*, in 1928, had celebrated the fictional "Girl" Dixie Dugan, the paper now described the real-life embodiment of this type as a bygone "image of a time that seems to have passed for far longer than it actually did."[108]

---

106. Katta Launisch (i.e., Polly Tieck), "Die Gestrige," *Tempo*, 12 May 1932, 5.

107. Nancy Ballogh and Lisa Matthias, "Glanz und Untergang eines Filmstars," *Tempo*, 6 April 1932, 3.

108. Ballogh and Matthias, "Glanz und Untergang eines Filmstars," *Tempo*, 26 April 1932, 5.

Another illustrative example of this shift is the rebuke "Frau Christine" gave to a representative of the "New Woman" ideal of the 1920s. In her letter, the successful director of a fashion store, who had used the nom de plume "a thoroughly rational woman" (*eine durch und durch Sachliche*), mocked the romantic ideals of other women writing in to "Frau Christine." She voiced her concerns that they were about to give up their hard-earned new freedoms, including more equal relations with men and, not least, the modern fashion of short skirts and short hair. In her answer, "Frau Christine" was outspoken in her rejection of rational womanhood, companionate marriage, the *Bubikopf*, and the flapper dress, favoring old-fashioned values of devotion and matrimony that, according to her, the more reasonable girls of the 1930s now subscribed to:

> You still adhere to values and emotions of 1928, which are now out of style. Working in the fashion industry, you could not help but notice the dropping hemlines and the return of more feminine hairstyles. But you had no eyes for the changes in women's emotional lives. . . . The girls of today are thinking too highly of themselves to only be a sexual object or a "companion" and they do not want to bear this horrible spiritual emptiness any longer. They long for the one—and I repeat: one—great, strong and profound experience that prepares them for marriage and life as a married woman.[109]

The explicit rejection of the defining features of the independent "New Woman" and of *Sachlichkeit* as the guiding ideal for gender relationships amounted to a renunciation of *Tempo*'s own programmatic emphasis on youth, gender equality, and modernity that the paper had formulated in 1928—a year that "Frau Christine" now treated as a symbol of an outdated cult of rationality. Apart from a more conservative dress code, as "Frau Christine" explained to a reader who had complained that the new fashion no longer allowed her to use her shapely legs to attract men, the defining characteristic of this new model of femininity was characterized by a deep emotionality and sincere devotedness.[110]

This new feminine ideal was also expressed in a comic strip that portrayed the young woman of today, in contrast to *Tempo*'s "Brigittchen," not as a clever, sexually independent flapper anymore, but as a girl still yearning, despite all

---

109. "Frau Christine: Die Sachliche," *Tempo*, 9 April 1932, 8.
110. "Fragen Sie Frau Christine: Die verlorene Chance," *Tempo*, 4 June 1932, 8.

Figure 28. Ottmar Starke, "Kleiner *Tempo*-Bilderbogen: Des Mädchens Wandlung," *Tempo*, 8 August 1932, 7. © Axel Springer AG. Used with permission.

modern achievements, for a protective, virile lover (Fig. 28). *Tempo*'s collectible series of film stars that constructed a natural, down-to-earth masculinity also portrayed German and international actresses as domesticated. Marlene Dietrich was described as being "attached in great love to her five-year-old little daughter" and Gloria Swanson as "very fond of children."[111] According to *Tempo*, Olga Chekhova's home was "a model of intimate family life" and the paper told its readers that Joan Crawford, besides her successful acting career, was also a "brilliant housewife."[112] In contrast to the 1920s, when the paper described such highly accomplished and internationally famous female actresses mainly as exotic and attractive "Girls," it now stressed their domestic-

---

111. "Ist das ihr Film-Typ?," *Tempo*, 7 May 1932, 6; 6 July 1932, 6.
112. "Ist das ihr Film-Typ?," *Tempo*, 27 July 1932, 6; 8 August 1932, 6.

ity. The image of femininity expressed in these portraits was more demure, motherly, and down-to-earth, embodying a more relatable modern woman during times of unprecedented economic crisis and political retrenchment.

Over the course of 1932, the shifts in *Tempo*'s vision of a German consumer modernity that had set in after September 1930 continued. Rather than a progressive, modern, and prosperous democracy, Germany's future was imagined in more conservative terms as a family-oriented consumer community that cared for the physical as well as the spiritual well-being of its members. Rather than the young generation, older men and down-to-earth women were now constructed as the ideal representatives of this vision. This moderate modernity still clashed, however, with the visions for Germany's future that the Nazis were starting to put into practice in the following year.

30 January 1933: Ullstein under Hitler

Ullstein's hopes of an end to Weimar's political crisis were shattered after Hindenburg finally appointed Hitler as chancellor of a coalition government on 30 January 1933. Nevertheless, Schäffer still kept the Ullstein publications on a line of "loyal opposition" and constructive criticism.[113] Surprisingly, *Tempo* did not comment directly on Hitler's appointment, but it continued to inform its readers about Nazi assaults, ongoing court cases against violent brownshirts, and the improper conduct of NSDAP deputies.[114] However, the governmental involvement of the Nazis did not turn out to be the beginning of their downfall, as Schäffer had hoped. Only two days after being sworn in, Hitler asked the president to dissolve parliament again. In an address to the German people broadcast on the same day, Hitler attacked the previous governments and the Republic itself as "fourteen years of Marxism" that had reduced Germany to a "field of rubble."[115] Schäffer later claimed that this speech made it clear to him that there would be no free press under the new regime.[116] In the end, he was a

---

113. Schäffer diary, 6 March 1933, in LBI, AR 7177/MF 512, 10, Nr. 4, fol. 4.

114. "Krawalle im Reich," *Tempo*, 31 January 1933, 10; "Politische Schreckenstat in Bahnmeisterei," *Tempo*, 1 *February* 1933, 10; "Zwei Tote in der vergangenen Nacht," *Tempo*, 4 February 1933, 10; "Sechzehn SA-Leute im Verhör," *Tempo*, 5 February 1933, 2; "Lärm-Szenen gegen Löbe," *Tempo*, 7 February 1933, 1–2; "Sturm-Szenen gegen Löbe," *Tempo*, 14 February 1933, 1–2.

115. Adolf Hitler, *Das junge Deutschland will Arbeit und Frieden. Reden des Reichskanzlers Adolf Hitler, des neuen Deutschlands Führer* (Berlin: Liebheit & Thiesen, 1933), 3.

116. Schäffer diary, 1933, in LBI, AR 7177/MF 512, 10, Nr. 2, fol. 2.

civil servant at heart who believed in the primacy of order and reason and saw politics as a rational management of problems. The irrationality of National Socialist ideology was completely alien to him and, as he later admitted, he ultimately underestimated Hitler.[117]

On 4 February, a new emergency decree granted the government extensive powers to ban newspapers and in the following days it used them mostly to suppress the party press of the SPD and the German Communist Party, the Nazis' biggest competitors in the upcoming Reichstag elections.[118] But Ullstein, always a prime target for Nazi aggression, was also attacked. On 16 February, Schäffer himself published an article calling for restraint in the political in-fighting and tried to debunk several myths touted by the right aimed at discrediting the Republic, including Hitler's image of a "field of rubble."[119] On the same day, and just a day after he was appointed as the new chief of the Berlin police, Magnus von Levetzow, a high-profile Reichstag deputy for the NSDAP, banned *Tempo* for a week.[120] Goebbels' *Angriff* reported on the ban on its front page, citing a recent article "that compromised vital interests of the state" as the reason.[121] The Nazi paper referred to an inside source, who described the ban as a reaction to Ullstein's supposedly methodical attacks on Germany's international credit standing by defeatist reports in the business sections of the company's newspapers. The company had also artificially inflated prices for lard, the *Angriff* claimed, by encouraging panic buying among the readers, and then blaming the rising costs on the government. *Tempo* had indeed criticized the impact of new tariffs for imported lard imposed by economics minister Hugenberg.[122] However, the government's move was an obvious attempt to silence a newspaper that had long been an outspoken political enemy, and Ullstein challenged the ban in the Supreme Court, which lifted it retroactively, charging the Prussian state for the incurred costs.[123] *Tempo*'s ban was an unmistakable warning shot: if Ullstein continued to offer even moderate criticism, the government was prepared to even use illegal means to silence its publications and to bankrupt the company.

---

117. Wandel, *Schäffer*, 236.
118. Koszyk, *Geschichte*, 354–55.
119. "Kampf dem Schlagwort," *Vossische Zeitung*, 16 February 1933, 1–2. See also Schäffer diary, 1933, in LBI, AR 7177/MF 512, 10, Nr. 4, fol. 2.
120. *Tempo*, 24 February 1933, 1.
121. "Gegen die Hetze der Journaille. *Tempo* verboten," *Der Angriff*, 17 February 1933, 1–2.
122. "Teueres Schmalz," *Tempo*, 10 February 1933, 8.
123. "*Tempo*-Verbot aufgehoben," *Tempo*, 25 February 1933, 1.

The Reichstag fire of 27 February 1933 and the following emergency decrees did away with the rest of press freedom that had still existed in Germany and firmly cemented the Nazi regime in power. In the run-up to the general election in March, the government made frequent use of its new powers, banning left-wing newspapers throughout Germany.[124] *Tempo* had effectively been purged of any liberal or even any overtly political content after its ban in February. However, on the eve of the general election in March, the paper urged its readers for a last time not to let themselves be intimidated or bewitched by propaganda, but to do their duty as citizens and vote according to their personal conviction:

> The free and secret ballot is only subject to the inner dictate of the voter's political opinion. The ruling parties were able to use the whole power of a mighty propaganda machine to strengthen their supporters' opinions and influence the opinions of those they want to win over. The opposition did not have access to such propaganda. . . . This is why everybody must vote according to their personal convictions, unfazed by all influences that cannot have an effect against an attitude founded in reflection, education, and experience.[125]

Even if it no longer could defend Weimar's democratic institutions, *Tempo* championed the idea of individual freedom, personal responsibility, and rationality as the cornerstones of citizenship. The rational voter as the embodiment of these values remained at the core of the paper's political vision, in which the Republic appeared as a manifestation of the will of the electorate.

On 5 March 1933, the NSDAP expanded its share of the vote to nearly 44 percent. It is difficult to speak of a democratic discourse after this date, not only because the effective suspension of the freedom of the press made it virtually impossible but also because the liberal forces had evidently lost the battle for the Republic and a debate about the right form of democracy seemed like a pointless exercise. The liberal journalists who did comment on the political situation could offer nothing more than a vague consolation in a hopefully brighter future.[126] After this victory was secured, the regime turned its attention to the liberal press. On the night of the election, Heinz Ullstein was arrested by

---

124. Koszyk, *Geschichte*, 356–57.
125. "Jeder übe sein Stimmrecht aus!," *Tempo*, 4 March 1933, 1–2.
126. Sösemann, *Ende*, 172–75.

the stormtroopers and brought to the NSDAP's Berlin headquarters for questioning. According to Schäffer, Heinz voted against reporting the incident in the company's papers after he was released the next day: "He does not ... feel obliged to play the martyr for opinions the company used to entertain against his will."[127] This direct rejection of the company's liberal-democratic tradition by a senior member of the management is a telling sign of the ideological confusion at the Ullstein house and shows—despite *Tempo*'s frequent calls to arms—how far the company had moved from its democratic ethos. A few days after the election, Ferdinand Bausback, chairman of the Ullstein supervisory board, reported that the government was drawing up plans for how to deal with the company, which involved the dismissal of Jewish employees.[128] According to Bausback, Goebbels was intent on systematically ruining the company with bans of its publications and attacks on advertising clients until the Nazis could cheaply buy up Ullstein's printing plant, while Hermann Göring wanted to preserve the company's press as an oppositional fig leaf. When the government sent a list of demands to the Ullstein management, Göring's plan seemed to have won out.[129] Ullstein was allowed to keep up a modest, yet loyal opposition, under condition of fundamental changes in the company's management, including the dismissal of Schäffer and the admission of several people with close ties to the government. After a short deliberation, the Ullsteins accepted. On 13 March 1933, Schäffer left the company.[130]

However, it was not only the new government applying pressure on the company: by now, there were many among the staff who sympathized with the new regime. The Ullstein works council was dominated by Nazis, and on 12 May the council organized a protest, demanding a quicker dismissal of all Jewish employees, which resulted in disruption of the printing of the evening papers.[131] In a reply to the council's demands, the management confirmed the termination of its contracts with Gustav Kauder, Hanns G. Lustig, Moritz Goldstein, and eleven other Jewish colleagues.[132] Another twelve were in the process of leaving the company, including Manfred Georg and Julius Elbau. The circular ended with a promise to continue to purge the staff of Jewish workers. By then, any residue of critical coverage had been purged from *Tempo*

---

127. Schäffer diary, 6 March 1933, in LBI, AR 7177/MF 512, 10, Nr. 4, fol. 6.
128. Schäffer diary, 8–10 March 1933, in LBI, AR 7177/MF 512, 10, Nr. 4, fols. 12–16.
129. Schäffer diary, 11 March 1933, in LBI, AR 7177/MF 512, 10, Nr. 4, fols. 17–20.
130. Schäffer diary, 11 March 1933, in LBI, AR 7177/MF 512, 10, Nr. 4, fol. 20.
131. Eksteins, *Limits*, 288.
132. Undated circular, in BArchL, N2193 Misch, Nr. 13, fol. 83.

and replaced with glowing reports about Goebbels's work as minister, Hitler's tireless efforts to rebuild the battered nation, and a supposedly jubilant population welcoming the government's reforms.

After Schäffer's departure, Ullstein needed another political helmsman, and this time it had to be someone with good connections to the Nazi regime. When Eduard Stadtler, a Nazi member of parliament, contacted the Ullsteins and offered his services, he was hired as "political director" on 1 July.[133] On 12 July, Stadtler was granted an audience with Hitler to discuss Ullstein's "Aryanization," in which the new chancellor agreed to keep the name of the company for "reasons of foreign policy."[134] In a general staff meeting a few days later, Stadtler passed on Hitler's greetings to Ullstein's employees and prepared them for the coming "reorganization" of the company.[135] However, the fact that Stadtler was able to meet Hitler says more about the Nazi leader's personal interest in the company than about Stadtler's real influence. He was an opportunistic turncoat, whose allegiance had shifted from the DVP to the DNVP over the course of his political career. Stadtler was elected to the Reichstag for the National Conservatives in July 1932 but joined the NSDAP parliamentary group after March 1933. Because of this ideological flexibility his application for party membership had been rejected. In his new position as Ullstein's political leader, he tried to ingratiate himself with the regime by accelerating the *Gleichschaltung* (synchronization) of the company. In 1934, after he had done his duty and the Ullstein family had withdrawn from executive positions and the majority of the shares had been transferred to people close to the new government, Stadtler was dropped by Hitler and had to leave the company.[136]

"Everybody Will Have Their Own Car!"
Dreams of a *"Volkswagen"* in *Tempo*

At the beginning of 1933, liberal commentators had seen hopeful signs that the period of democratic "hibernation" might be over. Not only had the popularity

---

133. For Stadtler, see Eksteins, *Limits*, 288–90.
134. "Die Neuordung des Verlages Ullstein 1933/34," UAS, Ullstein files, f. 2. The government files concerning the *Gleichschaltung* of the Ullstein company can be found in BArchK, R 43 II, 469c. See also Robert M. W. Kempner, "Hitler und die Zerstörung des Hauses Ullstein. Dokumente und Vernehmungen," in Freyburg and Wallenberg, *Hundert Jahre Ullstein*, 3:267–92.
135. "Ein Abend der NSBO-Zelle Ullstein," *Tempo*, 19 July 1933, 3.
136. State Secretary Lammers to Stadtler, 24 May 1934, in BArchK, R 43 II, 469c, fol. 53.

of the NSDAP seemed to have reached a climax, but the economy had shown the first signs of recovery.[137] *Tempo* added its usual optimism: during the traditional sales weeks in January, the paper painted the picture of spend-happy consumers storming the shops and "cranking up" the economy, with women leading the charge.[138] Hitler's shocking appointment at the end of the month ended the hopes of a democratic consolidation, but *Tempo* kept its positive outlook in economic terms and continued to call on its audience to consume. When Berlin's International Automobile and Motorcycle Exhibition opened again in February 1933 after it had been canceled the year before, *Tempo* touted the aim of mass motorization with undiminished enthusiasm, proclaiming "Everybody will have their own car!" and lauding new models for under 2,000 marks.[139] A few days later, in a regular column that commented on current affairs in rhyme, *Tempo* published an imagined conversation of a young white-collar couple visiting the auto show and dreaming of buying one of the compact cars.[140] Fulfilling this dream, they tell each other, has never been easier: even though he is unemployed at the moment, they are optimistic that the tide will soon turn in their favor. They could pay for it in installments, the couple tell themselves, and they could soon drive to the office and take it on holiday to Bavaria or Pomerania. A final report on the auto show praised the high number of cars sold, which supposedly reflected the optimism of German consumers.[141] While the German auto industry had been recovering since late 1932, this account itself was again overly optimistic. Only after April 1933 did the German auto industry experience a real boom, fueled by significant tax breaks introduced by the Hitler government.[142]

The automotive industry always played a central role in Nazi economic policy.[143] In his opening speech at the International Automobile and Motorcycle Exhibition, just days after he had been appointed as chancellor, Hitler emphasized the historic significance of the car and pledged his support for the aim of mass motorization.[144] In an article on the opening ceremony, *Tempo*

---

137. Sösemann, *Ende*, 163–65.
138. G.O., "'Polizeiwidrig billig!'," *Tempo*, 2 January 1933, 3; "Inventurschlacht hat begonnen," *Tempo*, 2 January 1933, 10; "Frau im Ausverkauf . . . ," *Tempo*, 3 January 1933, 3.
139. "Jeder soll sein Auto haben!," *Tempo*, 10 February 1933, 3–4.
140. Tom, "Ich mach mir meinen Vers: Der kleine Wagen," *Tempo*, 14 February 1933, 6.
141. "Bilanz der Auto-Schau," *Tempo*, 24 February 1933, 10.
142. Edelmann, *Luxusgut*, 149, 68.
143. Steinbeck, *Motorrad*, 212–25; Edelmann, *Luxusgut*, 173–80; Overy, "Economic Recovery," 474–76.
144. Edelmann, *Luxusgut*, 157–58.

reported in detail on Hitler's speech, citing the passages in which he described the German auto industry as a victory of entrepreneurial spirit over government regulation and promised to lower taxes on new cars and motorcycles.[145] When the government abolished all taxes on new motor vehicles a few months later, *Tempo* described the move as exceeding all expectations and "extraordinarily beneficial" for the German car industry.[146] By that time, the German press was already under intense pressure by the new government but, as *Tempo*'s calls on the democratic sense of the population during the elections in March showed, tempered criticism was still possible. However, in this case, *Tempo* could not have found much to disagree with, as the government had fulfilled one of its longest-held demands. For *Tempo*'s audience, who had always been told that only high taxes and unnecessary regulation stood in the way of mass motorization, this news could only be interpreted as an important step toward fulfilling their dream of owning their own *Volksauto*—something the former governments had not managed to do.

The paper's usual optimistic promotion of holiday and weekend bliss also continued unchanged. However, foreign holiday destinations had now completely vanished from *Tempo*'s narrative, while the supposed role of leisure time in building a national community was put in focus. The paper reported in detail on a trade fair, organized under the auspices of Goebbels's new Ministry of Public Enlightenment and Propaganda, that promoted Germany as a holiday destination and was supposed "to point out the beauty of the German homeland to the German people (*Volksgenossen*)."[147] In his opening speech, which *Tempo* reproduced in the report, Goebbels argued that the times when Germans considered going on a holiday abroad as the proper thing to do were over. According to the paper, the nation agreed. At the beginning of summer, *Tempo* announced on its front page that "the optimists were proven right again," as sunshine and warm weather all over Germany supposedly led to a strong "onrush of the travel-happy" on Berlin's train stations.[148] The enthusiastic vacationers were streaming from the capital to all corners of the nation, from the Baltic Sea to the Harz mountains, the paper reported. In a diary published in *Tempo*, the author Traute Wittmann described how she happily swapped luxury hotels and palm trees for a humble room on a farm in the German countryside.[149]

---

145. F.R.L., "Die Eröffnung der Autoschau," *Tempo*, 11 February 1933, 3.
146. "Steuerfreie Wagen und Motorräder," *Tempo*, 8 April 1933, 10.
147. "Besucht das schöne Deutschland!," *Tempo*, 18 May 1933, 3.
148. "Die frohe Pfingstbotschaft: Schönwetter in ganz Deutschland," *Tempo*, 3 June 1933, 1–2.
149. Traute Wittmann, "So eine Fahrt in die Sommerfrische . . . ," *Tempo*, 29 June 1933, 5.

Berlin's nightlife also still played a central role in *Tempo* in the form of the numerous reviews of new shows and films as well as the regular news about the entertainment industry that were published in the paper. However, after Hitler's appointment, the image of Berlin as cesspool of sin and hedonism, often used by German right-wingers to discredit the Weimar Republic and which *Tempo* had rejected vehemently before, crept into the paper.[150] In March, when Berlin's police chief, who had banned *Tempo* in February, closed most of the well-known gay bars in the city, the paper reported in detail on this "great battle against indecency."[151] The rest of the city's nightlife was not portrayed as an exciting, titillating, glamorous demimonde any more, but as a respectable "oasis in confused times" that provided much-needed joy to a downtrodden population.[152]

Youthful Pessimism: Young Men and Women under Chancellor Hitler

After Hitler's appointment, *Tempo*'s image of the nation's young men was characterized by despair. They did not even appear as dangerous radicals anymore—robbed of their future by an unprecedented economic breakdown, they either fled into hedonism and a life of crime or perished in the face of a cruel world that had no place for them.[153] A report on young German emigrants painted an especially bleak picture. The introduction to the five-part series described Weimar's young men in terms that were very similar to the ones of *Tempo*'s manifesto of 1928: rational, *sachlich*, and flexible. However, the optimism that had then pervaded the paper's outlook for young people had now made way for resignation:

> Our youth has no room to live. This horrible insight is particularly common among the age group born between 1906 and 1914. Grown up with war, hunger, and political chaos, they had to make their way through life on their own. These young people took every opportunity offered to them, they took every job they could get, they overcame all prejudices of their

---

150. For the representation of Berlin in right-wing discourse, see Dorothy Rowe, *Representing Berlin: Sexuality and the City in Imperial and Weimar Germany* (London: Routledge, 2017), 130–81; Andrew Lees, "Berlin and Modern Urbanity in German Discourse, 1845–1945," *Journal of Urban History* 17, no. 2 (1991): 153–80.
151. "Grosskampf gegen die Unsittlichkeit," *Tempo*, 4 March 1933, 12.
152. V. Z., "Oase der Musik in wirrer Zeit," *Tempo*, 7 February 1933, 6.
153. M.m., "Wenn junge Herren Geld brauchen," *Tempo*, 5 January 1933, 2; R.M., "Lesen Sie: Georg Glaser: 'Schluckebier'," *Tempo*, 2 March 1933, 6.

family background and thus became men prematurely—tough, capable, and experienced.[154]

The fact that the young generation only consists of men here is noteworthy, as it directly contradicts *Tempo*'s earlier inclusion of women in its generational narrative. The series ended without any hope. Not only was this hardened, rational, and *sachlich* generation forced to leave their country to have any hope of a decent life, but the young emigrants failed miserably. In the end, Germany's young men return in rags to their impoverished homeland that does not offer them a future.[155] In *Tempo*, rather than modern consumer-citizens, Weimar's young men had become the embodiment of the nation's demise.

On 30 January 1933, Lucy von Jacobi, writing one of her last articles for the paper, was reduced to using sarcasm when describing the return of an overtly feminine style in women's fashion. Her column reads like the closing words in the battle for the modern woman and a fatalistic comment on the political news of the day, Hitler's appointment as chancellor:

> It is the wish of every very modern woman today to look like an old portrait. Feminine, humble, and helpless—that is the latest fashion in fashion! A small cape, a cap and a muff made from fur, or any curly fabric will let you fall into line with this fashion without much personal cost. The cape gives you the broader shoulders demanded today, the cap looks just like something out of one of great-granny's photos and the muff is meant to create the illusion that women's mostly very busy hands have nothing else to do than to rest idly inside it.[156]

Most strikingly, the idea of "modernness" had changed from a keyword for equality and progress to a notion of opportunistic complicity with a reactionary concept of femininity—and thus, she implied, with the recent political shift to the right. This was the end result of *Tempo*'s shift in the representation of moderately modern femininity: a more conservative, yet still "modern" figure, combining high fashion, emotional independence, and a busy working life with a demure appearance and political restraint—a type "Frau Christine" would have supported, but Jacobi clearly did not approve of.

---

154. Fred Troje, "... Und so zogen wir nach Kanada," *Tempo*, 9 March 1933, 3.
155. Fred Troje, "... Und so zogen wir nach Kanada," *Tempo*, 11 March 1933, 4; 13 March 1933, 4; 14 March 1933, 3; 15 March 1933, 3.
156. "Tempo der Mode: Ganz wie ein altes Bild," *Tempo*, 30 January 1933, 7.

However, the Hitler government enforced an even more reactionary ideal of femininity than the image *Tempo* had cultivated after 1930. The ideal Nazi woman did not use cosmetics, rejected modern fashion, and refrained from smoking to save her body for the national duty of producing children.[157] In the months following Hitler's appointment, *Tempo* tried to find a compromise between the Nazi ideal of women as natural housewives and mothers and its own moderately modern femininity. In May 1933, "Frau Christine" still reprimanded a female reader, who had boasted about the way in which she filled the "natural" role of a subordinate housewife, for lacking self-confidence and "female dignity."[158] In the first half of the year, *Tempo* ran another series about female pioneers in male-dominated jobs, such as the astronomer Margarete Güssow, the driving instructor Eve Liebert, and the film laboratory technician Herta Jülich (Fig. 29).[159] These women were presented as professionals in their working environment, handling complicated machinery, but their demeanor in the photos was demure, not looking directly into the camera. They were praised for their quiet resilience, optimism, and assertiveness, but already the title of the series—"the first and only ones"—made it clear that these women were not necessarily examples to be followed by the common German woman, but rather interesting outliers. In a short series of articles published in the same month, *Tempo* pondered the question of whether "the woman of today" had to adapt to the changed times. In its answers, the paper defended certain aspects of modern femininity and tried to reconcile them with the Nazi ideal.[160] For example, the paper challenged the claim that smoking did not suit the German woman, and while it admitted that French fashion did not fit the supposedly sturdier frame and "earthy" nature of German females, *Tempo* spoke out for still adhering to an internationally respected "global taste" and against wearing traditional costumes (*Tracht*) in an urban setting. After the news broke that aviatrix Marga von Etzdorf, whom *Tempo* had always presented as a symbol of emancipated womanhood and the dynamism of youth, had died in an accident on her solo flight to Australia, the paper defended such daring and dangerous occupations for women:

---

157. Irene Guenther, *Nazi Chic? Fashioning Women in the Third Reich* (Oxford: Berg, 2004), 91–141; Matthew Stibbe, *Women in the Third Reich* (London: Arnold, 2003), 40–46.

158. "Fragen Sie Frau Christine: Der verhimmelte Mann," *Tempo*, 27 May 1933, 8.

159. S. W.-N., "Die Ersten und Einzigen," *Tempo*, 25 March 1933, 6; *Tempo*, 27 March 1933, 5; 29 March 1933, 5; 30 March 1933, 6; 3 April 1933, 6; 5 April 1933, 6.

160. L. D., "Muss die Frau von heute umlernen?," *Tempo*, 11 May 1933, 7; 22 May 1933, 3–4; 7 June 1933, 3.

Are women not allowed to be brave, capable, and competent? It is impossible to order or ban such traits! . . . To stand by yourself, your ideals and aims against all attacks, that is the most important duty of the German woman.[161]

However, from June onward, such attempts to rescue at least some parts of women's hard-won freedoms in a fusion of the Nazi ideal of the blonde, natural, motherly female and *Tempo*'s "modernized Gretchen" made way for articles determinedly supporting the government's policies. At the beginning of the month, the government introduced so-called *Ehestandsdarlehen*, interest-free loans of up to 1,000 marks for furniture and other domestic items, to enable young couples to marry and start a household. However, the new law was primarily aimed at taking women off the labor market as "double earners" and at boosting the birth rate, as the loan was only available for employed women and paid on the condition that they stop working as soon as they got married, with a quarter of the loan being forgiven for each living child the marriage produced.[162] *Tempo* lauded the plans as being "of utmost significance in terms of demographic and economic policy."[163] The loans were a first step toward securing the nation's future, which was threatened by a worrying decline in the birth rate and the reproduction of people with inferior genetic material, the paper argued. If Germany was to escape the fate of great civilizations such as ancient Greece or Rome, another article concluded, more needed to be done to create a culture of respect for mothers and the coming generations they produced, by promoting a positive attitude toward motherhood as well as an "extermination of all abnormal genomes by the sterilization of the retarded and mentally deficient."[164]

The change in *Tempo*'s image of modern femininity—from glamorous "Girls" to modernized "Gretchens," and from humble "weekend brides" to prolific mothers—is the most striking of all the discursive shifts that took place in the paper between 1928 and 1933. It reflected the political changes of the time as well as the economic crisis that had ended modern Germany's admiration for all things American. The modern woman remained—in contrast to modern masculinity, which was only connotated negatively—a symbol for

---

161. L. D., "Der Mut zur Tat," *Tempo*, 7 June 1933, 3. Etzdorf had actually survived the accident, but had killed herself hours later, a fact the government tried to cover up, see Rieger, *Technology*, 150–55.
162. Stibbe, *Women*, 40–41.
163. Pn–, "Dreihunderttausend Mädchen sollen heiraten," *Tempo*, 11 July 1933, 5.
164. "Gegen den Fluch des Geburtenrückgangs," *Tempo*, 24 June 1933, 3.

Figure 29. Detail from S. W.-N., "Die Ersten und Einzigen," *Tempo*, 25 March 1933, 6. © Axel Springer AG. Used with permission.

Tempo's vision of the future, even in its humbler, moderated version. However, even if its image of modern femininity had changed considerably since 1928, when the newspaper was forced to adopt the Nazi ideal of womanhood in 1933, the break with its earlier vision was stark.

In sum, *Tempo*'s vision of a German consumer society was flattened even further into an image of a modest yet content national community of consumers after January 1933. The newspaper's belief that consumer optimism, even in the face of widespread destitution, was the solution to economic decline remained the same, however, and it continued to frame consumption as a national duty. This did not change even when its worst nightmare of a Chancellor Hitler—and the consequences of this appointment for Weimar democracy—became reality. After this point, the pressure on Ullstein to report glowingly about the initiatives of the new government grew constantly, which explains some of the praise found in *Tempo* for Nazi policies. However, the government's nationalistic vision, embodied most prominently in the idea of the *Volksauto*, was in many respects not too far apart from the moderate modernity *Tempo* had constructed over the past years. Between 1928 and 1933, this vision had shifted from an optimistic, youthful, prosperous, and open democracy to a more modest, socially conservative state steered by a strong, unifying leader. The representatives of this vision also changed, from young, modern male and female white-collar consumers to older, dependable men and determined, yet humble and domestic women.

The End of *Tempo*

On 5 August 1933, *Tempo* ceased publication. It was the first newspaper of the Ullstein company to be discontinued after Hitler's appointment. There were sound commercial reasons for this: the paper had still sold over 100,000 copies a day in January 1933 and its circulation had actually gained slightly in the following months, despite its ban in February. But from April, when the Nazi government tightened its grip on public life and readers of democratic newspapers were intimidated by stormtroopers, its circulation rapidly declined.[165] When it was discontinued, *Tempo*'s daily circulation stood at 54,540 copies. With Ullstein's losses skyrocketing, the paper's lifeline had to be cut.[166] However, another reason for *Tempo*'s early demise was its high profile as a mega-

---

165. Eksteins, *Limits*, 281–82.
166. *Ullstein-Chronik*, 1933, unpaginated.

phone for democracy and as a resolute enemy of National Socialism. The Nazi newspaper *National-Zeitung* had already reported on the impending closure a few days earlier, triumphantly announcing the end of the paper: "The disappearance of this rag, which for a long time led the slanderous battle against the National Socialist movement, will be the beginning of the end for the whole Ullstein company."[167] In fact, *Tempo* did not disappear completely, but was effectively transformed into an afternoon edition of the well-established tabloid *B.Z. am Mittag*.[168] Stadtler reacted with alarm to the *National-Zeitung*'s report and forced the paper to publish a statement in which the *B.Z.*'s new edition was described as "a modern replacement" for *Tempo*.[169] The times had changed so drastically, Stadtler's intervention implied, that *Tempo*, the paper that was supposed to be the manifestation of speed, progress, and modernity, had become *unmodern*.

---

167. "Ullstein-Verlag kracht zusammen," *National-Zeitung*, 2 August 1933, 1.
168. *Ullstein-Chronik*, 1933, unpaginated.
169. Stadtler to Reich Chancellery, 16 August 1933, in BArchL, R43 II, 469c, fol. 1; "Ullstein-Verlag macht in Optimismus. *Tempo* ist vollständig verschwunden," *National-Zeitung*, 7 August 1933, 1.

Conclusion

Creative Adaptations of Modernity in the Interwar Period

The moderate modernity constructed by *Tempo*, its shifting meaning, and the ways its readers tried to put it into practice are examples of the "creative adaptation" that lies at the heart of the concept of alternative modernities. As Dilip P. Gaonkar has remarked, the spaces of creative adaptations of modernity—such as *Tempo*—should be seen as a "site where a people 'make' themselves modern, as opposed to being 'made' modern by alien and impersonal forces, and where they give themselves an identity and a destiny."[1] *Tempo* was an attempt by Ullstein to give modernity a positive meaning and it provided a forum to its readers to engage with this offer to construct themselves as citizen-consumers. It is important not to see such attempts to take ownership of the process of modernization as merely a defensive, passive reaction to soften its impact. People do not see modernity only as threatening force of change, it is "more often perceived as lure than as threat" and people from all walks of life "rise to meet it, negotiate it, and appropriate it in their own fashion."[2] In the history of the Weimar Republic, the negative reactions to modernity have been given outsized attention, while the optimistic appropriations, such as *Tempo*'s, have often been neglected. The identity constructed by *Tempo*'s authors and readers was that of a modern, young German citizen, who expressed their citizenship through participation in a burgeoning consumer society. They treasured and defended liberal values, such as individual freedom and the rule of law, and supported progressive culture and ideas—as long as they did not threaten the existing norms of German society.

---

1. Gaonkar, "On Alternative Modernities," 16.
2. Gaonkar, "On Alternative Modernities," 16.

While the general trajectory of *Tempo*'s vision of a German modernity remained stable, some elements of this vision changed considerably over the five years of the paper's existence.

Tempo's ideal of democracy shifted markedly over the course of its lifetime, from parliamentarianism modeled after Western nations like France, Britain, or the United States to a more authoritarian system of direct democracy that circumvented parliament. To be sure, this rather vague idea, embodied by Reich president Hindenburg, was never developed into a programmatic manifesto, but was a reaction to the deteriorating economic and political climate in the Weimar Republic. The hope remained that representative democracy could be revived after the crisis had passed, as long as its foundation, the Constitution and free and fair elections, survived.

Tempo's ideas about the role of the modern man as an embodiment of responsible democratic consumer-citizenship also changed quite profoundly between 1928 and 1933. While the self-appointed representatives of male youth like Zehrer and Gründel used the same vocabulary of *Sachlichkeit* and materialism as *Tempo*'s journalists did, the paper initially offered a far more affirmative and constructive idea of generational solidarity—not against the present order, but as part of its leadership; not to radically change the world, but to find a place in it. To be sure, *Tempo* effectively retreated from the discourse about modern masculinity after 1930 and left the field to publications like *Die Tat*. Still, *Tempo*'s image of levelheaded, unromantic, and constructive young men and *Die Tat*'s vision of a detached, reticent, yet emotionally charged "Young Front" were two sides of the same coin and cannot be understood without each other. They must be interpreted as reflections of two competing generational units arguing over the dominant interpretation of Weimar modernity. However, the liberal voices in this debate, such as *Tempo*, have been largely ignored by historians in the reconstruction of the contemporary discourse.[3]

Contrary to its relatively early abandonment of the discourse about modern masculinity, *Tempo* tried to influence the public debate about women's role in society until the paper's demise in 1933. Most importantly, *Tempo*'s image of modern femininity was often negotiated between the paper and its audience. In particular, its contest "The Beauty of the Working Woman" and the "Ask Frau Christine" columns show how male and female middle-class readers processed the interpretations offered to them in other parts of the paper, creating a hybrid image of moderately modern femininity consisting of new and traditional aspects of womanhood.

---

3. See also Hung, "'Der deutschen Jugend!'," 112–18.

When it came to its ideal of a German consumer society, *Tempo* did not lose any of its enthusiasm over the years. On the contrary, the more it was undermined by the deteriorating economy, the more optimistic its coverage of affordable holidays, modern consumer goods, and a supposedly imminent mass motorization became. The symbol for this vision was the *Volksauto*, a cheap compact car available for the "little man." It is clear from Ullstein's general editorial policy that behind this unrealistic vision stood the Keynesian belief in consumer spending as the solution for Weimar's economic slump, which threatened its democratic institutions. However, for *Tempo*'s middle-class readership, this policy created a gap between the paper's continued support for the political status quo and its discourse about modernity, which had changed dramatically after 1930: instead of an accelerated, urban lifestyle, Western democracy, and an "American" consumer society, it had been transformed into a German consumer community flanked by more traditional aspects such as the fatherly Hindenburg and the slowness of "Old Berlin." With this vision, *Tempo* reacted to the increasing disillusionment of many Germans with the Weimar Republic's democratic system, which they blamed for the downsides that seemed to come with modern life, such as rationalization, unemployment, economic chaos, and social destabilization. However, it was obvious that liberal forces were not able to deliver this new vision of a German consumer modernity without its threatening features, and a more authoritarian style of governing seemed a more promising path. In Italy, for example, the fascist leader Benito Mussolini had already proven with the establishment of the leisure and recreational organization Opera Nazionale Dopolavoro that the rule of an autocratic regime could go hand in hand with the development of an—albeit humble—consumer society.[4] In Germany, the Nazi utopia of the "Third Reich" promised a modern lifestyle similar to the American "people of plenty" with a simultaneous return to a more traditional social order, where mass society would be dissolved in a "people's community" and a woman would focus on "her husband, her family, her children, and her home" again.[5] As Hans-Ulrich Wehler has argued, at the end of the Weimar Republic, this promise of a people's community that granted access to organized leisure, modern consumer goods, and, not least, a *Volkswagen* replaced the fading liberal ideal of "bourgeois society."[6] While National Socialism would soon

---

4. Victoria De Grazia, *The Culture of Consent: Mass Organisation of Leisure in Fascist Italy* (Cambridge: Cambridge University Press 1981), 187–224.

5. *Hitler: Reden und Proklamationen, 1932–1945*, ed. Max Domarus (Wiesbaden: Löwit, 1973), 1:451.

6. Wehler, *Gesellschaftsgeschichte*, 4:306.

unleash its potential as, in Peukert's words, "modernity's most fatal developmental possibility," in 1933 it also promised to tame the downsides of modernization, which Weimar's liberal forces did not seem able to do.[7] *Tempo*, as a commercial product and a political project, needed to reflect this fact through the shifts in its vision of a moderate German modernity.

Such considerations inevitably lead to the question of the political significance of the moderate modernity that *Tempo* constructed. Which role did it play in the breakdown of Weimar democracy? Did it unwittingly pave the way for the Nazis' rise to power? It cannot be denied that there are some overlaps and similarities between *Tempo*'s liberal vision and the "alternative modernity" of the Nazis. Most of all, there is a peculiar continuity of the consumerist vision created by Ullstein and the "virtual consumption" that characterized National Socialist politics. The "virtual consumption" offered by *Tempo*—the prospect of affordable automobiles and household appliances—to shore up popular support for the Weimar Republic was the same tactic, described by Hartmut Berghoff, that the Nazi regime used to create support and consent only a few years later.[8] *Tempo*'s advertisement of an American-style German consumer society turned out to be readily compatible with National Socialist ideology. Hitler's admiration for Ford is well documented and the American vision of prosperity remained the ideal even under the Nazis, who pushed for the increased production of radios and other electrical appliances, the further popularization of mass tourism, and, most famously, the introduction of an affordable "people's car," to catch up with the high standard of living in the US.[9] As recent research has shown, Hitler's regime rejected the disciplining of consumption that had still characterized much of Weimar politics before 1933, and that *Tempo* had so often criticized.[10] The belief in stimulating consumer demand was a central factor in Nazi economic policies before 1939, and the virtual consumption created by building up a dreamland of unlimited prosperity beckoning after the

---

7. Detlev Peukert, *Max Webers Diagnose der Moderne* (Göttingen: Vandenhoeck & Ruprecht 1989), 82.

8. Berghoff, "Enticement and Deprivation," 165–84.

9. Berghoff, "Träume," 269–80. For the role of Fordism in Nazi ideology and politics, see the excellent overview in Stephan Link, "Rethinking the Ford-Nazi Connection," *Bulletin of the German Historical Institute* 49 (2011): 135–50.

10. S. Jonathan Wiesen, *Creating the Nazi Marketplace: Commerce and Consumption in the Third Reich* (Cambridge: Cambridge University Press, 2011); Berghoff, "Träume," 268–88; Wolfgang König, *Volkswagen, Volksempfänger, Volksgemeinschaft: "Volksprodukte" im Dritten Reich. Vom Scheitern einer nationalsozialistischen Konsumgesellschaft* (Paderborn: Schöningh, 2004); Shelley Baranowski, *Strength through Joy: Consumerism and Mass Tourism in the Third Reich* (Cambridge: Cambridge University Press, 2004)

"final victory" played a significant role in Nazi propaganda.[11] While their motivation and end goals couldn't have been more different, Ullstein and the Nazi regime both tied their political ideal to a consumer's paradise located in the near future, and relied on the hope for the imminent arrival of its blessings—the "confidence that ownership was just around the corner."[12] In the case of the Weimar Republic, this hope turned to a rejection of the political order when the promised consumer society did not materialize. After the inflated expectations, boosted by a visual consumer culture of newspaper advertising, shop displays, and commercial cinema, could not be met in the reality of an unstable economy, disenchanted consumers challenged the legitimacy of Weimar's democratic institutions and started blaming the state for its inability to deliver the desired standard of living.[13]

In this view, *Tempo*'s attempts to stimulate an unsatisfiable demand with its optimistic claims of affordable holidays and the imminent arrival of the *Volksauto* could be interpreted as indirectly undermining Weimar democracy. In a similar vein, it could be argued that *Tempo*'s promotion of a demurer femininity after 1930 prepared the ground for an acceptance of National Socialist policies and ideology, and that its support for Hindenburg over parliamentarianism made it easier for Hitler to ultimately install himself as an authoritarian *Führer*. In fact, many such claims were made after 1933. A representative example is Theodor Adorno, who argued in 1944 that the worldview disseminated by Ullstein and other liberal publishers after the mid-1920s was little different from that of the Nazis:

> At the latest with the stabilization of the German currency . . . German culture stabilized itself in the spirit of the Berlin illustrated magazines, which yielded little to that of the Nazis' "Strength through Joy," Reich autobahns, and jaunty exhibition-hall Classicism. The whole span of German culture was languishing, precisely where it was most liberal, for its Hitler, and it is an injustice to the editors of Mosse and Ullstein . . . to reproach them with time-serving under Nazism. They were always like that, and their line of least resistance to the intellectual wares they produced was continued undeflected in the line of least resistance to a politi-

---

11. For the concept of "virtual consumption" in Nazi Germany, see Berghoff, "Träume," 285; Berghoff, "Enticement and Deprivation," 167–71.
12. Pamela Swett, "Preparing for Victory: Heinrich Hunke, the Nazi Werberat, and West German Prosperity," *Central European History* 42 (2009): 675–707, at 677.
13. Torp, *Konsum und Politik*, 315–35; Torp, "Janusgesicht," 266.

cal regime among whose ideological methods, as the Führer himself declared, comprehensibility to the most stupid ranked highest.[14]

We do not know whether Adorno had an opinion on *Tempo* in particular, but in this view, it surely appears as one of the most vivid representatives of this dumbed-down "culture of least resistance."

It is important, however, not to read any path-dependent developments into creative adaptations of modernity. *Tempo*'s image of a moderate modernity—including, as it did, unrealistic ideas of consumer affluence and a wish for the curtailing of a supposed "excess" of parliamentary democracy—might have undermined Weimar's status quo in some respects, but it did not clear the path for the Third Reich. This becomes evident if we put *Tempo* and its construction of modernity into a broader, comparative context. Many interwar societies followed a path of a moderate modernity. Arguably, this idea was the dominant way to engage with the modern in interwar Britain. Both a hereditary monarchy with a deeply entrenched social hierarchy and the cradle of industrialization, the country had always fused tradition and modernity in its self-image and popular discourse.[15] Even in its long democratic tradition, the interwar era represented a profound shift in Britain's political culture, just like in Germany, turning from a limited, property-based franchise into a mass democracy with the introduction of universal male suffrage in 1918 and universal female suffrage in 1928. The popular press assumed a central role in the communication and mobilization of this new kind of mass politics.[16] Despite this transformation, conservative politics dominated interwar Britain.[17] However, underneath this conservative hegemony an intense debate was raging about the exact nature of democracy. Just like in Weimar Germany, people in Britain "lived in what nearly all agreed was a democracy. They were not, how-

---

14. Theodor Adorno, *Minima Moralia: Reflections from a Damaged Life* (London: New Left Books, 1974), 57.

15. Peter Mandler, "The Consciousness of Modernity? Liberalism and the English 'National Character', 1870–1940," in *Meanings of Modernity: Britain from the Late-Victorian Era to World War II*, ed. Bernhard Rieger and Martin Daunton (Oxford: Berg, 2001), 119–44; Alan O'Shea, "English Subjects of Modernity," in *Modern Times: Reflections on a Century of English Modernity*, ed. Mica Nava and Alan O'Shea (London: Routledge, 1996), 7–37.

16. Laura Beers, "Education or Manipulation? Labour, Democracy, and the Popular Press in Interwar Britain," *Journal of British Studies* 48, no. 1 (2009): 129–52.

17. Helen McCarthy, "Whose Democracy? Histories of British Political Culture between the Wars," *Historical Journal* 55, no. 1 (2012): 221–38.

ever, necessarily agreed on what democracy meant or should mean."[18] One of the competing narratives in this debate was a middle-class vision of British democracy as "individualist, liberal and self-consciously 'modern'," a definition that ultimately won out to dominate much of the country's political culture after 1945.[19] This was a moderate modernity characterized by conservative politics and a modest consumer society, described by J. B. Priestley in his popular novel *English Journey*:

> This is the England of arterial and by-pass roads, of filling stations and factories that look like exhibition buildings, of giant cinemas and dancehalls and cafés, bungalows with tiny garages, cocktail bars, Woolworths, motor-coaches, wireless, hiking, factory girls looking like actresses, greyhound racing and dirt tracks, swimming pools, and everything given away for cigarette coupons.[20]

For many British citizens, the lived practice of being modern was, first and foremost, the consumption of mass media, fashion, and durable goods such as home appliances and cars that Priestley described. Through these consumer goods, they took part in a modernizing discourse of material betterment and a rising standard of living. This was even true for the working class: although workers only really enjoyed the benefits of a developed consumer society after 1945, the "aspiration for consumer goods," expressed for example through window shopping, was widespread in interwar Britain.[21] Advertising and the illustrated press played a crucial role in spreading the ideal of consumer modernity. For women in particular, who were still excluded from many aspects of public life, shopping and reading magazines were important ways to make themselves modern.[22] The way "British modernity" was constructed and experienced was very much influenced by existing discourses, particularly that of class. In interwar Britain, the middle classes attached particular importance

---

18. Ross McKibbin, *Classes and Cultures: England 1918–1951* (Oxford: Oxford University Press, 2000), v.
19. McCarthy, "Whose Democracy?," 225.
20. J. B. Priestley, *English Journey* (London: William Heinemann, 1934), 401.
21. O'Shea, "English Subjects of Modernity," 29. See also Frank Trentmann, "Bread, Milk and Democracy: Consumption and Citizenship in Twentieth-Century Britain," in Daunton and Hilton, *Politics of Consumption*, 129–63.
22. Penny Tinkler and Cheryl Krasnick Warsh, "Feminine Modernity in Interwar Britain and North America: Corsets, Cars, and Cigarettes," *Journal of Women's History* 20, no. 3 (2008): 113–43.

to distinguishing themselves from other social strata and among each other.[23] Both home appliances and cars were used to redraw and entrench existing class distinctions: rather than signaling affiliation with a classless, "American" modernity, vacuum cleaners and family sedans projected and strengthened the middle-class identities of their owners.

Despite higher rates of ownership, the automobile was as much a symbol of modernity as in Germany. However, the reality of the British car market was very far removed from the American model of mass ownership. Just as in Germany, the car remained an exclusive luxury good, and British car manufacturing was based on craft skills and short production runs.[24] This was reflected in the way the car was marketed, stressing tradition and craftsmanship. In contrast to Weimar Germany, the car did not embody the dream of a unified, classless society; on the contrary, the status consciousness of middle-class consumers meant that the cheapest cars were generally shunned, as they suggested diminished affluence and miserliness. A flourishing "body-building" trade supplied British car owners with the opportunity to remodel their mass-produced car to fit in with their social group, catering to their needs of social distinction.[25] The automobile magazine *The Autocar* pointed out how these costly alterations showed a particular national approach to the automobile:

> Of course, you have to pay for it in the same way a woman has to pay for a dress from one of the great *couturieres*. But, like her, you get something different, and you won't take someone else's car from a park by mistake. All of which is very nice to us English, a distinction loving people if ever there was one.[26]

In the domestic sphere, British middle-class women used high technology to make themselves modern while retaining traditional bourgeois respectability. Electric home appliances like the vacuum cleaner contributed to recasting the middle-class home "as a clean and scientifically managed modern space"

---

23. Simon Gunn and Rachel Bell, *Middle Classes: Their Rise and Sprawl* (London: Phoenix, 2003), 58–89; McKibbin, *Classes and Cultures*, 44–105.
24. Tinkler and Warsh, "Feminine Modernity," 121.
25. Sean O'Connell, *The Car and British Society: Class, Gender and Motoring, 1896–1939* (Manchester: Manchester University Press, 1998), 23.
26. *The Autocar*, 16 December 1933, cited in Sean O'Connell, "The Social and Cultural Impact of the Car in Interwar Britain" (PhD diss., University of Warwick, 1995), 23.

and the housewife as an agent of modernity.[27] In this setting, vacuum cleaners acted not only as markers but also as instruments of social distinction. After 1918, with rising standards of cleanliness in the modern home and the increasing difficulty of hiring domestic servants to meet them, home appliances helped middle-class housewives in Britain to maintain their social status.[28] This focus on the technological modernization of a domestic setting characterized by conventional gender hierarchies amounted to a "conservative embrace of modernity."[29] The case of the Electrical Association for Women is instructive in this regard. Founded in 1924 by progressive middle-class reformers to promote the electrification of the home and ease the burden of housework, its members still accepted the social role of domesticity for women. According to Carroll Pursell, this made the Electrical Association for Women a representative expression of "conservative modernity."[30] This approach was also visible in industry: at the same time that the home was recast as a modern space, the factory was increasingly domesticated through facilities such as cozy restrooms and an aestheticization of the shop floor, in order "to reconcile modernity with tradition."[31] In any case, the lived experience of most housewives was quite different from the ideal constructed by advertisers, industry organizations, and educational groups like the Electrical Association for Women. Rather than creating modern, laboratory-like homes, new appliances were introduced into traditional homes, creating "transitional spaces that would have often incorporated a mix of old and new."[32]

As in Weimar Germany, gender relations were a central field in which the meaning of modernity was negotiated. The relationship between men and women in Britain was characterized by more equality after 1918, with the ideals of companionate marriage, mutuality, and sexual compatibility replacing the contentious "sex war" of the prewar period.[33] As a consequence, ideas of

---

27. Emily Hankin, "Buying Modernity? The Consumer Experience of Domestic Electricity in the Era of the Grid" (PhD diss., University of Manchester, 2012), 102.

28. Martin Pugh, *We Danced All Night: A Social History of Britain between the Wars* (London: Vintage, 2009), 179–80; Hankin, "Buying Modernity," 104.

29. Bernhard Rieger and Martin Daunton, "Introduction," in *Meanings of Modernity: Britain from the Late-Victorian Era to World War II*, ed. Bernhard Rieger and Martin Daunton (Oxford: Berg, 2001), 8.

30. Carroll Pursell, "Domesticating Modernity: The Electrical Association for Women, 1924–86," *British Journal for the History of Science* 32, no. 1 (1999): 48.

31. Vicky Long, "Industrial Homes, Domestic Factories: The Convergence of Public and Private Space in Interwar Britain," *Journal of British Studies* 50, no. 2 (2011): 434.

32. Hankin, "Buying Modernity," 140.

33. Claire Langhamer, "Love and Courtship in Mid-Twentieth-Century England," *His-*

femininity and masculinity changed dramatically. The figure of the "modern young woman" featured prominently in public debates and the popular press played an essential role in its construction.[34] Just like the readers of *Tempo*, British women "often sought to emulate these media images, assimilating definitions of 'modern' behavior into their own lives."[35] Priestley's observation about working-class women copying film stars is one example of how this worked in practice. As Tom Glancy has shown, this emulation did not mean a straightforward "Americanization," but rather a complex interaction, in which the audience played an active part and which resulted in a peculiarly British take on what it meant to be fashionable and modern.[36] At the same time, with rising home ownership and the growing importance of the nuclear family, the housewife became a "highly valued and 'modern' role for women" during the 1920s and 1930s, recasting a conservative focus on women's place in the domestic sphere.[37] Despite the more modern definition of heterosexual marriage in terms of companionship, it also remained the only accepted long-term "career" for women of all classes.[38] The conservative British interpretation of modern womanhood is also reflected in the so-called keep-fit movement of the interwar era. This fitness culture aimed at women stressed a modern and rational approach to the female body, while emphasizing their reproductive and maternal role. Its most popular organization, the Women's League of Health and Beauty, taught its target group of "business girls and busy women" the importance of a healthy, trained body to prepare for childbirth and to defend "racial health."[39]

British interwar masculinity was ambiguously constructed between the poles of a "re-domestication" after the violent experience in the trenches and a

---

torical Journal 50, no. 1 (2007): 173–79; Marcus Collins, *Modern Love: Personal Relationships in Twentieth-Century Britain* (Newark: University of Delaware Press, 2006), 39–56.

34. Selina Todd, *Young Women, Work, and Family in England 1918–1950* (Oxford: Oxford University Press, 2005), 1–18; Adrian Bingham, *Gender, Modernity, and the Popular Press in Inter-War Britain* (Oxford: Oxford University Press, 2003), 47–83.

35. Bingham, *Gender, Modernity, and the Popular Press*, 49.

36. Mark Glancy, "Temporary American Citizens? British Audiences, Hollywood Films and the Threat of Americanization in the 1920s," *Historical Journal of Film, Radio and Television* 26, no. 4 (2006): 461–84.

37. Judy Giles, "A Home of One's Own: Women and Domesticity in England 1918–1950," *Women's Studies International Forum* 16, no. 3 (May 1, 1993): 239–53.

38. Langhamer, "Love and Courtship," 179.

39. Jill Julius Matthews, "They Had Such a Lot of Fun: The Women's League of Health and Beauty between the Wars," *History Workshop*, no. 30 (1990): 22–54.

body culture centered around physical fitness and soldierly camaraderie.[40] The ambivalent masculinity of T. H. Lawrence, the celebrated hero of the Middle Eastern theater of the First World War, is a good example of these tensions.[41] Conventional masculinity seemed to be in crisis, undermined by the war experience, economic uncertainty, and a new, challenging femininity, which sparked fears of a national effeminacy. Particularly for young, lower middle-class men, working in distinctly unheroic professions like clerk or shopworker, bohemian youth culture and organized sports became a field in which they could take part in constructions of modern masculinity.[42] At the same time, a new ideal of involved fathers who "take their share in the life of the home" was discussed in the popular press, which opened their problem pages to issues of masculinity and attracted a mixed audience looking for advice on companionate marriage and modern fatherhood.[43]

In France, generational conflict, transformations of gender images, and the alleged influence of American culture generated similar debates as in Germany during the interwar years. The war experience had created a deep-seated cultural pessimism among middle-class intellectuals, who felt that European civilization and its supposed superiority had died in the trenches. The postwar world seemed to be out of joint, with all aspects of modern life that used to be fixed and stable—particularly the role of men and women in society—now in upheaval.[44] The figure of the "garçonne"—the modern, free-spirited, independent young woman blurring distinctive gender roles—was one of the cultural icons embodying these discourses. Through the success of Victor Margueritte's novel *La Garçonne*, the cultural influence of this French image of modern femininity radiated beyond the country's borders, including Germany, the UK, and the US, where translations were published in the 1920s. However, as Marie

---

40. Ina Zweiniger-Bargielowska, "Building a British Superman: Physical Culture in Interwar Britain," *Journal of Contemporary History* 41, no. 4 (2006): 595–610; Michael Roper, "Between Manliness and Masculinity: The 'War Generation' and the Psychology of Fear in Britain, 1914–1950," *Journal of British Studies* 44, no. 2 (April 2005): 343–62; Bingham, *Gender, Modernity, and the Popular Press*, 216–43; Martin Francis, "The Domestication of the Male? Recent Research on Nineteenth- and Twentieth-Century British Masculinity," *Historical Journal* 45, no. 3 (September 2002): 637–52.

41. Graham Dawson, *Soldier Heroes: British Adventure, Empire and the Imagining of Masculinities* (Abingdon: Routledge, 1994), 191–207.

42. Peter Bailey, "White Collars, Gray Lives? The Lower Middle Class Revisited," *Journal of British Studies* 38, no. 3 (1999): 281–82.

43. Bingham, *Gender, Modernity, and the Popular Press*, 217–41.

44. Mary Louise Roberts, *Civilization without Sexes: Reconstructing Gender in Postwar France, 1917–1927* (Chicago: University of Chicago Press, 1994), 1–16.

Louise Roberts has pointed out, Margueritte's heroine returns to conventional womanhood at the end of the novel, "appeas[ing] cultural and gender anxieties."[45] In fact, the whole debate about gender roles in France was an "attempt to negotiate change with continuity, to reconcile old and new worlds."[46] This was particularly reflected in the attempts of the French fashion industry to construct a "hybrid modernity" that combined modern fabrics and straighter lines with classical femininity to appeal to broad swathes of the female population.[47] In both France and Germany, Adam Stanley has shown, popular culture constructed a "femininity that combined elements of the new and modern with idealized tradition."[48] In both countries, most women were still restricted to their traditional social roles as wives and mothers, but they actively sought to combine this with a sense of modernness, particularly through the use of new consumer products.

Since the Revolution, debates about modern French masculinity were closely related to—and often disguised as—definitions of citizenship. In the interwar era, when this supposedly natural connection was questioned, there were many attempts to redefine French masculinity. Among them were new masculine ideals by centrist parties that focused on youthfulness and "manly republicanism . . . in defense of the Republic and democracy."[49] One of the central characteristics of this democratic manhood in interwar France was sangfroid, the quality of keeping "a cool head in the face of challenges of all kind," which echoes the importance of *Sachlichkeit* in Weimar Germany.[50]

Despite the fact that a mass consumer society remained a promise rather than a reality, interwar France saw the development of a consumerist mentality.[51] The introduction of consumer credit for cars and home appliances and the opening of the modern one-price store chains Uniprix, Monoprix, and Prisunic at the end of the 1920s created an embryonic French consumer culture. While

---

45. Roberts, *Civilization without Sexes*, 214.

46. Roberts, *Civilization without Sexes*, 216.

47. Mary Lynn Stewart, *Dressing Modern Frenchwomen: Marketing Haute Couture, 1919–1939* (Baltimore: Johns Hopkins University Press, 2008).

48. Adam C. Stanley, *Modernizing Tradition: Gender and Consumerism in Interwar France and Germany* (Baton Rouge: Louisiana State University Press, 2008), 8.

49. Geoff Read, *The Republic of Men: Gender and the Political Parties in Interwar France* (Baton Rouge: Louisiana State University Press, 2014), 78.

50. Geoff Read, "Des Hommes et des Citoyens: Paternalism and Masculinity on the Republican Right in Interwar France, 1919–1939," *Historical Reflections/Réflexions Historiques* 34, no. 2 (2008): 92.

51. Robert L. Frost, "Machine Liberation: Inventing Housewives and Home Appliances in Interwar France," *French Historical Studies* 18, no. 1 (1993): 112.

real demand still remained minimal, manufacturers, advertisers, and the press invented a mass consumer as an ideal, middle-class citizen, and this figure, showing an optimistic future for a crisis-ridden France, became a model to aspire to for many people.[52] Paid vacations and mass tourism in particular were part of this new idea of consumer-citizenship in interwar France. While not yet a mass social practice, tourism was seen as a right of citizenship, "enact[ing] a democratic model for vacations," which had only been the pursuit of the elite before.[53] The idea of mass consumption in general was closely linked to modern French femininity.[54] Home appliances in particular became a way for women to take part in modern society while being shut out of other avenues, such as politics. French women were denied the vote after the First World War, but at the same time the domestic sphere was reimagined as a site of modernity, where women acted as rational managers and sovereign users of modern machinery.[55] The outspoken goal was a reconciliation of "tradition and modernity" that would support a pronatalist, nationalist policy of boosting the birth rate to safeguard the "strength of the nation" and the "strength of the race."[56]

Beyond the Western world, the creative adaptation of modernity also often took the form of a fusion of old and new. In interwar Japan, for example, the urban middle class integrated ancient customs and local history into their modern identities in order to have a sense of ownership over the modernization process that had transformed the country since the Meji Restoration in the second half of the nineteenth century.[57] This process included beef sukiyaki and other products of a fusion of Western and Japanese cuisine as well as attempts to marry Western technology with Asian spirituality and the design of Western-style clothing adapted to Japanese bodies.[58] As in the Western context,

---

52. Frost, "Machine Liberation," 127–30.

53. Ellen Furlough, "Making Mass Vacations: Tourism and Consumer Culture in France, 1930s to 1970s," *Comparative Studies in Society and History* 40, no. 2 (1998): 250.

54. David H. Walker, *Consumer Chronicles: Cultures of Consumption in Modern French Literature* (Liverpool: Liverpool University Press, 2011), 168–80.

55. Frost, "Machine Liberation," 117; Ellen Furlough, "Selling the American Way in Interwar France: 'Prix Uniques' and the Salons des Arts Menagers," *Journal of Social History* 26, no. 3 (1993): 503–10.

56. Furlough, "Selling the American Way in Interwar France," 508–9.

57. Louise Young, *Beyond the Metropolis: Second Cities and Modern Life in Interwar Japan* (Berkeley: University of California Press, 2013), 141–54.

58. Andrew Gordon, "Consumption, Consumerism, and Japanese Modernity," in *The Oxford Handbook of the History of Consumption*, ed. Frank Trentmann (Oxford: Oxford University Press, 2012), 495–96; Harry D. Harootunian, *Overcome by Modernity: History, Culture, and Community in Interwar Japan* (Princeton: Princeton University Press, 2000), 164.

femininity was an important space in which interwar modernity was negotiated: the *moga* (modern girl), closely related to the rise of modern Japanese mass consumer culture and criticized for her supposedly shallow materialism and individualistic hedonism, was the representation of what it meant to be modern in interwar Japan.[59] The mass media that spread awareness of the *moga* throughout Japan "offered women an opportunity to participate actively in the creation of this burgeoning culture" and a space to make themselves modern.[60] Even in provincial places like Okinawa, with poorly developed consumer culture and far from the modern metropolis of Tokyo, young middle-class women aspired to be modern, combining existing values with new influences.[61]

Finally, even in the United States, which many people in Europe and the rest of the globe saw as the center of utmost modernism, people often practiced their own moderate modernity, trying to reconcile tradition with change and progress. While the figure of the hedonistic and self-confident flapper often dominated the image of modern femininity, most American women only embraced it very selectively. They roundly rejected the idea of sexual promiscuousness, and while they often enjoyed more freedoms than most of their European counterparts, they did not challenge the mores and traditions of their own society: marriage, respectability, and a domestic life was still the dominant life plan, particularly for white middle-class women.[62] In contrast to radically modern representatives of the Jazz Age, such as Anita Loos's Lorelei Lee and F. Scott Fitzgerald's Nicole Diver, mainstream authors such as Kathleen Norris, Temple Baileyn, and Dorothy Speare, who were read widely at the time, offered "a picture of more widely shared experiences; their fast-talking,

---

59. Barbara Sato, *The New Japanese Woman: Modernity, Media, and Women in Interwar Japan* (Durham, N.C.: Duke University Press, 2003), 45–77; Barbara Sato, "The Moga Sensation: Perceptions of the Modan Gāru in Japanese Intellectual Circles during the 1920s," *Gender & History* 5, no. 3 (1993): 363–81.

60. Sato, "Moga Sensation," 377.

61. Ruri Ito, "The 'Modern Girl' Question in the Periphery of Empire: Colonial Modernity and Mobility among Okinawan Women in the 1920s and 1930s," in Weinbaum et al., *The Modern Girl around the World*, 240–62.

62. Isabel Heinemann, "Preserving the Family and the Nation: Eugenic Masculinity Concepts, Expert Intervention, and the American Family in the United States, 1900–1960," in *Masculinities and the Nation in the Modern World: Between Hegemony and Marginalization*, ed. Pablo Dominguez Andersen and Simon Wendt (New York: Palgrave Macmillan, 2015), 71–92; Tinkler and Warsh, "Feminine Modernity"; Whitney Walton, "American Girls and French Jeunes Filles: Negotiating National Identities in Interwar France," *Gender & History* 17, no. 2 (2005): 325–53; Lynn Dumenil, *The Modern Temper: American Culture and Society in the 1920s* (New York: Hill and Wang, 1995), 127–44.

short-skirted flappers became sensible girls, and they did what sensible girls were supposed to do: fall in love with good men, and marry them."[63] The balancing of modernity and tradition was succinctly expressed in an article by the journalist Harriet Abbott published in the *Ladies' Home Journal* on 19 August 1920, reacting to the ratification of women's suffrage the day before:

> To-day we are building steadily and surely, brick by brick, a new philosophy that grows from, yet is not consubstantial with, the postulates of the woman movement so called. We are creating a new-woman faith typical of the newest new-woman movement.... It is an eclectic choosing of all that is sanest in the sweep of the last century toward a new freedom for women, combined with the persisting older ideas. It is a philosophy that stands on the foundation stones of old, tested, true experiences, so it is stable; but it is not made up of superstition and tradition; it couples to itself the best of what is new and so it is flexible.[64]

Even though most women followed this moderate line, American interwar masculinity was constructed mainly as a reaction to the specter of the brash flapper encroaching on male-only domains, like the workplace and nightlife establishments.[65] Other perceived challenges to dominant—meaning white, middle-class, heterosexual—masculinity were mass immigration, particularly from Asia, and the increasingly bureaucratized and industrialized nature of modern life itself.[66] These influences led to a rejection of traditional Victorian ideals of rationality and duty in favor of more modern ideas of the individualist "self-made man" relying on his "guts" and skill.[67] New stereotypes of rugged, physically strong manliness, such as "the caveman" or "the sheikh," the latter referring to Rudolph Valentino's most famous role, embodied these ideas in

---

63. Linda Simon, *Lost Girls: The Invention of the Flapper* (London: Reaktion Books, 2017), 221.
64. Harriet Abbott, "What the Newest New Woman Is," in *The American New Woman Revisited: A Reader, 1894–1930*, ed. Martha H. Patterson, Eileen Boris, and Vicki L. Ruiz (New Brunswick, N.J.: Rutgers University Press, 2008), 223.
65. Andrew P. Smiler, Gwen Kay, and Benjamin Harris, "Tightening and Loosening Masculinity's (k)Nots: Masculinity in the Hearst Press during the Interwar Period," *Journal of Men's Studies* 16, no. 3 (2008): 268.
66. Heinemann, "Preserving the Family and the Nation," 73; Gaylyn Studlar, *This Mad Masquerade: Stardom and Masculinity in the Jazz Age* (New York: Columbia University Press, 1996), 25.
67. Heinemann, "Preserving the Family and the Nation," 73; Smiler, Kay, and Harris, "Tightening and Loosening Masculinity's (k)Nots," 268.

popular culture.[68] Yet many American men evidently sought to combine these new ideals with existing ones: stars like Douglas Fairbanks, whose screen persona was arguably directed more at a male audience, personified an "ideal merger of traditional moral values associated with feminine tenderness and altruism with the 'masculine primitive' of rugged physicality and instinctual impulsivity."[69] Most importantly, Fairbanks—but also modern athletes and representatives of the thriving interwar bodybuilding culture, such as Charles Atlas—showed that modern masculinity was "self-made" and potentially achievable for everyone.[70]

While the United States boasted a highly advanced consumer society in comparison with the rest of the world, its existence and meaning were highly contentious at home.[71] During the interwar years, citizenship was closely linked to consumption and "the American learned that he was largely to think of himself as consumer," but the spreading of consumerism was widely regarded as a threat to civilization.[72] Intellectuals like Stuart Chase and Samuel Strauss offered a critique of the new world of consumption, worrying about increasing conformity and the degradation of political culture.[73] Their solution was not a completely different society, such as the one being built in the Soviet Union, but a more controlled consumer society in which the state would take a prominent role, tampering the worst excesses of consumerism.

However, despite its harrowing fallout, the Depression, rather than completely transforming American society, entrenched and clarified existing trends.[74] The vision of controlled consumption solidified with the onset of the

---

68. John Pettegrew, *Brutes in Suits: Male Sensibility in America, 1890–1920* (Baltimore: Johns Hopkins University Press, 2012), 15–120; Smiler, Kay, and Harris, "Tightening and Loosening Masculinity's (k)Nots," 270.

69. Studlar, *This Mad Masquerade*, 33.

70. Brian M. Ingrassia, "Manhood or Masculinity: The Historiography of Manliness in American Sport," in *A Companion to American Sport History* (Chichester: Wiley-Blackwell, 2014), 479–99; Pettegrew, *Brutes in Suits*, 306–18; Studlar, *This Mad Masquerade*, 239.

71. Meg Jacobs, "The Politics of Plenty in the Twentieth-Century United States," in Daunton and Hilton, *Politics of Consumption*, 223–39; Lawrence B. Glickman, "Born to Shop? Consumer History and American History," in *Consumer Society in American History: A Reader*, ed. Lawrence B. Glickman (New York: Cornell University Press, 1999), 1–14; Dumenil, *Modern Temper*, 76–97.

72. Warren I. Susman, *Culture as History: The Transformation of American Society in the Twentieth Century* (Washington, D.C.: Smithsonian Institution Press, 2003), 111.

73. Joe Renouard, "The Predicaments of Plenty: Interwar Intellectuals and American Consumerism," *Journal of American Culture* 30, no. 1 (2007): 54–67.

74. Rita Barnard, *The Great Depression and the Culture of Abundance: Kenneth Fearing, Nathanael West, and Mass Culture in the 1930s* (Cambridge: Cambridge University Press, 1995), 3–14.

crisis: mass consumption and leisure were accepted, in Keynesian terms, as an important factor in combatting the economic and social crisis, but only the state seemed able to wield this instrument effectively.[75] The "right"—meaning wholesome and controlled—way of consuming "became central to the adjustment to modernity."[76] In the harsh climate of the 1930s, the flapper vanished as an influential ideal, but ideas about gender roles still sought to combine aspects of modern femininity and masculinity with more conventional or traditional values.[77] In terms of democratic culture, the critical view of a supposed ineffectual parliamentarism was widespread in the United States during the interwar years, just as it was in Europe.[78] In Franklin D. Roosevelt, many Americans saw what Germans saw in Hindenburg or Hitler: a strong leader who addressed these problems of procedural democracy, uniting the country while sidelining an ineffectual parliament.[79]

Despite the ambivalence toward modernity in the United States, "America" was still the most important model that provided the blueprint in the UK, France, and Japan for their own creative adaptations, at least until the Great Depression. But while the American model of modernity—or what local intellectuals, politicians, and mass media constructed as such—was popular and influential, middle classes all over the world rarely saw it as the best solution for their own societies.[80] Instead, they adapted this model to their particular

---

75. Susan Currell, *The March of Spare Time: The Problem and Promise of Leisure in the Great Depression* (Philadelphia: University of Pennsylvania Press, 2010); Renouard, "The Predicaments of Plenty," 64–65; Bruce Lenthall, *Radio's America: The Great Depression and the Rise of Modern Mass Culture* (Chicago: University of Chicago Press, 2007); Cohen, *Consumers' Republic*, 18–61; McGovern, *Sold American*, 221–300.

76. Currell, *March of Spare Time*, 6.

77. Lubben, "New American Ideal," 291–308; Julie Human, "A Woman Rebels? Gender Roles in 1930s Motion Pictures," *Register of the Kentucky Historical Society* 98, no. 4 (2000): 405–28; Alice Kessler-Harris, "Gender Ideology in Historical Reconstruction: A Case Study from the 1930s," *Gender & History* 1, no. 1 (1989): 31–49; Susan Ware, *Holding Their Own: American Women in the 1930s* (Boston: Twayne, 1982).

78. Wilson Kaiser, "Partial Affinities: Fascism and the Politics of Representation in Interwar America" (PhD diss., University of North Carolina, 2011), 31–61; Alpers, *Dictators, Democracy, and American Public Culture*, 15–76. See also Moritz Föllmer, "Führung und Demokratie in Europa," in Müller and Tooze, *Normalität und Fragilität*, 177–97.

79. Kiran Klaus Patel, *The New Deal: A Global History* (Princeton: Princeton University Press, 2016), 45–120; Wolfgang Schivelbusch, *Three New Deals: Reflections on Roosevelt's America, Mussolini's Italy, and Hitler's Germany, 1933–1939* (New York: Picador, 2006), 17–48.

80. Glancy, "Temporary American Citizens"; Harootunian, *Overcome by Modernity*, 47–65; Victoria de Grazia, "Americanization and Changing Paradigms of Consumer Modernity:

sociocultural context in an optimistic embrace of its promise. In this respect, Ullstein's vision of a liberal, moderate German consumer modernity was part of a global, transnational debate. While we should not overemphasize the similarities of these very different national contexts, this brief comparative overview highlights the openness and contingency of the trajectory of these moderate modernities during the interwar years. The moderate modernity constructed in *Tempo* did not pave the way for the Third Reich. Rather, it was a vision of the future, competing with the alternative modernities of the Nazis and other groups, over the definition of a modern German society. The simultaneous existence and vigorous competition of these visions is what makes the Weimar era such a rich and fascinating period.

France, 1930–1990," *Sites: The Journal of Twentieth-Century/Contemporary French Studies Revue d'études Français* 1, no. 1 (March 1997): 191–213.

Bibliography

ARCHIVES

Akademie der Künste Berlin, Lucy von Jacobi papers.
Bundesarchiv Berlin-Lichterfelde, R 43 I-II Reichskanzlei files; N2193 Carl Misch papers.
Bundesarchiv Koblenz, N1012 Erich Koch-Weser papers.
Deutsches Literaturarchiv Marchbach, Manfred Georg papers.
Institut für Zeitgeschichte München, F 110 Carl Jödicke papers.
Leo Baeck Institute New York, AR 7177 Hans Schäffer papers; AR 7023 Hans Schäffer-Eckhardt Wandel collection.
Unternehmensarchiv Axel Springer AG Berlin, Ullstein files.
Wissenschaftliche Sammlungen der Humboldt-Universität zu Berlin, Lautarchiv.

PUBLISHED WORKS

Abelshauser, Werner, and Dieter Petzina. *Deutsche Wirtschaftsgeschichte im Industriezeitalter. Konjunktur, Krise, Wachstum.* Königstein: Athenäum, 1981.
"Alexander Roda Roda." In *Wer ist's?*, edited by Herrmann Degener, 1278–79. Berlin: Degener, 1928.
Alpers, Benjamin L. *Dictators, Democracy, and American Public Culture: Envisioning the Totalitarian Enemy, 1920s-1950s.* Chapel Hill: University of North Carolina Press, 2003.
Aurich, Rolf, Irene Below, Wolfgang Jacobsen, and Ruth Oelze, eds. *Lucy von Jacobi. Journalistin.* Munich: edition text + kritik, 2009.
Bailey, Peter. "White Collars, Gray Lives? The Lower Middle Class Revisited." *Journal of British Studies* 38, no. 3 (1999): 273–90.
Barnard, Rita. *The Great Depression and the Culture of Abundance: Kenneth Fearing, Nathanael West, and Mass Culture in the 1930s.* Cambridge: Cambridge University Press, 1995.
Barndt, Kerstin. *Sentiment und Sachlichkeit. Der Roman der Neuen Frau in der Weimarer Republik.* Cologne: Böhlau, 2003.
Barth, Boris. *Dolchstoßlegenden und politische Desintegration. Das Trauma der deutschen Niederlage im Ersten Weltkrieg 1914—1933.* Düsseldorf: Droste, 2003.

Barth, Boris. *Europa nach dem Großen Krieg. Die Krise der Demokratie in der Zwischenkriegszeit 1918–1938*. Frankfurt/Main: Campus, 2016.

Bavaj, Riccardo. "Pluralizing Democracy in Weimar Germany: Historiographical Perspectives and Transatlantic Vista." In *Transatlantic Democracy in the Twentieth Century: Transfer and Transformation*, edited by Paul Nolte, 53–73. Munich: Oldenbourg, 2016.

Bavaj, Riccardo, and Martina Steber. "Introduction: Germany and 'the West': The Vagaries of a Modern Relationship." In *Germany and "the West": The History of a Modern Concept*, edited by Riccardo Bavaj and Martina Steber, 1–37. New York: Berghahn, 2015.

Beers, Laura. "Education or Manipulation? Labour, Democracy, and the Popular Press in Interwar Britain." *Journal of British Studies* 48, no. 1 (2009): 129–52.

Below, Irene. "Wege der Professionalisierung." In *Lucy von Jacobi. Journalistin*, edited by Rolf Aurich, Irene Below, Wolfgang Jacobsen, and Ruth Oelze, 15–114. Munich: edition text + kritik, 2009.

Benninghaus, Christina. "Das Geschlecht der Generation. Zum Zusammenhang von Generationalität und Männlichkeit um 1930." In *Generationen. Zur Relevanz eines wissenschaftlichen Grundbegriffs*, edited by Ulrike Jureit and Michael Wildt, 127–58. Hamburg: Hamburger Edition, 2005.

Berghoff, Hartmut. "Consumption Politics and Politicized Consumption: Monarchy, Republic, and Dictatorship in Germany, 1900–1939." In *Decoding Modern Consumer Societies*, edited by Hartmut Berghoff and Uwe Spiekermann, 125–48. Worlds of Consumption. New York: Palgrave Macmillan, 2012.

Berghoff, Hartmut. "Enticement and Deprivation: The Regulation of Consumption in Pre-War Nazi Germany." In *The Politics of Consumption: Material Culture and Citizenship in Europe and America*, edited by Martin Daunton and Matthew Hilton, 165–84. New York: Berg, 2001.

Berghoff, Hartmut. "Träume und Alpträume. Konsumpolitik im Nazionalsozialistischen Deutschland." In *Die Konsumgesellschaft in Deutschland 1890–1990*, edited by Heinz-Gerhard Haupt and Claudius Torp, 268–88. Frankfurt/Main: Campus, 2009.

Bertschik, Julia. *Mode und Moderne. Kleidung als Spiegel des Zeitgeistes in der deutschsprachigen Literatur (1770–1945)*. Cologne: Böhlau, 2005.

Bingham, Adrian. *Gender, Modernity, and the Popular Press in Inter-War Britain*. Oxford: Oxford University Press, 2003.

Bleaney, Michael. *Under-Consumption Theories: A History and Critical Analysis*. London: Lawrence & Wishart, 1976.

Boak, Helen. *Women in the Weimar Republic*. Manchester: Manchester University Press, 2013.

Borrmann, Jennifer, ed. *Manfred George: Journalist und Filmkritiker*. Munich: edition text + kritik, 2014.

Borscheid, Peter. "Agenten des Konsums. Werbung und Marketing." In *Die Konsumgesellschaft in Deutschland 1890–1990. Ein Handbuch*, edited by Heinz-Gerhard Haupt and Claudius Torp, 79–96. Frankfurt/Main: Campus, 2009.

Borscheid, Peter. *Das Tempo-Virus. Eine Kulturgeschichte der Beschleunigung*. Frankfurt/Main: Campus, 2004.

Bosch, Michael. *Liberale Presse in der Krise. Die Innenpolitik der Jahre 1930 bis 1933 im Spiegel des Berliner Tageblatts, der Frankfurter Zeitung und der Vossischen Zeitung*. Frankfurt/Main: Peter Lang, 1976.
Bucher, Peter. *Der Reichswehrprozess. Der Hochverrat der Ulmer Reichswehroffiziere, 1929–1930*. Boppard: Boldt, 1967.
Büttner, Ursula. "Politische Alternativen zum Brüningschen Deflationskurs. Ein Beitrag zur Diskussion über 'ökonomische Zwangslagen' in der Endphase von Weimar." *Vierteljahrshefte für Zeitgeschichte* 37, no. 2 (1989): 209–51.
Büttner, Ursula. *Weimar. Die überforderte Republik 1918–1933*. Stuttgart: Klett-Cotta, 2008.
Canning, Kathleen. "Claiming Citizenship: Suffrage and Subjectivity in Germany after the First World War." In *Weimar Publics/Weimar Subjects: Rethinking the Political Culture of Germany in the 1920s*, edited by Kerstin Barndt, Kathleen Canning, and Kristin McGuire, 116–37. New York: Berghahn, 2010.
Canning, Kathleen. "War, Citizenship, and Rhetorics of Sexual Crisis: Reflections on States of Exception in Germany, 1914–20." In *German Modernities from Wilhelm to Weimar: A Contest of Futures*, edited by Geoff Eley, Jennifer L. Jenkins, and Tracie Matysik, 235–57. London: Bloomsbury, 2016.
Canning, Kathleen, and Sonya O. Rose. "Gender, Citizenships and Subjectivities: Some Historical and Theoretical Considerations." In *Gender, Citizenships and Subjectivities*, edited by Kathleen Canning and Sonya O. Rose, 1–17. Oxford: Blackwell, 2002.
Chakrabarty, Dipesh. *Provincializing Europe: Postcolonial Thought and Historical Difference*. Princeton: Princeton University Press, 2000.
Childers, Thomas. "Languages of Liberalism: Liberal Political Discourse in the Weimar Republic." In *In Search of a Liberal Germany: Studies in the History of German Liberalism from 1789 to the Present*, edited by Konrad J. Jarausch and Larry E. Jones, 323–59. New York: Berg, 1990.
Cohen, Coleen, Richard Wilk, and Beverly Stoeltje. "Introduction." In *Beauty Queens on the Global Stage: Gender, Contests, and Power*, edited by Coleen Cohen, Richard Wilk, and Beverly Stoeltje, 1–11. New York: Routledge, 1996.
Cohen, Lizabeth. *A Consumers' Republic: The Politics of Mass Consumption in Postwar America*. New York: Vintage, 2003.
Collins, Marcus. *Modern Love: Personal Relationships in Twentieth-Century Britain*. Newark: University of Delaware Press, 2006.
Confino, Alon, and Rudy Koshar. "Régimes of Consumer Culture: New Narratives in Twentieth-Century German History." *German History* 19, no. 2 (2001): 135–61.
Conze, Werner. "Demokratie." In *Geschichtliche Grundbegriffe. Historisches Lexikon zur politisch-sozialen Sprache in Deutschland*, edited by Otto Brunner, Werner Conze, and Reinhart Koselleck, 1:837–99. Stuttgart: Klett, 1972.
Cott, Nancy F. "The Modern Woman of the 1920s, American Style." In *A History of Women in the West*, vol. 5, edited by Françoise Thébaud, 86–87. Cambridge: Harvard University Press, 1994.
Currell, Susan. *The March of Spare Time: The Problem and Promise of Leisure in the Great Depression*. Philadelphia: University of Pennsylvania Press, 2010.

Bibliography

Dawson, Graham. *Soldier Heroes: British Adventure, Empire and the Imagining of Masculinities*. Abingdon: Routledge, 1994.

Demant, Ebbo. *Hans Zehrer als politischer Publizist. Von Schleicher zu Springer*. Mainz: Hase & Koehler, 1971.

Didczuneit, Veit. *Miss Germany. Eine schöne Geschichte*. Bonn: Haus der Geschichte der Bundesrepublik Deutschland, 2000.

Dinghaus, Angela. "Frauenfunk und Jungmädchenstunde. Ein Beitrag zur Programmgeschichte des Weimarer Rundfunks." PhD diss., University of Hannover, 2002.

Disko, Sasha. *The Devil's Wheels: Men and Motorcycling in the Weimar Republic*. New York: Berghahn, 2016.

Dreyer, Michael. "Weimar as a 'Militant Democracy.'" In *Beyond Glitter and Doom: The Contingency of the Weimar Republic*, edited by Jochen Hung, Godela Weiss-Sussex, and Geoff Wilkes, 69–86. Munich: iudicium, 2012.

Dumenil, Lynn. *The Modern Temper: American Culture and Society in the 1920s*. New York: Hill and Wang, 1995.

Edelmann, Heidrun. *Vom Luxusgut zum Gebrauchsgegenstand. Die Geschichte der Verbreitung von Personenkraftwagen in Deutschland*. Frankfurt/Main: Verband der Automobilindustrie, 1989.

Ehmer, Josef. *Bevölkerungsgeschichte und historische Demographie 1800–2000*. Enzyklopädie Deutscher Geschichte 71. Munich: Oldenbourg, 2004.

Eisenstadt, Shmuel N. "Multiple Modernities." *Daedalus* 129, no. 1 (2000): 1–29.

Eksteins, Modris. "The Frankfurter Zeitung: Mirror of Weimar Democracy." *Journal of Contemporary History* 6, no. 4 (1971): 3–28.

Eksteins, Modris. *The Limits of Reason: The German Democratic Press and the Collapse of Weimar Democracy*. Oxford: Oxford University Press, 1975.

Eley, Geoff. "What Was German Modernity and When?" In *German Modernities from Wilhelm to Weimar: A Contest of Futures*, edited by Geoff Eley, Jennifer L. Jenkins, and Tracie Matysik, 59–82. London: Bloomsbury, 2016.

Eley, Geoff, Jennifer L. Jenkins, and Tracie Matysik, eds. *German Modernities from Wilhelm to Weimar: A Contest of Futures*. London: Bloomsbury, 2016.

Eley, Geoff, Jennifer L. Jenkins, and Tracie Matysik. "Introduction: German Modernities and Contest of Futures." In *German Modernities from Wilhelm to Weimar: A Contest of Futures*, edited by Geoff Eley, Jennifer L. Jenkins, and Tracie Matysik, 1–27. London: Bloomsbury, 2016.

Eley, Geoff, and Jan Palmowski, eds. *Citizenship and National Identity in Twentieth-Century Germany*. Stanford: Stanford University Press, 2008.

Eley, Geoff, and Jan Palmowski, "Citizenship and National Identity in Twentieth-Century Germany." In *Citizenship and National Identity in Twentieth-Century Germany*, edited by Geoff Eley and Jan Palmowski, 3–23. Stanford: Stanford University Press, 2008.

Erdman, Barbara. "See You in the Funnies! An Analysis of Representation." *Journal of Visual Literacy* 13, no. 2 (January 1, 1993): 51–60.

Falter, Jürgen W. "'Anfälligkeit' der Angestellten—'Immunität' der Arbeiter? Mythen über die Wähler der NSDAP." In *Die Schatten der Vergangenheit. Impulse zur Historisierung des Nationalsozialismus*, edited by Uwe Backes, Eckhard Jesse, and Rainer Zitelmann, 265–90. Berlin: Ullstein, 1992.

Falter, Jürgen W. *Hitlers Wähler*. Munich: C.H. Beck, 1991.

Flik, Reiner. *Von Ford lernen? Automobilbau und Motorisierung in Deutschland bis 1933.* Cologne: Böhlau, 2001.

Flink, James J. *The Automobile Age.* Cambridge, Mass.: MIT Press, 1988.

Föllmer, Moritz. "Auf der Suche nach dem eigenen Leben. Junge Frauen und Individualität in der Weimarer Republik." In *Die "Krise" der Weimarer Republik. Zur Kritik eines Deutungsmusters*, edited by Moritz Föllmer and Rüdiger Graf, 287–317. Frankfurt/Main: Campus, 2005.

Föllmer, Moritz. "Führung und Demokratie in Europa." In *Normalität und Fragilität. Demokratie nach dem Ersten Weltkrieg*, edited by Tim B. Müller and Adam Tooze, 177–97. Hamburg: Hamburger Edition, 2015.

Föllmer, Moritz. *Individuality and Modernity in Berlin: Self and Society from Weimar to the Wall.* Cambridge: Cambridge University Press, 2013.

Föllmer, Moritz, and Rüdiger Graf, eds. *Die "Krise" der Weimarer Republik. Zur Kritik eines Deutungsmusters.* Frankfurt/Main: Campus, 2005.

Frame, Lynne. "Gretchen, Girl, Garçonne? Weimar Science and Popular Culture in Search of the Ideal New Woman." In *Women in the Metropolis: Gender and Modernity in Weimar Culture*, edited by Katharina von Ankum, 12–40. Berkeley: University of California Press, 1997.

Francis, Martin. "The Domestication of the Male? Recent Research on Nineteenth- and Twentieth-Century British Masculinity." *Historical Journal* 45, no. 3 (September 2002): 637–52.

Frevert, Ute. *Frauen-Geschichte. Zwischen bürgerlicher Verbesserung und neuer Weiblichkeit.* Frankfurt/Main: Suhrkamp, 1986.

Frevert, Ute. *"Mann und Weib, und Weib und Mann". Geschlechter-Differenzen in der Moderne.* Munich: Beck, 1995.

Freyburg, W. Joachim, and Hans Wallenberg, eds. *Hundert Jahre Ullstein, 1877–1977*, 3 vols. Berlin: Ullstein, 1977.

Fritsch, Werner. "Republikanische Partei Deutschlands (RPD)." In *Lexikon zur Parteiengeschichte. Die bürgerlichen und kleinbürgerlichen Parteien und Verbände in Deutschland 1789–1945*, vol. 4, edited by Dieter Fricke, 94–96. Cologne: Pahl-Rugenstein, 1986.

Fritzsche, Klaus. *Politische Romantik und Gegenrevolution. Fluchtwege in der Krise der bürgerlichen Gesellschaft: Das Beispiel des Tat-Kreises.* Frankfurt/Main: Suhrkamp, 1976.

Fritzsche, Peter. "Did Weimar Fail?" *Journal of Modern History* 68, no. 3 (1996): 629–56.

Fritzsche, Peter. "Historical Time and Future Experience in Postwar Germany." In *Ordnungen in der Krise. Zur politischen Kulturgeschichte Deutschlands 1900–1933*, edited by Wolfgang Hardtwig, 141–64. Munich: Oldenbourg, 2007.

Fritzsche, Peter. *A Nation of Fliers: German Aviation and the Popular Imagination.* Cambridge: Harvard University Press, 1992.

Frost, Robert L. "Machine Liberation: Inventing Housewives and Home Appliances in Interwar France." *French Historical Studies* 18, no. 1 (1993): 109–30.

Frye, Bruce B. *Liberal Democrats in the Weimar Republic: The History of the German Democratic Party and the German State Party.* Carbondale: Southern Illinois University Press, 1985.

Furlough, Ellen. "Making Mass Vacations: Tourism and Consumer Culture in France, 1930s to 1970s." *Comparative Studies in Society and History* 40, no. 2 (1998): 247–86.

Furlough, Ellen. "Selling the American Way in Interwar France: 'Prix Uniques' and the Salons des Arts Menagers." *Journal of Social History* 26, no. 3 (1993): 491–519.

Führer, Karl Christian. "Politische Kultur und Journalismus. Tageszeitungen als politische Akteure in der Krise der Weimarer Republik 1929–1933." *Jahrbuch für Kommunikationsgeschichte* 10 (2008): 26–51.

Führer, Karl Christian, and Corey Ross, eds. *Mass Media, Culture and Society in Twentieth-Century Germany*. Basingstoke: Palgrave Macmillan, 2006.

Fulda, Bernhard. "Industries of Sensationalism: German Tabloids in Weimar Germany." In *Mass Media, Culture and Society in Twentieth-Century Germany*, edited by Karl Christian Führer and Corey Ross, 183–203. Basingstoke: Palgrave Macmillan, 2006.

Fulda, Bernhard. *Press and Politics in the Weimar Republic*. Oxford: Oxford University Press, 2009.

Gaonkar, Dilip Parameshwar. "On Alternative Modernities." In *Alternative Modernities*, edited by Dilip Parameshwar Gaonkar, 1–23. Durham, N.C.: Duke University Press, 1999.

Gay, Peter. *Weimar Culture: The Outsider as Insider*. London: Penguin, 1968.

Giles, Judy. "A Home of One's Own: Women and Domesticity in England 1918–1950." *Women's Studies International Forum* 16, no. 3 (May 1, 1993): 239–53.

Gillis, John R. *Youth and History: Tradition and Change in European Age Relations, 1770-Present*. New York: Academic, 1981.

Glancy, Mark. "Temporary American Citizens? British Audiences, Hollywood Films and the Threat of Americanization in the 1920s." *Historical Journal of Film, Radio and Television* 26, no. 4 (2006): 461–84.

Glickman, Lawrence B. "Born to Shop? Consumer History and American History." In *Consumer Society in American History: A Reader*, edited by Lawrence B. Glickman, 1–14. Ithaca: Cornell University Press, 1999.

Gordon, Andrew. "Consumption, Consumerism, and Japanese Modernity." In *The Oxford Handbook of the History of Consumption*, edited by Frank Trentmann, 485–504. Oxford: Oxford University Press, 2012.

Graf, Rüdiger. *Die Zukunft der Weimarer Republik. Krisen und Zukunftsaneignungen in Deutschland, 1918–1933*. Munich: Oldenbourg, 2008.

Grazia, Victoria de. "Amerikanisierung und wechselnde Leitbilder der Konsum-Moderne (consumer-modernity) in Europa." In *Europäische Konsumgeschichte. Zur Gesellschafts- und Kulturgeschichte des Konsums (18. bis 20. Jahrhundert)*, edited by Hannes Siegrist, Hartmut Kaelble, and Jürgen Kocka, 109–37. Frankfurt/Main: Campus, 1997.

Grazia, Victoria de. "Americanization and Changing Paradigms of Consumer Modernity: France, 1930–1990." *Sites: The Journal of Twentieth-Century/Contemporary French Studies Revue d'études Français* 1, no. 1 (March 1997): 191–213.

Grazia, Victoria de. "Empowering Women as Citizen-Consumers." In *The Sex of Things: Gender and Consumption in Historical Perspective*, edited by Victoria de Grazia and Ellen Furlough, 275–86. Berkeley: University of California Press, 1996.

Grazia, Victoria de. *Irresistible Empire: America's Advance through Twentieth-Century Europe*. Cambridge: Harvard University Press, 2006.

Grendi, Edoardo. "Micro-Analisi e Storia Sociale." *Quaderni storici* 12, no. 35 (2) (1977): 506–20.

Griffin, Roger. *Modernism and Fascism: The Sense of a Beginning under Mussolini and Hitler*. London: Palgrave Macmillan, 2007.

Grossmann, Atina. "Girlkultur or Thoroughly Rationalized Female: A New Woman in Weimar Germany?" In *Women in Culture and Politics: A Century of Change*, edited by Judith Friedlander, Alice Kessler-Harris, Carroll Smith-Rosenberg, and Blanche Wiesen Cook, 62–80. Bloomington: Indiana University Press, 1986.

Grout, Holly. "Between Venus and Mercury: The 1920s Beauty Contest in France and America." *French Politics, Culture & Society* 31, no. 1 (2013): 47–68.

Guenther, Irene. *Nazi Chic? Fashioning Women in the Third Reich*. Oxford: Berg, 2004.

Gunn, Simon, and Rachel Bell. *Middle Classes: Their Rise and Sprawl*. London: Phoenix, 2003.

Gusy, Christoph. "Demokratisches Denken in der Weimarer Republik—Entstehungsbedingungen und Vorfragen." In *Demokratisches Denken in der Weimarer Republik*, edited by Christoph Gusy, 11–36. Baden-Baden: Nomos, 2000.

Gusy, Christoph. "Selbstmord oder Tod? Die Verfassungsreformdiskussion der Jahre 1930–1932." *Zeitschrift für Politik* 40, no. 4 (1993): 393–417.

Hake, Sabine. "In the Mirror of Fashion." In *Women in the Metropolis: Gender and Modernity in Weimar Culture*, edited by Katharina von Ankum, 185–201. Berkeley: University of California Press, 1997.

Hale, Oron J. *The Captive Press in the Third Reich*. Princeton: Princeton University Press, 1964.

Hankin, Emily. "Buying Modernity? The Consumer Experience of Domestic Electricity in the Era of the Grid." PhD diss. University of Manchester, 2012.

Harlander, Tilman, Katrin Hater, and Franz Meiers. *Siedeln in der Not. Umbruch von Wohnungspolitik und Siedlungsbau am Ende der Weimarer Republik*. Hamburg: Christians, 1988.

Harootunian, Harry D. *Overcome by Modernity: History, Culture, and Community in Interwar Japan*. Princeton: Princeton University Press, 2000.

Heinemann, Isabel. "Preserving the Family and the Nation: Eugenic Masculinity Concepts, Expert Intervention, and the American Family in the United States, 1900–1960." In *Masculinities and the Nation in the Modern World: Between Hegemony and Marginalization*, edited by Pablo Dominguez Andersen and Simon Wendt, 71–92. Global Masculinities. New York: Palgrave Macmillan, 2015.

Henderson, Susan R. "Self-Help Housing in the Weimar Republic: The Work of Ernst May." *Housing Studies* 14, no. 3 (May 1999): 311–28.

Hengstenberg, Hans-Eduard. "Sachlichkeit." In *Historisches Wörterbuch der Philosophie*, edited by Joachim Ritter and Rudolf Eisler, 8:1100–1102. Darmstadt: Wissenschaftliche Buchgesellschaft, 2004.

Herbert, Ulrich. "Europe in High Modernity: Reflections on a Theory of the 20th Century." *Journal of Modern European History* 5, no. 1 (2007): 5–21.

Heß, Jürgen C. *"Das ganze Deutschland soll es sein." Demokratischer Nationalismus in der Weimarer Republik am Beispiel der Deutschen Demokratischen Partei*. Stuttgart: Klett-Cotta, 1978.

Hessler, Martina. *"Mrs. Modern Woman": Zur Sozial- und Kulturgeschichte der Haushaltstechnisierung*. Frankfurt/Main: Campus, 2001.

Hessler, Martina. "Visionen des Überflusses. Entwürfe künftiger Massenkonsumgesellschaften im 20. Jahrhundert." In *Wirtschaftsgeschichte als Kulturgeschichte. Dimensionen eines Perspektivenwechsels*, edited by Hartmut Berghoff and Jakob Vogel, 455–80. Frankfurt/Main: Campus, 2004.

Hewitson, Mark, "The Kaiserreich and the Kulturländer. Conceptions of the West in Wilhelmine Germany, 1890–1914." In *Germany and "the West": The History of a Modern Concept*, edited by Riccardo Bavaj and Martina Steber, 55–68. New York: Berghahn, 2015.

Hong, Young-Sun. *Welfare, Modernity, and the Weimar State, 1919–1933*. Princeton: Princeton University Press, 1998.

Human, Julie. "A Woman Rebels? Gender Roles in 1930s Motion Pictures." *Register of the Kentucky Historical Society* 98, no. 4 (2000): 405–28.

Hung, Jochen. "'Bad' Politics and 'Good' Culture: New Approaches to the History of the Weimar Republic." *Central European History* 49, nos. 3–4 (2016): 441–53.

Hung, Jochen. "'Der Deutschen Jugend!' The Newspaper *Tempo* and the Generational Discourse of the Weimar Republic." In *Beyond Glitter and Doom: The Contingency of the Weimar Republic*, edited by Jochen Hung, Godela Weiss-Sussex, and Geoff Wilkes, 105–18. Munich: iudicium, 2012.

Hung, Jochen. "The Modernized Gretchen: Transformations of the 'New Woman' in the Late Weimar Republic." *German History* 33, no. 1 (2015): 52–79.

Hung, Jochen. "The 'Ullstein Spirit': The Ullstein Publishing House, the End of the Weimar Republic and the Making of Cold War German Identity, 1925–77." *Journal of Contemporary History* 53, no. 1 (2018): 158–84.

Hung, Jochen, Godela Weiss-Sussex, and Geoff Wilkes, eds. *Beyond Glitter and Doom: The Contingency of the Weimar Republic*. Munich: iudicium, 2012.

Huyssen, Andreas. *After the Great Divide: Modernism, Mass Culture, Postmodernism*. Basingstoke: Macmillan, 1986.

Ilgen, Volker. "Sei sparsam Brigitte, nimm Ullstein-Schnitte!" In *125 Jahre Ullstein. Presse- und Verlagsgeschichte im Zeichen der Eule*, 54–61. Berlin: Axel Springer, 2002.

Ingrassia, Brian M. "Manhood or Masculinity: The Historiography of Manliness in American Sport." In *A Companion to American Sport History*, 479–99. Chichester: Wiley-Blackwell, 2014.

Ito, Ruri. "The 'Modern Girl' Question in the Periphery of Empire: Colonial Modernity and Mobility among Okinawan Women in the 1920s and 1930s." In *The Modern Girl around the World: Consumption, Modernity, and Globalization*, edited by Alys Eve Weinbaum, Lynn M. Thomas, Priti Ramamurthy, Uta G. Poiger, Madeleine Y. Dong, and Tani E. Barlow, 240–62. Durham, N.C.: Duke University Press, 2008.

Jacobs, Meg. "The Politics of Plenty in the Twentieth-Century United States." In *The Politics of Consumption: Material Culture and Citizenship in Europe and America*, edited by Martin Daunton and Matthew Hilton, 223–39. Oxford: Berg, 2001.

James, Harold. *A German Identity: 1770 to the Present Day*. London: Phoenix Press, 2000.

Jensen, Erik Norman. *Body by Weimar: Athletes, Gender, and German Modernity.* Oxford: Oxford University Press, 2013.
Jones, Larry E. *German Liberalism and the Dissolution of the Weimar Party System, 1918–1933.* Chapel Hill: University of North Carolina Press, 1988.
Jung, Otmar. *Direkte Demokratie in der Weimarer Republik. Die Fälle "Aufwertung," "Fürstenenteignung," "Panzerkreuzerverbot" und "Youngplan."* Frankfurt/Main: Campus, 1989.
Kaelble, Hartmut, Jürgen Kocka, and Hannes Siegrist, eds. *Europäische Konsumgeschichte. Zur Gesellschafts- und Kulturgeschichte des Konsums (18. bis 20. Jahrhundert).* Frankfurt/Main: Campus, 1997.
Kaiser, Wilson. "Partial Affinities: Fascism and the Politics of Representation in Interwar America." PhD diss., University of North Carolina, 2011.
Kämper, Heidrun. "Demokratisches Wissen in der frühen Weimarer Republik." In *Demokratiegeschichte als Zäsurgeschichte. Diskurse der frühen Weimarer Republik*, edited by Heidrun Kämper, Peter Haslinger, and Thomas Raithel, 19–96. Berlin: de Gruyter, 2014.
Kämper, Heidrun, Peter Haslinger, and Thomas Raithel, eds. *Demokratiegeschichte als Zäsurgeschichte. Diskurse der frühen Weimarer Republik.* Berlin: de Gruyter, 2014.
Keitz, Christine. "Die Anfänge des modernen Massentourismus in der Weimarer Republik." *Archiv für Sozialgeschichte* 33 (1993): 179–209.
Kessemeier, Gesa. *Sportlich, sachlich, männlich. Das Bild der "Neuen Frau" in den Zwanziger Jahren. Zur Konstruktion geschlechtsspezifischer Körperbilder in der Mode der Jahre 1920 bis 1929.* Dortmund: Ebersbach, 2000.
Kessler-Harris, Alice. "Gender Ideology in Historical Reconstruction: A Case Study from the 1930s." *Gender & History* 1, no. 1 (1989): 31–49.
Kettler, Sabine, Eva-Maria Stuckel, and Franz Wegener. *Wer tötete Helmut Daube? Der bestialische Sexualmord an dem Schüler Helmut Daube im Ruhrgebiet 1928.* Gladbeck: Kulturförderverein Ruhrgebiet, 2000.
Klautke, Egbert. *Unbegrenzte Möglichkeiten. "Amerikanisierung" in Deutschland und Frankreich, 1900–1933.* Stuttgart: Steiner, 2003.
Klein, Michael *Georg Bernhard. Die politische Haltung des Chefredakteurs der Vossischen Zeitung, 1918–1930.* Frankfurt/Main: Lang, 1999.
Koebner, Thomas, Rolf-Peter Janz, and Frank Trommler, eds. *Mit uns zieht die neue Zeit." Der Mythos Jugend.* Frankfurt/Main: Suhrkamp, 1985.
Kolb, Eberhard. *The Weimar Republic.* Abingdon: Routledge, 2005.
König, Wolfgang. *Geschichte der Konsumgesellschaft.* Stuttgart: Steiner, 2000.
Koshar, Rudy. "Cars and Nations: Anglo-German Perspectives on Automobility between the World Wars." *Theory, Culture & Society* 21, nos. 4–5 (2004): 121–44.
Köster, Roman. "Vor der Krise. Die Keynes-Rezeption in der Weimarer Republik." *Mittelweg 36* 22, no. 3 (2013): 32–46.
Koszyk, Kurt. *Deutsche Presse 1914–1945.* Vol. 3. 4 vols. Geschichte der deutschen Presse. Berlin: Colloquium, 1972.
Koszyk, Kurt. *Deutsche Presse im 19. Jahrhundert.* Vol. 2. 4 vols. Geschichte der deutschen Presse. Berlin: Colloquium, 1966.
Koszyk, Kurt. *Zwischen Kaiserreich und Diktatur. Die sozialdemokratische Presse von 1914 bis 1933.* Heidelberg: Quelle & Meyer, 1958.

Bibliography

Krabbe, Wolfgang. *Die gescheiterte Zukunft der Ersten Republik. Jugendorganisationen bürgerlicher Parteien im Weimarer Staat.* Opladen: Westdeutscher Verlag, 1995.

Kracauer, Siegfried. *The Mass Ornament: Weimar Essays*, trans. Thomas Levin. Cambridge: Harvard University Press, 1995.

Kühne, Thomas. *Kameradschaft. Die Soldaten des nationalsozialistischen Krieges und das 20. Jahrhundert.* Göttingen: Vandenhoeck & Ruprecht, 2006.

Lacey, Kate. *Feminine Frequencies: Gender, German Radio, and the Public Sphere, 1923–1945.* Ann Arbor: University of Michigan Press, 1996.

Lange, Thomas. "Der 'Steglitzer Schülermordprozess' 1928." In *"Mit uns zieht die neue Zeit." Der Mythos Jugend*, edited by Thomas Koebner, Rolf-Peter Janz, and Frank Trommler, 412–37. Frankfurt/Main: Suhrkamp, 1985.

Langenscheidt, Florian, ed. *Deutsche Standards: Marken des Jahrhunderts.* Wiesbaden: Gabler, 2004.

Langewiesche, Dieter. *Liberalismus in Deutschland.* Frankfurt/Main: Suhrkamp, 1988.

Langhamer, Claire. "Love and Courtship in Mid-Twentieth-Century England." *Historical Journal* 50, no. 1 (2007): 173–96.

Laqueur, Walter. *Young Germany: A History of the German Youth Movement.* London: Routledge & Kegan Paul, 1962.

Lees, Andrew. "Berlin and Modern Urbanity in German Discourse, 1845–1945." *Journal of Urban History* 17, no. 2 (1991): 153–80.

Lenk, Carsten. *Die Erscheinung des Rundfunks. Einführung und Nutzung eines neuen Mediums 1923–1932.* Opladen: Westdeutscher Verlag, 1997.

Lenthall, Bruce. *Radio's America: The Great Depression and the Rise of Modern Mass Culture.* Chicago: University of Chicago Press, 2007.

Leonhard, Jörn. "Semantische Deplazierung und Entwertung. Deutsche Deutungen von *liberal* und *Liberalismus* nach 1850 im europäischen Vergleich." *Geschichte und Gesellschaft* 29, no. 1 (2003): 5–39.

Lepsius, Oliver. "Staatstheorie und Demokratiebegriff in der Weimarer Republik." In *Demokratisches Denken in der Weimarer Republik*, edited by Christoph Gusy, 366–414. Baden-Baden: Nomos, 2000.

Lethen, Helmut. *Cool Conduct: The Culture of Distance in Weimar Germany.* Berkeley: University of California Press, 2002.

Lethen, Helmut. "Freiheit von Angst. Über einen entlastenden Aspekt der Technik-Moden in den Jahrzehnten der historischen Avantgarde 1910–1930." In *Literatur in einer industriellen Kultur*, edited by Götz Grossklaus and Eberhard Lämmert, 72–98. Stuttgart: Cotta, 1989.

Lethen, Helmut. *Neue Sachlichkeit 1924–32. Studien zur Literatur des "Weißen Sozialismus."* Stuttgart: Metzler, 1970.

Levi, Giovanni. "On Microhistory." In *New Perspectives on Historical Writing*, edited by Peter Burke, 93–113. Cambridge: Polity, 1991.

Lindner, Erik, ed. *125 Jahre Ullstein. Presse- und Verlagsgeschichte im Zeichen der Eule.* Berlin: Axel Springer, 2002.

Llanque, Marcus. "Massendemokratie zwischen Kaiserreich und westlicher Demokratie." In *Demokratisches Denken in der Weimarer Republik*, edited by Christoph Gusy, 38–70. Baden-Baden: Nomos, 2000.

Llanque, Marcus. *Politische Ideengeschichte. Ein Gewebe politischer Diskurse.* Munich: Oldenbourg, 2008.
Lobenstein-Reichmann, Anja. "Der völkische Demokratiebegriff." In *Demokratiegeschichte als Zäsurgeschichte. Diskurse der frühen Weimarer Republik*, edited by Heidrun Kämper, Peter Haslinger, and Thomas Raithel, 285–306. Berlin: de Gruyter, 2014.
Long, Vicky. "Industrial Homes, Domestic Factories: The Convergence of Public and Private Space in Interwar Britain." *Journal of British Studies* 50, no. 2 (2011): 434–64.
Lubben, Kristen. "A New American Ideal: Photography and Amelia Earhart." In *The New Woman International*, edited by Elizabeth Otto and Vanessa Rocco, 291–308. Ann Arbor: University of Michigan Press, 2011.
Lüdtke, Alf, Inge Marszolek, and Adelheid von Saldern, eds. *Amerikanisierung. Traum und Alptraum im Deutschland des 20. Jahrhunderts.* Stuttgart: Steiner, 1996.
Lustig, Jan. *Ein Rosenkranz von Glücksfällen. Protokoll einer Flucht.* Bonn: Weidle, 2001.
Maase, Kaspar. *Grenzenloses Vergnügen. Der Aufstieg der Massenkultur 1850–1970.* Frankfurt/Main: Fischer, 1997.
Maase, Kaspar. "Massenmedien und Konsumgesellschaft." In *Die Konsumgesellschaft in Deutschland 1890–1990*, edited by Heinz-Gerhard Haupt and Claudius Torp, 62–78. Frankfurt/Main: Campus, 2009.
Magnússon, Sigurður Gylfi, and István M. Szíjártó. *What Is Microhistory? Theory and Practice.* London: Routledge, 2013.
Maier, Charles S. "Between Taylorism and Technocracy: European Ideologies and the Vision of Industrial Productivity in the 1920s." *Journal of Contemporary History* 5, no. 2 (1970): 27–61.
Mandler, Peter. "The Consciousness of Modernity? Liberalism and the English 'National Character,' 1870–1940." In *Meanings of Modernity: Britain from the Late-Victorian Era to World War II*, edited by Bernhard Rieger and Martin Daunton, 119–44. Oxford: Berg, 2001.
Marchand, Roland. *Advertising the American Dream: Making Way for Modernity, 1920–1940.* Berkeley: University of California Press, 1985.
Marshall, P. David, and Joanne Morreale. *Advertising and Promotional Culture: Case Histories.* London: Red Globe Press, 2017.
Matthews, Jill Julius. "They Had Such a Lot of Fun: The Women's League of Health and Beauty between the Wars." *History Workshop*, no. 30 (1990): 22–54.
McCarthy, Helen. "Whose Democracy? Histories of British Political Culture between the Wars." *Historical Journal* 55, no. 1 (2012): 221–38.
McCormick, Richard. *Gender and Sexuality in Weimar Modernity: Film, Literature and 'New Objectivity.'* New York: Palgrave Macmillan, 2001.
McElligott, Anthony. "Political Culture." In *Weimar Germany*, edited by Anthony McElligott, 26–49. Oxford: Oxford University Press, 2009.
McElligott, Anthony. "Rethinking the Weimar Paradigm: Carl Schmitt and Politics without Authority." In *Beyond Glitter and Doom: The Contingency of the Weimar Republic*, edited by Jochen Hung, Godela Weiss-Sussex, and Geoff Wilkes, 87–101. Munich: iudicium, 2012.

McElligott, Anthony. *Weimar Germany*. Oxford: Oxford University Press, 2009.
McGovern, Charles. "Consumption and Citizenship in the United States, 1900–1940." In *Getting and Spending: European and American Consumer Societies in the Twentieth Century*, edited by Susan Strasser, Charles McGovern, and Matthias Judt, 37–58. Cambridge: Cambridge University Press, 1998.
McGovern, Charles F. *Sold American: Consumption and Citizenship, 1890–1945*. Chapel Hill: University of North Carolina Press, 2009.
McKibbin, Ross. *Classes and Cultures: England 1918–1951*. Oxford: Oxford University Press, 2000.
Mendelssohn, Peter de. *Zeitungsstadt Berlin. Menschen und Mächte in der Geschichte der deutschen Presse*. Berlin: Ullstein, 1982.
Mergel, Thomas. *Parlamentarische Kultur im Reichstag der Weimarer Republik. Politische Kommunikation, symbolische Politik und Öffentlichkeit im Reichstag*. Düsseldorf: Droste, 2002.
Milatz, Alfred. *Wähler und Wahlen in der Weimarer Republik*. Bonn: Bundeszentrale für politische Bildung, 1968.
Mommsen, Hans. "Generationskonflikt und Jugendrevolte in der Weimarer Republik." In *"Mit uns zieht die neue Zeit." Der Mythos Jugend*, edited by Thomas Koebner, Rolf-Peter Janz, and Frank Trommler, 50–67. Frankfurt/Main: Suhrkamp, 1985.
Möser, Kurt. "World War I and the Creation of Desire for Automobiles in Germany." In *Getting and Spending: European and American Consumer Societies in the Twentieth Century*, edited by Susan Strasser, Charles McGovern, and Matthias Judt, 195–222. Cambridge: Cambridge University Press, 1998.
Mosse, George L. *The Image of Man: The Creation of Modern Masculinity*. Oxford: Oxford University Press, 1996.
Müller, Tim B. *Nach dem ersten Weltkrieg. Lebensversuche moderner Demokratien*. Hamburg: Hamburger Edition, 2014.
Müller, Tim B., and Adam Tooze. "Demokratie nach dem Ersten Weltkrieg." In *Normalität und Fragilität. Demokratie nach dem Ersten Weltkrieg*, edited by Tim B. Müller and Adam Tooze, 9–33. Hamburg: Hamburger Edition, 2015.
Müller, Tim B., and Adam Tooze, eds. *Normalität und Fragilität. Demokratie nach dem Ersten Weltkrieg*. Hamburg: Hamburger Edition, 2015.
Mulligan, William. "The Reichswehr and the Weimar Republic." In *Weimar Germany*, edited by Anthony McElligott, 78–101. Oxford: Oxford University Press, 2009.
Nolan, Mary. *Visions of Modernity: American Business and the Modernization of Germany*. Oxford: Oxford University Press, 1994.
Nora, Pierre. "Generation." In *Realms of Memory: Rethinking the French Past*, edited by Pierre Nora, translated by Arthur Goldhammer, 1:499–612. New York: Columbia University Press, 1996.
O'Connell, Sean. *The Car and British Society: Class, Gender and Motoring, 1896–1939*. Manchester: Manchester University Press, 1998.
Oldenziel, Ruth, Adri Albert de la Bruhèze, and Onno de Wit. "Europe's Mediation Junction: Technology and Consumer Society in the 20th Century." *History and Technology* 21, no. 1 (March 1, 2005): 107–39.
Ong, Aihwa. "Cultural Citizenship as Subject-Making: Immigrants Negotiate Racial

and Cultural Boundaries in the United States." *Current Anthropology* 37, no. 5 (1996): 737–62.
Oschilewski, Walther G. *Zeitungen in Berlin. Im Spiegel der Jahrhunderte.* Berlin: Haude und Spenersche Verlagsbuchhandlung, 1975.
O'Shea, Alan. "English Subjects of Modernity." In *Modern Times: Reflections on a Century of English Modernity*, edited by Mica Nava and Alan O'Shea, 7–37. London: Routledge, 1996.
Overy, Richard J. "Cars, Roads, and Economic Recovery in Germany, 1932–8." *Economic History Review* 28, no. 3 (1975): 466–83.
Passerini, Luisa. "The Ambivalent Image of Woman in Mass Culture." In *A History of Women in the West*, edited by Françoise Thébaud, translated by Joan Bond Sax, 5:324–42. Cambridge: Harvard University Press, 1994.
Patel, Kiran Klaus. *The New Deal: A Global History*. Princeton: Princeton University Press, 2016.
Peltonen, Matti. "Clues, Margins, and Monads: The Micro-Macro Link in Historical Research." *History and Theory* 40, no. 3 (2001): 347–59.
Perry, Joe. "Consumer Citizenship in the Interwar Era: Gender, Race, and the State in Global-Historical Perspective." *Journal of Women's History* 18, no. 4 (2006): 157–72.
Pettegrew, John. *Brutes in Suits: Male Sensibility in America, 1890–1920*. Baltimore: Johns Hopkins University Press, 2012.
Peukert, Detlev J. K. "Das Mädchen mit dem 'wahrlich metaphysikfreien Bubikopf'. Jugend und Freizeit im Berlin der zwanziger Jahre." In *Im Banne der Metropolen. Berlin und London in den zwanziger Jahren*, edited by Peter Alter, 157–75. Göttingen: Vandenhoeck & Ruprecht, 1993.
Peukert, Detlev J. K. "The Genesis of the 'Final Solution' from the Spirit of Science." In *Nazism and German Society, 1933–1945*, edited by David F. Crew, 420–57. London: Routledge, 1994.
Peukert, Detlev J. K. *Jugend zwischen Krieg und Krise. Lebenswelten von Arbeiterjungen in der Weimarer Republik.* Cologne: Bund, 1987.
Peukert, Detlev J. K. *The Weimar Republic: The Crisis of Classical Modernity.* Translated by Richard Deveson. New York: Hill and Wang, 1992.
Priamus, Heinz-Jürgen. *Angestellte und Demokratie. Die nationalliberale Angestelltenbewegung in der Weimarer Republik.* Stuttgart: Klett-Cotta, 1979.
Pugh, Martin. *We Danced All Night: A Social History of Britain between the Wars.* London: Vintage, 2009.
Pursell, Carroll. "Domesticating Modernity: The Electrical Association for Women, 1924–86." *British Journal for the History of Science* 32, no. 1 (1999): 47–67.
Ramsbrock, Annelie. *The Science of Beauty: Culture and Cosmetics in Modern Germany, 1750–1930.* Basingstoke: Palgrave Macmillan, 2015.
Read, Geoff. "Des Hommes et des Citoyens: Paternalism and Masculinity on the Republican Right in Interwar France, 1919–1939." *Historical Reflections/Réflexions Historiques* 34, no. 2 (2008): 88–111.
Read, Geoff. *The Republic of Men: Gender and the Political Parties in Interwar France.* Baton Rouge: Louisiana State University Press, 2014.

Reimus, Klaus. "'Aber das Reich muss uns doch bleiben!' Die nationale Rechte." In *Politische Identität und nationale Gedenktage. Zur politischen Kultur in der Weimarer Republik*, edited by Detlef Lehnert and Klaus Megerle, 231–53. Opladen: Westdeutscher Verlag, 1989.

Renouard, Joe. "The Predicaments of Plenty: Interwar Intellectuals and American Consumerism." *Journal of American Culture* 30, no. 1 (2007): 54–67.

Retterath, Jörn. "Der Volksbegriff in der Zäsur des Jahres 1918/19." In *Demokratiegeschichte als Zäsurgeschichte. Diskurse der frühen Weimarer Republik*, edited by Heidrun Kämper, Peter Haslinger, and Thomas Raithel, 97–122. Berlin: de Gruyter, 2014.

Reulecke, Jürgen. "*Ich möchte einer werden so wie die . . .*": *Männerbünde im 20. Jahrhundert*. Frankfurt/Main: Campus, 2001.

Reulecke, Jürgen. "Neuer Mensch und neue Männlichkeit. Die 'junge Generation' im ersten Drittel des 20. Jahrhunderts." In *Jahrbuch des Historischen Kollegs 2001*, 109–38. Munich: Oldenbourg, 2002.

Reuveni, Gideon. "Lesen und Konsum. Der Aufstieg der Konsumkultur in Presse und Werbung Deutschlands bis 1933." *Archiv für Sozialgeschichte* 41 (2001): 97–117.

Reuveni, Gideon. "Reading, Advertising and Consumer Culture in the Weimar Period." In *Mass Media, Culture and Society in Twentieth-Century Germany*, edited by Karl Christian Führer and Corey Ross, 204–16. Basingstoke: Palgrave Macmillan, 2006.

Reuveni, Gideon. "Wohlstand durch Konsum. Straßenhandel und Versicherungszeitschriften in den zwanziger Jahren." In *Die "Krise" der Weimarer Republik. Zur Kritik eines Deutungsmusters*, edited by Moritz Föllmer and Rüdiger Graf, 267–86. Frankfurt/Main: Campus, 2005.

Reynolds, Moira Davidson. *Comic Strip Artists in American Newspapers, 1945–1980*. Jefferson, N.C.: McFarland, 2003.

Riedel, Manfred. "Generation." In *Historisches Wörterbuch der Philosophie*, edited by Joachim Ritter and Rudolf Eisler. Vol. 1. Darmstadt: Wissenschaftliche Buchgesellschaft, 1974.

Rieger, Bernhard, and Martin Daunton. "Introduction." In *Meanings of Modernity: Britain from the Late-Victorian Era to World War II*, edited by Bernhard Rieger and Martin Daunton, 119–44. Oxford: Berg, 2001.

Rieger, Bernhard. *Technology and the Culture of Modernity in Britain and Germany, 1890–1945*. Cambridge: Cambridge University Press, 2005.

Roberts, Mary Louise. *Civilization without Sexes: Reconstructing Gender in Postwar France, 1917–1927*. Chicago: University of Chicago Press, 1994.

Roebling, Irmgard. "'Haarschnitt ist noch nicht Freiheit'. Das Ringen um Bilder der Neuen Frau in Texten von Autorinnen und Autoren der Weimarer Republik." *Jahrbuch zur Literatur der Weimarer Republik* 5 (1999/2000): 13–76.

Rohkrämer, Thomas. *Eine andere Moderne? Zivilisationskritik, Natur und Technik in Deutschland 1880–1933*. Paderborn: Schöningh, 1999.

Roper, Michael. "Between Manliness and Masculinity: The 'War Generation' and the Psychology of Fear in Britain, 1914–1950." *Journal of British Studies* 44, no. 2 (April 2005): 343–62.

Rosa, Hartmut. *Beschleunigung. Die Veränderung der Zeitstrukturen in der Moderne*. Frankfurt/Main: Suhrkamp, 2005.

Roseman, Mark. "National Socialism and the End of Modernity." *American Historical Review* 116, no. 3 (2011): 688–701.

Rosenhaft, Eve. "Lesewut, Kinosucht, Radiotismus: Zur (geschlechter-)politischen Relevanz neuer Massenmedien in den 1920er Jahren." In *Amerikanisierung. Traum und Alptraum im Deutschland des 20. Jahrhunderts*, edited by Alf Lüdtke, Inge Marszolek, and Adelheid von Saldern, 119–43. Stuttgart: Franz Steiner, 1996.

Rosenhaft, Eve. "The Unemployed in the Neighbourhood: Social Dislocation and Political Mobilisation in Germany 1929–33." In *The German Unemployed: Experiences and Consequences of Mass Unemployment from the Weimar Republic to the Third Reich*, edited by Richard J. Evans and Dick Geary, 194–227. London: Routledge, 2015.

Ross, Corey. *Media and the Making of Modern Germany: Mass Communications, Society, and Politics from the Empire to the Third Reich*. Oxford: Oxford University Press, 2008.

Ross, Corey. "Visions of Prosperity. The Americanization of Advertising in Interwar Germany." In *Selling Modernity: Advertising in Twentieth-Century Germany*, edited by Pamela Swett, S. Jonathan Wiesen, and Jonathan R. Zatlin, 52–77. Durham, N.C.: Duke University Press, 2007.

Rossol, Nadine. *Performing the Nation in Interwar Germany: Sport, Spectacle and Political Symbolism 1926–36*. Basingstoke: Palgrave Macmillan, 2010.

Rowe, Dorothy. *Representing Berlin: Sexuality and the City in Imperial and Weimar Germany*. London: Routledge, 2017.

Rusinek, Bernd A. "Krieg als Sehnsucht. Militärischer Stil und 'junge Generation' in der Weimarer Republik." In *Generationalität und Lebensgeschichte im 20. Jahrhundert*, edited by Jürgen Reulecke, 127–44. Munich: Oldenbourg, 2003.

Sack, Heidi. *Moderne Jugend vor Gericht. Sensationsprozesse, "Sexualtragödien" und die Krise der Jugend in der Weimarer Republik*. Bielefeld: transcript, 2016.

Saldern, Adelheid von. "'Art for the People': From Cultural Conservatism to Nazi Cultural Policies." In *The Challenge of Modernity: German Social and Cultural Studies, 1890–1960*, translated by Bruce Little, 299–347. Ann Arbor: University of Michigan Press, 2002.

Saldern, Adelheid von. "Transatlantische Konsumleitbilder und Übersetzungspraktiken 1900–1945." In *Die Konsumgesellschaft in Deutschland 1890–1990*, edited by Heinz-Gerhard Haupt and Claudius Torp, 389–402. Frankfurt/Main: Campus, 2009.

Saldern, Adelheid von. "Volk and Heimat: Culture in Radio Broadcasting during the Period of Transition from Weimar to Nazi Germany." *Journal of Modern History* 76, no. 2 (2004): 312–46.

Sato, Barbara. "The Moga Sensation: Perceptions of the Modan Gāru in Japanese Intellectual Circles during the 1920s." *Gender & History* 5, no. 3 (1993): 363–81.

Sato, Barbara. *The New Japanese Woman: Modernity, Media, and Women in Interwar Japan*. Durham, N.C.: Duke University Press Books, 2003.

Savage, Jon. *Teenage: The Creation of Youth Culture*. New York: Viking, 2007.

Scheffler, Robin Wolfe. "Interests and Instrument: A Micro-History of Object Wh.3469 (X-Ray Powder Diffraction Camera, ca. 1940)." *Studies in History and Philosophy of Science* 40, no. 4 (December 1, 2009): 396–404.

Schiller, Hans von, and Hans G. Knäusel. *Zeppelin. Aufbruch ins 20. Jahrhundert.* Bonn: Kirschbaum, 1988.
Schivelbusch, Wolfgang. *Three New Deals: Reflections on Roosevelt's America, Mussolini's Italy, and Hitler's Germany, 1933–1939.* New York: Picador, 2006.
Schmidt, Jens. "Sich hart machen, wenn es gilt." *Männlichkeitskonzeptionen in Illustrierten der Weimarer Republik.* Münster: Lit, 2000.
Schmidt, Klaus Werner. "Die Tat (1909–1939)." In *Deutsche Zeitschriften des 17. bis 20. Jahrhunderts*, edited by Heinz Dietrich Fischer, 349–63. Pullach: Verlag Dokumentation, 1973.
Schmitz-Scherzer, Reinhard. *Freizeit.* Stuttgart: Teubner, 1985.
Schottmann, Christian. *Politische Schlagwörter in Deutschland zwischen 1929 und 1934.* Stuttgart: Hans-Dieter Heinz, 1997.
Schug, Alexander. "Wegbereiter der modernen Absatzwerbung in Deutschland. Advertising Agencies und die Amerikanisierung der deutschen Werbebranche in der Zwischenkriegszeit." *WerkstattGeschichte* 34 (2003): 29–52.
Schulz, Andreas, and Gundula Grebner. "Generation und Geschichte. Zur Renaissance eines umstrittenen Forschungskonzepts." *Historische Zeitschrift Beiheft* 36 (2003): 1–23.
Schulz, Günther. *Die Angestellten seit dem 19. Jahrhundert.* Munich: Oldenbourg, 2000.
Schulze, Volker. "Vorwärts (1876–1933)." In *Deutsche Zeitungen des 17. bis 20. Jahrhunderts*, edited by Heinz Dietrich Fischer, 329–47. Pullach: Dokumentation, 1972.
Sharp, Ingrid. "Riding the Tiger: Ambivalent Images of the New Woman in the Popular Press of the Weimar Republic." In *New Woman Hybridities: Femininity, Feminism and International Consumer Culture, 1880–1930*, edited by Margaret Beetham and Ann Heilmann, 118–41. London: Routledge, 2004.
Siegel, Tilla. "It's Only Rational: An Essay on the Logic of Social Rationalization." *International Journal of Political Economy* 24, no. 4 (1994): 35–70.
Siegrist, Hannes. "Konsum, Kultur und Gesellschaft im modernen Europa." In *Europäische Konsumgeschichte. Zur Gesellschafts- und Kulturgeschichte des Konsums (18. bis 20. Jahrhundert)*, edited by Hartmut Kaelble, Jürgen Kocka, and Hannes Siegrist, 13–48. Frankfurt/Main: Campus, 1997.
Siemens, Daniel. "Kühle Romantiker. Zum Geschichtsverständnis der 'jungen Generation' in der Weimarer Republik." In *Die Kunst der Geschichte. Historiographie, Ästhetik, Erzählung*, edited by Martin Baumeister, Moritz Föllmer, and Philipp Müller, 189–214. Göttingen: Vandenhoeck & Ruprecht, 2009.
Simon, Linda. *Lost Girls: The Invention of the Flapper.* London: Reaktion Books, 2017.
Slater, Don. *Consumer Culture and Modernity.* Cambridge: Polity, 1997.
Smiler, Andrew P., Gwen Kay, and Benjamin Harris. "Tightening and Loosening Masculinity's (k)Nots: Masculinity in the Hearst Press during the Interwar Period." *Journal of Men's Studies* 16, no. 3 (2008): 266–79.
Smith, Alison K. "A Microhistory of the Global Empire of Cotton: Ivanovo, the 'Russian Manchester'" *Past & Present* 244, no. 1 (August 1, 2019): 163–93.
Sneeringer, Julia. "The Shopper as Voter: Women, Advertising, and Politics in Post-Inflation Germany." *German Studies Review* 27, no. 3 (2004): 476–501.

Sneeringer, Julia. *Winning Women's Votes: Propaganda and Politics in Weimar Germany*. Chapel Hill: University of North Carolina Press, 2002.
Söll, Änne. *Der neue Mann? Männerporträts von Otto Dix, Christian Schad und Anton Räderscheidt 1914–1930*. Paderborn: Wilhelm Fink, 2016.
Sontheimer, Kurt. "Der Tatkreis." *Vierteljahrshefte für Zeitgeschichte* 7, no. 3 (1959): 229–60.
Sösemann, Bernd. *Das Ende der Weimarer Republik in der Kritik demokratischer Publizisten. Theodor Wolff, Ernst Feder, Julius Elbau, Leopold Schwarzschild*. Berlin: Colloquium, 1976.
Spode, Hasso. "Der Aufstieg des Massentourismus im 20. Jahrhundert." In *Die Konsumgesellschaft in Deutschland 1890–1990*, edited by Heinz-Gerhard Haupt and Claudius Torp, 114–28. Frankfurt/Main: Campus, 2009.
Spree, Reinhard. "Angestellte als Modernisierungsagenten. Indikatoren und Thesen zum reproduktiven Verhalten von Angestellten im späten 19. und frühen 20. Jahrhundert." *Geschichte und Gesellschaft. Sonderheft* 7 (1981): 279–308.
Stachura, Peter D. *The German Youth Movement 1900–1945: An Interpretative and Documentary History*. London: Macmillan, 1981.
Stambolis, Barbara. *Mythos Jugend—Leitbild und Krisensymptom. Ein Aspekt der politischen Kultur im 20. Jahrhundert*. Schwalbach: Wochenschau, 2003.
Stang, Joachim. *Die Deutsche Demokratische Partei in Preußen 1918–1933*. Düsseldorf: Droste, 1994.
Stanley, Adam C. *Modernizing Tradition: Gender and Consumerism in Interwar France and Germany*. Baton Rouge: Louisiana State University Press, 2008.
Steffen, Kirsten. *"Haben Sie mich gehasst?" Antworten für Martin Beradt (1881–1949). Schriftsteller, Rechtsanwalt, Berliner jüdischen Glaubens*. Oldenburg: Igel, 1999.
Steinbeck, Frank. *Das Motorrad. Ein deutscher Sonderweg in die automobile Gesellschaft*. Stuttgart: Franz Steiner, 2012.
Steiner, Frank C. "Manfred George: His Life and Works." PhD diss., State University of New York, 1977.
Steinmetz, Willibald. "Anbetung und Dämonisierung des 'Sachzwangs'. Zur Archäologie einer deutschen Redefigur." In *Obsessionen. Beherrschende Gedanken im wissenschaftlichen Zeitalter*, edited by Michael Jeismann, 293–333. Frankfurt/Main: Suhrkamp, 1995.
Stewart, Mary Lynn. *Dressing Modern Frenchwomen: Marketing Haute Couture, 1919–1939*. Baltimore: Johns Hopkins University Press, 2008.
Stibbe, Matthew. *Women in the Third Reich*. London: Arnold, 2003.
Stöber, Rudolf. *Deutsche Pressegeschichte. Einführung, Systematik, Glossar*. Constance: UVK, 2000.
Strasser, Susan, Charles McGovern, and Matthias Judt, eds. *Getting and Spending: European and American Consumer Societies in the Twentieth Century*. Cambridge: Cambridge University Press, 1998.
Struve, Walter. "Hans Zehrer as a Neoconservative Elite Theorist." *American Historical Review* 70, no. 4 (1965): 1035–57.
Studlar, Gaylyn. *This Mad Masquerade: Stardom and Masculinity in the Jazz Age*. New York: Columbia University Press, 1996.

Susman, Warren I. *Culture as History: The Transformation of American Society in the Twentieth Century*. Washington, D.C.: Smithsonian Institution Press, 2003.
Sutton, Katie. "From Dandies to Naturburschen: The Gendering of Men's Fashions in Weimar Germany." *Edinburgh German Yearbook* 2 (2008): 130–48.
Sutton, Katie. *The Masculine Woman in Weimar Germany*. New York: Berghahn, 2011.
Sylvester, Nina. "Before *Cosmopolitan*: The Girl in German Women's Magazines in the 1920s." *Journalism Studies* 8, no. 4 (2007): 550–54.
Sylvester, Nina. "Das Girl: Crossing Spaces and Spheres. The Function of the Girl in the Weimar Republic." PhD diss., University of California, 2006.
Syon, Guillaume de. *Zeppelin! Germany and the Airship, 1900–1939*. Baltimore: Johns Hopkins University Press, 2002.
Theweleit, Klaus. *Male Fantasies*. Minneapolis: University of Minnesota Press, 1987.
Tinkler, Penny, and Cheryl Krasnick Warsh. "Feminine Modernity in Interwar Britain and North America: Corsets, Cars, and Cigarettes." *Journal of Women's History* 20, no. 3 (2008): 113–43.
Todd, Selina. *Young Women, Work, and Family in England 1918–1950*. Oxford: Oxford University Press, 2005.
Torp, Claudius. "Das Janusgesicht der Weimarer Konsumpolitik." In *Die Konsumgesellschaft in Deutschland 1890–1990*, edited by Heinz-Gerhard Haupt and Claudius Torp, 250–67. Frankfurt/Main: Campus, 2009.
Torp, Claudius. *Konsum und Politik in der Weimarer Republik*. Göttingen: Vandenhoek & Ruprecht, 2011.
Trentmann, Frank. "Bread, Milk and Democracy: Consumption and Citizenship in Twentieth-Century Britain." In *The Politics of Consumption: Material Culture and Citizenship in Europe and America*, edited by Martin Daunton and Matthew Hilton, 129–63. Oxford: Berg, 2001.
Trommler, Frank. "Mission ohne Ziel. Über den Kult der Jugend im modernen Deutschland." In *"Mit uns zieht die neue Zeit." Der Mythos Jugend*, edited by Thomas Koebner, Rolf-Peter Janz, and Frank Trommler, 14–49. Frankfurt/Main: Suhrkamp, 1985.
Trommler, Frank. "Technik, Avantgarde, Sachlichkeit." In *Literatur in einer industriellen Kultur*, edited by Götz Grossklaus and Eberhard Lämmert, 46–71. Stuttgart: Cotta, 1989.
Ullstein, Hermann. *The Rise and Fall of the House of Ullstein*. New York: Simon and Schuster, 1943.
Usborne, Cornelie. *The Politics of the Body in Weimar Germany: Women's Reproductive Rights and Duties*. Basingstoke: Macmillan, 1992.
Von Ankum, Katharina, ed. *Women in the Metropolis: Gender and Modernity in Weimar Culture*. Berkeley: University of California Press, 1997.
Von der Goltz, Anna. *Hindenburg: Power, Myth, and the Rise of the Nazis*. Oxford: Oxford University Press, 2009.
Walker, David H. *Consumer Chronicles: Cultures of Consumption in Modern French Literature*. Liverpool: Liverpool University Press, 2011.
Walton, Whitney. "American Girls and French Jeunes Filles: Negotiating National Identities in Interwar France." *Gender & History* 17, no. 2 (2005): 325–53.
Wandel, Eckhard. *Hans Schäffer. Steuermann in wirtschaftlichen und politischen Krisen*. Stuttgart: Deutsche Verlagsanstalt, 1974.

Ward, Janet. *Weimar Surfaces: Urban Visual Culture in 1920s Germany*. Berkeley: University of California Press, 2001.
Ware, Susan. *Holding Their Own: American Women in the 1930s*. Boston: Twayne, 1982.
Wehler, Hans-Ulrich. *Deutsche Gesellschaftsgeschichte*. 5 vols. Munich: Beck, 1987–2008.
Weinbaum, Alys Eve, Lynn M. Thomas, Priti Ramamurthy, Uta G. Poiger, Madeleine Y. Dong, and Tani E. Barlow. "The Modern Girl as Heuristic Device: Collaboration, Connective Comparison, Multidirectional Citation." In *The Modern Girl around the World: Consumption, Modernity, and Globalization*, edited by Alys Eve Weinbaum, Lynn M. Thomas, Priti Ramamurthy, Uta G. Poiger, Madeleine Y. Dong, and Tani E. Barlow, 1–24. Durham, N.C.: Duke University Press, 2008.
Weitz, Eric D. *Weimar Germany: Promise and Tragedy*. Princeton: Princeton University Press, 2007.
Weniger, Kay. *"Es wird im Leben dir mehr genommen als gegeben..." Lexikon der aus Deutschland und Österreich emigrierten Filmschaffenden 1933 bis 1945*. Hamburg: Acabus, 2011.
Widdig, Bernd. *Culture and Inflation in Weimar Germany*. Berkeley: University of California Press, 2001.
Wildt, Michael. "Generation als Anfang und Beschleunigung." In *Generationen. Zur Relevanz eines wissenschaftlichen Grundbegriffs*, edited by Ulrike Jureit and Michael Wildt, 160–79. Hamburg: Hamburger Edition, 2005.
Wildt, Michael. *Generation des Unbedingten. Das Führungskorps des Reichssicherheitshauptamtes*. Hamburg: Hamburger Edition, 2002.
Wipplinger, Jonathan O. *The Jazz Republic: Music, Race, and American Culture in Weimar Germany*. Ann Arbor: University of Michigan Press, 2017.
Wirsching, Andreas. *Die Weimarer Republik. Politik und Gesellschaft*. Munich: Oldenbourg, 2000.
Wirsching, Andreas. "From Work to Consumption. Transatlantic Visions of Individuality in Modern Mass Society." *Contemporary European History* 20, no. 1 (February 2011): 1–26.
Wohl, Robert. *The Generation of 1914*. London: Weidenfeld & Nicolson, 1980.
Young, Lisa Jaye. "Girls and Goods: Amerikanismus and the Tiller-Effekt." In *The New Woman International: Representations in Photography and Film from the 1870s through the 1960s*, edited by Elizabeth Otto and Vanessa Rocco, 252–69. Ann Arbor: University of Michigan Press, 2012.
Young, Louise. *Beyond the Metropolis: Second Cities and Modern Life in Interwar Japan*. Berkeley: University of California Press, 2013.
Zegenhagen, Evelyn. *"Schneidige deutsche Mädel." Fliegerinnen zwischen 1918 und 1945*. Göttingen: Wallstein, 2007.
Zeidler, Manfred. *Reichswehr und Rote Armee, 1920–1933. Wege und Stationen einer ungewöhnlichen Zusammenarbeit*. Munich: Oldenbourg, 1993.
Zweiniger-Bargielowska, Ina. "Building a British Superman: Physical Culture in Interwar Britain." *Journal of Contemporary History* 41, no. 4 (2006): 595–610.

Index

12-Uhr-Blatt, 65–66
8-Uhr-Abendblatt, 36, 42, 65, 73, 99

Abbott, Harriet, 236
Adorno, Theodor W., 15, 226–27
Advertising, 5, 10, 22, 56, 66, 93–94, 105, 109, 140, 150, 152–53, 155, 172
Alexanderplatz, 1
Allen, Mary, 101
Alsberg, Max, 187
Altonaer Blutsonntag, 183
America, 16–17, 21–23, 47–49, 62, 71, 103, 157–58, 163, 180, 194, 224–25, 229
Americanism, 16, 41, 106
Americanization, 5, 22, 28, 63, 92, 105, 157, 231
Amlinger case, 136, 139, 187
Angriff, Der, 1, 209
Anti-Semitism, 28, 29, 49, 126, 131
Arbeiter Illustrierte Zeitung (AIZ), 29–30
Arnheim, Rudolf, 65–66
Automobile, 16, 29, 46–47, 50–52, 60, 147–52, 182, 213–14, 225, 228–29, 233

Babylon Berlin, 12
Baileyn, Temple, 235
Baker, Josephine, 2, 96
Bausback, Ferdinand, 211
Beauty contests, 105, 114–21, 168, 171–72, 179, 223
Berliner Morgenpost, 27, 141, 149, 188
Berliner Illustrirte Zeitung, 27

Berliner Tageblatt, 33, 41, 139
Bergner, Elisabeth, 41
Bernhard, Georg, 30, 32, 34–35, 41, 76, 124–25, 136, 186–88
Blatt der Hausfrau, 108
Böß, Gustav, 71–72
Bonn, Moritz Julius, 204
Bow, Clara, 63, 106
Braun, Otto, 186
Brecht, Arnold, 163
Brecht, Bertolt, 85
Brennessel, Die, 29
Brigitte, 106–8, 118
Brigittchen, 106–10, 118, 206
Brooks, Louise, 106, 109–10
Brüning, Heinrich, 24, 127, 132, 134–38, 140–45, 148–49, 152, 161–62, 183, 186, 188–89
Bülow, Bernhard Wilhelm von, 187
B.Z. am Mittag, 41, 141, 142, 191, 221

Car. *See* automobile
Chekhova, Olga, 207
Citizenship, 20–23, 32–33, 40, 60, 73, 75, 82, 122, 126, 133, 150, 189, 210, 233, 237
Citizen-consumer, 21-23, 60, 82, 106, 121, 160, 192, 216, 223, 234
Communists, 5, 7, 29–30, 78, 81, 143, 147, 190, 195, 201
Communist modernity, 15–16
Communist Party of Germany (KPD), 7, 122, 129, 190, 193, 209
Compact car, 147–48, 152, 224
Companionate marriage, 95–96, 174–77, 206, 230–32

Companionship, 96, 98, 231
Constitution, 18, 20, 32–33, 47, 75, 79, 82, 126, 128, 134, 139–40, 184, 188, 190, 194–95, 223
  Constitution Day, 77–8, 127–28, 134, 139
Consumption, 21–23, 37, 46–49, 56, 101, 149–55, 195–220, 225, 234, 237–38
  Consumer, 21–23, 38, 44, 46–49, 51–52, 82, 147–51, 156, 197–98, 213, 220–29, 233–35
  Consumer citizenship. *See* citizen-consumer.
  Consumer culture, 90, 105–6, 149, 226, 233, 235
  Consumer democracy, 24
  Consumer community, 159, 208, 224
  Consumerism, 10, 18, 21, 23, 29, 49, 52, 54, 73–74, 103–4, 106, 150, 197, 225, 233–35
  Consumer modernity. *See* modernity
  Consumer products/goods/durables, 44–47, 56, 60–61, 147–49, 165, 195, 197–98, 224, 228
  Consumer society, 16, 21, 24, 45–46, 49–50, 60–61, 65, 92, 146, 156, 158–59, 168, 180, 220–28, 233, 235
  Virtual consumption, 46–47, 51, 56, 59–60, 106, 225–26
  Worker-consumer, 49
Crawford, Joan, 207
Curtius, Julius, 136, 139

Daily Mirror, 37
Daily News, 37
Dame, Die, 105
Democracy, 10–11, 18–20, 24, 32–33, 36, 73, 80–82, 126–28, 132–35, 145, 157–59, 163, 180, 184–88, 191–95, 202, 208–10, 220–21, 223–28, 233, 238
  Democracy of goods, 22, 47, 60
  Direct democracy, 20, 80, 140
  Liberal democracy, 13, 150, 163–64
  Parliamentary democracy, 20, 76, 82, 126–27, 194, 227
DDP, 30–33, 40, 71, 74–76, 79, 125–26, 137, 149, 187–89

Diederichs, Eugen, 88
Dietrich, Marlene, 168, 207
Diver, Nicole, 235
Dugan, Dixie, 106–7, 109–10, 157, 205
Dumb Dora, 1067
DNVP, 76, 124, 129, 140, 212
Doppelverdiener, 170, 178
DStP, 125–27, 129, 132–33, 160, 178, 180, 185, 187, 189
DVP, 74–76, 129–32, 212

Earhart, Amelia, 171
Economic crisis. *See* Great Depression
Eggebrecht, Axel, 42
Ehestandsdarlehen, 218
Einfach, Hans, 200–202
Einstein, Albert, 63
Eisdielenjugend, 92, 162, 167
Elbau, Julius, 10, 136, 140–41, 211
Elsberg, Paul, 197
Entertainment, 29, 44, 52, 63, 68, 85, 94–95, 105, 108, 198
  Entertainment industry, 55–56, 152, 215
  Entertainment section, 38, 106, 205,
Erkelenz, Anton, 149
Erzberger, Matthias, 73
Eschmann, Ernst Wilhelm, 164–65
Etzdorf, Marga von, 86, 100, 217–18

Fall Hußmann, 91–92
Femininity, 82–86, 95–122, 167–81, 205–8, 216–20, 223, 231–38
Fitzgerald, F. Scott, 235
Flapper, 108, 117, 157, 205–6, 235–36, 236–38
Ford, Henry, 5, 49, 64, 137, 225
Fordism, 106
Frankfurter Zeitung, 33
Frau Christine, 171–79, 202, 206, 216–17, 223
Freizeit. *See* leisure
Friedrichstraße, 5, 6
Fritsch, Willy, 203

Garçonne, 99–101, 102, 105, 117, 121, 171, 175, 205, 232–33
Geiger, Theodor, 133
Gender relations, 16, 84, 101, 121, 164–66, 174–79, 206, 230

Gender roles, 92, 97, 102, 111, 175–79, 232–33, 238
Generational conflict, 83–84, 92, 174, 232
Georg, Manfred, 41–42, 85, 93–94, 113, 157, 190, 204, 211
German Democratic Party. *See* DDP
German National People's Party. *See* DNVP
German People's Party. *See* DVP
German State Party. *See* DStP
Gert, Valeska, 41
Giese, Fritz, 105–6
Girl, 103–10, 113–14, 117–20, 157, 163, 168–79, 202–7, 218, 235
Glaeser, Ernst, 84, 89, 94
Gleichschaltung, 212
Goebbels, Joseph, 138, 144, 209, 211–12, 214
Goldstein, Moritz, 185, 211
Göring, Hermann, 211
Gräfenberg, Rosie, 124
Great Depression, 10, 14, 22–24, 123–25, 146–49, 157–59, 168, 178–79, 182–83, 195, 200–203, 237–38
Gretchen, 99, 101–3, 121, 171, 218
Groener, Wilhelm, 138–39, 142
Großmann, Stefan, 40, 42, 102, 128
Gründel, Ernst Günther, 164–65, 223
Gründgens, Gustav, 41
Grüne Post, 27

Haller-Revue, 109
Haus Vaterland, 55–56
Heaven, 41, 81, 92, 129, 131, 163, 190
Hessel, Franz, 41
Hilferding, Rudolf, 186
Hindemith, Paul, 85
Hindenburg, Paul von, 29, 127–28, 141, 151, 180, 183, 187–91, 202, 204, 223–26, 238
Hitler, Adolf, 24, 25, 77, 128, 133, 137, 142–45, 167, 183–84, 188–89, 202, 208–9, 212–17, 220, 225–26, 238
Höllering, Franz, 141–45, 186, 191
Hollywood, 17
Home, 46, 103, 114, 230
Home appliances, 46, 228–29, 233–34
Homosexuality, 101

Hoover, Herbert, 72
Horn, Camilla, 168
Horwarth, Ödon von, 41
Housewife, 63, 102–3, 108, 112, 115, 168, 170, 174, 178, 183, 198, 207, 217, 230–31
Hugenberg, Alfred, 76–77, 80–81, 124, 140, 209

Ice-cream-parlor youth. *See* Eisdielenjugend
Image telegraphy, 39, 68
Individualism, 54, 159, 163–64, 179, 228, 235–36
International Air Show, 61
International Automobile and Motorcycle Exhibition, 50, 150–51, 213
International Broadcasting Exhibition, 63, 147, 158, 201, 213
Inflation, 84, 90, 133, 139, 150, 157, 205

Jacobi, Lucy van, 41–42, 103, 112, 152, 182, 216
Jazz, 17, 45, 55, 60, 235
Jödicke, Carl, 184–85
Jugendbewegung. *See* Youth Movement
Jungdeutscher Orden, 2, 125–26, 149, 161
Jünger, Ernst, 70

Kameradschaftsehe. *See* companionate marriage
Kästner, Erich, 5, 41
Kauder, Gustav, 41, 81, 105, 136, 139, 190, 192–94, 201, 211
Kaus, Gina, 41, 96
Kelen, Emery, 79
Keun, Irmgard, 6
Keynes, John Maynard, 48, 149–50, 224, 238
Kleinsiedler, 197
Klemperer, Otto, 85
Koblenzer Nationalblatt, 128
Koch, Erna, 118–21, 171
Kochstraße, 36, 66, 123
Koch-Weser, Erich, 76, 187–68
Krakauer, Siegfried, 55, 60, 65, 105
Krantz, Paul, 91–92, 164
Kurfürstendamm, 1

Index

Lachmann, Fritz, 190
Lamprecht, Gerhard, 5–7
Landshoff, Ruth, 86
Lang, Fritz, 5–6
Lassdas, Lieschen, 153, 156
Lee, Lorelei, 105, 109, 235
Leipziger Tageblatt, 137
Leisure, 52–56, 59–61, 101, 152–53, 156, 197, 214, 224, 238
  Leisure culture, 24, 53, 152, 198
Leitner, Maria, 40, 54, 63, 113
Levetzow, Magnus von, 209
Lewinsohn, Richard, 35
Ley, Robert, 128, 185, 199
Liberalism, 32, 47, 75, 81, 125–27, 132–33, 136, 146, 160, 164, 180
Literarische Welt, 42
Löbel, Joseph, 97–98
Lokal-Anzeiger, 124
Loos, Anita, 96, 105, 109–10, 235
Luna-Park, 56–57
Luther, Hans, 70, 186
Lustig, Hanns G., 41–42, 86, 90–91, 112, 137, 140, 211

Mann, Erika, 40–41, 51, 86, 99–100, 175
Mann, Heinrich, 84, 90
Mann, Klaus, 86
Mann, Thomas, 41, 86
Mannheim, Karl, 70–71
Margueritte, Victor, 99, 232–33
Martius, Georg, 187
Masculinity, 86–99, 160–67, 202–5, 218, 223, 231–33, 236–38
  Military masculinity, 98, 163–67
Matzke, Frank, 163–65
McEvoy, Joseph P., 106, 109
Misch, Carl, 141–2, 185
Miss Germany, 105, 115
Modernity, 14, 17, 21, 23–24
  Alternative modernity, 13–16, 222, 225, 239
  Classical modernity, 13
  Consumer modernity, 21, 23, 159, 224, 239
  German modernity, 24, 43, 44, 114
  Hybrid modernity, 233
  Moderate modernity, 15, 17, 24–25
  Multiple modernities, 14

Modernization, 13, 21, 64, 70, 87, 98, 222, 230, 234
Mommsen, Wilhelm, 32–33
Montag Morgen, 124
Montgelas, Albrecht Graf, 35
Mosse publishing house, 33, 37, 226
Motorcycle, 51, 214
Motorization, 50–52, 150, 197, 213–14, 224
Müller, Richard A., 184

Nachtausgabe, 36, 73
National Socialist Workers' Party of Germany (*see* Nazis: NSDAP)
Nazis, 9, 13–15, 20–25, 30, 43, 72, 78, 81, 123, 128–33, 138, 142–46, 153, 160–67, 183–95, 200–201, 208–26, 239
National Socialism, 136, 144–45, 165, 184–85, 188, 209, 221, 224–25
National Socialist modernity, 16
NSDAP, 77, 81, 122, 128, 132–33, 161, 167, 184–85, 189–90, 193–95, 208–13
Neher, Carola, 96
New Objectivity. *See* Neue Sachlichkeit
New Woman, 103, 205–6
Nightlife, 55–56, 60, 152, 215, 236
Nilfisk, 172
Norris, Kathleen, 235

Oehme, Walther, 144
Optimism, 16, 23, 60, 69, 82–84, 90, 95, 132–37, 146–57, 179–83, 190, 197, 200, 213–17, 220–6, 239
Osborn, Max, 35
Ossietzky, Carl von, 42, 143, 186

Page, Anita, 168–69
Papen, Franz von, 183, 186, 189, 190–97, 200
Parliamentarianism, 33, 72, 89, 167, 180, 183, 223, 226, 238
Parteiismus, 126
People's community, 126
People's Car. *See* Volksauto
People's National Reich Association, 125
Photography, 57–60

Pol, Charlotte, 86, 96, 170, 175, 178
Polgar, Alfred, 106
Potsdamer Platz, 1, 159
Preuß, Hugo, 32
Priestley, J. B., 228, 231
Progress, 8, 13–17, 26, 36, 44–46, 52, 74, 83, 98, 101–3, 135, 148, 158, 160, 163, 179, 180, 190, 202, 208, 216, 221–22, 230, 235
Progressivism. *See* progress
Pünder, Hermann, 138–39

Radicalization, 9, 94, 145, 161, 167, 170, 180
Radio, 16, 42, 44–47, 54–56, 63–64, 102, 147, 158–59, 198, 201, 225
Rationalization, 13, 46, 54, 87, 95, 97, 146, 158, 224
Rathenau, Walther, 70, 73
Red Army, 87
Redslob, Erwin, 77, 128
Rehfisch, Hans José, 112–13
Reichsbanner Schwarz-Rot-Gold, 77, 185
Reichskunstwart. *See* Redslob, Erwin
Reichswehr, 136–39, 162, 183, 187
Reichswehrprozess. *See* Ulm Reichswehr trial
Reiner, Josef, 136, 141
Reinhold, Peter, 137–38
Reissner, Larissa, 29
Reznicek, Paula von, 51, 96
Robolsky, Otto, 141–42, 149
Roda Roda, Alexander, 41, 73, 79, 128, 190
Roosevelt, Franklin D., 238
Rundt, Arthur, 109–10, 157–58

SA. *See* stormtroopers
Sachlichkeit, 18, 69–72, 82–86, 89–91, 96–98, 103, 126–29, 135, 165, 202, 206, 223, 233
  Neue Sachlichkeit, 70
Schäffer, Hans, 140–41, 186–92, 208–12
Schleicher, Kurt von, 138, 186, 189, 195
Schlesinger, Paul, 35, 71
Scholem, Gershom, 185
Schmeling, Max, 41
Schmitt, Carl, 70

Schnitzler, Arthur, 105
Schwarzschild, Leopold, 125
Schwarzwald, Eugenie von, 41
Sexuality, 38, 92, 97, 99, 101, 103, 109, 112, 166, 175, 176, 179, 202, 206, 230, 235
"Sky," 41, 72, 79, 80, 190
Social Democrats, 25, 30, 32, 40, 102, 132
Social Democratic Party of Germany. *See* SPD
Sombart, Werner, 64–66, 70
Sonnemann publishing house, 33
Speare, Dorothy, 235
SPD, 30, 36, 49, 129, 137, 183, 185, 188–9, 193, 199, 209
Speed, 7–8, 45, 64–69, 86, 159, 201–2, 221
Spengler, Oswald, 62
Sports, 38, 54, 57, 64, 79, 84, 95, 97, 99, 103, 106, 165, 174, 232
Stadtler, Eduard, 212, 221
Stahlhelm, 78, 195
Steglitzer Schülermordprozess, 91
Stein, Fritz, 143, 187
Stormtroopers, 143–44, 211, 220
Strasser, Georg, 84
Strasser, Otto, 136
Strength through Joy, 226
Stresemann, Gustav, 74–82, 127, 135
Suhrkamp, Peter, 203
Swanson, Gloria, 207
Sydow, Georg, 34–35, 49

Tage-Buch, Das, 124, 204
Tat, Die, 2, 40, 88–89, 125, 157, 165, 223
Tatkreis, 88, 90, 94, 125
Taylor, Frederick Winslow, 64
Technology, 7, 16, 23–24, 39, 57, 60–65, 68–70, 84–86, 99, 103, 147, 158–59, 165, 201, 229, 234
"Technology Everybody Needs," 44–46, 50, 147, 197
Teenager, 63, 92, 162
Third Reich, 9, 13, 133, 224, 227, 239
Threepenny Opera, 85
Tieck, Polly, 151–53, 156, 205
Tourism, 53, 59–60, 96, 152, 175, 178, 197, 200, 214, 234

Torres, Raquel, 168
Treviranus, Gottfried, 136
Tucholsky, Kurt, 2, 40

Ufa. *See* Universum Film AG
Ullstein publishing company, 13, 15, 24, 25–43, 49, 59, 66–71, 123, 126–27, 135–146, 183–90, 208–12, 212, 220–6
  Ullstein affair, 124–25, 136–37, 140
  Ullstein-Berichte, 37, 93, 149, 195
  Ullstein, Franz, 26, 76, 124, 136, 140, 184
  Ullstein, Hans, 26, 68
  Ullstein, Heinz, 136–37, 143, 184, 210–11
  Ullstein, Hermann, 26, 30, 145
  Ullstein, Karl, 68
  Ullstein, Leopold, 26, 28
  Ullstein, Louis, 26, 124, 184
  Ullstein management, 40, 123–24, 139, 142–5, 185, 190, 211
  Ullstein Rudolf, 26
Ulm Reichswehr trial, 138, 143, 162
United States of America, 14, 16–17, 20–27, 45–52, 82, 100, 105, 109, 123, 157–58, 180, 223, 235–38
Universum Film AG, 137, 140
Unruh, Fritz von, 42
Unter den Linden, 50

Vacations. *See* holiday
Vacuum cleaner, 172, 197, 229–30
Veidt, Conrad, 203
Velde, Theodor van de, 97–98, 103
Velocity. *See* speed
Vetter, Karl, 42
Volksauto, 148, 180, 214, 224–26
Volksgemeinschaft. *See* people's community
Volksnationale Reichsvereinigung. See People's National Reich Association
Volkswagen. *See* Volksauto

Vorwärts, 30, 36
Vossische Zeitung, 27, 30, 33, 35, 49, 73, 88, 124, 126, 132, 136, 140–41, 143, 184, 186, 188

Wallenberg, Ernst, 190–91
Wandrey, Conrad, 28
War youth generation, 164–67
Wassermann, Jakob, 91
Weekend, 53–56, 95, 152–55, 170, 198, 200, 214
Weekend bride, 170, 218
Weill, Kurt, 85
Weisenborn, Günther, 93
Welk, Ehm, 54
Wels, Otto, 185, 199
Welt am Abend, 36, 66, 73, 80
Welt am Montag, 65
Weltbühne, Die, 42, 94, 124, 143
Wessel, Horst, 143
White-collar culture, 55, 98, 153, 156
White-collar workers, 37–38, 51, 54–56, 58, 68, 70, 87, 95, 100, 104–6, 111–12, 133, 146, 161, 173–74, 198
Wilder, Billy, 5, 40, 86
Wilmersdorfer Straße, 124
Wochenende. *See* weekend
Wolf, Friedrich, 113, 170
Wolff, Theodor, 10, 41
Wong, Anna Mae, 106

Young, Chic, 106
Young front, 89, 223
Young generation, 82, 86–87, 160, 164–65, 204, 206, 216
Young Plan, 79–81, 162
Youth Movement, 16, 88, 91–92

Zehrer, Hans, 88–90, 125, 162–66, 223
Zeppelin, 2, 62–63, 103
Zimmermann, Ferdinand Friedrich, 41, 88, 125, 157, 166